MODERNIST PATTERNS

Modernist Patterns
in Literature and the Visual Arts

Murray Roston

NEW YORK UNIVERSITY PRESS
Washington Square, New York

© Murray Roston 2000

First published in the U.S.A. in 2000 by
NEW YORK UNIVERSITY PRESS
Washington Square
New York, N.Y. 10003

This book is printed on paper suitable for recycling and
made from fully managed and sustained forest sources.

Library of Congress Cataloging-in-Publication Data
Roston, Murray.
Modernist patterns in literature and the visual arts / Murray
Roston.
p.   cm.
Includes bibliographical references and index.
ISBN 0–8147–7527–6 (cloth)
1. English literature—20th century—History and criticism.
2. Modernism (Literature)—Great Britain.   3. Art and literature—
Great Britain—History—20th century.   4. Art and literature—
United States—History—20th century.   5. American literature—20th
century—History and criticism.   6. Modernism (Literature)—United
States.   7. Art, Modern—20th century.   8. Modernism (Art)
I. Title.
PR478.M6R67   1999
820.9'112—dc21   98–45373
                                                        CIP

Printed in Great Britain

Contents

List of Illustrations

Photographs and permission for Figures 5, 9, 10, 19, 24, 25, 28 and 29 were supplied by Art Resource.

Acknowledgments

Once again, I should like to express my appreciation to my home university for granting me leaves of absence, and to the English department at UCLA for generously inviting me to teach there at regular intervals through the years. In addition to the pleasure of exchanging ideas with colleagues and students, those invitations have granted me access to more extensive libraries than are available to me in Israel. Professor Thomas Wortham, the department chair, has been unfailingly kind in the support and hospitality he has extended to me, not least in initiating my appointment as a permanent Adjunct Professor in the department in order to ensure the continuation of such visits.

Chapter 3 includes some material originally published in *Studies in the Novel* and recently reprinted in Jerome Meckier (ed.), *Critical Essays on Aldous Huxley* (Prentice-Hall, 1996). I have made use of it here, in considerably developed form, by kind permission of the editors.

Mr Timothy Bartlett, Mr Timothy Farmiloe and Ms Charmian Hearne have, from both sides of the Atlantic, continued to provide generous editorial encouragement and support.

Lastly, and as always, I should like to express my affectionate thanks to my wife, Faith, for her stimulating company, valuable critical comments, and lively humour – qualities ever-present, but especially appreciated during our shared visits to art centres throughout the world.

Bar Ilan University   MURRAY ROSTON
Ramat Gan, Israel

The author and publishers are grateful to the following for permission to reproduce copyright material: the Estate of Ernest Hemingway and Charles Scribner's Sons as detailed below: *The Sun Also Rises* (Copyright 1926 by Charles Scribner's Sons, Copyright renewed 1954 by Ernest Hemingway); *For Whom the Bell Tolls* (Copyright 1940 by Ernest Hemingway, Copyright renewed 1968 by Mary Hemingway); 'Big Two-Hearted River' *In Our Time: Stories by Ernest Hemingway*; also appears in *The Nick Adams Stories* (Copyright 1925 by

Introduction

A colleague recently enquired, with a hint of exasperation, why books exploring the relationship between literature and the visual arts invariably begin with an apology, a defence of intermedia investigation, when the principle behind such enquiry is so self-evident. In all eras, he remarked, both writer and artist create their work from within the same cultural setting and hence inevitably express to a larger or lesser extent the dominant concerns of their time.

The complaint is, it would seem, justified in relation both to the themes selected for treatment and to the style adopted in works produced contemporaneously by writers and artists. Milton's *Paradise Lost* clearly partakes of the same mythological grandeur, cosmic range and baroque dynamism as Rubens' magnificent *Fall of the Damned*, the latter depicting the archangel Michael driving myriads of rebel angels in terrified flight through infinite space to the hell that awaits them below; while in contrast, during the following century, Pope's *Rape of the Lock* focused down from heaven to earth, revealing, on smaller scale, an amused interest in human society and its fashions, in a manner resembling Watteau's depictions of the aristocracy at leisure or Canaletto's Gulliver-like overviews of public celebrations in Venice. Yet whoever has followed the checkered history of such interdisciplinary study will have encountered the entrenched opposition of critics, their assertion that crossing the borders separating the media is an intrinsically invalid procedure. It is a resistance that remains strong in our own day, even though the reasons motivating it have been largely discredited by the leading critical ideologies of our time. It may be helpful to trace briefly the fluctuations in such critical evaluations.

Horace's casual comment, *ut pictura poesis*, from which interdisciplinary studies used to draw their authority, was, in its original context, far more limited in intent than has generally been assumed. His *Ars Poetica* merely noted that art resembles literature insofar as one work may please while another displeases; one painting may be admired briefly, another permanently.[1] But during the European Renaissance the phrase he employed, extracted from its context,

1

became, as one historian has termed it, the keynote to all critical
writing of that time. Leonardo Da Vinci justified his art by echoing
the tradition on which Horace's dictum had drawn, regarding poetry
and painting simply as variations of each other: 'If you call painting
"dumb poetry", then the painter may say of the poet that his art
is "blind painting".' In England, too, the principle was eagerly
espoused at that time, and by the early eighteenth century, Joseph
Warton could declare unhesitatingly that a particularly fine passage
in Dryden's poetry was, in effect, a verbal painting. To translate that
passage into pictorial form, he claimed, 'the painter has nothing to
do but to substitute colours for words, the design being finished to
his hands.'[2]

That marked the high-point of the principle's acceptance, the tide
soon beginning to turn. Edmund Burke drew attention in 1756 not
to the similarities between the media but to the disparities. Painting,
he pointed out, is an essentially mimetic art, striving for meticulous
realism, while poetry, in contrast, gains its strength from its lack of
detail. Poetry employs allusiveness and the emotive connotations of
language as substitutes for what cannot be apprehended visually,
those substitutes providing the distinctive ingredients of literary
form.[3] But it was, of course, Lessing's treatise, *Laokoön*, published in
1766, that vigorously contested the traditional analogy between the
media, insisting that the contrasting use of spatial and temporal factors in those art forms made any comparison between them highly
suspect. Such comparisons had led critics to encourage a false merger
of the two media: 'In poetry, a fondness for description, and in painting, a fancy for allegory, has arisen from the desire to make the one a
speaking picture without really knowing what it can and ought
to paint, and the other a dumb poem, without having considered
how far painting can express universal ideas without abandoning its
proper sphere and degenerating into an arbitrary method of writing.'
From that time onward, little was to be heard of Horace's maxim.

The one aspect of such intermedia study that did survive this
reversal was the study of sequential 'influence' – investigations of
writers who may have been affected stylistically by their admiration
for painters or for pictorial traditions from previous eras, those links
usually acknowledged by the writers themselves and hence historically irrefutable. But that approach carefully avoided synchronic
comparison, the connecting of authors and painters from the same
generation, a form of inquiry which, apart from minor instances,
went into eclipse.[4]

The transformation that has occurred during the last few decades has been dramatic, justifications for renewed study of the subject converging from a number of unexpected sources. The rise of semiotics as a leading component of literary theory has, by its recognition that language consists not of lexicographically defined words but of signs needing to be interpreted in terms of their contemporary or local context, bestowed new importance upon the social matrix of the period, a knowledge of which was now seen as indispensable for a valid understanding of linguistic communication. The concept of intertextuality emerged simultaneously, the recognition that each literary work is a tissue of references and allusions to other literary works, drawing upon an infinite web of discourses – the discourses of power, sex, family, science and religion. And with that conception arose a ratification, on basically new grounds, of the interdependence of contemporary acts of creativity, the belief, as Stephen Greenblatt has put it, that there exists in each generation 'a shared code, a set of interlocking tropes and similitudes' essential for interpreting the signs employed in the artistic works of the time. That awareness has reauthenticated, although with different terminology, the earlier concern with the dominant patterns of each era. And Michel Foucault's adoption of the word *episteme* to categorise that cultural matrix, the self-enclosed system of knowledge that he saw each generation as developing, has, by offering a semiotic substitute for the discarded term 'periodisation', lent new prestige to research into the social, economic, aesthetic and philosophical settings within which writers and artists produce their work.[5]

While literary studies were being revolutionised by the emergence of semiotics and structuralism, art history, in contrast, was slower to respond, many in the profession remaining faithful to its traditional archival concerns, the documenting of the sales of paintings and the cataloguing of their sequential locations. Gombrich's *Art and Illusion*, while it marked a turning point in art history by focusing upon the role of the viewer in art, suffered from a static conception of that viewer, failing to acknowledge, as Norman Bryson has shown, how essential it is to recognise cultural shifts from generation to generation, to acknowledge that the viewer, too, changes in accordance with the altered concepts of the time. The spectator implied by medieval church art is quite different from the viewer implied by a Raphael or Vermeer. If the pervasive influence of Gombrich functioned in the direction of dehistoricising art, recent years have seen a counter movement, the emergence of the so-called New

Art History, with its plea for a more sensitive reading of art in terms
of its relationship to the evolving circumstances of contemporary
society. It marks a new concern with the fluctuating codes of visual
interpretation prevalent in each era, codes that affect not only viewer
response but also the painter's strategies in addressing such contemporary expectations. Michael Baxandall has thus insisted that
we recognise how different are the assumptions and patterns of
thought that each generation brings to art, noting that 'the mental
equipment a man orders his visual experience with is variable, and
much of this variable equipment is culturally relative, in the sense of
being determined by the society which has influenced his experience'.[6] In all such approaches there is a clear sense of art as an
expression of current attitudes and assumptions. Yet the disqualification of 'periodisation' has continued to dominate postmodernist
criticism as if these fundamental changes in critical approach had
not occurred.

   That continued opposition may arise from the fact that revalida-
tions of the contextual matrix have not addressed directly one of
the main objections to them – the suspicion that the idea of a cultural
pattern existent in each era is liable to lend a monolithic quality to
our reading of it, the sense of a paradigmatic framework to which
each creative artist is seen to conform thereby implying the existence of a dull uniformity among such writers and painters. The
methodology adopted in this present study, as in my investigation
of earlier eras, attempts to answer that objection. It assumes the
presence of a more subtle and, for the historian, a more stimulating
configuration. It posits the existence in each generation of a central
complex of inherited assumptions, of emergent ideas and of urgent
contemporary concerns; but it sees each creative artist and writer
as reacting individually to those assumptions and challenges.
Each poet, novelist, painter and sculptor may choose to accept the
dominant ideas and priorities of his or her time, may question
them, may even vigorously deny them, but will inevitably in some
sense acknowledge and react to them. Even when the writer or
artist resists them most forcefully, those impulses will, as matters of
immediate pressure, continue to affect, often without their awareness, aspects of the art produced. What all writers and artists
share are the problems specific to their time; and a close study of
the techniques they develop in order to deal with those contemporary challenges and the themes and symbols which they choose,
each modified to suit the needs of the specific medium, can prove

enriching to our understanding of the works produced within each generation.

My interest lies not merely in identifying the analogies between the media in each period, but in moving a stage beyond – attempting to employ such perceived affinities as a means of obtaining insights into the literary works themselves, insights that might not be available from other sources and that may at times suggest possible solutions to as yet unsolved critical problems. In order not to encroach on the area to be examined in this book, I should like to offer an instance from a period slightly later than the Modernist, Edward Albee's *Who's Afraid of Virginia Woolf?*, which was first performed in the 1960s. Riveting as it is dramatically, the play has been docketed by almost all critics as little more than the representation of a sado-masochistic marriage, the conflict between a small-town university professor and his earthy wife, the latter flaunting her sexual promiscuity before her husband but eventually subjected in her turn to his vengeful shattering of her consolatory pretence, the fiction that she possesses a child. A leading reviewer at the time of its first performance described the play (with remarkable myopia) as a 'frighteningly well-observed picture of a matrimonial *corrida*, with the scarred and bloody husband at last taking the cow by the horns after a long, liquor-logged evening' – a comment that has appeared on the cover of the Penguin edition of the play for the past thirty years, presumably on the assumption that it offers a valid summary of the work. That this reading has continued to hold its place in criticism is evidenced by the fact that the article on that play selected for inclusion in a recently published collection of essays on Albee, a piece written by John Galbraith, while acknowledging the play's 'harrowing dramatic power', similarly concludes by dismissing it as merely portraying a matrimonial sex duel.[7] Neither of these reviews, nor other studies of the play, explain the reasons for its profound impact on the stage and the immediate recognition among audiences of its extraordinary relevance to contemporary concerns. Such summaries, moreover, ignore a contradiction of that reading existent within the play itself, the deep affection between the married couple, their warm, shared sense of humour, and, not least, the tender mutual concern that accompanies and appears to refute the seeming cruelty and vengefulness existing between them. Such readings overlook, for example, Martha's admission to an incredulous Nick of her abiding love for her husband underlying all the pain of their relationship, her confession that the only person she really cares for is

George who is out somewhere there in the dark...George who is good to me, and whom I revile; who understands me, and whom I push off; who can make me laugh, and I choke it back in my throat; who can hold me, at night, so that it's warm, and whom I will bite so there's blood; who keeps learning the games we play as quickly as I can change the rules; who can make me happy, and I do not wish to be happy, and yes I do wish to be happy.[8]

Nor do they enquire what connection exists between this supposed marital sex conflict and the strange title of the play?

In the course of this brief introduction, I can only hint at a different reading of the play, a reading based upon a change occurring simultaneously in the plastic arts of that time. It was in the 1960s, just when the play was being first produced, that Richard Rogers of England and Renzo Piano of Italy were commissioned to design the Pompidou Cultural Centre of Paris, a structure that, like Albee's play, shocked the public by its harsh break with previous tradition; for it provocatively placed on the outside of the building those elements which had, throughout the centuries, been so carefully concealed within. Water-supply pipes coloured green criss-cross the outer walls of the building, intersecting with giant ventilation ducts painted in bright blue to ensure that their presence cannot be missed, while conduits for electric wiring marked in yellow cut across elevators in red to provide full external exposure of the 'bowels' of the building.

That innovation was no mere shock tactic but, like most such changes in art form, expressed a cultural shift, an alteration in current thinking. By the mid century, psychiatric counseling had become endemic in leading Western countries, an integral part of the life-style of the middle and upper classes, the principle having now been accepted that the cloaking of inner anxieties, pressures and fears, a failure to acknowledge the traumas of childhood, and, even more so, the repression of such experiences when once recognised could be severely damaging to mental health. Everything hidden within was now to be exposed, not only to oneself and to one's psychiatrist but, more effectively, by public divulgence, as in the sessions of group therapy widely conducted at that time, in which participants were encouraged to disclose in open forum the most secret guilts and terrors of their inner world, as well as the most intimate details of their sexual lives. So here, while the principle of laying bare the sewage system of a building to the visitor's gaze might not produce beauty in any traditional sense of that term, it

expressed in architectural form the contemporary desire for psychological honesty, offering an unembarrassed confrontation with the
previously subterranean utilities, essential to the building's function
but formerly hidden away as distasteful to the sight.

With that architectural innovation in mind, we may return to the
play, and to the recognition that the real distinction there between
the central marital pair and the 'yuppie' couple with whom they are
contrasted is the deep conviction of George and Martha that, no
matter how agonising the task, how painful the operation, each
must assist the other in stripping away all illusions, in tearing out
hidden fears and secret longings, and in learning to live in total honesty with themselves and with each other. It is, they recognise,
insufficient to perform that process in privacy, where the effect
would be mitigated. The disclosures must be performed publicly.
Hence Martha's exposure before the young couple of George's covert sense of academic failure and his repressed guilt towards his
dead parents; and hence, at the end of the play, George's shattering
of Martha's pretence that she possesses a son. That pretence George
has tenderly tolerated for a time as a consoling recompense for their
tragic failure to bear a child, a device valid as long as they both *knew*
that it was make-believe; but the moment Martha shares the pretence with the visitors, he perceives that she has crossed the danger-
ous borderline into self-delusion, and the fiction must be publicly
cauterised, however harsh the procedure.

Their supposed sadomasochism is thus, in the deepest sense, an
expression of mutual love, no less painful to each because of that
underlying affection. Disclosures arouse momentary fury and resentment each time a secret is uncovered, yet it is a process felt as profoundly necessary for their spiritual well-being. As George explains
to a totally uncomprehending Honey as she drunkenly peels off
the label from a brandy bottle, the uncovering of hidden psychoses
must be unrelenting:

> *George*: We all peel labels, sweetie; and when you get through the
> skin, all three layers, through the muscle, slosh aside the organs...
> them which is still sloshable – and get down to bone...you
> know what you do then?
> *Honey*: [terribly interested]: No!
> *George*: When you get down to bone, you haven't got all the way
> yet. There's something inside the bone...the marrow...and
> that's what you gotta get at [a strange smile at Martha].

Honey: Oh! I see.
George: The marrow. But bones are pretty resilient, especially in
    the young. Now take our son...
Honey: [strangely]: Who?
George: Our son...Martha's and my little joy![9]

That urgent need to expose the world of repressed inner experience
is the justification for the title – a seemingly facetious play on the
nursery rhyme of the 'big bad wolf' but concealing, as the concluding
words of the play indicate, Martha's profound fear of the confrontation with the inner self which Virginia Woolf had characterised in
her writings, and yet her own recognition of its unavoidable necessity, however agonising the task. A knowledge of contemporary
architecture and of the motivation for its innovative techniques can
thus provide valuable insights into the principles underlying a leading drama of the time, since they are both responding, in their creative forms, to an altered configuration, the need both to confront
and to express artistically a fundamentally new conception germane
to their generation.

    That same methodology will be applied in this present book to the
period that has come to be known as Modernism, the period from
1900 to the outbreak of the Second World War in 1939.[10] Probably no
period in history has produced such far-reaching changes in both literature and the arts. The human figure, for the first time in centuries,
in effect disappeared from canvases as painters experimented with
abstract and geometrical forms. In the novel, the long-established
interest in society, especially in its class relations, became supplanted
in the 1920s by a penetration into the inner consciousness of the
individual, the flow of unarticulated thought occurring behind the
façade presented to others. Architecture deserted the classical and
Gothic forms that had, despite the introduction of new building
techniques, continued to predominate during the nineteenth century,
and it now branched out into such revolutionary structures as the
Bauhaus, the prairie style and the skyscraper. And verse writing
underwent no less of a revolution both thematically and stylistically
after the advent of Imagism and Vorticism, and the break with the
lyrical traditions of the past which those movements inaugurated.

    From our present standpoint at the end of the century, we possess
the inestimable privilege of distance, of an ability to assess that period
with some degree of historical hindsight, free from the immediate
pressures of that time. My concern here, it must be emphasised, is not

with conscious interactions between the media, such as a writer's deliberate attempt to provide a literary counterpart to some new stylistic technique emerging within the plastic arts. I am interested rather in the ways in which writers, often oblivious of the changes being introduced in the painting or sculpture of their day or unaware of their relevance to their own work, developed their own independent reactions to the stresses of the time and, although tailoring their responses to the needs of their verbal medium, frequently in that process paralleled innovations being introduced in the plastic and visual media. It is hoped that the placing of literary works within the context of the far-reaching changes occurring in contemporary painting, architecture and sculpture may shed fresh light upon our understanding of the writings produced in that period; and at the same time, by a reverse process, help also to identify the cultural changes that generated stylistic innovations within the visual arts themselves.

1
Conrad's Stylistic 'Mistiness'

Before attempting to relate a specific aspect of Conrad's narrative method to contemporary painting, I should like to examine briefly the intermedia connections that have interested critics until now. The question of Conrad's stylistic affiliation to Impressionism and the degree to which his own literary innovations may have drawn upon techniques developed by that school of painters did, in fact, stimulate considerable critical interest, as well as critical puzzlement, during his lifetime. And the evidence supporting such affinities might indeed seem to be strong. Ford Madox Ford, his friend and close literary collaborator, affirmed categorically that Conrad acknowledged the indebtedness, describing him as a writer 'who avowed himself impressionist'.[1] But as Eloise Knapp Hay has warned, even if Ford's report is correct – and Ford candidly admits to lapses of memory in his reminiscence of their partnership, as well as to an occasional confusing of his own and Conrad's views – the avowal remains problematic, as the implications and connotations of the term 'impressionist' at the turn of the century were by no means identical with those current in our own day.[2]

The conception we now have of Impressionist painting as an art form dedicated to freshness of aesthetic vision and responsiveness to the transforming play of light had not yet come into vogue. When not dismissed as unworthy of consideration, the productions of that school had, in the final decades of the century, been associated with a striving for optical accuracy in a manner unshackled by the academic rules of the past. It was seen as an attempt to reproduce the way objects impinge upon the human retina; and in that regard there was little to connect Conrad with such forms of depiction.[3] Furthermore, Ford's usage of the term had relied less on its association with painting than on its vaguer and much-debated transference to literature, as writers sought for a verbal counterpart to the new style in art. Ferdinand Brunetière, in an 1879 essay on 'Impressionism in the Novel', had, with mingled admiration and admonition, set the direction for such debate by his assumption that the distinguishing mark of such painting was (as its name implied) the artist's attempt to capture on canvas the optical sensation or impression produced by an initial glance at a scene. Applying the concept to literature, he had praised Alphonse Daudet for 'encountering' characters, for deserting the tradition of an omniscient narrator providing full descriptions of his fictional figures and for presenting them instead as if he were meeting them for the first time – although Brunetière did condemn the tendency in such writing to concern itself primarily with externals or surfaces. Both Ford and Conrad owed many of their critical conceptions to this early exposition of 'literary impressionism', Conrad's own article on Daudet, written in 1898, not only echoing the ideas but employing the phraseology of Brunetière's essay.[4] Yet even within the context of this literary version of impressionism, Ford's description of Conrad as wholeheartedly subscribing to its stylistic tenets is clearly an exaggeration in the light of the latter's conscious dissociation from that movement, as in his deprecatory remark in 1897 that Stephen Crane was '*only* an impressionist'.[5]

To the school of painting itself, the acknowledged model for the literary version, Conrad was unequivocally hostile. In 1891 he had visited Madame Parodowska in Paris, where she was temporarily residing in an apartment belonging to her cousin Paul Cachet. The latter, the physician and amateur painter who had attended Van Gogh in his last years, had charitably acquired a number of unsaleable paintings from that group of artists. Conrad wrote to her shortly after his visit expressing his relief that she had now left that apartment, as the paintings by Monet, Renoir, Cézanne, Sisley and Van Gogh hanging upon its walls were, he suggested, the work of lunatics: 'Truly, I did not like knowing that you were in the Doctor's apartment. It had a nightmarish atmosphere, with its paintings of the Charenton school.' (Charenton was a mental asylum near Paris). Towards the art movement at large, Conrad was equally scornful: 'For the moment, we may well laugh at it all, but on the whole, the final impression is painful.'[6]

On the other hand, he did not, it would seem, reject outright his classification by others as a member of the allied literary movement. There is a ring of authenticity in Ford's account of the way they became reconciled to that charge:

We accepted without much protest the stigma 'Impressionist' that was thrown at us. In those days Impressionists were still considered to be bad people: Atheists, Reds, wearing red ties with which

to frighten householders. But we accepted the name because...
we saw that Life did not narrate, but made impressions on our
brains. We in turn, if we wished to produce on you an effect of
life, must not narrate but render...impressions.[7]

However imprecise the terminology (since Ford's usage here shifts
from the capitalised form, indicating a specific school, to an uncap-
italised, more general designation), their employment of the word at
a time when its primary application was to a group of painters and
their recognition that they did bear some affinity to that mode
encouraged critics to pursue the relationship. In 1932 Joseph Warren
Beach's widely read study of the twentieth-century novel gave cur-
rency to the association by entitling one chapter 'Impressionism:
Conrad', even though, within the chapter itself, his discussion of the
relationship proved disappointingly thin, a brief mention of the
principle adopted by both Conrad and Ford that an author should
'get his character in first with a strong impression' before filling in
details of its past.[8]

One of the most interesting commentaries on this supposed
affiliation was a brief essay by Ramon Fernandez, published in
France in 1924, which praised as a specifically Impressionist quality
Conrad's focus upon the inner world of his characters. In contrast
to Balzac, the essay maintained, Conrad's writing 'does not trace
the reality before the man but the man in the face of reality; it
evokes subjectively integrated experiences because the impression
is equivalent to the totality of the perception'. Fernandez quotes, as
an authorial or narratorial enunciation of this principle, Marlow's
remark in *Chance*: 'I saw him only on that one occasion I told you of.
But it may be that a glimpse and no more is the proper way of
seeing an individuality.' Fernandez' development of this insight
was to prove even more thought provoking, his identification, as a
literary device peculiar to Conrad's writings, of the principle of
'delayed apprehension'. Incidents in the novels are, he pointed
out, frequently presented as puzzling first impressions, enigmatic
events, whose significance is only grasped later by the fictional
viewer. Primacy is thereby accorded to the initial fleeting glance, or
to the instantaneous reaction before the mind has had time to
absorb the impression or to establish logical connections, the original blurred response being, as in contemporary painting, valued
above explicit, detailed depiction. Hence the account in *The Shadow
Line*:

I became bothered by curious, irregular sounds of faint tapping on the deck. They could be heard single, in pairs, in groups. While I wondered at this mysterious devilry, I received a slight blow under the left eye and felt an enormous tear run down my cheek. Raindrops. Enormous. Forerunners of something...

As Ian Watt has, more recently, redefined that technique in his own sensitive study of Conrad, again relating it to Impressionist and Post-Impressionist painting, the individual's sensations of the external world are, by a process of delayed decoding, translated subsequently into the causal and conceptual terms which make them retroactively understandable to the observer and, by extension, to the reader.[9]

This is an insight undoubtedly valuable in defining Conrad's narrative method, but one wonders how justified it is to connect it, as both Fernandez and Watt do, to the French school of painters. Monet's swift 'impressions' of scenes, such as his sequential views of *Rouen Cathedral*, were indeed aimed at capturing transitory effects; but there was no attempt on his part to create a sense of delayed comprehension. On the contrary, the artist's concern was with the *initial* impact upon the eye, not with any retrospective elucidation. And the same holds true for his fellow painters. Upon more leisurely inspection, the viewer may appreciate the process whereby, in a canvas by Manet or Sisley, the visual effect has been achieved, the way in which a distant horse or sailboat consists in fact of a mere daub of paint or cluster of dots. But each of those objects is recognisable as such at first glance, subsequent analytical scrutiny forming no part of the artist's aesthetic purpose. To identify as Conrad's main indebtedness this technique of 'delayed apprehension' involves a misunderstanding of the paintings themselves.

There may be more truth in a remark by Sir Hugh Clifford cited by Fernandez, his observation that Conrad's depictions of the Malays 'were the result, as it were, of a series of flash-light impressions absorbed by a mind of strangely sensitive and imaginative quality'.[10] But the significance of that comment is to be found less in its connection with the Impressionists, as Fernandez claims, than in the image of the flashlight, suggesting as it does an indebtedness to contemporary photography. The flash illumines a scene so briefly and so dazzlingly that both eye and mind require a moment to absorb and apprehend it – a process closely paralleling Conrad's narrative strategy of delayed apprehension; but it is a process that had no relevance to Impressionist painting. Manet, Dégas and their contemporaries learned much from photography, as will be discussed later. But such lessons could not have included the principle of the eye's delayed reaction to flashlight, as magnesium flash was only in the embryonic stages of development when the Impressionists were at work. An experiment with magnesium flash for a group portrait by Fantin-Latour in 1884 proved a failure and was hence discarded by him when the photograph, after processing, revealed that 'almost everyone had abruptly shut their eyes'.[11]

This problematic use of the term Impressionism in relation to Conrad is deepened by its confusion with Symbolism during the 1890s. There were indeed shared elements that encouraged the merger and even the interchangeability of the terms, both movements resisting traditional forms of mimesis, although they tended to move in different directions. Jean Moréas' *Symbolist Manifesto* of 1886, which aimed at dissociating the movement from Impressionism, insisted that, in contrast to the Impressionists' striving for optical accuracy, their purpose was to present in perceptible form ideas existing beyond reality, in the world of the imagination.[12] Yet their paths did converge to some extent as the Impressionists, despite their conscious commitment to objective truth, began increasingly to express the transmuting of vision as filtered through the personality of the beholder, in a manner reflecting the delving into the inner self in the writings of Verlaine, Huysmans, Baudelaire and Mallarmé. The anti-establishment stance which these movements shared furthered their accord. The Symbolist journal *Révue Indépendante* openly acknowledged the Neo-Impressionist painters as fellow avant-gardists, reproducing in its pages canvases by Renoir, Signac and Seurat, and organising in its editorial office exhibitions of their paintings, with prominence accorded there to Manet, Pissarro, Morisot and Van Gogh.[13]

Yet here too the supposed connection of Conrad with Symbolism is tenuous, even though he was aware of the ideas of the movement, then being widely promulgated in England by Arthur Symons' study. The Symbolist concern with hallucination may have some slight bearing on Conrad's novels, such as Marlow's feverish condition, with its 'dream-sensation that pervaded all my days at that time'. But where the purpose of a leading Symbolist such as Gustav Moreau was to divorce himself entirely from the real world and to create instead, as in his *Evening and Sorrow* of 1882, an imagined mythological or allegorical entity, the dream element in Conrad's novels is a literary device to heighten the shock of discovery within the actual world, the revelation of the horrors of imperialism that he himself had witnessed. Such exposure of the social evils of his time is far removed from the Symbolist creed, as enunciated by Gustave Kahn, 'we are tired of the quotidian, the near-at-hand, and the compulsorily contemporaneous; we wish to be able to place the development of the symbol in any period whatsoever, and even in outright dreams'.[14] It has been suggested, for example, that the jungle setting, the voyage of discovery, and the ambiance of nightmare in Conrad's work resemble the atmosphere of Baudelaire's *Le Voyage* and Rimbaud's *Bâteau ivre*; but even allowing for the differences between poetry and prose (the translator in the following passage, despairing of capturing the highly intricate and compressed poetic images, was compelled to resort to poetic prose), the placing of any passage from the *Bâteau ivre* beside Conrad's work reveals the gulf that lies between:

> I who ran, spotted with electric crescents, a mad plank, escorted by the black sea-horses, when the Julies with bludgeon brought down in collapse the ultramarine skies with their ardent funnels; I who trembled, hearing whimper fifty leagues off the rut of Behemoths and the dense Maelstroms, eternal weaver of blue immobilities . . . [15]

There is in such writing an impassioned frenzy of drug-like intoxication, which Rimbaud himself termed a 'cultivation of insanity', foreign to Conrad's calm narrator, half-apologetically recalling his feverishness as perhaps clouding the accuracy of his account, but by that very means revealing his concern with a meticulous recording of the truth. If Conrad belongs to the Symbolists at all, it is, as Ian Watt finally admits, in a very limited and eclectic way, and there seems little to be gained by associating him with that school.[16]

All these attempts to establish a relationship with Impressionism have, then, by general consensus, proved unsatisfactory, only the theory of 'delayed apprehension' continuing to interest critics, while the relevance even of that aspect to the French school of painters is, as I have suggested, highly dubious. Michael Fried's essay on *Almayer's Folly*, subtitled: *on 'Impressionism' in Conrad, Crane, and Norris*, an essay resulting from Fried's earlier study of 'disfiguration' in the literature of the time, may appear from the title to continue the pursuit of such parallels; but in fact he specifically states that he is

employing the term only in a heuristic sense, having failed to be persuaded by the many critical attempts to relate the literature of the
late nineteenth century to French painting.[17] In my own suggestion
of the affinity between Conrad's writing and the French school of
painters, I should like to focus upon a specific problem that has arisen
in connection with his work and, through a close examination of
that problem, to suggest a fresh line of enquiry.

* * *

The high critical rating accorded to Conrad's novels throughout this
century has, from the first, been accompanied by persistent condemnation of a supposed defect in his writing, a defect so serious as
potentially to disqualify the author from any claim to literary distinction. E. M. Forster's review, published in 1921, before Conrad's
reputation had become firmly established, presented an assessment
of his work that was to be endorsed repeatedly by subsequent
critics, a castigation of the pervasive vagueness and abstractness of
his language. Conrad, he maintained, 'is always promising to make
some general philosophic statement about the universe, and then
refraining with a gruff disclaimer...sentence after sentence dis-
charges its smoke screen into our abashed eyes'. The result, he
claimed, was a half-dozen great books inspired by something noble,
heroic and beautiful, but so obscure at their vital moments that one
must conclude the author to be 'misty in the middle as well as at the
edges, that the secret casket of his genius contains a vapour rather
than a jewel'.[18]

Conrad's reputation survived the attack, but the stigma remained.
When F. R. Leavis, supplying for his generation the stamp of authoritative critical approval, identified Conrad as one of the four major
figures epitomising the 'great tradition' of the English novel, he
began, paradoxically enough, by admitting with exasperation his
own sense of a grave literary blemish in the writings, a failing so
severe that he had, until that point, set aside any attempt to provide
a critical study of the work. Only on coming across Forster's cen-
sorious review had he felt relieved of the need to deal with that flaw,
and free to concentrate upon Conrad's merits. The so-called profund-
ity so often imputed to Conrad's writings and deriving from the
mistiness of his allusive terms, was, he insisted, in reality the very
reverse, a reprehensible imperfection. The virtues of his style were to
be found instead, he argued on New Critical principles, in the con-

crete particularisation of his narration, in the vividness with which
The Heart of Darkness conveyed the experience of the author's own
journey into the Congo. Accordingly Leavis deplored the adjectival
insistence, the circumlocutory avoidance of precision represented by
such phrases as 'inconceivable mystery', 'unspeakable rites' and
'monstrous passions' as muffling the final effect, and producing a
cheapening of tone that was 'little short of disastrous' for the novel
as a whole.[19]

Such disapproval finds repeated echoes in subsequent criticism, as
in Edward Said's condemnation of the 'affected garrulity' in the
novels, interpreted by Said on psychological grounds as Conrad's
attempt to 'hide himself within the rhetoric' in order to camouflage
his own deep sense of guilt, a guilt identified there (with surprising
lack of evidence) as deriving from the desertion of his homeland and
the abandonment of his career at sea.[20] James Guetti saw that same
flaw as arising from a discrepancy between the moral assumptions
of the fictional narrative and the amoral reality which the journey
reveals.[21] And with the advent of postmodern critical strategies, the
charge remained essentially the same, while the terminology altered
accordingly. The mistiness of language began now to be interpreted
by J. Hillis Miller and others in deconstructionist formulation as representing the apocalyptic or parabolic quality of the work, the series
of ironic revelations that sequentially conceal rather than disclose
the promised truth.[22]

In a recent study, that perception of inner dialogical conflict,
while again being seen as a failing, has been attributed more specifically to the ambivalence detectable in Conrad's response to the
post-Nietzschean world. Daphna Erdinast-Vulcan, adopting the
postmodernist assumption of a conflict between text and subtext,
has suggested that Conrad's reluctant recognition of the universe as
devoid of God was countered by a submerged desire to reassert
Christian myth. The religious symbolism in the story, ironically
applied to the faithless Europeans whom he identifies as 'pilgrims',
'apostles' and supposed 'emissaries of light', implies by contrast that
Marlow himself is engaged on a more valid quest, a pilgrimage in
search of moral meaning. That quest, constantly undermined by the
accompanying note of scepticism and despair, is eventually frustrated
by the recognition that no final truth can be attained. And one result
of that dialogical tension, she maintains, is the unfortunate haziness
of language, symptomatic of the author's own unresolved spiritual
predicament. Acknowledging that such stylistic imprecision could

indeed prove damaging to the effectiveness of the work, she turns elsewhere for the story's redeeming quality, attributing the enduring nature of the tale to Marlow's affirmation of his task, his pledge of commitment to the role of the narrator.[23]

This dissatisfaction with the nebulousness of Conrad's style at the climactic moments of his narrative, a charge potentially so damning to a writer, manifests itself almost invariably, one notes, within critical studies that acknowledge, either overtly or by implication, that Conrad remains in the final analysis a novelist of the highest rank. Perhaps it is time to enquire whether that supposed fault should be reassessed, whether it should be seen instead as an integral and ultimately positive aspect of his artistic achievement. In that regard, Jerry Wasserman, in one of the most perceptive essays on Conrad in recent years, provides a valuable starting point. Instead of condemning the impenetrability of language, he has argued that it represents in this story the author's ambivalence towards the effectiveness of words, since, as Marlow perceived, rhetoric had become in his generation a tool of imperial expansion, an unsavoury instrument of civilisation that, instead of defining and clarifying, is employed to obfuscate. As the story itself notes, natives are arbitrarily designated 'rebels' or 'criminals' whenever such nomenclature aids the oppressive practices of the imperialists. As part of Marlow's distrust of language, Wasserman notes that his most effective means of communication are non-linguistic – the blowing of the steam whistle at a moment of crisis, the gestures whereby he conveys meaning to the natives – while the expressive silence of the forest reveals to him the poverty of human speech. In that context, the eloquence which Marlow so admires in Kurtz constitutes an enviable ability to use words that he himself lacks, the final cry of horror representing for him a courageous affirmation of speech. Had he been faced with such darkness, Marlow concludes, 'I would have nothing to say. This is the reason why I affirm that Kurtz was a remarkable man. He had something to say. He said it.'[24]

That more positive response to the impenetrability of language as an intrinsic aspect of the story has wider connotations, especially when placed within the setting of contemporary art movements. Descriptive clarity and a striving for mimetic fidelity belong in general, as Wilhelm Worringer argued cogently at the beginning of this century, to generations placing their trust in the validity of tangible, observable phenomena or to generations assuming the existence of an ultimate harmony between man and the world about him. Those are qualities characteristic of the Italian quattrocento, with Alberti's Neoplatonic description of beauty as consisting of the harmony of all the parts 'fitted together with such proportion and connection that nothing could be added, diminished or altered but for the worse'. They are to be found in the work of the Dutch seventeenth-century painters, reflecting their confidence in a materialistic, moneyed bourgeoisie; in Defoe's verisimilitude of detail during the rationalism of the early eighteenth century; and, as Linda Nochlin has shown, in Courbet and Flaubert when attempting to capture in their respective media the social actualities of their time with the truthfulness of objective observers.[25]

Leavis's condemnation of Conrad's stylistic vagueness formed part of a similar, if later phenomenon, as New Criticism, attempting to parallel the objectivity of the empirical sciences, sought in the mid-twentieth century to develop within literary investigation a method of analysis reliant upon close scrutiny of texts, and accurate identification of the connotations and ambivalences of words. Accordingly it developed a preference, as in the revived contemporary interest in Donne's poetry, for authors who employed those linguistic interrelationships with precision.[26] Hence arose the dissatisfaction of such critics with Conrad's stylistic 'vagueness', however readily they might acknowledge his other virtues. But that approach involved a fundamental misconception of his purpose. For the empirically based principles by which they were evaluating his writing were diametrically opposed to those Conrad was consciously cultivating, as an early and leading exponent of a movement countering the empiricist tendencies of his time, and projecting a disturbed awareness of the imponderables in human existence, of mysteries upon which the new science could shed little light.

In turning to the visual arts, we shall need to resort to a major principle governing this present investigation. Those critics attempting to identify Impressionist tendencies in Conrad, whether related to the pictorial or the literary versions of that term, have searched for signs of a personal indebtedness to his predecessors, for ways in which his writing may have absorbed elements derived from those painters and writers who were active in the generation prior to his own. If, however, pursuing the synchronic approach, we focus not upon his predecessors but upon his immediate contemporaries, those artists confronting similar problems and challenges in the kindred media, the enquiry becomes redirected from the Impressionists, active a generation before Conrad's major phase, and towards their successors,

the Post-Impressionists of his own time. Paul Gauguin, acknowledged by that latter group as their leading theoretician and artistic
innovator,[27] may prove particularly valuable here, not as a source of
Conrad's characteristic traits and stylistic innovations, but as a fellow artist simultaneously exploring, during the peak years of his
own activity from 1896 to his death in 1903, many of the author's
profoundest concerns, and introducing into his paintings elements
close to those being developed within the stories and novels of Conrad's major period, from *Almayer's Folly* in 1898 to *Nostromo* in 1904.
Our main focus will be upon the stylistic changes they initiated, of
fundamental importance to the movement of Modernist art at large,
and, most of all, upon their desertion of the perceptual in favour of
the conceptual. But that stylistic change is intimately related to their
thematic concerns, as New Art History theory has led us to perceive.

The study of semiotics, particularly the theory of art as representation rather than mimesis, has, as noted in the Introduction to this
volume, encouraged a fundamental reinterpretation of painting and
literature, perceiving them as a series of communicative *signs* creating discourse between the creative artist and the receptor. Since
signs, to be recognisable, rely necessarily upon associations shared
by the perceptors, the discourse generated is seen to be determined
in large part by the cultural, economic and social setting of the time;
and prominent among those hidden assumptions is the nature of contemporary patronage, a patronage that exploits the arts as a means
of exerting power. Julia Kristeva, for example, has revealed how
Giotto's use both of colour and of spatial composition in his frescoes
in the Arena Chapel in Padua reflect the 'liberating' humanist
renewal of Christianity during the early fourteenth century, and the
contemporary dominance of the Florentine upper-middle class.[28] But
as Norman Bryson and others have shown, the creative artist is not
shackled by the connotations of a sign.[29] Sensitive to approaching
change, and at times even helping to instigate it, the artist can alter
or adapt the associations of such signs both stylistically and thematically. I would like to suggest that it is this very process of sensitivity
to cultural change and the shared resistance of Conrad and Gauguin
to the power play of the time that produced in their work stylistic
innovations expressing their instinctive opposition to concepts current in their day.

Central in the work of both was a withdrawal from the civilised
world of urban Europe into the mystery and fascination associated
with the primeval, their journey into the residues of the past serving

as a voyage of self-discovery and revelation. Intrinsic to this with-drawal from civilisation – and remarkable in the contrast it afforded to the accepted modes of their time – was the respect accorded to the 'natives' in the accounts of their respective voyages. Even among professional ethnologists in the later decades of the nineteenth cen-tury, interest in the culture and rituals of surviving tribal societies was at that time condescending, even disdainful, such study prov-ing useful, it was implied, only in the evidence it provided of the impressive progress made by mankind since such crude beginnings. In the realm of art history, Gottfried Semper's *Der Stil in den tech-nischen und taktonischen Kuensten* of 1861, which was to dominate research until the end of the century, deplored the non-mimetic quality of early art, attributing its cause to the inflexibility of artisans unable to free themselves from limitations inherent in the original technical processes of manufacture, those restrictions persisting even when the earlier processes had been improved upon or even discarded. And Alfred Haddon's *Evolution in Art* of 1895, as its title suggests, reflected the general view of history at that time, as a grad-ual progression from savagery to civilisation. The non-mimetic qual-ity of tribal totem poles and cave drawings are ascribed in his work to early man's incompetence, an inability to copy objects effectively, that latter skill being mastered only by later generations.[30] The schol-arly attitude of *noblesse oblige* predominated, with only few excep-tions, throughout the century,[31] characterising even the London Colonial Exposition of 1887 and the Paris Exhibition of 1889, where harpoons, arrows and axes used by early societies or employed by surviving African and New Guinea tribes were displayed, together with a limited number of artifacts, to illustrate the crude beginnings of mankind's attempt to achieve mechanical advancement.

Gauguin's response to the 1889 Paris Exhibition was refreshingly different, the visit constituting for him an artistic revelation, a turn-ing point in his aesthetic development. Fascinated by the pristine vigour of the Aztec sculpture displayed there, he began admiringly to incorporate its forms into his own work, searching for similar instances in artifacts from other ancient cultures. As he explained in a letter to Daniel de Monfreid in 1897, he viewed the supposed crudity of such works as resulting not from lack of skill but from the crafts-man's deliberate 'deformation' of nature in order to convey the mys-terious power of the gods represented.[32] The sense of mystery he discerned there was to be of vital importance to his own artistic development, and forms a fundamental part of the present argument.

Indeed his conception of the tribal craftsman as consciously re-
nouncing mimetic representation in favour of stylised forms was
to mark a turning point in Western regard for such ancient arts,
inaugurating the validation of such pristine works as models for
painting and sculpture in the twentieth century.[33]

For our own era, with its demand that alternative cultural traditions –
such as African, Mexican or American Indian – be incorporated
into the curriculum of studies as equally worthy of respect, the
trail-blazing work of Gauguin deserves especial esteem. Almost
alone, he responded some hundred years ago to those so-called
'primitive' art forms not only without condescension but with deep
admiration for their superiority to his own artistic tradition, perceiving there a process of non-mimetic representationalism sorely lacking in the West. Indeed, as so often in the history of such changes,
his adoption of certain of their techniques is to be seen less as an
'influence' upon his work than as his discovery in them of authority
for his own emergent desire to forego the principle of illusionist verisimilitude, a principle that had dominated Western painting from
the time of the Renaissance and (if in altered form) had continued to
motivate the Impressionists' attempt to capture with accuracy the
fugitive effects of changing light.[34] Instead, Gauguin saw in totemic
sculpture a model for his own wish to represent in art the cerebral
as opposed to the objective, to discard literalist representation in
favour of the envisioned. It encouraged in his art intimations of the
mysterious, the submerged, the abstract essence beyond the merely
visible that was soon to become so central to Modernist art. And it is,
I would suggest, in the context of that new principle, the allusive
gesturing towards an idea in place of literalist or accurate depiction,
that Conrad's much maligned stylistic 'nebulousness' should be
placed.

Gauguin first came across the 'tiki' patterns on Marquesan decor-
ated staffs in Tahiti (he did not visit the Marquesan islands themselves until some ten years later), and he became fascinated by their
facial forms, consisting of enlarged eyes and exaggerated nostrils in
a manner far removed from the mimetic. In assimilating them into
his woodcut of *The Crucifixion* in 1891 (Figure 1), he was not only
adopting an admired artistic technique but, by deliberately merging
the pagan with the Christian, implying that they were cross-cultural
facets of the same basic human concerns. He was intrigued, for
example, by the resemblance between the cross-legged, seated posture
in representations of Indonesian deities (he possessed photographs

of such sculpture) and the pose of idols worshipped by the Polynesians; and his linking of such early art with the Christian Crucifixion placed them on essentially the same level. His enthusiasm for such art at a time of the general disdain towards it was to affect his contemporaries directly. It was, for example, his painting of a Tahitian woman beside a Polynesian totem that Roger Fry selected for the poster advertising the famed Post-Impressionist exhibition at the Grafton Gallery in 1910, and that led to Fry's influential essays, published soon afterwards, in which he validated for his generation 'Negro Sculpture' and 'The Art of the Bushman', essays later incorporated into his widely read *Vision and Design*.[35] And the interest in primitivist art that Gauguin inaugurated was, filtered through his friends and admirers, to culminate in the elongated sculptures by Modigliani based on the African totem pole, as well as in Picasso's *Les Demoiselles D'Avignon*, one figure of which derived from the Marquesan 'tiki' sculpture owned by the painter and on permanent display in his studio.

Conrad evinced little interest in totemic statues or artifacts; but at this time of general condescension towards such tribal cultures he did manifest a positive response to the extraordinary power and beauty of the primeval. As Chinua Achebe has reminded us in a very moving essay, Conrad was not free from certain racist prejudices common to his generation. He tends at times to regard the natives as children, he refers to the 'babble' of their language and the 'frenzy' of their dances in a manner that is indeed offensive by the standards prevailing in our own day.[36] Moreover, postmodern criticism has revealed the innate tendency of human beings to misrepresent the 'otherness' of persons alien to themselves and to attach to foreign cultures exotic myths and fantasies closer to their own imaginative needs than to the reality of the alien world; and there was without doubt some degree of misrepresentation in this instance. Similarly Marianna Torgovnick deplores Conrad's failure to follow through, to deal with the 'really radical themes' of colonial exploitation and feminist principles raised in this work.[37] But that, surely, is to judge him by concepts generated and broadly adopted only during the latter part of our century, with its antipathy to all forms of imperial subjugation. Viewed within the context of the early 1900s, the sympathy and genuine admiration Conrad felt towards the natives was not only exceptional; it marked, as we now know, a revolution in the attitude to colonialism itself, a revolution that contributed greatly to the standards now prevalent in our own time with its condemnation of all forms of repression. Echoing behind our present denunciation of imperialist expansion as being an unjustified imposition of a supposedly superior civilisation upon an authentic native way of life is the famous phrase from the enveloping narrative of *Heart of Darkness*, that imperial conquest constitutes no more than the taking away of land 'from those who have a different complexion or slightly flatter noses than ourselves'. Marlow admires the natural 'statuesque repose' of the bronzed, muscular natives before they were starved to skeletons by their oppressors or reduced to absurdity by the loincloths prudishly forced upon them, loincloths whose 'short ends behind waggled to and fro like tails'. And the women he depicts as embodiments of primordial truths, of passions rooted in the enigmatic power of the primeval world in a manner elevating them above the sheltered women of Europe, the latter so hopelessly out of touch with reality:

> She walked with measured steps, draped in striped and fringed cloths, treading the earth proudly, with a slight jingle and flash of barbarous ornaments. She carried her head high . . . She looked at all of us as if her life had depended upon the unswerving steadiness of her glance.[38]

Elsewhere, through his fictional Lingard, Conrad described the jungle itself with awed admiration:

> . . . the landscape of brown golds and brilliant emeralds under the dome of hot sapphire; the whispering big trees; the loquacious nipa-palms that rattled their leaves volubly in the night breeze, as if in haste to tell him all the secrets of the great forest behind them. He loved the heavy scents of blossoms and black earth . . . [39]

This shared respect for primitive culture may have its source, partly at least, in a biographical similarity between the two men, a detail well-known in relation to Conrad but less so for Gauguin – that they had both begun their careers as professional seamen and had pursued that calling for many years. Gauguin, like Conrad, signed on for a career at sea at the age of seventeen, and continued in the profession for more than six years before choosing a more settled life ashore. Their personal acquaintance with native cultures in the course of their sea journeys no doubt endowed them with an ability to evaluate their own societies by criteria drawn from a broader cultural

range than was available to their peers, especially as their own con-
tacts ashore were untainted by the social superiority to the natives
experienced by colonial administrators. In that latter regard, there
may appear to be a fundamental difference between the two, that
Gauguin represented his Tahiti as a Paradise, a languorous Eden,
while Conrad's Congo was depicted as a Hell on Earth. But in fact,
even in this respect, their responses were remarkably close, Gauguin's natives depicted in a world as yet untouched by the corrup-
tions of civilisation, while Conrad's Inferno portrays them after
aggressive colonialist incursion.

Gauguin's response to imperialism is, like his seafaring experience, less widely known to the general public, his reaction, with no
less abhorrence than Conrad's, to the hypocritical greed and appalling cruelty that he saw motivating the colonial process itself, at a
time when imperialism was traditionally regarded as a noble cause,
bringing Christian morality, justice and cultural advancement to the
backward places of the earth. By chance, Gauguin's arrival in Tahiti
had coincided with the death of its country's native king, Pomeré
the Fifth, a king who had made acceptance of French protectionism
for the colony conditional on the recognition of his monarchal rights
throughout the period of his lifetime. His demise, therefore, only
four days after Gauguin landed on the island, removed that protective barrier, unleashing upon the Polynesians the full force of
French colonial power. With growing disgust, Gauguin witnessed
the unimpeded rush of petty officials, of police, clergy and missionaries to fill the monarchal vacuum, harshly imposing their rule, ruthlessly suppressing local customs, and exploiting the natives with
unbridled rapacity, corruption and self-interest. In his *Intimate
Journals*, Gauguin records how the gendarmes now demanded sexual
gratification from the native women under threat of arrest for
imputed infringements of the law, a law for the most part incomprehensible to the island's inhabitants. The courts, where such arrests
were tried, Gauguin saw as a grotesque parody of justice, with the
judge

in a hurry to pass sentence knowing nothing, nothing of what the
natives are like. Seeing before him a tattooed face, he says to himself, 'There's a cannibal brigand,' especially when the gendarme,
who has an interest in the matter, tells him so. The trial concludes
with the imposition of an absurdly large fine, equivalent to the
entire yield of the valley. Is this humane, is this ethical?

The clergy and missionaries, from whom some higher level of morality might have been expected, behaved no better, acting, in his eyes, as lackeys of an insatiably cruel and corrupt Church:

> The missionary is no longer a man, a conscience... They say to him, 'Kill!' – and he kills. 'It is God who wills it!'
> 'Seize that region,' – and he seizes it.
> 'Seize that inheritance,' – and he seizes it.
> Your wealth? There is not a square inch of land that you have not extorted from the faithful by the promise of heaven, obliging them to give you the fruits of everything that is sold, even the fruits of prostitution.

Of colonialism itself Gauguin caustically remarked, 'they cut people's throats under the pretext of spreading civilization. When they are tired of firing at rabbits, they fire at the blacks.'[40]

Conrad may write with quieter irony, but the impact is no less chilling. With withering scorn Marlow, recalling his meeting with a drunken colonial officer who had announced importantly that he was responsible for the upkeep of the road, comments wrily: 'Can't say I saw any road or any upkeep, unless the body of a middle-aged negro, with a bullet-hole in the forehead, upon which I absolutely stumbled three miles farther on, may be considered as a permanent improvement' (p. 20).

The Edenic world of Gauguin's paintings was thus an impassioned reaction to colonial abuse, an attempt to capture, before its disappearance, an admired world of mutual respect and affection, of unembarrassed nakedness, of simple daily activities in a Tahitian village as yet untouched by the encroaching exploiters. Gauguin who, on his arrival, was initially welcomed into the community of white Europeans, deserted it almost immediately in protest at the cruelty he had witnessed, moving, to the strong disapproval of his compatriots, into a native village and transferring his sympathies unreservedly to its inhabitants. In contrast to the avarice of the colonials, he learned to respect the natives' generosity, the hospitality they extended to visitors from neighbouring villages, gratitude being neither offered nor expected even when the visitors were total strangers. Stealing, he adds, with a side-glance at his own country, was a crime entirely unknown among them. He studied their language, lauding the surprising flexibility of its vocabulary, and, as a gesture of the need to preserve their culture from suppression by the invaders, began from this point to title his canvases in Polynesian dialect, incomprehensible though it was to potential purchasers in Europe.

The similarity between the two men outlined here may seem primarily thematic, a convergence of artist and writer in their sympathy for the natives. But it arose from impulses highly significant for the stylistic innovations they introduced to their respective media, impulses revealing, in addition to the humanitarian, their responsiveness to a major cultural shift of their time. In contrast to the 'noble savage' movement of the eighteenth century, the idealisation of the primitive that, as Hoxey N. Fairchild pointed out many years ago, emerges cyclically in generations wearied by intellectual sophistication,[41] the new movement was rooted in a fundamentally new conception of human development. It marked a reaction to the dominant mode, a reaction whose ultimate significance was not always perceived by those scholars most active in promulgating it. For the contemporary arrogance towards the native reflected, and to a large extent resulted from, the 'optimistic' interpretation of Darwinian evolution as an upward progression, moving through the centuries from the crude and aboriginal to the civilised and refined. It was a prejudice so marked among Victorian intellectuals that their attitude, in the extremity of the sentiments expressed, reads today almost as a parody of racism. So eminent a personality as James Hunt, the first president of the British Anthropological Society, declared as axiomatic in his opening address in 1863 that negroes were closer to the ape than were the Europeans and hence were incapable of being civilised. In a debate held at the same Society some three years later, one member advocated, to the applause of the group at large, the massacring of savages as 'a philanthropic principle' benefiting mankind at large. And in his influential study *Prehistoric Times* of 1865, which has been categorised as second only to Lyell's work in its impact upon the Victorian intellectual, John Lubbock described the savage as 'neither free nor noble; he is a slave to his own wants, his own passions; ... ignorant of agriculture, living by the chase, and improvident in success'.

Such early societies were seen as, by nature, morally undeveloped and hence inferior. Henry Sidgwick's *An Outline of the History of Ethics* (1886), J. G. Romanes' *Mental Evolution in Man* (1888) and Henry Drummond's *The Ascent of Man* (1894), all well-known Victorian studies, assumed as unquestionable the superiority of their own culture to those of earlier eras. Only towards the turn of the century, at a time when both Conrad and Gauguin were expressing

their own sympathies, did Edward Burnett Tylor begin to suggest a
relativist approach for anthropology, a respect for pluralism in
culture, arguing that tribal behaviour which through Western eyes,
might appear irrational or purposeless, could often be discerned as
perfectly acceptable within the context of the society itself.[42] But
there can be no doubt that the more contemptuous attitude continued to prevail, as in the essays by James G. Frazer published at
that time and forming the groundwork for his major study, *The
Golden Bough*. As J. W. Burrow has rightly remarked, it was ironical
that men who had sufficient scientific detachment to treat primitive
ritual and religion as elements integral to social life were, by their
own distrust of the Christian faith, least likely to appreciate what
religion meant to the worshippers themselves.[43] Hence the condescension in Frazer's work as, with the confidence of an enlightened
intellectual, he examined analytically the 'absurd' superstitions of
the past, arising from the terrors to which the worshippers were
subject in their exposure to the vicissitudes of nature and which, he
implied, had ceased to be relevant to more advanced man. For such
beliefs, whether pagan or Christian, Frazer had nothing but disdain,
summarising his study as 'the melancholy record of human error
and folly'.

Conrad was familiar with contemporary anthropological research,
not least through his friend and fellow Polish exile Branislaw
Manilowski, who was a disciple of Frazer.[44] But in place of Frazer's
confident superiority – his habit of writing as an enlightened intellectual addressing other enlightened intellectuals – Conrad recognised a reverse reading implicit in that condescending approach. For
if Christianity, from which the Western world had, through the centuries, derived its social and moral principles, was now defined as
emanating from primitive vegetative impulses shared with the most
'barbaric' of African tribes, then perhaps the enlightened civilisation
of the nineteenth century at large, upon which Frazer's generation
so obviously prided itself, was vulnerable to the same withering
scrutiny. Perhaps, for all the eloquence and noble ideals to which it
subscribed, it was motivated by the same greeds and lusts, the same
egocentric impulses as Frazer attributed to primordial man – with
the one notable reservation that the 'savage', aware of those impulses,
had to some extent, been able, to control them.

This shared perception leads us into the central concern of this chapter, the stylistic effect of their new ideas upon both writer and artist,
and the similarities in the way such views manifested themselves in

their work. While style has always been seen by critics as integral to content, as being, at its best, not imposed upon the material but as developing organically from it, recent theory has granted to rhetoric an even more performative and manipulative function than was previously accorded. Terry Eagleton and others have come to see it in terms of cultural relativism, as reflecting and perhaps modifying the economic, philosophical and political assumptions of each generation. Richard Rorty, taking that view much further, denies altogether the existence of transcendental absolutes, interpreting the rhetorical strategies of texts as devices for creating substitute values in a world of shifting criteria. Truth, he argues, is not to be seen as a vertical relationship between representations and what is represented, but should be regarded

> horizontally – as the culminating reinterpretation of our predecessors' reinterpretation of their predecessors' reinterpretation. . . . It is the difference between regarding truth, goodness, and beauty as eternal objects which we try to locate and reveal, and regarding them as artifacts whose fundamental design we often have to alter.[45]

It is in that context that the stylistic innovations of Gauguin and Conrad should be examined, as expressions of their shared perception of the inscrutability of the primeval, their sense, in contrast to the rationalists of their time, of mysterious, uncontrollable elements existing beyond the factual and both deepening and enriching human experience. Gauguin's notebooks and the personal records of his Tahitian experience may highlight the erotic attractions the island held for him, the physical delight afforded him by its amenable native women, including his beloved mistress Tahura, of whom he wrote: 'And the Eve of this Paradise became more and more docile, more loving. I was permeated by her fragrance – noa, noa'; and the entire work of that name is a paean to the erogenous, paradisial quality of the island.[46] But the translation of that experience on to his canvases is Edenic in a very different sense. His nude women have none of the sexual voluptuousness of Renoir's fleshly models, nor indeed of those depicted more coyly in Victorian art, in the Roman canvases of Alma-Tadema or the allegorical scenes by Lord Leighton. Gauguin's are Edenic not in the alluring quality of their nudity but in their *remoteness* from the actuality of this world, their elevation above life. His female figures, indeed, are not merely untouched by civilisation; they are themselves transmuted into enigmatic artifacts.

That effect of remoteness was achieved by the importation into his art of a technique that was to prove, in addition to his admiration of totems, a major influence on his contemporaries, the principle of 'cloisonism'. Inspired by the tradition of medieval enamels and stained glass, where shaped pieces consisting of a single, unvaried colour were held in place by metal surrounds, Gauguin introduced into his own paintings boldly outlined areas of unmodulated colour, free from the delicate shading traditionally employed from the time of the Renaissance onward to create illusions of solidity and depth. If Renaissance perspective had been primarily mimetic, aimed, in Da Vinci's words, at 'nothing else than seeing a place or objects behind a pane of glass, quite transparent, on the surface of which the objects behind that glass are drawn', Gauguin was deserting that tradition of art as a window on reality in favour of art as deliberate stylisation.[47] It was a process reinforced for him by the discovery that Japanese painting employed a similar technique – simple areas of colour, demarcated by dark contours. Its attraction for him derived, as in the Aztec sculpture he so admired, from the implied rejection of naturalism in favour of ritualised forms. Like the medievalist, if from different motives, he wished to represent in his paintings a truth existing beyond the tactile and the visible. And cloisonism facilitated that end. It provided him with an essentially new artistic approach, which his friend Van Gogh admiringly imported into his own canvases and was to be adopted before long as a primary ingredient of Post-Impressionist painting.

Semiotically, *Te Aa No Areois – The Seed of the Areois* (Figure 2) covertly transmits three signals to the viewer, each of them divorcing the painting from the Western tradition of female nudes. The firm dark line bounding her figure, reminiscent of the metal outlining of stained-glass windows, stylises the representation, isolating her from the real world. Then, the flat colour-wash of her limbs, exempting them from shadow or the fall of light on shaped surface, divests them of depth-illusion, freeing the image from the kind of fleshliness associated with the erotic. And the angle of view from below further enhances her dignity, raising her to the status of some occult demi goddess, with the allusive title hinting at her primal, life-giving powers. The Eden he creates in his canvases is hence mythic in quality, divorced from the merely mimetic. Visual fidelity was no longer the aim, as it had been even for so non-naturalistic a painter as

Cézanne, striving as he did to capture the optical distortions created by the adjacency of objects. The artist has moved beyond that into the conception of art as conveying the quintessence of objects and scenes, an intangibility existing behind the visible, but imaginatively perceived by the artist. Indeed Gauguin contrasted the principles he adopted for his Post-Impressionist painting with those assumed by the Impressionists, commenting drily that his predecessors had, for all their innovations, retained 'the shackles of verisimilitude'. And, in a passage seminal in its implications for the twentieth century, he rejected the long-established naturalistic tradition of Western art, advising the painter to 'think more of the creation that will result than of nature'.

Seurat and Pissarro may have analysed the bark of a tree into its component dots of colour in an attempt to recreate with greater optical accuracy the effect upon the human retina, but there is no such purpose behind Gauguin's blue tree trunks – vegetation such as has never existed in nature – nor in the splashes of red and green vaguely indicative of shrub or lawn in the dream world of his art. The bright colours characterising his canvases contributed to their distancing from actuality, suggesting the cryptic quality of the scene, its enchanting indeterminacy: 'One does not use colour to draw but always to give the musical sensations which flow from itself, from its own nature, from its mysterious and enigmatic interior force.'[48] Strindberg was among the first to perceive this non-naturalistic quality in Gauguin's paintings, initially with some antagonism but, as he admitted in the course of a letter to the artist, with a growing recognition of its essential originality:

> I saw on the walls of your studio that confusion of sun-flooded paintings which pursued me this night in my sleep. I saw trees that no botanist would ever discover, animals that Cuvier never suspected the existence of, and men that you alone have been able to create. A sea that might flow from a volcano, a sky in which no god could live. Monsieur (said I in my dream), you have created a new earth and a new heaven...[49]

The technique Gauguin introduced was to function in Modernist art in various ways, adapted by each subsequent painter to serve his or her individual needs within the larger motif of transcending the literal or naturalistic. Toulouse-Lautrec, in a manner brilliantly suited to the art of the poster, used the bold outlining of unvariegated patches of colour to convey the garishness of Parisian nightlife; Matisse created delicate arabesques of contoured pastel hues even further removed from reality, and, together with his fellow Fauvists, adopted Gauguin's unrepresentational use of vivid tones. But Gauguin, as the initiator, employed his innovations in a different way, to transform his scenes into icons of a far-off Eden, an Eden haunted by impalpable forces lurking behind the façade of the physical. As Mallarmé remarked of one of Gauguin's Tahitian canvases, 'It is amazing that one can put so much mystery in so much brilliance.' And Gauguin himself defined his purpose as an attempt to depict that part of nature which one does not see:

> ... the primitive soul, the unearthly consolation of our sufferings to the extent that they are vague and incomprehensible before the mystery of our origin and of our future.[50]

Mahana no Atua – The Day of God (Figure 3) of 1893 thus becomes transmuted into a hieratic image. The stylised poses of the figures to the left echo the wall paintings in Egyptian tombs, the flat, unvaried patches of colour endow the localised landscape with archetypal significance, while the idol dominating the scene, based on the Easter Island figures of which he had read in J. A. Moerenhoet's *Voyages aux îles du grand océan* (1837), creates an effect paralleling Conrad's famed description of the dark forest of the Congo as 'the stillness of an implacable force brooding over an inscrutable intention'.

In the context of this shared concern with the impenetrable forces of mystery, to censure Conrad for stylistic imprecision, for a rhetoric that merely obfuscates, is as inappropriate, I would suggest, as to judge Gauguin's paintings by the criterion of Courbet's realism. For Conrad's 'nebulousness' derives, like Gauguin's mysterious Eden, from his attempt to hint at larger, arcane powers beyond the perceptual, the primeval forces motivating mankind whose unfathomability forms part of their being. Moreover the literary process Conrad employs to create this effect in his writings bears close comparison to that adopted by Gauguin. As the dusky female in *Te Aa No Areois* is elevated by cloisonist technique above the real world into a symbol of the Earth's primitive fertilising powers, so Kurtz's native mistress is exalted above the real world, endowed with an intangible grandeur and menace derived from the hidden, unplumbed regions of the primeval, of which she becomes at that moment the allegorical embodiment:

She was savage and superb, wild-eyed and magnificent; there was something ominous and stately in her deliberate progress. And in the hush that had fallen suddenly upon the whole sorrowful land, the immense wilderness, the colossal body of the fecund and mysterious life seemed to look at her, pensive, as though it had been looking at the image of its own tenebrous and passionate soul.[51]

It has become a cliché of modern criticism, since the appearance of Albert Guerard's study in the 1950s,[52] to assume that Marlow's voyage to the Congo was a process of discovery, revealing to him profound truths of which he had previously been unaware. But the text offers clear indications to the contrary, a difference very relevant to our present concerns. For it presents the narrator, Marlow, not as making some profound discovery in the process of his journey but, like Gauguin, intuitively aware of the humanity of these dark-skinned 'rebels', and accordingly disgusted at the maltreatment meted out to them by the contemptuous Western colonisers. Even before he had set out on the journey, Marlow had already perceived Brussels, the Western capital from which the colonial administrators were despatched and by which they were controlled, to be a 'whited sepulchre,' outwardly pure but inwardly corrupt. While waiting for the boat that has yet to carry him into the jungle, he recognises the irony of the painting executed by Kurtz as a representation of the imperial ideal – a female figure bearing a lighted torch – and he notes its 'sinister' implications. And all this before he had encountered the cruelty of Belgian colonial rule. In that painting, Kurtz, paralleling traditional personifications of Justice, had depicted his female figure blindfolded. The result, however, as Marlow recognises, is a truer expression of imperialism than Kurtz had intended, with the supposed bearer of the light of civilisation unable herself to see the light. Above all there is Marlow's own account of the moment when he finally confronts the evidence of the human sacrifices that Kurtz has had offered up to him, the proof of the dreadful corruption of the imperial ideal. Gazing through binoculars at the supposed wooden knobs on the poles around Kurtz's house, he focuses upon one, suddenly recognising it as a human head. The sight causes him to throw his head back 'as if before a blow'. But as he explains a moment later: 'I was not so shocked as you may think. The start back I had given was really nothing but a movement of surprise. I had expected to see a knob of wood there, you know ...'.[53] His surprise was the timing, shock not at the discovery but at the nature of the evidence, the decapitated heads providing proof of a principle he had already acknowledged before setting out. The entire journey was for Marlow a search for confirmation, to authenticate his realisation that Western imperialism was, beneath its eloquent and noble ideals, motivated by crass economic greed. In that, Marlow (and indeed Conrad himself) resembled Gauguin in being almost alone in his intuitive recognition of the rights of the natives and his innate sympathy for their suffering at the hands of their colonial exploiters.

Gauguin's respect for the essential humanity of the natives was motivated to a large extent by a recognition that the rationalism of the Western world had deprived it of its sense of the arcane, of the mystic powers of nature to which a life at sea can, as we know from Conrad's writings, sensitise a thinking individual. That sensitivity was, moreover, strengthened by a new conception of mankind arising just at that time. For in place of the dominant nineteenth-century view of ancient tribes as culturally immature societies, a counter-movement began to emerge, of which Gauguin was the acknow-ledged pioneer – a growing recognition of what Jung was to term some twenty years later the 'collective unconscious', the idea that there exists an amalgam of mythic configurations fundamental to all human experience and underlying all cultures. His acknowledg-ment of that anthropological substratum, of patterns common to the variegated forms of human behaviour, including seasonal celebra-tions, social customs and religious beliefs, encouraged a perception of the universality of mankind, with the similarity between sacred practices in different creeds no longer casting doubt upon their validity but authenticating them, as satisfying the basic needs of human existence.

Gauguin's early recognition that the posture assigned to Indo-nesian deities resembled that of the Polynesian gods, as mentioned earlier, forms part of this approach, his introduction of Buddha-like figures into his paintings, as in his *Barbaric Tales*, his evocation of Egyptian painting within the Tahitian canvases and his validation of Aztec sculpture. But perhaps even more significant was his innov-ative treatment of Christianity itself. Generally regarded as an atheist, he did indeed reject the dogmas of the church. As we have seen, he was appalled by the behaviour of its priests and missionaries. Yet despite this ostensible dissociation from its practices, he repeatedly incorporated Christian elements as central motifs in his work. One out of every ten canvases he produced included such Christian themes, in a manner scarcely indicative of a rejection of the faith.[54]

Those motifs, significantly, were not presented in traditional form but in terms of universal, archetypal myth. *Te Tamari No Atua – The Birth of Christ, the Son of God*, now in the Neue Pinakothek in Munich, like the similar version in the Hermitage Museum, start-lingly transposed the Nativity scene to a Tahitian setting, depicting a dark-skinned woman delivered of a haloed baby within a stable, a canvas believed to have been painted at the time Gauguin's mistress Pahura gave birth to their short-lived child.[55] Such translation of Christian scenes into contemporary or local settings had, it is true, been endemic in late-medieval Christian art. European painters, such as the Limbourg brothers, could unconcernedly place within their representation of the biblical Bethlehem the churches of Notre Dame and Sainte Chapelle familiar to them from contemporary Paris.[56] In that transference of biblical locale to the immediate environ-ment, therefore, there was nothing intrinsically new. But Gauguin was painting long after Western art had rejected such anachronisms in favour of historical accuracy. Moreover he was not a native Tahit-ian, naively visualising a sacred scene from the past in terms of his own surroundings. He was a European producing canvases for sale to other Europeans, and was thus deliberately violating accepted practice, provocatively translating the scriptural scene into another culture, a culture considered at that time as distinctly inferior. He was thereby expressing the conviction that religious beliefs outreach divisions of race and country.

In *Ia Orana Maria – The Virgin with Child*, he again merged the Christian with the pagan, the two native women who offer homage to the Tahitian Madonna and Child incongruously adopting the Buddhist pose of prayer.[57] If Gauguin had divorced himself from Christianity, rejecting its claim to be the only true faith, he perceived, as in his *Self-Portrait with the Yellow Christ* with its pagan deity in the background, the underlying bonds uniting those three apparently polarised figures – the Christian, the pagan and the modern seeker after truth. In acknowledging the centrality of this phenomenon in the work of Conrad as well as that of Gauguin, we may recall the description of the narrator Marlow, in both the opening and closure of his Congo story, the sole participant perceiving the hidden truths of civilisation, as seated 'in the pose of a meditating Buddha', embodying within the Western setting the inscrutability and wis-dom of an ancient, oriental faith.

The relativism implicit in his merger of religious concepts may have a bearing too upon the prominence of the *Doppelgänger* figure in Conrad's work, the splitting of the central character into two, as in Leggatt's mirroring of the captain in *The Secret Sharer* or the implied identification of Marlow with Kurtz ('No, they did not bury me...'). As Michael Levenson has wisely commented, such 'doubling' of central figures is to be seen as an aspect of modernist pluralism, the individual no longer able to appraise life from a single authoritative standpoint, moral or otherwise, but disturbingly aware instead of manifold, often contrasting norms that compel him to project himself into a second figure, into an alternative vantage point.[58] Within postmodernist theory, this sense of the divided self has become a central concern, with Michel Foucault offering Bentham's Panopticon as a vivid image of such self-division. In that specific form of prison, in which a guard, situated aloft in a tower, is able to watch all the inmates while remaining hidden from them, each prisoner within his cell develops a twofold conception of self. He is simultaneously conscious of his own inner being, while at the same time aware of the way he is viewed from outside. Jacques Lacan, developing a similar concept from Freudian 'narcissist' theory, saw as especially significant the moment when a child first perceives itself in a mirror, a unified self suddenly observed from without. From that moment onward, he argues, the individual tends to define himself to some extent in terms of the 'other', the latter providing either a contrast to or a reflection of self.[59]

That twofold perception, the projection of self into an outside entity, occupies its place not only in the *Doppelgänger* element in Conrad's writings, but in Gauguin's paintings too. *Christ in the Garden of Olives* of 1889, endows the figure of Jesus at the time of his Agony in the Garden with the artist's own features, suggesting by that identification a degree of shared experience, the figure itself functioning both as 'other' and as self. Gauguin admitted unreservedly: 'There I have painted my own portrait', explaining in connection with that canvas that he too was, in his artistic struggles, involved in the process of 'climbing a rough Calvary'.[60] A similar projection of himself as the 'other' was to be found in the strange drinking vessel of glazed stoneware he produced in the same year, a work he entitled, *Jug in the Form of a Head, Self Portrait*, in which, shortly after witnessing the execution of a prisoner by guillotine, he depicted himself as a blood-stained, severed head, again implying (this time in allusion to John the Baptist) that he be viewed as a martyr to the cause of art. Thus they both reveal in their work this emergent Modernist sensitivity to the split consciousness of the self.

Sympathetic as both Gauguin and Conrad were to the beauty of the jungle and the Tahitian world, they were conscious too of the more ominous aspects of those scenes, which, as part of the sense of the archetypal, reflected too the submerged, less-attractive elements in civilised man. *Rave Te Hiti Ramu – The Idol* of 1898 depicts a wildly staring figure, half idol and half human, too naturalistically depicted to be a carved totem and hence uncomfortably suggestive of a living man-monster, an image of human savagery within an untamed landscape of twisting, intertwining branches. More significantly for our purposes here, his *Parahi Te Marae – The Sacred Mountain* of 1892 (Figure 4) presents a tribal god brooding over a landscape, the smoke from a sacrificial fire rising before it. And surrounding the enclosure is (need one comment further?) a wooden fence, sur- mounted by human heads. The *Marae*, as the artist explained to the uninitiated viewer, was a temple area reserved for the practice of human sacrifice.[61]

The similarity between this scene and the climactic moment of Conrad's story, the discovery of the human heads displayed on wooden poles and testifying to the 'unspeakable rites' performed by Kurtz, is not fortuitous, both writer and artist responding, here too, to an aspect of the cultural shift we have been examining. Through- out the eighteenth and nineteenth centuries, Western civilisation had revealed an obsessive interest in cannibalism, both as a symbol of civilised man's superiority to the despicable impulses believed to characterise savage societies and as a reminder of the dangers to be encountered by the explorer, missionary or coloniser. The West, in fact – as has been noted by Dorothy Hammond and Alta Jablow – was far more addicted to tales of cannibalism than the Africans ever were to cannibalism itself, its incidence on that continent being extremely rare, with some anthropologists now claiming that it never existed at all.[62] The difference between the traditional treatment of that theme and its treatment in the works we are studying lies in the indulgence with which both Conrad and Gauguin regarded it, the assumption that the practice was, within certain limits, understand- able in a jungle setting, however unforgivable it might be among civilised men. At one point, when a shriek from the bank seems to indicate the slaughter of some enemy natives, the young black head- man snaps at Marlow:

'Catch 'im. Give 'im to us.' 'To you, eh?' I asked; 'what would you do with them?' 'Eat 'im!' he said curtly, and, leaning his elbow on

the rail, looked out into the fog in a dignified and profoundly pensive attitude. I would no doubt have been properly horrified, had it
not occurred to me that he and his chaps must be very hungry:
that they must have been growing increasingly hungry for at least
this month past . . . [63]

The source of the natives' sustenance, lumps of a 'dirty lavender colour' resembling half-cooked dough which they carried wrapped in
leaves, though referred to euphemistically as hippopotamus meat,
are, Marlow hints, suspect in origin; but as the authorial voice
remarks, they at least kept the natives alive at a time when they
were being paid by their white employers with pieces of worthless
wire, lacking in nutriment. Marlow's amazement is evoked, one
notes, not by the practice of cannibalism itself but (with a droll
twinge of vanity) by the natives' remarkable ability, in the loneliness
of the jungle and in their famished condition, to resist regarding him
as an 'appetising morsel' and taking appropriate action. For him
their self-control is an enigma, part of the haunting mystery of the
primeval world, paralleling in literary form Gauguin's visual representations of its brooding inscrutability:

> Restraint! I would just as soon have expected restraint from a hyena
> prowling amongst the corpses of a battlefield. But there was the
> fact facing me – the fact dazzling, to be seen, like the foam on the
> depths of the sea, like a ripple on an unfathomable enigma, a mys-
> tery greater – when I thought of it – than the curious, inexplicable
> note of desperate grief in this savage clamour that had swept by us
> on the river-bank, behind the blind whiteness of the fog. [64]

The extraordinary 'restraint' the natives exercise derives, Marlow
perceives, from their limiting of cannibalism to the consumption of
the bodies of those already dead, like that of the steersman whose
corpse Marlow prefers to throw to the fish lest it become a 'first-class
temptation' to them – and all this in contrast to the horrific practice
of supposedly civilised man, murdering humans for pecuniary gain or
the mere gratification of vanity. As Lacan would put it, the 'other'
becomes the contrast against which we attempt to measure and define
ourselves. So Gauguin describes sympathetically in his *Noa Noa* how
cannibalism had in times past been forced upon the natives by dire
famine, at a period when their rate of reproduction greatly out-
stripped the supply of food, adding that, on discovering alternative

methods of coping with the problem, they henceforth abandoned the practice. With this more understandable process he contrasts the actions of Western man, in the harsh comment: 'Civilized? You are proud of not eating human flesh?...To make up for it, you eat the heart of your neighbour every day.'[65] If Conrad's *Heart of Darkness*, too, reveals as its primary message the barbarity lurking within supposedly civilised man, the savagery shrouded within Kurtz's eloquence, its parallel is to be found in a bas-relief Gauguin sculpted in 1896 depicting a cultured European, bearing the artist's own features, yet sardonically entitled *Oviri – The Savage*, a term he was to use of himself henceforth as a kind of battle cry in his rebellion against establishment culture.

All these elements, Gauguin's mysterious elevation of his scenes through 'cloisonism', the ritualistic poses evocative of archetypal myth, the hints of ominous elements even in the Edenic scenes, suggest, in the parallels they afford to Conrad's own writings, that the stylistic 'vagueness' to which critics have so strenuously objected is not a flaw, but performs in the latter's work a positive function, of central significance for their time. Marlow's remark that the whole meaning of seamen's yarns lies within the shell of a cracked nut has long been a focus of attention for critics analysing his work; but it is surely the subsequent statement that is more telling, that Marlow, as Conrad informs us, 'was not typical (if his propensity to spin yarns be excepted)', that to him

> the meaning of an episode was not inside like a kernel but outside, enveloping the tale which brought it out only as a glow brings out a haze, in the likeness of one of these misty halos that sometimes are made visible by the spectral illumination of moonshine.[66]

It is this enveloping glow, the nebulousness of language itself, which in Conrad's writing acts as a veil through which profound truths can be discerned, truths which, as Emily Dickinson once wrote, would prove too blinding if presented in their naked form:

> Tell all the Truth but tell it slant –
> Success in Circuit lies
> Too bright for our infirm Delight
> The Truth's superb surprise
> As Lightning to Children eased

> With explanation kind
> The Truth must dazzle gradually
> Or every man be blind –[67]

Hence the impact of Marlow's lie to the Intended at the end of the story, his decision not to inform her of Kurtz's appalling final words, 'The horror! The horror!' It is a decision that has appeared puzzling to many critics, some seeing it as evidence either of Marlow's failure or, by extension, of Conrad's deficiency as a novelist. But the 'haze' surrounding that decision, the seeming obscurity of his motive, deepens for the perceptive reader the subtlety of the message conveyed – that Marlow has learnt to apply to his own impulses the restraint that Kurtz so fatally lacked, to suppress his own deep-rooted hatred of a lie (recorded earlier in the story) in order to save her from the immense pain of confrontation with the truth. He knows of his obligation to that truth as well as his obligation to the memory of Kurtz, but the duties of restraint override them: 'Hadn't he said he only wanted justice? But I couldn't. I could not tell her. It would have been too dark – too dark altogether...' And if one imagines that he has thereby failed in his main task, in revealing these hidden truths to the world, we should recall that Marlow has related the full story to his fellow seamen on the yacht moored in the Thames and, even more importantly, that Conrad has provided the novel itself for the edification of the perceptive reader.

To summarise, therefore, if a prime innovation of Gauguin's canvases was their desertion of mimesis in favour of cloisonist stylisation, the allusiveness of Conrad's writing, both in the descriptive passages and in his hints of the profound implications to be derived from his scenes, similarly achieves a sense of elevation above the merely literalistic. As the steamer moves up the river, the frenzied activities of the natives on either bank are conveyed as isolated flashes, as iconic dream-like images stimulating deep and disturbing thoughts:

> as we struggled round a bend, there would be a glimpse of rush walls, of peaked grass-roofs, a burst of yells, a whirl of black limbs, a mass of hands clapping, of feet stamping, of bodies swaying, of eyes rolling, under the droop of heavy and motionless foliage. The steamer toiled along slowly on the edge of a black and incomprehensible frenzy. The prehistoric man was cursing us, praying to us, welcoming us – who could tell? We were cut off from the

comprehension of our surroundings. . . . We could not understand because we were too far and could not remember, because we were travelling in the night of first ages, of those ages that are gone, leaving hardly a sign and no memories.[68]

Both writer and artist are aware, well in advance of their contemporaries, of hidden elements beyond the visible and tactile, the existence of unknown urges and desires operating beneath human consciousness. Hence the transference of the setting of their works, away from the nineteenth-century recording of contemporary city life and social manners to an exploration of the primeval mysteries of the human heart in Tahiti and the African Congo, where the utter savagery:

> had closed round him, – all that mysterious life of the wilderness that stirs in the forest, in the jungles, in the hearts of wild men. There's no initiation either into such mysteries. He has to live in the midst of the incomprehensible.[69]

At times Gauguin's comments on his art not only approximate to Conrad's but even echo their terminology, strangers though they were to each other. He wrote on one occasion that it was not in the physical world of observable objects but 'in the dark corners of my heart, which are sometimes mysterious, that I perceive poetry',[70] while Conrad wrote similarly to his friend Curle:

> Explicitness is fatal to the glamour of all artistic work, robbing it of all suggestiveness, destroying all illusion. You seem to believe in literalness and explicitness, in facts and also in expression. Yet nothing is more clear than the utter insignificance of explicit statement and also its power to call attention away from things that matter in the region of art.[71]

So it was that Gauguin, in a letter to Fontainas in 1899, recorded his desire to explore certain elements rarely explored by previous artists – those same elements that Conrad found so fascinating and for which the latter has so often been castigated – the unfathomable, the infinite and the recondite:

> Here near my cabin, in complete silence, amid the intoxicating perfumes of nature, I dream of violent harmonies. A delight

enhanced by I know not what sacred horror I divine in the infinite. An aroma of long-vanished joy that I breathe in the present.
Animal figures rigid as statues, with something indescribably
solemn and religious in the rhythm of their pose, in their
strange immobility. In eyes that dream, the troubled surface of an
unfathomable enigma.[72]

In the long-standing critical debate over Conrad's supposed debt to
Impressionism, it may be wise to observe the strong affinities he
bears to a painter with whom he has never been closely compared,
but who, as an immediate contemporary, shared some of his most
fundamental concerns and innovative stylistic techniques.[73] We may
recall here Gauguin's own criticism of the Impressionist painters,
from whom he consciously divorced himself, his dislike of the fidelity
to optical effects that had motivated that earlier generation, their
desire to reproduce with accuracy the way the visible world impinges
upon the human eye. Despite their break with tradition, he argued,
they remained bound by the shackles of mere verisimilitude, unable
to see the world of the imagination beyond: 'For them the dream
landscape, created from many different entities, does not exist....
They heed only the eye and neglect the mysterious centres of
thought...'[74] It was that dream landscape, and the mysterious
centres of thought stimulated by it, that fascinated Conrad too,
expressed by him stylistically in those 'misty' passages which have so
long disturbed the critics but were so integral to his art, his sense of
impalpable, enigmatic forces motivating even the most sophisticated
and seemingly civilised forms of human society.

2

T. S. Eliot and the Secularists

Even those critics suspicious of intermedia studies have come to acknowledge that the innovative aspects of T. S. Eliot's poetry cannot be divorced from the changes that were occurring simultaneously in the visual arts. Recognition of that relationship has been slow to emerge, but from the 1960s onwards the broken images of his verse, its crabbed allusiveness, the disorienting contiguity of incidents disparate in time and space and connected only by mental association have come to be linked with experiments with *collage* in Cubist painting, with the juxtaposition of the incongruous in Surrealism, and with the provocative unconventionality of the Dadaists. The irony in his verse, as one critic defined it, 'is due to a montage-principle of placing together statements having an entirely different poetic tone', while a more recent study of Eliot is subtitled *from skepticism to a surrealist poetic*, the author seeing the sudden contrasts and unexpected transitions in his verse as paralleling the shock tactics of the Breton school.[1] In all such forms of art, verisimilitude had been deserted in favour of cerebral affinities, objects no longer being considered as authentic in themselves but as elements interacting with other components, forming part of larger patterns or stimulating the connotative faculties of the viewer. All this, it is now recognised, occurred not simply as an artistic break with tradition by a generation tired of established modes, but, more integrally, as a series of responses within the respective media to altered concepts concerning the universe and the place of humankind within it.

In identifying the source of these far-reaching changes, it has become a commonplace of criticism to attribute the disjointed and dissonant elements in twentieth-century works to the contemporary rejection by scientists of the physical solidity of the world, their questioning of the substantiality of tactile reality such as had, since the Renaissance, validated in art and literature the principles of visual perspective and mimetic representation. The inauguration of molecular research, of quantum mechanics and of relativist theory propounded at that time by Bohr, Planck, Einstein and others had called into question the long-established reliance upon optical verification. The assumption that the evidence of sight and touch afforded the firmest authentication of actuality had become seriously undermined by the discovery that the human eye responds only to a narrow sector of the spectrum, the area existing between red and violet, hence providing only a partial and untrustworthy picture of mankind's environs. Molecular theory, the discovery of positive and negative electrons moving freely within even the most rigid materials, challenged confidence in the apparent solidity of objects, and the space-time concept of relativity served to weaken even further human faith in the data provided by sensory perception. The universe at large, including the immediate environs of mankind, which both artist and writer had for so long attempted to reproduce with some degree of fidelity to perceptual impressions, had now been revealed as far more intricate and perplexing, the ensuing distrust concerning the fixed rules and supposed order of the universe producing the harsh disjunctions and discontinuities of their art.[2]

Within this larger perception, the gradual recognition of the filaments connecting Eliot to Modernist painting as collective reactions to changes in universal concepts at that time, there is, one may note, a silent acknowledgment of a principle intrinsic to synchronic study – the notion that, for such shared responses to be recognised, no evidence is required of a conscious indebtedness to the plastic arts on the part of the writer, nor of any direct contact between them. For despite the patent parallels, Eliot himself seems to have been generally oblivious of the relevance of his own work to the aesthetic changes being initiated by contemporary painters. That insensibility is particularly remarkable as he was living in Paris and artistically active there from 1910–11, during the period when some of the most innovative and revolutionary paintings were being produced within that city. From 1909, Picasso and Braque had begun working together to inaugurate Cubism, the former creating in those years such influential canvases as his *Still Life with Liqueur Bottle*. Yet even after Modernist painting had achieved wide recognition and the British counterparts of the Cubists had already acquired their own reputations, Eliot displayed little interest in the painting of his time. The publication of some early poems in the second issue of Wyndham Lewis' Vorticist paper *Blast* in 1915 seems to have been arranged more through Pound's connection with that movement than through any sense of artistic affinity on Eliot's part;[3] and his indifference to such connections persisted. As Herbert Read was to record in later years, 'though I once or twice tried to establish some personal contact between him and artists like Henry Moore and Ben Nicholson, my efforts came to little or nothing. If pressed he would no doubt have admitted that the tradition that led from Poe and Baudelaire to Laforgue and Rimbaud and his own poetry could not be entirely divorced from the tradition that led from Delacroix and Cézanne to Matisse and Picasso, but he would not himself have made much of the comparison.'[4] There is, indeed, a light-hearted reference to a Post-Impressionist in his 'Sweeney Agonistes':

> Where the Gauguin maids
> In the banyan shades
> Wear palmleaf drapery
> Under the bam
> Under the boo
> Under the bamboo tree.

but the frivolous tone suggests no serious interest in the innovative qualities of those Tahitian canvases.[5] The fact that his American patron, John Quinn, was a prominent art collector, a major force in organising the seminal Armory Show of 1913, which was to introduce Impressionism and Post-Impressionism to the United States, appears to have sparked no reciprocal sympathy on Eliot's part; and neither did his personal acquaintance with Roger Fry and Clive Bell, both leading figures in encouraging England's responsiveness to the new art forms.[6] He was indeed, as might be expected from any self-respecting intellectual of that decade, familiar with the names of leading artists, remarking in a letter to Scofield Thayer in 1920 that if the latter required illustrations:

> Lewis, Wadsworth, John, Roberts, Sickert ought to be glad to have their drawings used. There are of course important people in Paris too: Picasso, Modigliani, Matisse, Marchand etc.[7]

but he betrayed no consciousness of their relevance to his own poetic activity.

In this present chapter I should like to explore an aspect of such affinity deriving from a phenomenon in contemporary painting that, in one respect at least, has only recently been afforded prominence. *The Waste Land* itself, because of its characteristic allusiveness, has produced a range of conflicting interpretations, the main disparity

concerning its ultimate message. For many readers, seizing upon it
as the testament of a disaffected generation, it came to be regarded
as a manifesto of twentieth-century nihilism, the weary protest
of a writer disillusioned by the collapse of traditional values, revealing, as I. A. Richards claimed at the time, the 'complete severance
between his poetry and *all* beliefs'. Eliot's public repudiation of that
assessment did little to counteract its broad acceptance, since he
employed in that denial, as in most of his comments on his own
poetry, a phraseology sufficiently vague to leave the matter open, in
this instance as if the discrepancy perceived by Richards were merely
a matter of formal definition:

> As for the poem of my own in question, I cannot for the life of me
> see the 'complete separation' from all belief – or it is something no
> more complete than the separation of Christina Rossetti from
> Dante. A 'sense of desolation' etc. (if it is there) is not a separation
> from belief; it is nothing so pleasant. In fact, doubt, uncertainty,
> futility, etc., would seem to me to prove anything except this
> agreeable partition; for doubt and uncertainty are merely a variety
> of belief.[8]

One should not miss, as so many of his contemporaries did, the
implications of that final phrase, that the doubt and uncertainty in
that poem formed aspects of his own desire for belief. His comment
of 1931, while more decisive in its rejection of the secular reading of
his poem, did little to clarify his aim:

> ... when I wrote a poem called *The Waste Land* some of the more
> approving critics said that I had expressed the 'disillusionment of
> a generation,' which is nonsense. I may have expressed for them
> their own illusion of being disillusioned, but that did not form
> part of my intention.[9]

His disavowal was never taken seriously, and the poem continued
to be seen in primarily secular terms, as voicing the disenchantment
of the time, the conclusion of *The Waste Land* being assumed to be
both depressing and negative in its import. George Williamson
deduced that the protagonist is left at the end in the 'helpless state
of the Fisher King'. Alvarez regarded the poem at large as asserting
'the impossibility of finding any solution', while more recently
Eloise Knapp Hay has marked the culmination of that interpretation

by commenting that the work 'can now be read simply as it was written, as a poem of radical doubt and negation'.[10]

In the opposite camp, the poem has been interpreted as expressing, at a submerged level, the protagonist's gradual movement towards a validation of religious experience. But that view has, over the years, won more limited support, in part through a suspicion that it constituted a retrospective rereading, an exploitation of hindsight. Had we not known of his later conversion, it was argued, we could not have discerned hints of such leanings within the text. Lyndall Gordon, convinced of the religious underpinning to the poem yet aware of the difficulty of substantiating that view from the text itself, attributed the apparent discrepancy to Eliot's diffidence. His innate reticence with regard to his personal life led him, she suggests, while revealing to his audience the lamentable condition of contemporary humanity, to keep his religious tendencies so subdued that the strategy of concealment backfired. Readers fastening on the signs of despair ignored their subordination in the poem to the protagonist's own craving for an ascetic, exemplary life. More recently Calvin Bedient has, in a close reading of the poem, argued staunchly in favour of the religious orientation of the work, adopting a similar explanation. He identifies the presence of 'different voices' within the poem as a diversionary tactic intended to preserve the poet's privacy. While those voices serve as 'theatrical' projections of Eliot's own doubts and uncertainties, they allow the protagonist of the poem, by the plurality of speakers, to find his way, behind the smoke screen they offer, to the threshold of a final spiritual redemption – to the recognition, if not yet the full experience, of a metaphysical reality beyond words into which Eliot feels it would be a satisfaction to die.[11]

Before turning to the visual arts for evidence that may throw light on this controversy, one should note that there do exist significant hints of a religious tendency in Eliot's earlier writings, suggesting that, long before the composition of *The Waste Land*, he was already moving in the direction of such commitment, evidence that would counter the charge that later events have been read back into the poem. In 1913 he composed some poems unquestionably religious in orientation – 'I am the Resurrection' and 'The Love Song of St Sebastian' – and was at that stage planning a further poem, never completed, on the theme of 'The Descent from the Cross'. His more general views on secular affairs seem even then to have been coloured by his personal propensities, the syllabus he prepared for his

1916 extension lectures revealing not only a somewhat ascetic preference for self-restraint and discipline but linking those principles to
Christian tradition:

> The beginning of the twentieth century has witnessed a return to
> the ideals of classicism. These may be roughly characterized as *form*
> and *restraint* in art, *discipline* and *authority* in religion, *centralization*
> in government (either as socialism or monarchy). The classicist
> point of view has been defined as essentially a belief in Original
> Sin – the necessity for austere discipline.[12]

In *Prufrock*, composed some ten years before *The Waste Land* and
over fifteen years before his acceptance into the church, as well as in
a period when the theme of the striving of the Christian soul for
spiritual fulfilment was conspicuously unfashionable in poetry, the
persona acknowledges there the intense devotionalism that had preceded his despair, in a passage where the protective, self-mocking
deprecation fails to conceal the throb of genuine emotion:

> … though I have wept and fasted, wept and prayed,
> Though I have seen my head (grown slightly bald) brought in
>   upon a platter,
> I am no prophet …

In the context of the larger image of the poem as an ironic 'love
song', presenting a Prufrock insecure towards women and filled
with hesitations about life, the sentiment reveals, in an age of doubt,
his unequivocal envy of the figure of John the Baptist, so steadfast in
faith that even the threat of death could not deter him from rejecting
Salome's immoral advances. And the central theme of that poem,
the repeated allusions to some indeterminate 'overwhelming question' bedevilling Prufrock, when it is finally articulated, emerges as his
yearning for some assurance concerning the Christian afterlife – irrelevant as that urgent problem may have seemed to his twentieth-
century peers, the latter represented here by the coldly sceptical
Modern Woman:

> And would it have been worth it, after all,
> After the cups, the marmalade, the tea,
> Among the porcelain, among some talk of you and me,
> Would it have been worth while,

To have bitten off the matter with a smile,
To have squeezed the universe into a ball
To roll it toward some overwhelming question,
To say 'I am Lazarus, come from the dead,
Come back to tell you all, I shall tell you all' –
If one, settling a pillow by her head,
Should say: 'That is not what I meant at all.
That is not it, at all.'

The marked contrast in the poem between Prufrock's spiritual yearnings and the supposed indifference of the contemporary intellectual raises the problem that will form the central theme of this chapter – why Eliot's poetry during the early decades of this century, especially his *Prufrock* and *The Waste Land*, should have held such immediate appeal for his contemporaries, for what was in fact a predominantly secular generation, among them his principal supporter, Ezra Pound, who had in 1910 publicly declared himself an agnostic. That it did have an immediate appeal needs little comment here – E. M. Forster acknowledged in 1936 the profound impact those poems had had on the younger generation of that time, for whom Eliot had become 'the most important author of their day, his influence is enormous'.

Some were indeed affected by the religious search within his writings – among those he influenced to follow his path towards conversion, or at least towards deep concern with religious belief, were such leading writers as Graham Greene, Evelyn Waugh, Christopher Isherwood and W. H. Auden. However, as another contemporary, Malcolm Cowley, was to recall, among the major section of that younger generation, ardent admiration for *The Waste Land* as a literary artifact was tempered by the discomfiting realisation that its religious subtheme was at discord with their own intellectual predispositions. They recognised that his verse marked a stylistic break with past poetic modes, they found in it a manifesto of their own loss of values, but, together with those qualities, the poem as a whole seemed patently at variance with the atheism, agnosticism, socialist fervour and dialectical materialism that had become the dominant philosophical tendencies among them. Those were tendencies remote from, if not antithetical to, the theme that motivated the poem, the pilgrimage of a twentieth-century Grail knight.[13] As Eliot was to hint in *The Journey of the Magi*, recounting his own movement towards religious commitment, his had been a progress intrinsically unpalatable to most of his peers, one that he felt compelled to pursue in privacy:

> At the end we preferred to travel all night
> Sleeping in snatches,
> With the voices singing in our ears, saying
> That this was all folly.[14]

the speaker returning, after his conversion, to a world far removed from his newly affirmed faith, 'the old dispensation/With an alien people clutching their gods.'

Together with that gap between Eliot's maturing Christian faith and the growing secularism of his readers, there is a further anomaly in the way he influenced his generation, that the two leading English poets whose reputations Eliot was primarily responsible for reviving at that time, winning them acclaim throughout the English-speaking world as the models most worthy of imitation by his peers, were John Donne, dean of St Paul's, and the Jesuit priest, Gerard Manley Hopkins, both of whom had devoted a major part of their verse to the same metaphysical yearning for union with the divine as motivated Eliot.[15] If the discrepancy between the predominant secularism of the time and Eliot's eventual conversion to the faith has led many to interpret *The Waste Land* as representing the general loss of spiritual belief during the opening decades of the century, this latter element, the revival of interest in the transcendental quality of Metaphysical poetry and the unequivocally Christian commitment of Hopkins, suggests there may have been subtler forces at work contributing to the swift acceptance of their verse – together with the writings of Eliot himself – as the new poetic models for the age.

Within the secular dispensation of the time, among both artists and writers, may be discerned a trend that in many ways paralleled his own, predisposing contemporary intellectuals to perceive within Eliot's poetic quest a process with which they could closely empathise despite any surface differences. One aspect of that trend has recently been investigated, although only in relation to painting. As Linda Henderson has shown in a penetrating study, there existed at the turn of this century a movement of major contemporary importance that had been almost forgotten by historians, a movement whose centrality was eclipsed in large part by a fortuitous change in terminology. Einstein's identification of time as the fourth dimension, an identification that revolutionised scientific thinking from

1919 onward, when confirmed by experiments at the Royal Society, has tended to obscure the earlier speculations on the nature of that fourth dimension, which in their own day had excited as much interest as the black-hole theory has in our own time. For prior to Einstein, mathematicians had, during the latter half of the nine-teenth century, been considering the possibility of a fourth dimen-sion of a very different kind, their hypotheses profoundly affecting writers and artists, not least because the new theories seemed to confirm that generation's dissatisfaction with the scientific pragmat-ism of their day.

Euclid's fifth postulate, that through a specific point only one line can be drawn parallel to any given line, had established for centuries the concept of a spatially determined universe with fixed, invariable rules. But in 1867 Georg F. B. Riemann suggested that perhaps a dis-tinction should be made between finite space, where Euclid's axiom holds true, and infinite space where it may not, where forms may 'squirm' or become malformed as they move about. Such reflections were not entirely hypothetical, but based on a process of logical induction. If, it was argued, a square extended perpendicularly within our finite world becomes a cube, then in an infinite world not restricted to three dimensions, a cube extended in space should become what was termed by these theorists a 'hypersolid', a geo-metrical shape not apprehensible to the mind, since human thought is limited to the conditions prevailing in the three-dimensional cos-mos. For those sceptical of such speculation on the ground that no concrete evidence had been adduced, Charles Howard Hinton offered a persuasive illustration, obtained by moving in a contrary direction. Had we been living in a two-dimensional world, he pointed out in 1904, a sphere passing through the plane we inhabit would be similarly incomprehensible, the visible evidence being restricted to the appearance of a spot on the surface of the plane, gradually expanding and then diminishing, from which no true conception of the sphere could be deduced.[16] We should therefore, he argued, pre-serve an open mind concerning the possibility of similar, non-visible phenomena occurring in a dimension beyond the three with which we are familiar.

Within the realm of painting, those theories played a surprisingly significant part in the development of Cubist art. In a lecture in 1911, later published as an essay, Apollinaire noted the centrality of this theory to contemporary aesthetics and the stimulus it had provided. He recorded the Cubist painters' preoccupation with 'new measures of space which, in the language of the modern studios are designated by the term *fourth* dimension' – the reference, of course, being not to Einstein, whose work only became known from around 1919, but to these hyperspace concerns. Jean Metzinger, the Cubist painter closest to Picasso and Braque during the period of their joint experimentation, learned of the new concepts from Maurice Princet, an actuary by profession, fascinated by these spatial conjectures and a regular member of their artistic circle. Princet was intrigued by the possibility, based upon this theory, that painting should reproduce not optical reality but the 'idea' of each object as it exists in hyperspace:

> You can easily represent a table by a trapezoidal form, to produce a sensation of perspective and create an image to correspond to the table you see. But what would happen if you decided to paint the table as an idea (*'le table type'*)?[17]

Together with Juan Gris, Metzinger began studying geometry under Princet's guidance in order to explore the application of non-Euclidean theory to painting. In the seminal essay *Du Cubisme*, published jointly by Metzinger and Albert Gleizes in 1912, appeared the categorical statement: 'If we wished to tie the painter's space to a particular geometry, we should have to refer it to the non-Euclidian scholars.'[18] Duchamp, usually connected (as in his famed *Nude Descending a Staircase*) with attempts to rival the way movement was captured in the newly emergent cinema, was, as he himself declared, concentrating primarily at this time on trying to depict the distortion of shape that forms were liable to undergo within the realm of infinity. And he was doing so in accordance with the new hyperspace theories, which he too had been studying under the tutelage of Princet. His pictorial experiments during this time were aimed, as he phrased it, at demonstrating the way geometrical figures could be extended into a realm beyond the visible. Of his *Portrait of Chess Players*, painted in 1911, he wrote, 'I painted the heads of my two brothers playing chess, not in a garden . . . but in infinite space', and defined his work during this period as being 'elemental parallelism': 'It was a formal decomposition; that is, linear elements following each other like parallels and distorting the object. The object is completely stretched out, as if elastic.' He explained that by 'elemental parallelism' he meant a 'Sort of parallel multiplication of the n-dimensional continuum to form the n+1 dimensional continuum.'[19] He read widely at this time in the literature of alchemy, the Tarot pack and occult symbolism, which, as we shall see, became closely connected with hyperspace theory, all of them assuming the existence of some metaphysical entity obscured from human sight.

When assessing the deeper impulses motivating such artists to turn to non-Euclidian geometry, one should bear in mind that the empirical sciences themselves were at this time moving beyond pragmatism and the physically verifiable into a new phase, where hypothetically conceived functions and elements within the universe were now accepted as authentic, even though they were not empirically provable. Eddington, in his 1927 Gifford Lectures, noted how reliance upon the visible and tangible was, at the turn of the century, being discarded by its previous main proponent, science itself, which now posited a universe discernible only in terms of symbolic relationships, the physical world of substance having been revealed as illusory. Until recently, he remarked,

> the physicist used to borrow the raw material of his world from the familiar world, but he does so no longer. His raw materials are aether, electrons, quanta, potentials, Hamiltonian functions.... Science aims at constructing a world which shall be *symbolic* of the world of commonplace experience.... The external world of physics has thus become a world of shadows. In removing our illusions we have removed the substance, for indeed we have seen that the substance is one of the greatest of our illusions.[20]

In the same year Wyndham Lewis, in a perceptive study of the implications of this new scientific approach for the artist, pointed out that molecular theory, the contention that an armchair is really a 'seething ocean of movement', had reduced the supposedly empirically provable from the status of solidity and reliability to the status of mere conjecture, the scientist's armchair now being in no sense more 'real' than the artist's imaginative representation of it:

> The scientific object, the simplest aspect of any given object, 'exists' in the same sense and on the same level of reality as the image. It is a world of hypothesis: it is what *should* be there if the empirical systems of fact could lead us to some absolute.[21]

The speculations of the fourth-dimensionalists can be seen retrospectively, therefore, as especially plausible at that time in the light of the developing sense within the sciences themselves of a system of wave patterns, formulae and energy strategies controlling the visible world in a manner hidden from the eye. In that context of growing distrust of physical reality, the conglomerate entity assumed to exist transcendentally came to be regarded as ultimately more authentic than the tangible world in which we live.

How far this rediscovered interest in hyperspace should lead us to change our conception of the dominant impulses of that era may be illustrated by the confident remark of a respected historian published in 1968. John A. Lester summarised this period as marking the collapse of faith in any reality beyond the physical: 'To know that there is an eternal truth consonant to man's being, and to know that man is gifted with a faculty capable of perceiving at least a glimmer of that truth – these were necessary axioms, and both were, or appeared to be, substantially demolished in the years between 1880 and 1914.'[22] In fact, both within the sciences and within the world of the secular layman, there had, as we now know, been a remarkable resurgence of faith in the existence of such extraterrestrial verities.

There have been some attempts to link the Cubist concern with hyperspace to Eliot's poetry, but only in a very restricted sense. Interest has focused upon the destabilising of perspective in that art form and its relationship to the poetic juxtaposing of fragments of city life as they appear in the 'Preludes'.[23] But there is, I believe, a far more profound link to be perceived. Proponents of hyperspace philosophy frequently invoked Plato's myth of the shadows, whereby the generality of mankind, like creatures existing permanently within a cave, see only the shadows cast on the wall by objects passing outside, whereas the philosopher, who ventures into the 'true' world outside, sees the absolutes themselves. The world as it appears to the eye is, in that allegory, regarded as less trustworthy than the ideal world beyond – as in the allusion to 'the world of shadows' in the passage from Eddington cited above. In accordance with that principle, advocates of hyperspace suggested that the human mind must sharpen its powers, relying less on mere physical observation and cultivating instead its intuitive faculty in order to discern the verities beyond, to become sensitive to the metaphysical entity now being seen as ultimately more authentic than the tactile universe in which we live. It was advice eagerly espoused by members of the Theosophical Society, who welcomed hyperspace theory as evidence in support of their own esoteric philosophy. Thus L. Revel, a leading exponent of that mystical sect, suggested in 1911, with reference to these fourth-dimension theories, that the idea of a metareality existing beyond the perceptible should encourage search for truth in two directions, both outward and inward:

> It is possible for human consciousness to liberate itself from its shackles...making use of transcendent faculties in order to soar up over the walls of its prison of flesh into the worlds of the beyond. Is not a human being capable of making use of such faculties conscious of a movement other than that which is visible with bodily eyes! The perceptions of a more subtle world interpenetrating those of a world inferior to it must at first result in an enlarging of the mind's notions about the dimensions of space, and then in an opening of a more inward vision, as if internal sight penetrated through objects.[24]

In more general terms, outside the parameters of Theosophy, such hyperspace theory seemed to offer confirmation from within science of the religious faith that empiricism had seemed so seriously to undermine. In 1910, W. F. Tyler's *The Dimensional Idea as an Aid to Religion* contended that scientific belief in the existence of a fourth dimension – a dimension invisible to the human eye and inconceivable to the human mind – could be seen as corroboration of the Christian belief in 'transcendental conditions...outside of our evolutionary track'.[25] But the impact of those theories upon the secularists of the time, including the Cubists and the Surrealists, was much greater, as Apollinaire and others testified. To assume that such painters engaged in their innovative experiments simply out of a desire for innovation, because, as has so often been argued, they were 'bored' with traditional perspective,[26] is to overlook this profounder motivation, the incentive of all great artists to express through their work shifts in the cultural perspective of their time – in this instance to depict not visible reality but an extraterrestrial or ideal reality now believed to exist beyond the haptic and discernible.

Recognition of this deeper impulse may throw some light on an aspect of art history that has proved disappointing to those attempting to correlate Cubist painting with explorations of the fourth dimension. For while Metzinger, Gris and Duchamp were consciously examining hyperspace theory and fully acknowledged their debt to it, Picasso denied any such interest, even though he must have been aware of the new theories, as Princet, who formed part of his circle, spoke of them, we are told by his companions, tirelessly and enthusiastically. But if we extrapolate the situation, this fascination

with hyperspace may be seen as itself an aspect of a larger issue relevant to painting, a contemporary reaching out to truths beyond the
pragmatically verifiable. A canvas such as Picasso's *Seated Nude* (Figure 5) of 1909–10, and indeed the entire movement towards abstract
art emerging at this time, reflect the advent of a kindred propensity,
the transfer of authenticity from the specific to the generic in a manner
markedly contrasting with the practice of earlier eras. If eighteenth-
century writers and artists had also striven to express 'universal'
truths valid for all generations, to deemphasise the merely local in
favour of the 'type', those truths or types were in that period
derived inductively from the observable, from those elements com-
monly agreed upon by mankind on the basis of everyday experience
and hence recognised as authentic. The poet's task, as Samuel Johnson defined it, was not to number the streaks of the tulip but to
exhibit those features 'which would recall the flower to every mind',
that is, to deduce the generic from the particular and thereby identify
the characteristics shared by all members of the species or type. And
for the medium of the plastic arts, his friend Sir Joshua Reynolds
propounded the same ideal, criticising Bernini's *David* on the ground
that the expression on the face of the statue is 'far from being
general. . . . He might have seen it in an instance or two; and he mis-
took accident for generality.'[27]

The twentieth-century search for the universal was fundamentally
different, arising from new and disturbing factors that had entered
into its calculations. It derived not only from the concept of relativity
and the discovery of invisible wave patterns, but also, as part of
that concern with the numinous, from an increasing recognition
that somewhere there existed mathematical formulae mysteriously
dictating events in the physical world, while leaving the specific
unpredictable. Developing out of the governmental fact-finding
committees beginning to be established around the 1850s and so
caustically satirised in Dickens' *Hard Times* as the new worship of
'hard facts', statistics had taken an increasingly prominent place in
society at the turn of the century. In medical, social and economic
research it was now becoming possible to determine with precision
the proportion of the population due to contract a disease, liable to
survive into old age, or fated to fall below the poverty line, even
though the destiny of the individual remained impossible to foretell.
Insurance companies could now gauge such possibilities by means
of actuarial tables. Similarly, if the result of a single spin of a coin
remained unpredictable, the ratio in a hundred instances was

now seen to be both constant and predetermined. The movement towards abstract, geometric and Cubist art expressed this growing awareness of a validity beyond the perceptible. Picasso's *Seated Nude* like so many of the works produced at this time, expressed this contemporary attempt to apprehend the concept of a female figure unlocalised in time and space. The head is a comprehensive form into which any specific face could be inserted in order to individualise it – the result being a figure embodying what Plato would have called the 'idea' of the female.[28] Only a generation earlier, Nietzsche had dismissed as invalid the Platonic principle of ideal forms, as he did the concept of generic truth expressed in the verbal labelling of objects:

> Just as it is certain that one leaf is never totally the same as another, so it is certain that the concept 'leaf' is formed by arbitrarily discarding these individual differences and by forgetting the distinguishing aspects. . . . We obtain the concept, as we do the form, by overlooking what is individual and actual.[29]

But his was a nineteenth-century response, evoked at a time when science was still essentially empirical. With the new movement towards abstraction both in the sciences and in hyperspace theory, Nietszche's dismissal of the 'idea' was no longer convincing, and the concept of universal paradigms became reauthenticated in a manner closely approximating to the Platonic.

Wilhelm Worringer's seminal study *Abstraction and Empathy* of 1908 provided a new perspective in its suggestion that, in all generations, humankind experiences the two contrary impulses indicated in its title. Together with a proclivity to identify with nature or physical reality, he argued, there always coexists a desire to remove the tactile object from its fortuitous setting and to relate it to the absolute. In a period of comparatively settled epistemology, when society, as in the Renaissance, is basically in harmony with the physical world, the tendency for empathy with nature predominates, its art then employing curvilinear and organic shapes in order to elicit from the viewer the sense of gazing upon a familiar world from which the imperfections of reality have been removed. Its aim then is 'to project the lines and forms of the organically vital, the euphony of its rhythm and its whole inward being, outward in ideal independence and perfection, in order, as it were, to furnish in every creation a theatre for the free, unimpeded activation of one's own sense of

life'. In societies less at peace with actuality, in primitive tribes fear-
ful of the threatening world around them, or in communities such as
that of ancient Egypt, highly civilised but, in its precarious reliance
upon the rise of the Nile in the midst of its desert surroundings
experiencing a distrust of nature, art 'seeks after pure abstraction as
the only possibility of repose within the confusion and obscurity of
the world-picture, and creates out of itself, with instinctive necessity,
geometric abstraction. Art under such conditions is the consummate
expression, and the only expression of which man can conceive, of
emancipation from all the contingency and temporality of the world-
picture.'[30] The result in periods tending towards the abstract, therefore, is a desire to redeem the individual object within the mundane
world by tearing it away from the accidents of its existence, producing stylised totem poles and artifactual images. As Braque remarked
in 1908 of his *Female Nude*, a painting that made no pretence at anatomical or mimetic accuracy, 'Nature is a mere pretext for decorative
composition, plus sentiment. It suggests emotion, and translates that
emotion into art. I want to express the Absolute, and not merely the
factitious woman.'[31]

   Worringer's theory, however, misses one important element.
The twentieth-century preference for abstraction in art was not only
the reflection of a fundamental spatial and temporal dislocation in the
world-view of the time, with Cubism expressing the fragmentation
of the tactile world. It also represented a more positive response, the
search for 'pure' and eternal forms not merely as a place of 'repose'
or emancipation, an escape from the dissatisfactions of actuality, but
out of a genuine belief in the truths existent there and a conviction
that the artist's task was now to represent an authenticity existing
beyond the corporeal and visible. As Olivier-Hourcade claimed in
1912 on behalf of the twentieth-century painter:

> the external appearance of things is transitory, fugitive and REL-
> ATIVE. Therefore one must search out THE TRUTH, and cease to
> make sacrifices to the pretty effects of perspective or of half-
> light.... One must seek the *truth* and stop making sacrifices to the
> banal illusions of optics.[32]

Much of the new movement was indeed motivated by a fascination
with form in its own right, a concern with the relationship of lines,
planes and colour. But the mystical, semireligious impulse formed
an essential ingredient. Wassily Kandinsky, who is generally acknow-

ledged as the inaugurator of abstract painting, made this point clearly by attributing the origin of the movement to the collapse of faith in soulless materialism and 'the building up of the psychic-spiritual life of the twentieth century which we are experiencing'. In his essay *Concerning the Spiritual in Art*, the title itself being significant, he rejected the traditional concern of the artist with the pursuit of personal fame, offering as his image of true art a spiritual triangle that blends into the scene at Mount Sinai:

> Despite this confusion, this chaos, this wild hunt for notoriety, the spiritual triangle moves ahead, slowly but surely, with irresistible strength moving ever forward and upward.
>
> An invisible Moses descends from the mountain and sees the dancing around the golden calf. But he brings to man fresh stores of wisdom.
>
> His voice inaudible to the crowd, is first heard by the artist.[33]

During the years 1908–11 he became deeply influenced by the Theosophical movement, notably by the writings of Rudolf Steiner, who had called for a form of revitalised Christianity; and the paintings he produced during this transitional phase, as he began to desert mimetic art in favour of abstract forms, repeatedly adopted religious motifs derived from such apocalyptic works as the Revelation of St John, picturing the dissolution of the physical world at the last trumpet. In his *All Saints' Day* of 1911 he included hints of trumpeting angels at three of its corners, with St George and St Vladimir towards the lower left. As Rose-Carol Long has pointed out, the reiterated themes of deluge and destruction during this phase represented to Kandinsky the nightmare of a materialistic world, the chaos of his own generation and the need for spiritual vision.[34] It was his version in visual terms of the despair with the mundane and material that Eliot was to represent poetically, paralleling in addition the latter's yearning for religious belief.

Nor was Kandinsky alone among painters in the inspiration he gained from Madame Blavatsky and her circle – Mondrian derived directly from them the philosophical basis for his grid-form canvases. In 1909 he had formally joined the Theosophical Society of Holland, and began reading widely in Madame Blavatsky's writings, together with those of Annie Besant, Krishnamurti and Rudolf Steiner; and although he allowed his membership in the movement to lapse in later years, he remained to the end a faithful supporter. Robert

Rosenblum has revealed the deep vein of mysticism that permeated Mondrian's work in those early years, his portraits emblematically depicting moments of spiritual communion with another world. After the dramatic moment in 1911 when he changed his own way of life and adopted a new artistic direction for his work, his decision to abandon naturalism arose from a desire to depict instead absolutes transcending the inferior 'relativist' world in which we live, a 'higher reality' beyond nature. Madame Blavatsky's *Isis Unveiled* of 1877 had pointed to the mystical qualities of geometrical symbols, seeing the vertical as the male principle, the horizontal as the female, and the cross, in its merger of those two forms, as representing life and immortality. It was on that basis that Mondrian began restricting his own canvases to grid-forms containing contrasts of primary colours within vertical, horizontal and cruciform lines. And it was to the world of the spirit that his art was directed. 'There are', he declared, 'two paths leading to the Spiritual; the path of learning, of direct exercises (meditation, etc.) and the slow certain path of evolution. The latter manifests itself in art.... Should these two paths coincide ... then one has attained the ideal art.' While his own generation had recognised the untenability of any fixed view of the perceptible and had acknowledged with anxiety the ultimate relativity of all elements, his own desire, he explained, was to nurture the intuitive within mankind, its 'desire for the absolute, the immutable'.[35]

If the Theosophical Movement remained suspect to many intellectuals, it should not be forgotten how prevalent at this time was the interest in a correlative movement, the revived study of spiritualism and extrasensory perception. The Society for Psychical Research, founded in 1882, attracted to its ranks some of the most distinguished thinkers of the day, drawn from a wide spectrum of society and including such leading figures as Sir Gilbert Murray, Prime Minister Arthur Balfour, A. C. Bradley, Henry Sidgwick, and the bishops of Carlisle and Ripon. That interest in spiritualism among scientists and intellectuals may seem strange today, but it had received notable impetus from a seemingly authoritative source. In 1888, the British scientist Sir Oliver Lodge, at approximately the same time as H. R. Hertz was conducting similar experiments in Germany, had demonstrated in his laboratory the existence in the air of invisible radio waves capable of transmitting information – a discovery that appeared to lend credence to the possible existence of mental waves passing from one person to another, and perhaps, even, permitting contact with the spirits of the dead. Lodge accordingly became a leading member of the association, whose main purpose, while rigorously exposing charlatanry in that field, was to collect evidence of extrasensory communication and mental telepathy. The motivation of its members, therefore, again reflected the current preoccupation of that generation in establishing contact with a supraterrestrial entity imperceptible to the human eye. As Lodge summarised his position, the newly discovered ether might be 'the universal connecting medium which binds the universe together, and makes it a coherent whole instead of a chaotic collection of independent isolated fragments'.[36]

Even when the impulse was not specifically religious or indebted to spiritualism and the occult, abstract art revealed a yearning for the absolute that was closely related to such religious or semireligious proclivities – and, I suggest, closely related to Eliot's own spiritual search. Roger Fry, whose authority carried considerable weight at this time, in his 'Essay on Aesthetics' in 1909 in fact used the term 'mystical' to describe his own entirely secular view of art:

> I think the artist might if he chose take a mystical attitude, and declare that the fullness and completeness of the imaginative life he leads may correspond to an existence more real and more important than that we know of in mortal life.

Art, he believed, represented a superior reality beyond the mundane, a form of life that temporal existence only rarely approaches: 'I mean this, that since the imaginative life comes in the course of time to represent more or less what mankind feels to be the completest expression of its own nature, the freest use of its innate capacities, the actual life may be explained and justified by its approximation here and there, however partially and inadequately, to that freer and fuller life.'[37] And in a widely read study, the art critic Sheldon Cheney emphasised in 1934 the occult quality in abstract painting, whereby the artist withdraws

> from the surrounding disorder of human physical life, into blissful self-identification with the divine spirit, experiencing the rapture of perfect realization of harmony and order. Whether one prefers to term this identification with God – in the Christian mystic's words – or merely elevation into a region of harmonious accord of spiritual and physical living, there is presupposed a realm beyond the comprehension of the senses, but open nonetheless to experience:

where there is total release from the bondage of material and worldly things, where the individual partakes of the life of the spirit.[38]

Once one becomes aware of this mystical impulse in modern art, the ramifications begin to stretch in all directions. In Russia, Malevich had learned of hyperspace theory through the philosopher P. D. Ouspensky, who, in his *Tertium Organum* of 1911, had described it not only as a geometrical or cosmological system but in wider and indeed spiritual terms as a means of escaping from death into the sphere of the soul. Malevich, marking a turning point in Modernist art, adopted the theory as a primary impulse for his own innovations, five of the canvases he exhibited in 1915 bearing subtitles specifically relating them to the concept of the fourth dimension. He had actually denied any allegiance in his art to established norms, traditions or beliefs, arguing that 'art no longer cares to serve the state and religion; it no longer wishes to illustrate the history of manners, it wants nothing further to do with the object as such, and believes it can exist, in and for itself, without things'.[39] But his development towards Suprematist art, which he inaugurated in the early 1920s, in some ways involved a contradiction of that refusal to serve religion in any form. In his rejection of the merely three-dimensional and logical, he declared in favour of a 'cosmic consciousness', that is, a faith not in religion in the established sense of Christian belief, but in the form of a transcendental universalism. One of his most famous works, *Suprematist Painting (Large Cross on White)* of 1920, while seemingly merely geometrical – a black rectangle superimposed on a red rectangle against a white background – was, as evidenced by its title, to some extent mystical in import, elevating the wooden cross from physical actuality into a symbol outreaching locality or time. It expressed his religio-philosophical faith in the authenticity of the non-objective in preference to the supposedly real, as propounded by the positivists.

Nor was this transcendental search among secularists confined to the painters. Yeats did not share Eliot's predilection for Christianity, having deserted that faith in his youth, but he described himself nonetheless as a person of markedly spiritual temperament who had been deprived of religion by nineteenth-century science. He recognised that by the desertion of that faith, the ladder was gone by which we could climb to a higher reality. And he found his alternative in the occult. Throughout his life the appeal of the esoteric as the key to the meaning of life affected him strongly:

> I was unlike others of my generation in one thing only, I am very religious, and deprived by Huxley and Tyndall, whom I detested, of the simple-minded religion of my childhood, made a new religion, almost an infallible church of poetic tradition . . .

Denying that he had been influenced by the French Symbolists, of whom he claimed he had known little, he found the sources of his poetic vision in hieratic philosophies, primarily medieval, including kabbalah, alchemy and the hermetic and Rosicrucian creeds, in the hope of finding there the surrogate faith he sought. As a member of the Dublin Hermetic Society, as he recalled in later years, he had belonged to

> their Esoteric Section, an inner ring of the more devout students, which met weekly to study tables of oriental symbolism. Every organ of the body had its correspondence in the heavens, and the seven principles which made the human soul and body corresponded to the seven colours and the planets and the notes of the musical scale.

It was a yearning that remained with him throughout his career, providing a major stimulus for his poetry. As Yeats was to summarise that tendency, 'An obsession more constant than anything but my love itself was the need of mystical rites – a ritual system of evocation and meditation – to reunite the perception of the spirit, of the divine . . .'[40] His reaching out to the occult influenced his friend Ezra Pound, whose interest in hermetic philosophy echoed many of Yeats' own preoccupations. If, as mentioned earlier, Pound had in 1910 declared that he was an agnostic, by 1921 he recorded in his 'Axiomatica' his belief in a 'Theos' that outstrips human consciousness, a divine force not necessarily identical with the Christian deity. It is clear that during the intervening period he had been moving in the direction of some sort of mystical faith not unrelated to his theories of art. As he maintained in terms closely reflecting the attempt by abstract painters to capture metaphysical concepts, one could either believe the artist was the perfect creator or 'on the contrary you could believe in something beyond man, something important

enough to be fed with the blood of hecatombs'.[41] His colleague in
founding the Imagist movement, Hilda Doolittle ('H. D.'), was also
deeply involved in hermetic philosophy, deriving much of her poetic
inspiration from its occult beliefs.

It becomes apparent, therefore, that while the overwhelming
majority of artists, writers and intellectuals of Eliot's generation
were indeed secular in disposition, in the sense that they rejected
the doctrines of Christian belief, they were, in contrast to our own
generation (at least in its post-hippy and post-guru phase), profoundly motivated by a search for a metareality, for a mystic belief,
which the emergence of hyperspace theory seemed to confirm. As
Apollinaire and others testified, artists were turning away from the
haptic and verifiable, now seen as no longer authentic, in favour of
the realm of the absolute, which they believed lay beyond.

In this context it should be less surprising that the images of saw-
dust restaurants, empty sandwich bags and butt-ends of cigarettes
in Eliot's poetry appealed to a generation increasingly convinced of
the hollowness of a merely terrestrial reality when unelevated by
numinous faith in some universal entity. The specifically Christian
version of such faith towards which Eliot was moving was not the
one they were seeking. But in its earlier form within these poems,
representing a dissatisfaction with urban materialism and a yearning for metaphysical truths that would answer the needs of the soul,
its appeal was considerable. The human spirit, as Eliot argued in a
manner remarkably consistent with the parallel impulse among the
secularists, strives to advance to a more satisfying sphere where the
dissensions of particularity might be harmonised:

> the life of a soul does not consist in the contemplation of one con-
> sistent world but in the painful task of unifying (to a greater or
> less extent) jarring and incompatible ones, and passing, when
> possible, from two or more discordant viewpoints to a higher
> which shall somehow include and transmute them.[42]

It has been suggested by critics such as Robert Klein that the distinguishing quality of Modernist art was its desertion of 'reference', its
abandonment of the attempt to reproduce objects outside itself,
leading to the substitution of that element by autonomy, by paintings that exist as self-justifying works, as art objects in their own
right. And J. Hillis Miller has, in the same vein, stated categorically
that an abstract painting 'does not "mean" anything in the sense of

referring beyond itself in any version of traditional symbolism. It is what it is.'[43] Those statements do indeed hold true for one area of abstract art, where the painter is concerned solely with the relationship of shapes and colours in an attempt to project or capture a mood in a manner divorced from actuality. As Meyer Schapiro argued long ago, that type of painter 'selects colors and patterns which have for him the strongest correspondence to his state of mind, precisely because they are not tied sensibly to objects but emerge freely from his excited fantasy. They are the concrete evidences, projected from within, of the internality of his mood, its independence of the outer world.'[44] But there is, in addition, a major form of abstract art that remains consciously referential, attempting to convey a reality sensed as existent outside the perceptible, depicting generic concepts that embrace and absorb the particulars of the tangible. Such art aims at incorporating the actual at the same time as it transcends it. Brancusi's charming statuette *The Kiss* (Figure 6) of 1912 has certainly deserted the mimetic; but it would be quite inaccurate to describe it as 'non-referential'. As its title confirms, it endeavours to capture the quintessence of the human kiss, to convey the 'idea' of it existent in an eternal dimension beyond spatial or temporal limitation. And that purpose formed an essential part of his art. Originally a Rumanian shepherd close to nature, Brancusi, like Mondrian, believed deeply in the existence of an insubstantial reality not visible to the human eye, and strove to express the relevance of objects to that further truth, stripping them of their physical appurtenances. It was a gradual process in the development of his art. He began his series of bird sculptures, produced from 1912 onwards, with his 'Maiastra', named after the miraculous bird of Rumanian folklore – a sculptural work that, although stylised, possesses a recognisable beak, body and tail. But step by step he moved away from such particulars towards increasingly abstract forms, a process culminating in his famed *Bird in Space* (Figure 7) of 1927, in which, by means of a delicately contoured, upward-curving form of polished bronze, he succeeded in conveying the concept of soaring flight in a symbol entirely divested of physical trappings and yet clearly referential in its thematic significance. True form, he argued,

> ought to suggest infinity. The surfaces ought to look as though they went on forever, as though they proceeded out from the mass into some perfect and complete existence.

That perfect or complete existence outside the realm of actuality was the ideal world that absorbed so much of the interest of Modernists. 'All my life', Brancusi wrote, 'I have been working to capture the essence of flight', adding:

> what is real is not the external form, but the essence of things. Starting from this truth, it is impossible for anyone to express anything essentially real by imitating its external surface.[45]

Brancusi's formulation of his art as intended to capture the 'essentially real' is thus diametrically opposed to the non-referentiality that Hillis Miller and others have seen as constituting the central element in Modernist, and especially Abstract art.

Such aesthetic concern with disembodied essence, of which the real is merely a specific instance, lay behind the fascination among many artists and writers of this time with the brilliant performances of the American dancer Loïe Fuller, whose graceful swirling of flowing, diaphanous veils beneath lights changing in colour created a strangely immaterial beauty. While that beauty derived from bodily movement, it seemed to symbolise the intangibility of art. As one contemporary described her performance:

> ...before our very eyes she turned to many coloured, shining orchids, to a wavering sea flower, and at length to a spiral-like lily, all the magic of Merlin, the sorcery of light, colour, flowing form.... I was entranced...she transformed herself into a thousand colourful images...

It was the exquisite insubstantiality of Fuller's performances that inspired Yeats' haunting query concerning the nature of beauty. Just as the splendour of a tree exists as an entity constituting so much more than the sum of its constituent parts, so the splendour of such dance, although created by corporal movement, exists as a puzzlingly numinous element surpassing the physical:

> O chestnut tree, great rooted blossomer,
> Are you the leaf, the blossom or the bole?
> O body swayed to music, O brightening glance,
> How can we know the dancer from the dance?[46]

And on the stage during this same period, Pirandello's ingenious drama, *Six Characters in Search of an Author* (1923), startlingly reversed norms by its similar assumption that the characters in a play have, as it were, pre-existed in some ideal, metaphysical reality before the writer struggles to apprehend their being and to translate them into visible form.

Within that contemporary context, therefore, it seems justified to assume that Eliot's *Waste Land* found an answering echo among the secular artists and writers of his generation not merely because the poem expressed a shared sense of disillusionment with the dreariness of twentieth-century urban existence, but because it represented a yearning for some overarching metaphysical truth that would lend meaning to the sterile actuality of human existence. The fact that his spiritual journey was, during that period, expressed in universal terms, incorporating elements from myth, from Hinduism and from major literary works, helped to make it more palatable to the non-religious. And it was only when Eliot took the final step of joining the established Church, henceforth accommodating his writings to the dogmas of Anglicanism, notably in *Ash Wednesday* and the *Four Quartets*, that the secularists began to temper their admiration or to withdraw it altogether.

It is within Eliot's tendency – visible in his earlier poems and shared with his fellow writers and artists – to search for universals capable of comprehending the specifics of human existence that a major innovation of *The Waste Land* should be seen, namely Eliot's substitution of the single, identifiable *persona*, the subjective 'I' traditional in poetry, by an elusively composite figure drawn from disparate eras, cultures and lands. To identify that change solely as expressing the Freudian fragmentation of the individual, a breakdown into the warring factions of the inner self, is to miss its more positive function, closely paralleling the mode emerging in contemporary painting, drama and sculpture. The subjective self, the controlling voice of a single integrated being, often closely identified with the poet, could no longer function effectively in the new configuration.[47] It was rejected by him as too narrowly specific and localised, needing to be replaced by an 'abstract' of mankind, by an amalgam comprehending the more universal elements in human history and its variegated imaginative creations, a figure assimilating the Grail knight, the bored modern typist, the classical Tiresias, the seedy clairvoyante, the prophet Ezekiel, the Fisher King, the tragic Tristan and the dubious Levantine merchant. Together they

constitute, like the painter's striving after abstract truths, an aggreg-
ate of the human condition, outstripping the limitations of time,
space or social class.

That desire on Eliot's part to conflate the disparate forms of the
specific finds a close counterpart in Modernist painting. Picasso's *Girl
Before a Mirror* of 1932 (Figure 8) evidences a similar attempt to merge
within one representation the diverse cultural, literary, anthropological and physiological aspects of womanhood. Ostensibly a portrait of the artist's current mistress, Marie-Thérèse Walter, and hence
in that sense contemporary in time, the figure is depicted not only
from different angles of vision (including the newly invented x-ray)
to suggest the anatomical facets of her being, but from heterogeneous historical, anthropological and cultural viewpoints too, in a
manner encompassing the multiple variety and range of her manifestations. The headdress is thus evocative of the Egyptian Nefertiti,
the ribs and apple-like breasts allude to the biblical Eve, the frontal
face, circular and partially eclipsed, suggests Diana the pagan
moon-goddess, her distended belly with egg-shaped content recalls
her biologically procreative function, while the darker reflection in
the mirror, delineating a primitive inner world beyond the detec-
tion even of x-rays, displays her profile as a tribal mask tattooed
with mystic emblems. And that primitivist reflection becomes symbolically unified with the female figure itself by the 'embrace' of her
extended arms.

This palimpsestic tendency, the superimposition of seemingly
contrary angles of vision to convey the manifold permutations of the
abstract or conceptualised self, is not restricted in Eliot's poem to the
persona. The opening to the 'Game of Chess' section, for example
(too lengthy to quote here in full), provides a similarly composite
portrait of the female lover in her diverse aspects of beauty, betrayal,
vanity, splendour, seductiveness and victimisation, the passage
ranging allusively throughout history, literature and myth to
encompass Cleopatra, Dido, Eve, Imogen, Bianca, Belinda and Phi-
lomela in a single synthesised image; and all this in a manner far
more complex than mere montage:

> The Chair she sat in, like a burnished throne.
> Glowed on the marble, where the glass
> Held up by standards wrought with fruited vines
> From which a golden Cupidon peeped out
> (Another hid his eyes behind his wing)

> Doubled the flames of sevenbranched candelabra
> Reflecting light upon the table as
> The glitter of her jewels rose to meet it . . .

The echo of Cleopatra, both Plutarch's and Shakespeare's, in the opening lines needs no comment. In the continuation of the passage (beyond the lines quoted here), *laquearia* echoes Virgil's account of Dido's feast in *Aeneid* (1:726); 'sylvan scene' hints at Milton's depiction of the Garden of Eden in *Paradise Lost* (4:140); the golden Cupids and the picture above the mantel allude to Iachimo's description of Imogen's bedchamber in *Cymbeline*; while the title of this section evokes Bianca's rape in Middleton's *Women Beware Women*.[48] As Eliot wrote in his doctoral thesis, during a period when he was beginning to formulate his own ideas of poetry, the self must now be conceived not in personal terms but as an abstraction of all past human experience:

> We have no right, except in the most provisional way, to speak of *my* experience, since the I is a construction out of experience, an abstraction from it, and the *thats*, the browns and hards and flats, are equally ideal constructions from experience, as ideal as atoms.[49]

One notes that final phrase – 'as ideal as atoms' – acknowledging the link between his new technique and the new world beyond the reach of human sight, recently revealed by the physicists.

Allied to this innovative process of replacing the poetic 'I' by an amalgam is the further strategy so characteristic of Eliot's verse, the superimposition of echoes from the past upon scenes from the present:

>   The nymphs are departed.
> And their friends, the loitering heirs of city directors;
> Departed, have left no addresses.
> By the waters of Leman I sat down and wept . . .
> Sweet Thames, run softly till I end my song,
> Sweet Thames, run softly, for I speak not loud or long . . .

In contrast to the process Harold Bloom has defined as 'misprision' – the attempt of writers to overcome the oppressive power of their predecessors, whom they desire oedipally to supplant[50] – Eliot's purpose is to incorporate the broader, more universal vision. He employs the contrivance most often as a means of denigrating the present, but the principle behind all such attempts is to reassert the validity of the past, of the more universal vision of human history. The splendour and dignity of the past is thus contrasted with the sordidness of the present in order to suggest the higher level to which his own generation should aspire – the purity and beauty of Spenser's conception of love in the *Prothalamium* juxtaposed to the casual profligacy of twentieth-century lovemaking. If, as Virginia Woolf recorded, his friends recognised the poem as 'Tom's autobiography – a melancholy one', containing allusions to his stay in Munich and to his wife's developing neurosis,[51] those more personal elements become transformed into paradigmatic form and absorbed into a larger pattern, a process which, like Brancusi's or Pirandello's, and indeed like the hyperspace theorists, moves away from the particular into the generic and universal.

The relevance of the new hyperspace concept for literature was influential in James Joyce's circle too. His disciple, Eugène Jolas, noted in his contribution to *Our Exagmination* how far the new experiments in the visual arts were concerned ultimately with space and how necessary it was that literature should echo that concern:

> While painting...has proceeded to rid itself of the descriptive, has done away with the classical perspective, has tried more and more to attain the purity of abstract idealism, and thus led us to a world of wondrous new spaces, should the art of the word remain static?[52]

And the tendency to move away from the particularised into the universal that Eliot had inaugurated in poetry formed an essential ingredient of *Ulysses* itself, published in the same year as *The Waste Land*. Joyce adopted that principle as its structural framework, combining past and present archetypally, as Stephen is figured as a Homeric Telemachus in search of a father figure, with the adultery of Molly in the final scene evoking (by contrast) her mythological counterpart, Penelope, faithfully awaiting her husband's return. As Eliot himself remarked on Joyce's correlation of the immediate world with ancient legend: 'Manipulating a continuous parallel between contemporaneity and antiquity...is simply a way of controlling, of ordering, of giving a shape and significance to the immense panorama of futility and anarchy which is contemporary history.'[53] He noted in that connection how the modern experience is represented there in all its triviality, aimlessness, sordidness and absurdity, yet redeemed by its allusion to a lost mythical world, by its perception of a preexistent structure and of human continuity between the two worlds. Only by placing the localised within the setting of the universal could any validity be achieved.

In painting as opposed to literature, such mythic polarities are generally more difficult to achieve. Picasso's haunting canvas of a refugee family, a woman fearfully clutching her child to her bosom, was not always recognised as ironically echoing the traditional pose of Madonna and Child. But in England, Eliot's poetic usage, his intertextual superimposition of present upon past, attracted immediate attention, its impact reinforced by his widely read essay 'Tradition and the Individual Talent', in which he argued of the poet that 'not only the best, but the most individual parts of his work may be those in which the dead poets, his ancestors, assert their immortality most vigorously'. He was, thereby, once again attempting to present, in place of the poet's subjective experience, which had so long served as one of the central topics of poetry, a more comprehensive theme, a merging of past and present that permitted a panoramic vision, disregarding the divisions of time and viewing contemporary existence *sub specie aeternitatis*.

His approach stimulated among writers and artists a new interest in such allusive intertextuality, by offering contrasts with previous eras as a means of highlighting the characteristics of the new. The effect of that stimulus was to be strikingly exemplified in Francis Bacon's *Study after Velázquez's Portrait of Pope Innocent X*. There the dignified portrait of Pope Innocent on Velázquez's seventeenth-century canvas (Figure 9), seated calmly and authoritatively upon his throne, is recalled to the viewer's memory by the title of the painting, thereby providing within the new work a similar contrasting of past and present, the seventeenth-century painting serving as an antithesis to the twentieth century – a Freudian conception of man (Figure 10) terrifiedly imprisoned in the claustrophobic restrictiveness of his clerical office, screaming in horror as the inhibiting throne is psychologically transformed for him into an electric chair. But Bacon's purpose is not merely to provide a contrast but to suggest a universal truth, that even the seventeenth-century Pope Innocent had experienced that terrifying loneliness beneath the robes of office. It is, Bacon suggests, not only at nightfall that each confirms the desperation and unutterable solitude of the inner self:

> ... I have heard the key
> Turn in the door once and turn once only
> We think of the key, each in his prison
> Thinking of the key, each confirms a prison ...

Eliot's version of such multiple allusiveness, the introduction into his verse of familiar quotations or snatches of extraneous dialogue, was, as has been recognised, a literary form of collage, echoing Picasso's introduction of a piece of printed oilcloth into his *Still Life with Chair Caning* in 1912, which marked the inauguration of so-called Synthetic Cubism. That process Eliot may have learned, in its literary form, from the friend and patron of that group of artists, Apollinaire, who had experimentally introduced into his own verse similar juxtapositions of overheard speech. Closer in time, as well as in intent, was the new process of photomontage inaugurated by the German, John Heartfield, and transformed into an art form by the Russian Constructivist, Alexander Rodchenko, who combined and superimposed variegated photo-images to create startling juxtapositions or incongruous combinations.[54] In Eliot's poem, however, there is, in addition to such contrast, a profounder effect, a sense of the telescoping of history itself, a recognition that both episodes belong to an overall unifying concept, a universal pattern transcending the local or particular. His purpose is both discriminatory and integrative, the integrative aspect being of greater significance than a mere shock tactic or incongruity; for he employed it as a means of collating past and present, sacred and profane, to produce an essentially new conception of myth – a conception especially relevant to the theme being pursued here, namely the peculiar attraction his poetry afforded for his secular peers.

The daring blending of sacred and profane in Eliot's verse, such as ' ... Belladonna, the Lady of the Rocks, The lady of situations ... ', merging the Madonna of the Rocks with the contemporary call girl – did have a major precedent in Western civilisation, the integration of classical and Christian mythology during the Renaissance; but that earlier coalescence had been fundamentally different, both in its nature and its purpose. In an attempt to provide an alternative model to Christianity during the fifteenth-century emergence from medievalism while ensuring that such a model would not countermand Christian faith, Pico della Mirandola had, with the support of Marsilio Ficino's Platonic Academy, promulgated a theory to validate the process, suggesting that the ancient Greeks and Romans, denied the privilege of biblical revelation, had been groping towards Christianity, seeing it as in a glass, darkly. In that context Hercules could be unembarrassedly welcomed as a classical adumbration of the biblical Samson; and Venus, accompanied by her child-god Cupid, could be identified with the Virgin Mary, the mother of the male god of Love. Botticelli's famed depiction of *The Birth of Venus*, the pagan Aphrodite born miraculously from the foam or *aphros* of the sea, might appear an incongruous choice for so deeply religious a painter were it not, for him as for the contemporary viewer, a pictorial representation of the Immaculate Conception, the dogma newly promulgated by papal authority that the Virgin Mary's birth had also been unblemished by sexual intercourse.[55] The fusing of the pagan and the holy in that period was thus a device, partly conscious, partly instinctive, to enable the importation into the Christian world of classical qualities essentially inimical to that tradition – including a delight in the beauty of the naked body.

Eliot's use of myth was, I would suggest, both in intent and in practice the antithesis of that Renaissance mode. For his was an attempt not to validate an ousted paganism by its incorporation into Christianity but, in reverse strategy, to authenticate a debilitated Christianity by reliance upon the patterns of paganism. The conflation within his poem of the Fisher King, the Hooded Man of the Tarot pack, the dismembered Osiris, the crucified Christ and the Phoenician Sailor is, on the one hand, as Franco Moretti has noted, an example of Lévi-Strauss's concept of '*bricolage*,' demonstrating how mythical thought builds up structures by fitting together the fossilised remains of events in the history of an individual, a society or a cultural tradition. But as Moretti himself remarks, in Eliot's poem it provides, in addition, a tension or two-directional force whereby history is, on the one hand, presented as a mere accumulation of debris and, on the other, transformed within the poem into a new construct, metamorphosed from signified to signifier.[56]

That usage is, however, more subtle than Moretti suggests. For one must recall the period that had preceded this innovation, when, towards the end of the nineteenth century, myth had been employed devastatingly as a means of undercutting the authority of the Scriptures, functioning there as an instrument no less damaging in that regard than Darwinism itself. Frazer's *Golden Bough*, although a study originally undertaken by a classics don at Oxford in a seemingly innocuous attempt to trace variations on the myth of Osiris, moved far beyond that original aim. His discovery, in the course of his investigation, of the extraordinary ubiquity of the Osiris myth in cultures ranging from the most primitive to the most civilised, its origins reaching back far beyond the period of ancient Greece, was sufficiently impressive in itself. It was, however, the implications for Christianity that were to be so momentous for his contemporaries, implications reinforced by the mordant sarcasm with which the author presented the results of his study – a sarcasm carefully phrased to protect him from charges of blasphemy while leaving the injurious purport of his comments patent to all.

His revelation that the Osiris myth – the killing of the god and his eventual restoration to life by the goddess Isis – was basically identical with the ritual killing or dismemberment of the king or god in tribal communities in order to symbolise the end of winter and, at their resurrection a few days later, to symbolise the advent of spring and the hope of a new harvest could itself have proved by implication severely damaging to Christian belief. It opened the possibility that what had for so long been revered as the most sophisticated and refined form of religious worship, with its central story of crucifixion and resurrection, was based upon a primitive fertility rite ignorantly sanctified by later generations. But the way Frazer presented such parallels throughout his work left nothing to the imagination. Christians and pagans, Frazer remarked, had at an early date become aware of the 'remarkable coincidence' both in the nature and in the timing of their various festivals, the pagans having, long before the advent of Christianity, celebrated the Virgin Birth of their god at the same seasonal time as the Christian Christmas. That coincidence, we are told, formed historically a theme of bitter controversy between the adherents of the rival religions. And Frazer sardonically comments:

> In these unseemly bickerings the heathen took what to a superficial observer might seem strong ground by arguing that their god was the older and therefore presumably the original, not the counterfeit, since as a general rule an original is older than its copy. This feeble argument the Christians easily rebutted. They admitted, indeed, that in point of time Christ was the junior deity, but they triumphantly demonstrated his seniority by falling back on the subtlety of Satan, who on so important an occasion had surpassed himself by inverting the usual order of nature.[57]

The withering scorn of such passages, in the work of a respected scholar relying upon seemingly irrefutable evidence, was potentially mortifying for the Christian intellectual, providing a grave obstacle to continued adherence to the faith. Yet in his notes to the poem, Eliot specifically records his indebtedness to Frazer, quite apart from his indebtedness to the latter's disciple Jessie Weston, as if the poem had been largely inspired by Frazer's findings:

> To another work of anthropology I am indebted in general, one which has influenced our generation profoundly; I mean *The Golden Bough*; I have used especially the two volumes *Adonis, Attis, Osiris*. Anyone who is acquainted with these works will immediately recognise in the poem certain references to vegetation ceremonies.

What may easily be missed here is Eliot's inversion of Frazer's conclusions, his subtle reconstituting of the implications of the new theories. As he wrote at this time in an essay in *The Dial*, Eliot approved of the main implications of Frazer's work, that '*all* art emulates the condition of ritual. That is what it comes from and to that it must always return for nourishment.'[58] But he rejected the 'unconscious fatalism' implied in Frazer's work, the assumption that there exist non-human forces to which man is subjected. Instead, employing Jung's more recent theory of the 'collective unconscious', the existence in all societies and individuals of archetypal patterns inherited by accumulation from the experience of their forebears, Eliot saw in the correspondence between the cardinal episodes of Christian doctrine and those of other religions, myths and cultures not a disqualification of the Christian creed but a corroboration, evidence of the conformity of the Christian faith to universal human experience, and hence of the satisfaction it could offer for the basic spiritual needs of Western man.[59] Robert Langbaum has justly noted that Eliot's use of Jung provided an appeal to our deeper being, 'that when we delve deep into the psyche we find an archetypal self and a desire to repeat the patterns laid out in the sort of myths described by Frazer and Jessie Weston'.[60] But the poem goes far beyond a desire merely to repeat patterns for their own sake. On the one hand, its replacement of the traditional narrator by an amalgam of figures drawn from different periods of history and literature did express to perfection the new concept of the unconscious, as defined by Jung:

If it were permissible to personify the unconscious, we might call it a collective human being combining the characteristics of both sexes, transcending youth and age, birth and death, and, from having at his command a human experience of one or two million years, almost immortal. If such a being existed, he would be exalted above all temporal change; the present would mean neither more nor less to him than any year in the one-hundredth century before Christ; he would be a dreamer of age-old dreams and, owing to his immeasurable experience, he would be an incomparable prognosticator. He would have lived countless times over the life of the individual, of the family, tribe and people, and he would possess the living sense of the rhythm of growth, flowering, and decay.[61]

But Eliot's deeper purpose was to explore by that new principle the possibility of reauthenticating the seemingly discredited beliefs of Christianity. He sought, by inverting the negative implications of the new anthropological insights, to suggest, however tentatively at this stage in his progress, their corroboration of those beliefs as belonging to larger universal truths acknowledged by mankind. If Jessie Weston had argued, with scholarly prestige deriving from both Frazer and Freud, that the symbols in the Christian Grail legend – the Lance, the Sword and the Dish – were patently sexual in their symbolism, and that the legend as a whole hence constituted the outgrowth of an ancient pagan fertility rite, Eliot, by placing that legend within a much broader range of myth, sought to suggest the confirmation it offered that religious images of sterility and rebirth, of death and resurrection, far from being mystical elements only tenuously related to reality, in fact expressed the most fundamental yearnings for human survival within the physical world, yearnings extended into the sphere of spiritual experience.

In the context of the contemporary preoccupation with the 'fourth dimension' in art and philosophy, with the belief even among secularists of a world existing beyond the real, Eliot perceived those shared mythic patterns of emasculation and healing, of aridity and fertility found within primitive tribal practices not as disqualifications of Christian faith but as essences or 'abstracts' of the human condition existent in an eternal context beyond the actual. Their recurrence in the Tarot pack, in ancient rituals, in Egyptian and classical mythology, constituted, in that view, local manifestations of transcendent truths, adapted to the regional needs and concepts of those cultures, while the Christian version formed their fullest and most sophisticated expression – and above all the version most relevant to his own spiritual needs and to those of his contemporaries in the Western world. In that, incidentally, he differed from many creative artists of his time, who were then incorporating into their painting and sculpture the newly admired masks and totem poles of African and other primitive societies, perceiving in them a primordial power superior to the jaded forms of Western art. For Eliot, an élitist by nature, interest in such past rituals, in slain idols and resurrected gods, lay not in the superiority of those primitive forms, but in their foreshadowing of the more valid rituals of worship embodied in Christianity.

Eliot was not alone in his perception of the authenticity such archetypal foreshadowings could offer for Christian belief. How stimulating the merging of mythological forms was to his generation, in the secular as well as the religious sphere, may be seen in D. H. Lawrence's remarkable story *The Man Who Died*, published in the same year as *The Waste Land*. In that story the Christ figure (reverentially never named in the narrative, as part of the author's continued respect for the faith) merges into that of the dismembered but reassembled Osiris, in vindication of the author's personal belief in the primacy of virility over celibacy. According to Egyptian legend, Osiris was, on the reconstruction of his scattered parts, found to lack the genitals, and Lawrence identified in that deprivation a link with the celibate Jesus and with the advocacy of continence in Pauline Christianity. In Lawrence's fictional sequel to the Christian story, Jesus learns through his meeting with the priestess of Isis and through the gentle stimulus of her touch, the error of having advocated chastity during his previous life:

> It was Isis; but not Isis, Mother of Horus. It was Isis Bereaved, Isis in Search. . . . She was looking for the fragments of the dead Osiris, dead and scattered asunder, dead, torn apart, and thrown in fragments over the wide world. And she must find his hands and his feet, his heart, his thighs, his head, his belly, she must gather him together and fold her arms round the re-assembled body till it became warm again, and roused to life, and could embrace her, and could fecundate her womb . . .
>
> Suddenly it dawned on him: 'I asked them all to serve me with the corpse of their love. And in the end I offered them only the corpse of my love. This is my body – take and eat – my corpse –'[62]

Here too the pagan story functions as a kindred archetype, revalidating the Christian narrative for the author's time. As Lawrence
remarked in his *Fantasia of the Unconscious* (1923):

> And so it is that these myths now begin to hypnotize us again. ...
> The soul must take the hint from the relics our scientists have so
> marvellously gathered out of the forgotten past, and from the hint
> develop a new living utterance. The spark is from dead wisdom,
> but the fire is life.[63]

The use of myth, in both Lawrence's work and in Eliot's, was closer
to Cubist art than may at first appear. Indeed Eliot's formulation of
his own philosophical position at the time when Cubist art was
emerging reveals the connection most clearly. The discovery of
some new viewpoint different from one's own, he argued, does not
necessarily mean that it should be adopted in the latter's place, oust-
ing the previous belief. Instead it was preferable to create a third
viewpoint that would include both ideas, provided the viewer
remained conscious of the amalgamation. In those terms, Frazer's revelation of the mythic substructure that Christianity shared with the
pagan world did not mean that Eliot was required to jettison his
own belief; nor, on the other hand, would continued confidence in
the superiority of his own faith in itself adequately acknowledge the
newly revealed archetypal validity of myth. What was needed was
the establishment of a third vantage point that, as he put it, 'some-
how contains' the other two viewpoints while displaying a conscious awareness of their continued existence.[64]

   That process, even in the image it employs, the merging of contrasting vantage points, corresponded closely to the technique of
multiple viewpoint in Cubism, not merely as an innovative method
of resisting established conventions of perspective, but also as a
means of reflecting the new synthesis of mythic archetypes, both
religious and pagan, with modern scientific perceptions. Picasso's
Girl Before a Mirror, as has been seen, follows essentially the same
procedure, adopting an artistic viewpoint that allows for the simultaneous incorporation of biblical tradition, of pagan myth, of medical x-ray, while deliberately creating thereby a third and overriding
modernist depiction, which both contrasts and assimilates those
viewpoints.

   In this period, however, one of those multiple viewpoints
received especial attention, namely the eternal essence assumed to

lie beyond the actual. Duchamp, for example, in attempting to represent the distortion spatial forms would undergo on their projection into that further dimension, did so on the assumption that those 'distortions' were closer to ultimate truth than the limited perception offered in the universe we inhabit. And in Eliot's poetry the same concept predominates. This contemporary search for an abstract reality, surpassing the limitations of the rational or of the empirically provable, lies at the source, I believe, of Eliot's haunting assertions of paradoxical, lambent mysteries that transgress logic – the dry rock that provides water, the corpse that sprouts in the earth, the drowning that represents baptismal rebirth – whereby the limitations of the physical are dwarfed by the paradoxes of transcendent truths. In this connection, it is perhaps significant that in the year prior to the publication of this poem, while Eliot was still engaged in its composition, his championing of the Metaphysical Poets focused upon an element intimately related to this interest. In his widely discussed essay on that school of poets he singled out John Donne, praising him for qualities that conformed closely to his own developing poetic creed. Donne, living in a period in many ways paralleling Eliot's, had been confronted by a scientific revolution that seemed similarly to negate religious faith, to 'call all in doubt'. The solar-centred universe proposed by Copernicus and recently confirmed by Galileo and Kepler, had seemed, by discrediting the harmoniously structured Ptolemaic universe, to reduce man to an insignificant insect on a minor planet spinning subserviently about the sun, and by that discovery to discredit too the hierarchical and moral order of an anthropocentric world:

> And freely men confess, that this world's spent,
> When in the Planets, and the Firmament
> They seeke so many new; they see that this
> Is crumbled out againe to'his Atomis.
> 'Tis all in pieces, all coherence gone;
> All just supply, and all Relation:
> Prince, Subject, Father, Sonne, are things forgot...[65]

Donne's response, presaging Eliot's, had been not to deny the factually based discoveries of the astronomers but to relegate and restrict their implications to the domain of a merely physical reality. By scorning that limited actuality, he reached out to a spiritual entity beyond, to a world of paradox unconstrained by the trammels of spatial, temporal or rational measurement. In *Goodfriday, 1613, Riding Westward*, the opening scene of planets orbiting elliptically in accordance with Kepler's scientific observations is countered by a meditative vision of a vastly different spiritual world, whose Son/ Sun magnificently contradicts the laws regulating our own heliocentric universe:

> There I should see a Sunne by rising set,
> And by that setting endlesse day beget;
> But that Christ on this Crosse, did rise and fall,
> Sinne had eternally benighted all.

It was this readiness on Donne's part to incorporate into his poetic response what lay beyond the tactile, namely the *meta-physical* in the literal meaning of that eponymic term, his willingness to temper the empirical and observable by the transcendent view and amalgamate the actual with philosophical speculation, that won Eliot's admiration in a passage that was to become seminal for twentieth-century criticism:

> A thought to Donne was an experience; it modified his sensibility. When a poet's mind is perfectly equipped for its work, it is constantly amalgamating disparate experience; the ordinary man's experience is chaotic, irregular, fragmentary. The latter falls in love, or reads Spinoza, and these two experiences have nothing to do with each other, or with the noise of the typewriter or the smell of cooking; in the mind of the poet these experiences are always forming new wholes.[66]

Donne's amalgamation of disparate experience, his ability to assimilate meditative thought and physical perception even when paradoxically contradicting the logical and verifiable, provided for Eliot a major attraction of his poetry.

In the same way, Eliot's *Journey of the Magi*, a reenactment of the Nativity in immediately contemporary terms – just as Donne had, in *Goodfriday 1613*, envisioned, as the title indicates, a vivid reenactment of the Crucifixion in the year he wrote it – parodies the petty definitions of the empiricists restricted to the limitations of time and space. 'There was a Birth, certainly,/We had evidence and no doubt', he comments mordantly, but by his capitalisation of the words Birth and Death he by-passes such paltry empirical distinctions to reach out to the metaphysical concepts of those events, representing their counterparts in a dimension beyond, a dimension possessing for him a value outstripping the factual:

> ... were we led all that way for
> Birth or Death? There was a Birth, certainly,
> We had evidence and no doubt. I had seen birth and death,
> But had thought they were different; this Birth was
> Hard and bitter agony for us, like Death, our death.

His rejection of empiricism was already embryonic in the doctoral dissertation he wrote in 1911–14, where he argued, in terms similar to those employed by the hyperspace theorists, that the scientific process of generalising from particulars ignores an essential difference between the physical objects from which they are generalised and the universal truths to which they must be related:

> every transformation of type involves a leap which science cannot take, and which metaphysics must take. It involves an *interpretation*, a transmigration from one world to another, and such a pilgrimage involves an act of faith.[67]

Such a statement may, once again, appear far removed from the experiments of Cubist painters; but if one places beside it a central passage from the essay *Du Cubisme* by Metzinger and Gleizes, the parallel becomes manifest. There they define Cézanne as marking the beginning of a movement away from the mimetic depiction of objects towards a higher truth, the representation of the 'profound essence' that both embraces and consummates the specificity of individual objects:

> If Cézanne did not attain those regions where profound realism imperceptibly becomes luminous spiritualism, then he left to us, who also seek this goal, a simple and wonderful method. He who understands Cézanne is close to Cubism. One may say that the difference between Cubism and previous manifestations is only one of intensity: it is sufficient to regard attentively the process of the passage of realism, moving away from the superficial realities of Courbet's realism and with Cézanne into profound essence, and overtaking the luminous unknowable, which has retreated.

If that same dissatisfaction with the 'superficial realities' of this physical world and the desire for the 'luminous unknowable' led Eliot towards a yearning for the metaphysical and, as part of that tendency, towards support of the seventeenth-century poets associated with that name, at precisely the time he was writing this poem there arose in Italy a school of painters, also oppressed with a sense of the loneliness and emptiness of the tactile world, who (not fortuitously) adopted for their work the name *pittura metafisica*. In 1917 a meeting occurred in a military hospital in Ferrara between the Futurist painter Carlo Carrà and Giorgio de Chirico. Impressed by the sense of the void in Nietzsche's writings and the description in his letters of the deserted piazzas of Turin, Chirico had begun to see in those Italian squares a source of 'strange and deep, infinitely mysterious and solitary poetry'. He sought to express in his paintings the vacuity of the contemporary world and his nostalgic longing for a more impressive, mystical entity that seemed to have existed in the past but had disappeared from the twentieth century. Where Eliot, with memories of Spenser's nymphs and the colourful pageantry of an earlier age, had written wearily of his own time:

> Shall I say I have gone at dusk through narrow streets
> And watched the smoke that rises from the pipes
> Of lonely men in shirt-sleeves, leaning out of windows?

Chirico's *The Melancholy and Mystery of a Street* (Figure 11) evokes not only the haunting sense of menacing shadows but also an architectural perspective suggestive of the deterioration from a majestic past to a desolate present. The Renaissance colonnades of the piazza, intended for the busy concourse of crowds, contrasts eerily with the emptiness of the square, an emptiness broken only by a girl playing with a hoop and by the dark, ominous shadow of a hidden figure. Moreover, where Eliot's sympathy with the earlier Metaphysical Poets had been based in large part on their shared validation of transcendent paradox, so Chirico, in reaction to the scientism of the day, chose instead the non-rational, maintaining that 'logical meaning must be eliminated from art'. As part of that rejection of reason, like Eliot he found in myth a more satisfying response to the ambiguities of human existence, and searched in Greek legend for the subject matter of his art, inserting below his self-portrait the inscription *Et quid amabo nisi quod aenigma est?*[68]

Hart Crane, too, while dissociating himself from the doubts implicit in Eliot's religious quest, shared the conviction that poetry, and life itself, must emerge from the restrictive scientism of the day to establish links with the metaphysical, to connect the mechanistic world with numinous experience. Profoundly affected in 1922 by a reading of Ouspensky's *Tertium Organum* (itself indebted, as has been noted, to hyperspace theory), he perceived a strong connection between his own mystic experiences and those of which the Russian had written. He read there that the founders of the religions of the world 'have all been bridgebuilders...between the *Finite* and the *Infinite*', and in *The Bridge* he himself searched for a means to respond to the 'higher' cosmic consciousness described by Ouspensky.[69]

Eliot's *Waste Land* deserves to be seen, therefore, not merely as an expression of twentieth-century disillusionment but within the context of this broader search for luminous truths surpassing reality, a search that dominated so much of art and literature in the early decades of this century. In that setting *The Waste Land* constitutes an account of his own painful yearning for and discovery of meaning in the spiritual vacuum of his day, the spring-time of his soul's awakening being for him an agonising experience, his April represented as

> ... the cruelest month, breeding
> Lilacs out of the dead land, mixing
> Memory and desire, stirring
> Dull roots with spring rain.

If, among the stony rubbish of the twentieth century, the dry stone gives no sound of water, no hint of salvation, and the journey to the Chapel Perilous seems at first to lead only to emptiness and dry bones, there is, at the conclusion of that passage,

> a flash of lightning. Then a damp gust
> Bringing rain.

That moment of revelation is in no sense capricious, but the culmination of a process developing throughout the poem, consummating the repeated allusions to rebirth from seeming death. The early reference to the dry bones, by its echo of Ezekiel's vision, associates them even at that stage with their approaching revitalisation. And the corpse of the drowned Phoenician, transformed into something

rich and strange ('Those are pearls that were his eyes') again hints at
a death that is really a rebirth.

Even though the poem was written before Eliot's formal conversion, there are lines clearly suggesting his contemplation of that
commitment. – 'The awful daring of a moment's surrender/Which
an age of prudence can never retract' – the 'surrender' to the
promptings of the heart rather than to the prudence dictated by the
intellect.[70] Above all, however, the motive force of the poem is his
growing perception of the ways in which the twentieth-century
intellectual, by a revalidation of myth, may be able in some way to
cope with the loss of faith seemingly dictated by science. The fragmentation of the individual, which has so often been seen as the
theme of this poem, the discredited faiths and mystical creeds
defined by Frazer and Freud as totems and taboos of primitive societies, no longer meaningful to a sophisticated age and jettisoned by
all right-thinking men, are gradually perceived as unified and
indeed authenticated by their participation in a higher universal
concept. The drowned Phoenician Sailor, the Fisher King, the
Hanged Man of the Tarot Pack are adumbrations, in disparate cultures, both of the Crucifixion and the Christian paradox of rebirth,
the idea of being born into the mortality of this world and of dying
into eternal life, with baptism as a 'drowning' that recreates. And the
thunder that heralds the life-giving rain echoes the thunder of the
Lord of Creation from the Upanishads, of Prajapati, whose message
Datte, dayadhvam, damyata – 'Give, sympathize, control' – is seen by
Eliot as paralleling the cardinal principles of Christianity – selfless-
ness, compassion and restraint. Moreover the climax of the Upanishads, the ideal to which those virtues are to lead – *Shantih, shantih,
shantih* – echoes, as he acknowledges in his notes, the Christian
'peace which passeth understanding'. It represented, however tentatively at this stage, the spiritual fulfilment within his own faith
that he was then seeking, these cultural fragments gathered from
such diverse sources intended to serve as bulwarks that could
'shore' up his ruins, strengthening the seemingly derelict, dilapidated
creed of his time and offering hope of a restored faith for the future.

The discomfort critics have experienced in dealing with this
anomaly – that a religious poem served as the catalyst for Modernist
verse – has expressed itself in an almost exclusive focus upon the
form of the poem, as if that alone constituted its appeal for his generation and as if that could be separated from the poem as an organic
whole. A. Walton Litz, on the occasion of the fiftieth anniversary of

the poem's publication, contended that its value does not lie in the thematic contrasts between two kinds of life and two kinds of death. 'If this were so, *The Waste Land* would be fit only for courses on religious ideas in literature. *The Waste Land* is not *about* spiritual dryness, it is about the ways in which that dryness can be perceived and expressed.'[71] If that were so, one might reply, its theme could have been restricted to parched deserts, carbuncular clerks and Shakespearean rags in a setting devoid of hooded Christ figure, Holy Grail and Chapel Perilous. The specifically religious journey that constituted the core of the poem may in itself have seemed irrelevant to the predominantly secular public. But what did attract that public, including its leading artists and writers, was, in addition to its weary acknowledgment of the bleakness of modern life, the stimulus provided by its central theme – its search for universal truths existent beyond human perception, truths untrammelled by the laws of logic, space and time. The feeling of betrayal experienced by many of Eliot's admirers on the announcement of his conversion arose, we may suspect, from disappointment that he had chosen to ally himself with traditional, orthodox Christianity, to join, as it were, the establishment, rather than to continue to represent the troubled search for enigmatic absolutes such as characterised the art of his generation.

But with an understanding not only of the centrality of hyperspace theory in Cubist painting but, in larger terms, of the attempt of artists to transcend the merely visible, to convey essences imperceptible to the human eye but ultimately more valid than material reality, it is possible to perceive a deeper bond than has previously been acknowledged between the secular and the religious experimenters during the early decades of this century, both groups acknowledging and attempting to represent verities existent beyond the merely tactile and visible, with many openly acknowledging the mystical quality of their search. And such knowledge may, more specifically, serve to suggest a fundamental correlation between the pioneering canvases of Duchamp, Metzinger, Malevich, Picasso, Chirico and Mondrian and the thematic, as well as the literary innovations of Eliot's *Waste Land*.

3

Huxley's Counterpoint

Although Aldous Huxley's *Point Counter Point* was received with international acclaim on its appearance and, as Isaiah Berlin, Kenneth Clark and others have testified, marked a turning point in the intellectual careers of many members of that generation, it has never fared well with critics in terms of its artistic achievement.[1] Some have, with reservation, applauded its amusing and irreverent parody of contemporary fashions; but any claim to its being a serious literary work, deserving to be placed among the major novels of the century, was rejected by David Daiches and others many years ago. The characters, Daiches argued, do not develop organically in the manner required by the novel genre, and the musical theme of counterpoint, which provides the structural frame of the novel, contributes little, he maintained, to the central theme of the work. E. B. Burgum echoed that view in his statement that 'No development takes place in the totality of relationships. These remain what they were at the beginning, a chaos of contrasts', concluding accordingly that the novel was 'an aesthetic failure, since the pattern promised by the title is never achieved'. And Laurence Brander claimed in 1969 that the novel has no plot, is grossly mismanaged, and is pieced together simplistically and arbitrarily.[2] These strictures have been repeated so frequently in subsequent years as to become a veritable chorus of condemnation, with only a lone voice here or there attempting, usually very hesitantly, to defend the novel from outright dismissal in terms of its literary or artistic achievement.

The principles behind that condemnation are, however, more than a little strange when placed within the aesthetic context of its time. In a period when the finest work in all art forms, including the novel, was essentially innovative, breaking away from established patterns to create stylistic forms suited to deal with new twentieth-century challenges, it seems scarcely justifiable to dismiss a novel of that era, as Daiches did, on the ground of its failure to conform to the traditional conventions of the genre. Neither *Orlando* nor *Ulysses* complied with the nineteenth-century requirements of organic, naturalistic development of character; yet because the latter were more

1. Gauguin, *The Crucifixion*.

2. Gauguin, *Te Aa No Areois –
The Seed of the Areois*.

3. Gauguin, *Mahana No Atua – The Day of God*.

4. Gauguin, *Parahi Te Marae – The Sacred Mountain*.

5. Picasso, *Seated Nude*.

6. Brancusi, *The Kiss*.

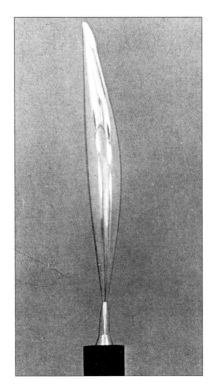

7. Brancusi, *Bird in Space*.

8. Picasso, *Girl Before a Mirror*.

9. Velázquez, *Portrait of Pope Innocent X.*

10. Bacon, *Study after Velázquez's Portrait of Pope Innocent X.*

11. Chirico, *The Melancholy and Mystery of a Street.*

12. Metzinger, *Tea Time.*

13. Picasso, *Head of a Woman*.

14. Picasso, *Weeping Woman*.

15. Picasso, *Three Musicians*.

16. Picasso, *Minotaur Carousing*.

patently experimental, more obviously innovative both in style and in treatment of subject, the criterion of organic development was never applied to them as a litmus test for authenticating or invalidating their literary worth. Within the pictorial arts, only the uninitiated would apply to the canvases of Braque or Kandinsky the yardstick of naturalism. Yet in judging Huxley's novel even his few more energetic supporters have refrained from defending him in terms of artistic innovation, preferring to seek ways of justifying his work on more conventional grounds, such as the apologetic argument that his moral stance and play with ideas offer some compensation for the lack of psychologically persuasive characterisation.[3]

That Huxley intended *Point Counter Point* to be a novel of experimentation, deserting conventional forms in order to inaugurate an innovative approach to the genre, cannot be dismissed as mere conjecture. There is patent testimony within the novel itself. The introduction there of the figure of Philip Quarles, an author engaged in planning an essentially new type of novel based on principles more suited to the needs of his time, is sufficient indication, Philip's reflections upon the kind of work he hopes to produce being presented in the form of lengthy italicised extracts from his notebook. But Huxley goes much further, confirming, in a subtly devised image, the validity of identifying those interior experiments with his own literary venture. Philip, contemplating the possibility of placing a novelist within his own novel, and perhaps another novelist within that inner novel, compares the result of that sequence to the picture on the front of the Quaker Oats carton of those days, which regularly displayed a benevolent Quaker holding in his hand a packet of that same cereal, on which was portrayed the figure of a smaller Quaker holding a packet... That series has been read most obviously in the direction of infinitesimal smallness. But it also functions, one should note, in the reverse direction, from the inner figure outwards, so that the internal novel being planned by Philip becomes itself a replica of Huxley's outer novel, *Point Counter Point*, in which Philip is a fictional participant. The innovations, therefore, that Philip Quarles designs for his own projected novel must be regarded, on that broad hint, as highly pertinent to Huxley's own experimentation with form.

The idea of 'contrapuntal plots', which Philip determines to adopt for his new work, has long been seen as in some way relevant to the outer novel, but almost invariably in a negative sense – not as an integral part of the fictional work but as a mere gimmick, offering facetious juxtapositions of antithetical scenes for the amusement of the reader or, alternatively, as part of the customary charge that the characters are mere mouthpieces for exaggeratedly contrasting view-points. Peter Quennell castigates Huxley for offering us only eccentrics taking their principles to extremes, and for ignoring the possibility of a middle path. Those characters, he remarks with exasperation, 'must either be exploring the heavens...or wallowing in the slime', with no hint of any marriage between heaven and hell.[4] Peter Fichow similarly perceives that contrastive element as essentially a play with the idea of diversity – Jones murdering his wife while Smith wheels the perambulator in the park. And Jerome Meckier, perceiving in those contrasts an extension of the musical subtheme of the work, suggests that the main theme of the novel is Huxley's satirical comparison of his own generation to an orchestra in which each character, by insisting on playing his own individual tune instead of working in harmony and unison with others, produces mere cacophony.[5] For such critics, therefore, the main thrust of the novel is social satire, an animadversion on the disparity of purpose among members of his generation, the polarity of their behaviour and their total inability to cooperate.

I should like to suggest that, beneath the surface banter, there is in this novel a profound theme, tragic in import as well as highly innovative in presentation, reflecting a major shift in contemporary thought and, in both respects – thematically and stylistically – providing for the novel a literary counterpart to changes occurring at precisely that time within the visual arts.[6]

The new spatial notation introduced by Analytical Cubism underwent a significant change during the 1920s. Earlier, when Braque and Picasso were first experimenting with the new approach, their purpose had been to desert mimetic representation of what is optically received in favour of cerebral perception. As Olivier Hourcade explained at the time, painting the rim of a teacup as an ellipse in accordance with Renaissance laws of perspective is a falsification of actuality in favour of mere visual impression. And this growing suspicion of the gap between what is registered on the optical nerve and actuality, between the way we see objects and our intellectual consciousness of their true shape, had its counterpart in the realm of philosophy. In his study *Our Knowledge of the External World*, published in 1914, Bertrand Russell argued that the effect of solidity bestowed upon objects by human ocular process is itself mere mental fabrication. Since the information received by the eye, the evidence we have of the object, is restricted to the single facet that confronts us, the mind compensates for that limitation by conjuring up composites, by *imagining* aspects derived from previous experience. Hence he argued (in line with the changes in science discussed in the previous chapter) that the so-called empirical evidence previously assumed to be provided by the visible – the doctrine of 'seeing is believing' – is inadmissible, based not on fact but on mere conjecture of those facets concealed from the eye: 'All the aspects of a thing are real', he claimed, 'whereas the thing is a mere logical construction'.[7] Braque put the concept no less forcefully in rejecting optical verisimilitude as the basis of art in an axiom later echoed by Picasso (although the latter may have been the originator of the phrase), namely that 'Art is not truth. It is a lie that makes us realize truth.'[8] As Jacques Rivière noted in 1912 in defence of the new art form, traditional depth-perspective in painting does no more than record the viewer's location:

> Perspective is as accidental a thing as lighting. It is the sign, not of a particular moment in time, but of a particular position in space. It indicates not the situation of objects, but the situation of a spectator.... But in reality we can change position: a step to the right and a step to the left complete our vision. The knowledge we have of an object is ... a complex sum of perceptions.[9]

The presentation of objects from a number of different angles thus became the new basis for their work, a process that they began to term 'simultaneity'. The purpose was not merely to offer a variety of angles of viewpoint but to suggest the equal validity of those views, a process discounting the previous precedence afforded to the artist's angle of vision. Where, for example, traditional perspective had granted primary importance to the foreground, always presented as larger than the receding areas behind, as in normal vision, Braque wished to preserve an equality of authenticity to all areas:

> The acute angles in the paintings I did at L'Estaque in 1908 were the result of a new conception of space. I said good bye to the 'vanishing point'. And to avoid any projection towards infinity I interposed a series of planes, set one on top of another, at a short distance from the spectator. It was to make him realize that objects did not retreat backwards into space but stood up close in front of one another. Cézanne had thought a lot about that. You have only

to compare his landscapes with Corot's, for instance, to see that he had done away with distance and that after him infinity no longer exists. Instead of starting with the foreground I always began with the centre of the picture. Before long I even turned perspective inside out and turned the pyramid of forms upside down so that it came forward to meet the observer.[10]

In Jean Metzinger's *Tea Time* of 1921 (Figure 12) planes are treated as if they were transparent, revealing further strata beyond those initially perceived, so that the various viewpoints from which the subject can be regarded are presented concurrently, the teacup, for example, being divided vertically to display two contrary angles of vision, neither awarded preference over the other.

Paul Laporte has attempted to connect such Cubist 'simultaneity' to Einstein's theory of relativity; but he admits somewhat ruefully that, in an interview with Einstein himself, the latter firmly rejected the comparison on the ground that the reverse was true – that the theory of relativity was aimed at casting doubt on such simultaneity, at the idea that contrasting views of an object differ only in the angle from which they are viewed. As he had argued in his early presentation of the theory, his treatise *On the Electrodynamics of Moving Bodies* (1905), in a relatively motioned world the event or object regarded in fact *changes* in accordance with the viewpoint: 'two events which, viewed from a system of co-ordinates, are simultaneous, can no longer be looked upon as simultaneous events when envisaged from a system which is in motion relatively to that system.' On those grounds, the supposed connection of Cubist art to Einstein's emergent theory, especially the suggestion that it derives from it, has been generally rejected.[11]

I would like to suggest that there is a relationship at a more subtle level, that both the theory itself and the emergent art form were, in their different ways, reflecting a contemporary transformation in philosophical concepts. As Karl Popper has shown so effectively, scientific theories, as well as scientific discoveries, have frequently resulted not from impartial, objective investigation but from hypotheses arising from or suggested by shifts in contemporary ideas, prognoses emerging from the predisposition of the scientists themselves, which, often unconsciously, they felt impelled to test or confirm. It is a pattern that could explain the frequent incidence in history of concurrent breakthroughs by contemporary investigators, such as the simultaneous proposition of the theory of evolution by Darwin and his lesser-known contemporary Alfred R. Wallace.[12] In that context of subconscious impulses directing scientific investigation, the theory of relativism itself may be seen as more integral to the time of its advocacy than has previously been thought, stimulated, in fact, by a shift in the more general perceptions of the time.

In earlier Cubist art, Braque and Picasso did indeed present a visual composite of the same object viewed from diverse angles, those aspects being, as it were, superimposed one upon the other. But at that period the principle was applied primarily to still life in order to challenge the principle of ocular monism. The Metzinger canvas *Tea Time*, one notes, had, in that tradition, treated the human sitter as a sculptural object rather than a living being, an item to be translated into the new terminology of art. As Metzinger commented in the article on Cubism, which he produced together with Albert Gleizes, the major purpose of that group of painters was to remove such items from temporal restrictions by 'moving around an object to seize from it several successive appearances which, fused into a single image, reconstitute it in time'.[13] In the late 1920s and the 1930s, however, as Leo Steinberg has recorded[14] – precisely, we may note, at the time of Huxley's novel, published in 1928 – a change occurred, as Picasso introduced an essentially innovative form of human portraiture, a dual-faceted human countenance offering simultaneously both profile and frontal view, in a manner rejecting volumetric fidelity in any conventional sense.

Probably the earliest hint of such facial duality had occurred in Picasso's *Les Demoiselles d'Avignon* of 1907, where the noses on two frontally viewed faces are inserted in profile, as triangular forms. But there the technique lacked the implications developed in the later phase. In Picasso's lithograph *Head of a Woman* of 1925 (Figure 13) the profile is so delicately accommodated within the frontal view that its presence can easily be overlooked unless the viewer consciously blocks off the right side of the face; but from that time onwards the interpenetration of diverse angles of viewpoint became increasingly evident in Picasso's portraits, as well as increasingly discordant, those contrary viewpoints representing conflicting facets of personality. The disharmony culminated in such characteristically disturbing canvases as his *Weeping Woman* (Figure 14), expressing a frenzied inner chaos, the depiction of warring internal tensions that have failed to achieve unity. The organisers of the exhibition entitled 'Picasso and the Weeping Women', held at the Los Angeles County Museum of Art in 1994, attributed the emergence of this theme to entirely personal elements in the artist's life, to the break-up of his marriage with Olga Koklava and his developing relationships with Marie-Thérèse Walter and Dora Maar. But Picasso's artistic originality, as evidenced by his impact upon contemporary painters, has always been of much wider significance than the merely personal, and such canvases as his *Girl in a Mirror* of 1932, discussed in the previous chapter, confirm that the emergence of the multifaceted portrait and the accompanying sense of inner discord in his *Weeping Women* also reflected the new Freudian division of the human self into its component parts, the ego, id, superego and libido, each striving for dominance within the individual's subconscious.

That aspect is indeed self-evident; but the conflicting angles of vision functioned also, one may perceive, as an expression of a broader conflict endemic to the period, and to which we may now return in connection with *Point Counter Point*.

The centrality of multiplicity of viewpoint as it emerged even in the earlier forms of Cubist art should itself cast doubt on the traditional criticism that its presence in Huxley's novel was a mere gimmick, ultimately irrelevant to the novel's development – or, as John Atkins has recently argued, marking the failure of a writer who was 'congenitally unable to provide a synthesized view of life'.[15] The emergence of this element in painting suggests instead that Huxley's adoption of multiplicity as the organising motif of his work was an attempt to express in literary terms a problem that was concerning the painter too. As Picasso moved into the 1920s phase with his adoption of facial duality in his portraiture, it is possible to discern in his work a sensitivity to a human split in personality quite different from the Freudian, a split simultaneously apprehended by Huxley, with remarkable shrewdness, and adapted by him to the genre of the novel. As Philip, seated with Elinor on the deck of a homeward-bound steamer, catches disconnected snatches of conversation from the passengers promenading past as part of their daily exercise – a truncated remark about missionaries, a giggling denial of flirtatiousness, a protest at the quality of flannel underwear – he perceives a new way of structuring a novel that might prove more true to life than even the most realistic works of previous traditions. His wife Elinor (forestalling the critics) wishes he would write 'a simple, straightforward story about a young man and woman who fall in love and get married'. But, brushing the suggestion aside as unworthy of consideration, he prefers exploring the exciting possibilities offered by the new technique.

What precisely is that new technique of multiplicity? Since he calls it half-humorously the 'musicalization of fiction', the primary focus in criticism has been either on the fugue-like reflection of similar situations in the plot structure, or, as we have seen, on the implications of the musical imagery of the novel in terms of orchestral disharmony. But within Philip's discussion with Elinor, what at first seems merely comic grows serious towards the end of the passage, suggesting the deeper, underlying theme that will function throughout the work:

> 'Well, as a matter of fact...these *camisoles en flanelle* and pickled onions and bishops of cannibal islands are really quite to the point. Because the essence of the new way of looking is multiplicity. Multiplicity of eyes and multiplicity of aspects seen. For instance, one person interprets events in terms of bishops; another in terms of the price of flannel camisoles; another, like that young lady from Gulmerg,' he nodded after the retreating group, 'thinks of it in terms of good times. And then there's the biologist, the chemist, the physicist, the historian. Each sees, professionally, a different aspect of the event, a different layer of reality. What I want to do is to look with all those eyes at once. With religious eyes, scientific eyes, economic eyes...'[16]

As the title of the outer novel implies, that multifaceted approach will provide an opportunity of investigating one of the problems most deeply disturbing for the contemporary intellectual – that no settled or controlling view appeared possible any longer. Every standpoint had now become, in a manner not experienced in previous eras, cancelled out by another approach, an approach diametrically opposed in its implications yet apparently equally valid. Every *point*, indeed, is now nullified by a *counterpoint*. The religious mystic, treasuring the individual's inner world as sacrosanct, insists on full responsibility for human choices, while Freudian psychology, splitting the human personality into constituent parts controlled by preconditioned reflexes, heredity and traumatic childhood experience, absolves the individual of such accountability. For the biologist, confined to the evidence of verifiable data, the ideas of beauty and harmony, so cherished by poet and painter, emerge as mere titillations of the nervous system, devoid of transcendental truth. The hierarchy of the Catholic priesthood, drawing its authority from the Pope, is now seen reductively by the zoologist as simply a human version of the 'pecking order' governing the poultry yard. From point A, the absurd untenability of point B is convincingly proved; then the process is reversed, to reveal from the second standpoint the utter irrationality of the first, that process of reciprocal cancellation leaving no valid criteria for living.

While this approach did resemble and, on Karl Popper's principle, may have instigated Einstein's theory denying the validity of objects, now seen as dependent on the changing position of the observer, it functioned also as a means of expressing the bewildering disparity of contemporary values. If we place it once again in the context of Braque's statement concerning the new perspective, in which divergent angles of viewpoint were to be presented as equally authentic, the fact that philosophically those contrasting viewpoints were mutually exclusive and that no controlling belief or set of moral principles was given preference, meant that the intellectual was left with nothing in which to place his or her faith. Love itself, the subject of countless poems extolling its splendour, marking it as the pinnacle of human experience, was, for example, now pitted against the Darwinian concept, gradually permeating the public consciousness, which, with all the authority of scientific evidence, reduced love to an illusory, physiological impulse. The female's choice of a paramour is, according to evolutionary theory, unconsciously dictated by her search for a person endowed with the most appropriate physical characteristics for breeding the new generation and ensuring the survival of the species. Male creatures, from alligators to stag beetles, fight each other, Darwin had pointed out, 'for a particular female who sits by, an apparently unconcerned beholder of the struggle, and then retires with the conqueror' to reproduce those qualities proven in battle to be in the best interests of her offspring. It is a dry, biologically based observation; but for the poet it constituted a crushing negation of the long-established chivalric tradition, with its knights in armour nobly fighting for the hand of the fair lady, a chivalric tradition absorbed into Western culture and preserved as a romantic element well into the twentieth century. Love, it appeared, was no longer the marriage of true minds that looks on tempests and is never conquered, the adoration of beauty, of charm, of grace, of noble thoughts and high ideals, but a subliminal search for the possessor of the most resilient genes in the battle for survival.[17]

For the creative artist and writer motivated emotionally by a belief in the transcendent authenticity of art, this nullification of traditional standards was particularly distressing, producing an unresolvable conflict between, on the one hand, an instinctive sense of the beauty and harmony of the world together with the sanctity of the individual within it and, on the other, an intellectual recognition that the intimidatingly authoritative evidence adduced by the scientists had disqualified and invalidated such inner conviction as a mere chimera. The battle between humanism and scientism, it must be stresssed, was no longer between two opposed camps, with the aesthetically oriented humanist crusading against the irreverent empiricist, but had become internalised within the individual, as a struggle between the emotional and the cerebral, as the writer was compelled intellectually to acknowledge the validity of these new discoveries while intuitively yearning for the older beliefs. The result was, as in Huxley's own case, a painful division of self, as his faith in the potential splendour of the world and of mankind within it seemed contradicted by a paralysing acknowledgment that rational analysis had witheringly disproved such belief.

In Huxley's *Ape and Essence*, Loola warns Poole in preparation for their love orgy: 'You mustn't think – if you think, it stops being fun.' But Huxley was congenitally unable to stop thinking, his analytical, scientifically oriented mind in constant conflict with his emotional impulses. Such, indeed, is the inner dissonance of his fictional author, Philip Quarles, unable to express his love for his wife Elinor, genuine though it is, not through inarticulateness, but because each time his heart prompts him to speak, his intellect, apprehending the new empirically based counterarguments, freezes the emotion, diverting his thoughts from the warmth of human love to the larger and emotionally petrifying biological context. As a result, Elinor's yearning for an expression of his affection is met instead by a learned disquisition on animal procreation. It was undoubtedly relevant to the modern conception of human sexual relations but scarcely congenial to her mood of the moment:

> 'There's nothing human quite analagous to heat in mares or she-dogs. Except,' he added, 'except perhaps in the moral sphere. A bad reputation in a woman allures like the signs of heat in a bitch. . . . Absence of heat is the animal's equivalent of the chaste woman's habits and principles . . .'
>
> Elinor listened with interest and at the same time a kind of horror. . . . It was amazing, it was unexpected, it was wonderfully interesting; but oh! she almost wanted to scream. (pp. 110–11)

The chilling process of intellectual analysis in the early twentieth century had spread across from the narrower realm of science to dominate humanist conceptions too. Five years earlier C. K. Ogden and I. A. Richards had published their seminal study *The Meaning of Meaning*, suggesting that the older conception of Nature, 'the belief in a world of Spirits and Powers which control events, and which can be evoked and, to some extent, controlled themselves by human practices', had now been definitely overthrown.[18] It was time, they maintained, to apply scientism to language, to recognise that true 'meaning' could only be assigned to words referring to tactile objects or events in the physical world, to concrete elements that are publicly verifiable. Within their nominalist approach to language there seemed little room for poetry, and a few years later I. A. Richards' *Science and Poetry* (1926) would attempt, somewhat lamely (he was later to repudiate his own reasoning), to carve out a more limited area for verse. Although poetry could make no claim to ultimate truth, he pleaded, it did attempt a form of 'pseudo-statement', limiting itself to the emotional response of the speaker: 'This is the way the "thing" looked – smelt, felt, sounded, etc. – to *me*, and this is what it made me think or feel.'[19] Any conception of literature as striving for an ultimate Truth or Beauty, the kind of cosmic verities that the Romantics (and Huxley) so deeply yearned for, seemed no longer feasible. This predominant preference for rational analysis, for splitting objects into definable subsections in a manner seeming to undercut all aesthetic assumptions, may indeed be seen as parodied in Magritte's wrily entitled *Eternal Evidence* of 1930. A female nude, traditionally symbolising in art the purest and noblest expression of beauty, is there ironically divided into isolated, separately framed sections, dissected, as it were, into component parts, that division irremediably destroying the sense of harmony and completeness that feminine beauty had represented in past eras.

The conflict in Philip Quarles between the instinctive promptings of his heart and the cerebral analyses of his empirically trained mind – a projection of Huxley's own inner discord – was especially distressing to one caught, as Aldous Huxley was, between the scientific traditions of his grandfather, Thomas Huxley (represented in his own day by his brother Julian, the distinguished biologist who kept him abreast of the most recent discoveries in that field)[20] and the traditions of his great-uncle Matthew Arnold, epitomising the humanist, liberal imagination. And to that was added his close relationship with his favourite aunt, Mrs Humphry Ward, whose novel *Robert*

Elsmere of 1888 had created a sensation when it first appeared, depicting with sympathy and understanding the religious dilemma of a young clergyman caught between traditional Christian faith and the new winds blowing in from the Oxford movement. His forebears, Thomas Huxley and Matthew Arnold, had indeed clashed directly on the topic so central to Aldous's concerns, the attempt to assign to literature and science their respective places in society. His grandfather claimed that literature should, and inevitably would, step down from its high place in education and hand over to the natural sciences, since the latter alone were able to supply practical knowledge for a practical age, including a basis for determining its ethical standards. It was in response to Thomas Huxley's claim that Arnold composed his trenchant essay 'Literature and Science' (1879), insisting that 'culture' was all-embracing, and that the rational pursuit of knowledge, of which science constituted one element, formed merely a subcomponent of such culture. Literature would therefore continue to express, as science could not, those larger powers 'which go to the building up of human life...the power of conduct, the power of intellect and knowledge, the power of beauty, and the power of social life and manners'.

That earlier debate had, however, occurred at a time when science was still in its infancy, not yet having achieved the intimidating authority of later years. For Aldous's generation, its nullifying of all extra-empirical experience now seemed finally to disqualify the cravings of the heart. Hence his choice of the epigraph for this novel, a quotation from Fulke Greville who, experiencing a seventeenth-century conflict in some ways comparable, a clash between traditional faith and the new scientism of the Copernican–Galilean universe, complained bitterly of the irreconcilable dichotomy of the human condition, of man torn between the incompatible claims of heart and mind:

> Oh, wearisome condition of humanity,
> Born under one law, to another bound,
> Vainly begot and yet forbidden vanity,
> Created sick, commanded to be sound.
> What meaneth Nature by these diverse laws
> Passion and reason, self-division's cause?

In his own verse Huxley expressed more personally that inner strife between passion and reason, between the heart and the mind, as a yearning for some metaphysical truth beyond the material, a craving

frustrated by the disheartening dictates of his own intellectualism
and expressed here, as usual in his writings, at first with a certain
flippancy but culminating in a throb of genuine emotion:

> Beauty for some provides escape,
>   Who gains a happiness in eyeing
> The gorgeous buttocks of the ape
>   Or Autumn sunsets exquisitely dying.
>
> And some to better worlds than this
>   Mount up on wings as frail and misty
> As passion's all-too-transient kiss
>   (Though afterwards – oh, *omne animal triste!*)
>
> But I, too rational by half
>   To live but where I bodily am,
> Can only do my best to laugh,
>   Can only sip my misery dram by dram.[21]

If Peter Quennell castigated Huxley for offering us, as part of his
contrapuntal technique, only eccentrics taking their principles to
extremes and ignoring the possibility of a middle path, it may be
argued that this very polarity, the sheer impossibility in his generation of finding any middle path, of discovering any way of reconciling these intrinsically conflicting perspectives, constitutes the primary
message of the novel. As Philip sadly remarks: 'I mistrust intellectualism, but intellectually, I disbelieve in the adequacy of any scientific
or philosophical theory, any abstract moral principle.... The problem for me is to transform a detached intellectual scepticism into a
way of harmonious all-round living.'[22]

Huxley is neither satirising his characters for their ridiculous idiosyncrasies nor condoning them, but exploring one of the most
urgent concerns of his modern condition, an *aporia* not of meaning –
not the disjunction or unresolved tension that Derrida and other
deconstructionists have seen as constituting text – but a cultural
aporia, a spiritual impasse. One of his characters, attending a chapel
service in an earlier novel, clearly reflects the conflict of emotion and
reason that the author was himself experiencing at the time:

No, but seriously, Gumbril reminded himself, the problem was
very troublesome indeed. God as a sense of warmth about the

heart, God as exultation, God as tears in the eyes, God as a rush
of power or thought – that was all right. But God as truth, God as
$2+2=4$ – that wasn't so clearly all right. Was there any chance of
their being the same? Were there bridges to join the two
worlds?[23]

As Philip remarks of his planned inner novel, the contrapuntal technique will not be a mere series of ironically contrasting situations
('While Jones is murdering his wife, Smith is wheeling the perambulator in the park') but, as he develops the idea more cogently, will
offer characters who are 'dissimilars solving the same problem', considering the central predicament from different and, it transpires,
incompatible viewpoints:

> The novelist can assume the god-like creative privilege and
> simply elect to consider the events of the story in their various
> aspects – emotional, scientific, economic, religious, metaphysical etc.
> He will modulate from one to the other – as, from the aesthetic to
> the physico-chemical aspect of things, from the religious to the
> physiological or financial. (pp. 408–9)

By offering within the novel a carefully structured superimposition
of these contrasting viewpoints, modulating from the emotional to
the scientific, from the economic to the religious often within a
single character, he provides a multifaceted representation of contemporary reality closely corresponding to the simultaneously multiple viewpoint of Cubist art.

There is, early in the novel, a passage in which this simultaneity,
the conflict between intuitive emotionalism and analytical logicality,
each claiming the exclusivity of its perceived truths, is expressed
particularly effectively. In a process of oscillation, each pulsating
expression of the heart is interrupted in parenthesis by the negating comment of the intellect. As the orchestra plays, the splendid
rondeau wafted through the air conjures up in the mind the romantic Wordsworthian image of a solitary girl singing to herself of the
loveliness of the natural world. Bach's music is

> a slow and lovely meditation on the beauty (in spite of squalor
> and stupidity), the profound goodness (in spite of all the evil),
> the oneness (in spite of such bewildering diversity) of the world.
> It is a beauty, a goodness, a unity that no intellectual research can

discover, that analysis dispels, but of whose reality the spirit is from time to time suddenly and overwhelmingly convinced. (pp. 42–3)

The final sentence in that passage contains, we may note, a melancholy reversal of expectation. The phrase 'that no intellectual research can discover' leads the reader to anticipate by rhythmic repetition 'and that no analysis can dispel', in confirmation of the ultimate superiority of such soulful harmony to scientific interference. Instead, however, comes the sober admission that analysis *does* dispel the assurance of the heart. And as the account of the concert continues, the 'certitude' created by her singing is ironically dissipated by the only description of the music that would be valid in the exclusively factual, empirically oriented terms required by the scientist: 'Is it illusion or the revelation of profoundest truth? Who knows? Pongileoni blew, the fiddlers drew their rosined horsehair across the stretched intestines of lambs...'[24]

How far this concern of Huxley's reflected the broader problems of the time is evidenced by Wallace Stevens' exploration of essentially the same conflict. Nurtured in a deeply religious household but himself rejecting Christianity at an early age, he was constantly exploring the place of poetry in a world seemingly devoid of a metaphysical dimension. In such an altered reality, is our sense of Nature's harmony and beauty, he asks, simply an illusion? He too, in a poem published in 1936, takes as his symbol the Wordsworthian scene of the solitary girl singing in the heart of nature, but in a changed dispensation. For his generation, she is now sadly perceived as merely reading *into* Nature her own unfounded preconceptions of its supposed harmonies:

> ...It may be that in all her phrases stirred
> The grinding water and the gasping wind;
> But it was she and not the sea we heard...
> It was her voice that made
> The sky acutest at its vanishing.
> She measured to the hour its solitude.
> She was the single artificer of the world
> In which she sang. And when she sang, the sea
> Whatever self it had, became the self
> That was her song, for she was the maker...[25]

The 'blessed rage for order' that impels mankind to envisage Nature as governed by benevolent harmony results, he regretfully concludes, only in a mental construct, an artifact with no basis in reality.

It is here that Picasso's new form of portraiture becomes so relevant. In his later canvases the superimposition or interpenetration of diverse angles of vision expressed not merely a physical multiplicity of viewpoint dependent on the location of the observer, but a representation of that larger intellectual impasse, the compression, into a single facial representation, of the disturbingly contending aspects of the individual in a manner paralleling the conflict between heart and mind expressed by Huxley and Stevens. E. H. Gombrich, arguing that the word-image conjured up by a verbal or visual sign depends upon the cultural context within which it is invoked, noted how the word 'house' produced different concepts when used in a Japanese as opposed to a European setting; and he offered as evidence of such diversity a view of the English Lake District by a visiting Chinese artist who instinctively translates the landscape into the patterns of his own culture, the willows overlooking the water becoming calligraphic ideograms.[26] But that principle should not be related merely to fixed cultural settings, a contrast between Chinese and European viewpoints, since the word-image in each culture is itself not static but fluctuates from generation to generation in accordance with changing conditions. So here the idea of a human portrait had changed fundamentally, no longer to be associated with a dignified tribute to the achievements or the authority of the sitter, but now offered in the twentieth century as an often unflattering representation of the dissonant elements contending within, as in Francis Bacon's *Pope Innocent X*.

There is, however, a distinction here between the media that may lead us to the central structural innovation of Huxley's novel; for where a painting, confined to a single moment of time, tended, as in the *Weeping Woman*, to present the conflict by a process of superimposition, in the novel, where space is less at a premium, Huxley devised an alternative process, polarising the inner conflict of the individual into separate characters who constitute inverse mirror images of each other. Each experiences the clash of incompatible values, the impossibility of achieving harmony, but in each a different aspect of the conflict is dominant. The same person is thus, in effect, viewed simultaneously from multiple angles.

Philip Quarles is patent self-portraiture – a novelist afflicted, in a manner painfully similar to Aldous's impairment of vision, with a physical disability that prevents him from competing in sports and hampers the development of close human contact. The proximity to Huxley's condition therefore invites comparison. But so too, we should note, does the character of Walter Bidlake, also a writer, working as the assistant editor of a literary periodical and fuming at the gross exploitation he experiences at the hands of his employer Burlap – the latter an evocation of Middleton Murry, for whom Huxley had once slaved on *The Athenaeum*. Walter's passionate infatuation with the coolly remote, sexually indulgent Lucy Tantamount, moreover, was an obvious modelling upon Huxley's own extramarital affair with Nancy Cunard.[27] However, this split is not an instance of the familiar *Doppelgänger* or *alter ego* figure – a tradition of 'doubling' of self in the novel recently examined in some detail by Karl Miller, whereby, as in Conrad's Marlow–Kurtz, the presence of a surrogate self leads by a process of eventual recognition to deeper self-understanding.[28] Instead Huxley employs the principle of bifurcation to present not a real and a surrogate self, but two contrasting and incompatible facets of his own being.

In a manner echoing the dissonance of Picasso's split portraits, the harsh, jagged lines and strident colours conveying the inner discord of contemporary man and woman, Huxley imparts by this process his own tragic inability to achieve fulfilment or to establish accord between the contending impulses of his mind and heart. For where Philip, the sceptic representing the rational facet of Huxley's being, consistently applies to the human condition an analytical objectivity incapacitating the promptings of the heart, Walter marks the reverse process, a projection of Huxley's innate romanticism, the Shelleyan longing for beauty and love painfully thwarted by the frigid intellectualism of his day, an intellectualism represented here by Lucy Tantamount. Impelled by such ardour, Walter insists on knowing, as they lie in bed together, whether she reciprocates his passion, repeatedly posing the question, only to be met by the condescending detachment of the New Woman, who scoffingly reminds him how 'absurdly unmodern' it is to seek for love in the fast world of airplanes, a world leaving no room for the old-fashioned baggage of romanticism. 'Not even for a heart?' asks Walter plaintively. No, she insists, not even for that (pp. 282–3). The scene is thus, with reversal of gender roles, a perfect mirror image of Elinor's unrequited demand for assurances of love from an intellectually detached Philip.

This process of polarising the incompatible elements of the self was not restricted to duality. The principle, as Philip repeatedly informs us, is *multiplicity* of viewpoints, an awareness of numerous inner selves, a multiplicity reflected in Picasso's developing art forms too. Identity or consciousness of self, as Michel Foucault has shown in his image of the Panopticon mentioned earlier, is fundamentally pluralistic as each individual is aware both of himself seen from within and of the alien view of the watcher or 'other.' But the result is not merely a dyad resulting from an awareness of an alien consciousness; for the external views can be many and varied, thus transforming the duality, Foucault argues, into multiplicity.[29]

The same holds true for the characters in this novel; for not only Walter and Philip but a number of other characters in the novel emerge as representing different facets of those manifold interpretations of life, each of whose seeming exclusive validity had posed a major crisis for the twentieth-century intellectual. Huxley projects into each of those figures aspects of himself as, indeed, Philip the novelist muses on his own crisis of identity: 'At different times in his life and even at the same moment he had filled the most various moulds. He had been a cynic and also a mystic, a humanitarian and also a contemptuous misanthrope; he had tried to live the life of detached and stoical reason and another time he had aspired to the unreasonableness of natural and uncivilized existence....Where was the self to which he could be loyal?' (pp. 268–9)

That Huxley intended this segmentation of the author to be recognised by the reader – however dilatory critics may have been in identifying it – is corroborated, it would seem, by a broadly amusing hint offered within the text. As Burlap awaits his first meeting with the authoress Romola Saville, whose poetry submitted to his journal he had come to admire, the door opens to admit not a single writer, but two, one remarkably thin, the other tending to plumpness:

> 'And which,...may I venture to ask, is Miss Saville?'
> 'Neither of us,' said the portly lady in a rather deep voice...
> 'Or both, if you like,' said the other...'We're the two parts of Romola Saville's dual personality.'

They are, it transpires, the joint authors of the poems, the Jekyll and Hyde, as they call themselves, of a compound authorial figure (pp. 320–1).

The gravity of that concern may appear to be undercut by the drollery with which it is so often treated in the novel; but we should recall that Picasso too, although the foremost inaugurator of new aesthetic modes for his time and acknowledged as passing through a similar period of emotional crisis in the 1920s and 1930s, has long been recognised as resorting to humour and parody in his art as a means of challenging accepted norms. There was his puckish remark about his enormously influential use of bicycle handlebars for the sculpture of a bull's head, that, when discarded as garbage, the sculpture may prove useful for a cyclist; or, as Robert Rosenblum has pointed out, there is his lighthearted punning in the truncated newspaper cuttings included in his collages.[30] So in Huxley's writing some of the instances are intended to seem initially ludicrous, some are presented more seriously; but together the bewildering variety of contradictions they produce and, above all, the grim failure of each representative character to achieve fulfilment, create the underlying anguish conveyed by the novel at large. As one of his characters complains in *Those Barren Leaves*, with obvious reference to Huxley himself, 'you make it very hard for your readers. You write sentimental tragedies in terms of satire, and they see only the satire.'[31]

The response of each of the main characters to that central twentieth-century concern highlights their function as variegated facets of the problem. Lucy, as the reversal of roles in the love scene indicates, functions in larger terms as a female counterpart to Philip, the intimidating New Woman of the 1920s; but with important distinctions. She too has perceived the changes wrought by the new science, having been born into a generation for whom 'God and Morals and all the rest of it' had been knocked out of everything, never to be reinstalled. Sceptically, she has come to recognise that love is merely a corporeal act devoid of spiritual ennoblement, a physiological impulse needing to be satisfied at the carnal level. In the opening scenes her hedonistic 'sleeping around', free from moral or romantic inhibitions, possesses a certain attractiveness in an era witnessing the emancipation of women and a growing liberalism in matters of sex. But her letter from Paris somewhat later in the novel points ominously to the fate Huxley sees in store for her. To vary the tedium of a life devoid of emotional satisfaction, she will, in her dependence on exclusively physical sensation, be driven to embark on a neurotic search for ever-new experiences – nymphomania, sadism, masochism – leading inevitably, as is suggested by her final account of an affair with a man she picked up in a street, to a dismal end in some brothel or madhouse.

He came at me as though he were going to kill me, with clen-
ched teeth. I shut my eyes, like a Christian martyr in front of a
lion. Martyrdom's exciting. Letting oneself be hurt, humiliated,
used, like a doormat – queer. I like it. Besides, the doormat uses
the user. . . . The marks are still there where he bit me on the neck.
I shall have to wear a scarf for days. (p. 493)

That subtle fictional structure, the juxtaposition of contrary responses to the same central challenges, animates the novel throughout. There is Mrs Quarles, who cannot conceive how anyone could
live in this world without God as comfort, contrasted with her
daughter-in-law, Elinor, for whom religion 'and, along with religion,
all transcendental morality, all metaphysical speculation' seemed
utterly nonsensical. There is Burlap, the residual Victorian, impervi-
ous to the preeminence of rationalism and, with the hypocrisy that
the Edwardians attributed to that age, extolling the ideals of the
heart and the asceticism of Franciscan poverty, while a moment later
advising Beatrice how to invest her gramophone shares. Yet if he
seems absurd, almost a caricature, one notes Philip's own admission
that Burlap does represent an element lost in the transition to
modernity, an element that he, as a novelist, sadly lacks: 'But the
heart, the heart. . . . The heart was Burlap's specialty. "You'll never
write a good book," he had said oracularly, "unless you write from
the heart." It was true; Philip knew it . . . '

And so the multiple variations continue. John Bidlake embodying
from a slightly different angle the sensuality we have seen in Lucy
and representing the current faith in Vitalism, places his trust in his
virile life-force, despising all forms of intellectualism as arid. A blend
of Renoir and Augustus John, he delights in visceral verve – a boom-
ing laugh, a robust figure, a dominating presence, until the moment
death lays a warning hand upon him and finds him utterly unpre-
pared, with no religious faith to support him, shrinking into childish
superstitions, into a terrified avoidance of his grandson's sickroom
and a pitiful refusal to confront his own condition. Lord Edward, on
the intellectual side, blithely engrafts a newt's tail on to the stump of
its amputated leg, unconcerned at the implications of such genetic
experiments (implications Huxley was to explore so devastatingly in
Brave New World), while his brother, futilely striving to reconcile the
scientific with the intuitive, attempts with ludicrous results to prove
the existence of God by mathematical calculation. And Illidge, Lord
Edward's assistant, exemplifying the faith of the younger generation

in Marxism as a means of reversing the unfair division of capital
and thereby committed to the political liquidation of unproductive
members of society, surreptitiously, and in flagrant contradiction to
his declared principles, pays a weekly allowance to his ageing mother.
For each, the painful dichotomy of the cerebral and the instinctive,
the impossibility of harmonising those antagonistic viewpoints, constitutes both their own dilemma and, Huxley implies, the broader
insoluble crisis of their generation.

The sole character in the novel who seems at times to have succeeded in reconciling the two worlds is the formidable Rampion, the
fictional version of D. H. Lawrence, who seems to represent the
long-sought answer to Huxley's predicament. This novel was written during the period when Huxley had come, at least temporarily,
to admire Lawrence for his seeming ability to reintegrate the body
and soul in a world that had divorced them; and Rampion does at
first appear to have achieved a wholesome and apparently satisfact-
ory answer for himself. Yet gradually we are led to perceive how
limited that solution really is. Rampion's only response to the spiritual ideals of Christianity, for example, is to dismiss St Francis con-
temptuously on psychological grounds as 'a smelly little pervert'
who gets a thrill out of licking other people's ulcers – that very fixing
in a formulated phrase that Prufrock had so abhorred. And what is
worse, the objective experimentalism of science, which occupies so
central a place in the concerns of the novel, is simply rejected by
Rampion out-of-hand as totally unworthy of consideration. For him
it does not constitute any form of threat and hence he is, by that
myopia, relieved of the conflict to which the other characters are
exposed. As Huxley was to write of Lawrence shortly after the latter's death in an article full of admiration for his qualities as an artist,
he lacked any awareness of the conflict implied by discoveries of science such as were causing Huxley himself his major problems:

> His dislike of science was passionate and expressed itself in
> the most fantastically unreasonable terms. 'All scientists are liars,'
> he would say, when I brought up some experimentally estab-
> lished fact, which he happened to dislike. 'Liars, liars!' It was a
> most convenient theory. I remember in particular one long and
> violent argument on evolution, in the reality of which Lawrence
> always passionately disbelieved. 'But look at the evidence, Law-
> rence,' I insisted, 'look at all the evidence.' His answer was char-
> acteristic. 'But I don't care about evidence. Evidence doesn't

mean anything to me. I don't feel it here.' And he pressed his two hands on his solar plexus. I abandoned the argument and thereafter never, if I could avoid it, mentioned the hated name of science in his presence.[32]

Philip, although at times he admires Rampion for having achieved a form of personal integrity, ruefully recognises towards the end of the novel that the latter's answer is not for him, and that he himself will need to struggle on further for a means 'to transform a detached intellectual scepticism into a way of harmonious all-round living'.

As the title of the novel suggests, and as the earlier discussion of the Bach concert had illustrated, music functions here not, in the words of so many critics, as an irrelevance but as a paradigm of this twentieth-century conflict and as integral to it. From the classical period onward, music had constituted a primary symbol of cosmic concord, the kind of universal harmony that seemed to Huxley to have been disrupted in his generation. In reliance upon Pythagoras's linking of the mathematical ratios of melodic chords with the perfection and proportion of the heavenly spheres, music had, for the Western world, come to typify the concept of an ideal perfection for which humankind strives. But in the exclusively physical terms to which the empiricist reduced music, as in the description of the rosined horsehair drawn across the intestines of lambs, music became not only denuded of its splendour but, even worse, was stripped of that divine or heavenly quality with which it had so long been associated, a quality now seen as a mere illusion. The wit of the title, therefore, lies in the ironic juxtaposition of terms. The word *counterpoint*, denoting the rich harmonies of the fugue, becomes nullified by its location beside the word *point*, the combination of terms now symbolising the process of reciprocal cancellation that forms the underlying theme of the novel, the idea noted earlier that for every *point* one may make, there is a *counterpoint* that vitiates it. The music wafted upwards to Lord Edward's study is, from the viewpoint of the physicist, no more than a series of vibrations:

Pongileoni's blowing and the scraping of the anonymous fiddlers had shaken the air in the great hall, had set the glass of the windows looking on to it vibrating; this in turn had shaken the air in Lord Edward's apartment on the further side. The shaking air rattled Lord Edward's *membrana tympani*; the interlocked *malleus*, *incus*, and stirrup bones were set in motion so as to agitate the membrane of the oval window and raise an infinitesimal storm in the fluid of the labyrinth. The hairy endings of the auditory nerve shuddered like weeds in a rough sea; a vast number of obscure miracles were performed in the brain, and Lord Edward ecstatically whispered 'Bach!'(p. 44).

On the other hand, Lord Edward's ecstatic murmur 'Bach!' as his auditory nerve registers the vibrations reminds us of the sublime inner experience to which such scientific analysis is blind. A little earlier we had been offered the biologist's version of such music as Lord Edward reads a passage reminding him that even a Mozart symphony could be traced physiologically to a piece of meat that had been transformed into brain cells:

> Bits of animals and plants became human beings. What was one day a sheep's hind leg and leaves of spinach was the next part of the hand that wrote, the brain that conceived the slow movement of the Jupiter Symphony. And another day had come when thirty-six years of pleasures, pains, hungers, loves, thoughts, music, together with infinite unrealized potentialities of melody and harmony, had manured an unknown corner of a Viennese cemetery, to be transformed into grass and dandelions, which in their turn had been transformed into sheep, whose hind legs had in their turn been transformed into other musicians, whose bodies in their turn.... It was all obvious – but to Lord Edward an apocalypse. (p. 39)

Perhaps ludicrous when described in such bald terms, it was nonetheless, as the reader was compelled to recognise, a description technically irrefutable; and what was worse in the context of such newly validated scientific reasoning, it appeared to cast grave doubt upon any possibility of believing in music as divine in inspiration, as capable of elevating the soul to celestial heights. It could now be seen only in terms of a temporary, physical stimulation of the senses.

The 'cacophony' in the novel is the result, therefore, not of society's lack of mutual cooperation, as Meckier has argued, with each player insisting upon his or her own tune oblivious of others, but the recognition of a more profound crisis in the age itself. As Huxley had remarked elsewhere, there existed for him a puzzling contrast between the seeming fortuitousness of the universe – in this specific instance the sound of a dripping tap – and his own instinctive and frustrated longing to discover within it some unifying harmony, some indication of the divine, beyond the order that the human forcibly imposes upon it – and here, we should recall, he is writing not fiction but an essay describing his own views:

> Drip drop, drip drap drep drop. So it goes on, this water melody for ever without an end. Inconclusive, inconsequent, formless, it is always on the point of deviating into sense and form. Every now and again you will hear a complete phrase of rounded melody. And then – drip drop, di-drep, di-drap – the old inconsequence sets in once more. But suppose there were some significance in it! It is that which troubles my drowsy mind as I listen at night. Perhaps for those who have ears to hear, this endless dribbling is as pregnant with thought and emotion, as significant as a piece of Bach. Drip-drop, di-drap, di-drep. So little would suffice to turn the incoherence into meaning. The music of the drops is a symbol and type of the whole universe; it is for ever, as it were, asymptotic to sense, infinitely close to significance but never touching it. Never, unless the human mind comes and pulls it forcibly over the dividing space. If I could understand this wandering music. If I could detect in it a sequence, if I could force it to some conclusion – the diapason closing full in God, in mind, I hardly care what, so long as it closes in something definite – then, I feel, I should understand the whole incomprehensible machine . . . [33]

Huxley's perception of this twentieth-century dichotomy, the discrepancy between music as evidence of universal harmony and its reductive definition in exclusively physical terms, is again closely paralleled in the paintings of the time; for one notes the proliferation, during the early decades of this century, of musical instruments as images of the cultural dissonance of the modern world – the Cubists' repeated incorporation of guitars, mandolins, violins, clarinets and cellos in the most stridently discordant and fragmented canvases of their time. Typical are Braque's *Clarinet and Violin* of 1913, Juan Gris's *Still Life with Guitar and Clarinet* of 1920 and, most influential of all, Picasso's *Three Musicians* of 1921 (Figure 15). Music had become not only splintered into disconnected components but, as in the latter canvas, diminished to the vaudevillian, a harlequin farce performed by dehumanised, clownish figures, the music itself represented by crude notational fragments. As Rampion scornfully comments towards the close of this novel:

the whole thing painted in the cubist manner so as to make quite
sure that there should be no life in it whatever. Nothing like modern art for sterilizing the life out of things. (p. 420)

If music seemed no longer capable of being identified as divine, the
cultural impasse held similar implications for the conception of
humankind itself and the long-cherished idea of the sanctity of the
individual. As Marjorie contemplates her pregnancy, the authorial
voice interrupts with a reminder of the biologist's claim that the
human embryo residually repeats in the stages of its development
within the womb the evolutionary processes that had produced it
millennia ago, a procedure reducing the human to the same level as
the myriads of other creatures swarming on land or sea, and hence
seeming to make the idea of man formed in the image of God not
only untenable but absurdly presumptuous:

> Six months from now her baby would be born. Something that had
> been a single cell, a cluster of cells, a little sac of tissue, a kind of
> worm, a potential fish with gills, stirred in her womb and would
> one day become a man – a grown man, suffering and enjoying,
> loving and hating, thinking, remembering, imagining. And what
> had been a blob of jelly within her body would invent a god and
> worship; what had been a kind of fish would create, and having
> created, would become the battle-ground of disputing good and
> evil; what had blindly lived in her as a parasitic worm would look
> at the stars, would listen to music, would read poetry. (p. 2)

In the context of that evolutionary process, man's behavioural patterns, his spiritual yearnings, his organisational achievements, even
his vices, are perceived merely as variations on the social habits of
the animal world at large, in a manner that, as Philip perceives,
strips them of their splendour and even of their perversity. The
modern factory, he records in his notebook, is now to be correctly
understood as a human version of the highly organised termitary;
the middle-classes' love of property in the light of the male warbler's
ferocious defence of its territory; and the depravity of the alcoholic
in the context of ants, which neglect their young for the sake of the
intoxicating liquor exuded by invading parasites. (p. 438)[34]

If mankind's anatomical descent from the ape had, for the nineteenth century, produced repercussions primarily in the religious
sphere, challenging the supposedly divine origin of the human

species, for Huxley's generation the problem had spread into the sociological, as man's imagined achievements in all spheres – his political frameworks, his technology, his commercial institutions and even his rituals of courtship and matrimony – were conceived anew, with disturbingly disparaging effect, as conforming in essentials to the social patterns prevailing among the lowest orders of insects, mammals and reptiles. Thus Philip, reading – in a recent biological study – of the female Angler-fish, which carries a dwarf parasitic male attached to her body, is at once reminded of the unhealthy relationship between Lucy and Walter.

In this connection it is surely not fortuitous that, in the same year as Huxley was composing this novel, Picasso, in the series of etchings commissioned by Vollard in 1927 and executed during the following few years, introduced a new figure, the Minotaur, half-man half-beast, symbolising the violence and grossness in the human, the bestial impulses of which the artist had now become conscious in his activities as a lover. In *Minotaur Carousing* (Figure 16), love between man and woman is, as elsewhere in the series, stripped of its delicacy and refinement to become associated with the couplings of brutes. Among the Surrealists, the Minotaur had shortly before this period become a symbol of the conflict between the conscious and the subconscious in human behaviour, and the stimulus for Picasso's Minotaur drawings was no doubt the invitation he received to design the cover for a new journal of that name, edited by André Breton and Paul Eluard. In his Vollard etchings the animalistic character either presides as a spectator at the orgies or participates actively in them. And to underscore the parallel with the new perception in Huxley's novel, in a companion series of etchings, *The Sculptor's Studio*, he depicted a naked man and woman engaged in love-making with, beside them, two horses in the act of copulation. In verse, that deepened awareness of man's kinship with the beast resulting from such zoological studies found similar expression in Delmore Schwarz's moving poem, *The Heavy Bear that Goes with Me*, with its weary sense of the ever-present brutish self within, apeing or parodying, like Picasso's Minotaur, the potential sensitivity and spiritual dignity of human love:

> That inescapable animal walks with me,
> Has followed me since the black womb held,
> Moves where I move, distorting my gesture,
> A caricature, a swollen shadow ...

Stretches to embrace the very dear
With whom I would walk without him near,
Touches her grossly, although a word
Would bare my heart and make me clear,
Stumbles, flounders, and strives to be fed
Dragging me with him in his mouthing care,
Amid the hundred million of his kind,
The scrimmage of appetite everywhere.[35]

That same impulse in Picasso's work may be responsible for the
phase following immediately upon the emergence of his twin-faceted
portraits, his depiction of human faces with grotesque animal snouts
or probosces, as in his *Portrait of Jaime Sabart* in 1937.

The conflict Huxley was exploring, between the zoogical affinities
of mankind suggested by scientific analysis and the instinctive
desires of the heart, perhaps, achieves, its fullest expression in this
novel in the figure of Spandrell, who brings together the diverse elements explored through other characters. Often dubbed a Satanist
or 'diabolic nihilist' by reviewers of the novel, it may be argued that
he is a far more complex figure. That critical definition has been
based largely on his resemblance to Baudelaire, on whom he was in
certain ways modelled.[36] But Huxley denied repeatedly that his
novels were intended as *romans à clef*, insisting that he used actual
people only as starting points from which to develop characters tail-
ored to the specific concerns of each fictional work. In the important
essay he wrote on Baudelaire at approximately the same time as
he composed this novel, he did indeed describe the latter as a diabolical nihilist, but added that he was a diabolist only in word, that
'his path was not strewn with seduced young girls, adulterous
wives, and flagellated mistresses'.[37] In this novel Huxley, in the
Freudian terms fashionable at the time, paralleled Ernest Jones'
Oedipal interpretation of *Hamlet* in tracing that diabolism to the
trauma experienced by Baudelaire in his youth, when an adored
mother remarried soon after being widowed. Those circumstances
he incorporated into Spandrell's early history. But there the parallel
ends, not only in the contrast of Spandrell's actual corruption of
innocent women and his fiendish seducing of Illidge into commit-
ting murder but in the impetus for such devilry and its significance
for the work at large.

As the reader learns towards the end of the novel (although there
are frequent hints earlier), he is in the deepest sense a *prêtre manqué*,

a devout ascetic with a missed vocation – he in fact appears, at one point in the novel, wearing a dressing gown of rough brown, 'like a monk's cassock'. Perhaps, in that regard, his difference from Baudelaire was not so marked, for T. S. Eliot maintained in an essay published that same year, 'the important fact about Baudelaire is that he was essentially a Christian, born out of his due time'.[38] Huxley's Spandrell, born into the twentieth century, is, like Prufrock, spiritually incapacitated for religious piety because for him faith in a divine Creator, upon which such Christian asceticism must rest, has been vitiated by the harsh light of rationalist empiricism. The medieval devotee, in line with Tertullian's *certum est quia absurdum est*, had been able to dismiss the evidence of his senses in favour of the richness of religious paradox, or, as in the spiritual exercises of Donne and El Greco in a later century, could make the physical world shimmer away to nothing before the vibrant power of inner spiritual vision. But in the modern setting Spandrell's intellect, trained to rely exclusively upon verifiable evidence, now demanded tangible or visible proof to counter the disbelief engendered by his mind. Without such proof he – as a 'reversed ascetic' representing the religious facet within the multiple viewpoints of the novel – is lost.

In that respect Spandrell may be seen as joining the rationalist Philip and the romantic Walter as diverse aspects of Huxley's own inner being, personifying, like the third non-identical reflection in Picasso's *Girl in the Mirror*, Huxley's crisis of values, his searching for some transcendental truth with which the intellect could come to terms, a search that was in fact to end in the mysticism dominating his later novels. If at this stage of his life he was only partially sympathetic to Spandrell's religious quest, that embryonic tendency was eventually to result in a firmer conviction, his belief that the spiritual sickness of his time arose from modern man's alienation from the Divine Reality or Godhead, and his categorical claim in *Time Must Have a Stop* that 'to realize this supreme identity is the final end and purpose of human existence'.[39]

'One way of knowing God', Spandrell maintains in the novel, 'is to deny Him' (p. 215), and his increasingly vicious acts of debauchery are, as we are led to understand retrospectively, pursued not for the pleasure they afford but as a desperate means of luring God out of His hiding place in order to provide the visible evidence he so sorely needs. He is hoping, as it were, for a thunderbolt from heaven to strike him in retribution for his sins, so that, in that fraction of a second in which he perceives it rushing towards him, he will have the immense satisfaction, even at the expense of the eternity of his own soul, of knowing with certainty that God exists, that God is not dead as Nietzsche had claimed. But he is repeatedly disappointed. Even after murdering the Nietzschean Webley – a sin even more Christianly damnable since he has seduced Illidge into participating in the crime – nothing happens, and God fails to appear:

> But no, but no, God was there, outside, absolute. Else how account for the efficacy of prayer – for it *was* efficacious; how explain providence and destiny? God was there, but hiding. Deliberately hiding. It was a question of forcing him to come out of his lair, his abstract absolute lair, and compelling him to incarnate himself as a felt experienced quality of personal actions... Spandrell had conjured him with violence to appear, and out of the bloody steam of the magically compelling sacrifice had emerged only a dust-bin. (pp. 588–9)

But perhaps God's refusal to appear was itself a test of faith, the failure of the incantation itself evidence that God was indeed there as providence, as destiny, not only as the giver but also as the *withholder* of grace. And with that final hope, Spandrell turns to his last resource, bringing to full circle the symbolic theme of music with which the novel began and which has so often been dismissed as a casual irrelevance in the work. Turning to Rampion, the sole person whose opinion he respects, he reverts to the fundamental question raised in that opening description of the rondeau – does the spiritual 'certitude' induced by music at its very finest constitute any ultimate evidence of a divine, benevolently ordered universe or is it only a baseless illusion created neurologically by a series of vibrations in the auditory nerve?

Accordingly he invites Rampion to listen with him to a recording of the superb *heilige Dankgesang* from Beethoven's A Minor quartet, which, he claims, 'proves all kinds of things – God, the soul, goodness – unescapably. It's the only real proof that exists...' Here the authorial voice reminds us, with an echo of the rosined hair drawn across the intestines of lambs, that the recorded music was, from a strictly scientific viewpoint, no more than a series of vibrations produced by a needle scratching the spiral grooves on a shellac surface. For Spandrell, in contrast, it represents the highest point of human participation in the divine, if only Rampion could confirm his view and soothe his intellectual doubts. For Spandrell the music, emotionally, remains convincingly divine: 'the beauty was unearthly, the convalescent serenity was the peace of God. The interweaving of Lydian melodies was heaven.' Significantly, in this scene Spandrell's thoughts gradually merge into those of the writer. Huxley's authorial voice takes over, a transition suggesting that the scene presents not merely Spandrell's yearning for proof but Huxley's too:

> It was as though heaven had suddenly and impossibly become more heavenly, had passed from achieved perfection into perfection yet deeper and more absolute. The ineffable peace persisted; but it was no longer the peace of convalescence and passivity. It quivered, it was alive, it seemed to grow and intensify itself, it became an active calm, an almost passionate serenity. The miraculous paradox of eternal life and eternal repose was musically realized.(pp. 595f.)

Rampion, however, to Spandrell's bitter disappointment, is unimpressed, insisting that, lovely as the movement may be, it proves nothing; and reverting to his obsessive concern with sexual fulfilment (and thereby being disqualified for the reader as the source of any valid solution to the central predicament of the novel), Rampion cynically dismisses the music, for all its beauty, as merely 'the art of a man who's lost his body.... Just a hymn in praise of eunuchism.'[40] Rampion's chilling reply leaves Spandrell with no further recourse. Without empirical proof to counter the negating force of his intellect, without tangible evidence for the divine source of such harmony, the conviction of heavenly serenity must be rejected as a chimera. Life under such circumstances ceases to be meaningful and he goes wearily to the suicide he has planned, a suicide conditional upon the result of this final test.

With our knowledge of Huxley's own movement towards mysticism in subsequent years, culminating in the Buddhist-inspired transcendental meditation that was to constitute the ideal in his novel *Island* (1962), it is significant that the sole person in this novel to achieve any degree of spiritual fulfilment is Marjorie. Under Rachel Quarles' tutelage she finds her way, through mystical contemplation, from despair to inner tranquillity, to 'the peace of God, the peace of God that passeth all understanding'. Huxley, in his own spiritual development, was not quite ready for that solution, and within this novel Marjorie's meditation is presented as slightly ridiculous – she lacks the intellectual apparatus necessary for a full understanding of the conflict, and her contemplation of the clouds leads her merely to forget to prepare Walter's supper. That scene is nonetheless a hint of the direction Huxley was taking. In the context of his movement towards mysticism it becomes apparent that Spandrell's yearning for faith, his longing for proof, through music, of the existence of a benevolent God in an ultimately harmonious universe, was not a satirical caricature of an outmoded creed but reflected, with due gravity, one aspect of Huxley's own multifaceted character, the predicament he was facing at that time. Indeed Huxley confirmed that more personal reading when, in later years, he remarked that the conclusion of *Point Counter Point* paralleled his own journey towards endorsement of the spiritual, his own recognition that the aesthetic, in this case the beauty of music, formed not a substitute for the spiritual but constituted an integral part of it. The conclusion of this novel was, he wrote, an expression

> of that kind of aesthetic mysticism which runs through the book and which is an analogue on another plane (perhaps even, to some extent, it is the homologue) of the ultimate spiritual mysticism. Anyhow, it was through the aesthetic that I came to the spiritual – having begun by rejecting the spiritual in favour of the aesthetic and by identifying it with the aesthetic, making the part include the whole.[41]

A charge repeatedly levelled against this novel, implicit in some of the negative comments quoted earlier and often stated more explicitly, is that it fails to come up with any answer, that for the moralist, as Bowering claims, Huxley regrettably 'offers no resolution. . . . It is here that the novel breaks down. . . . It is not so much that the novel fails to provide an answer but that it suggests there is no answer.'[42] One may well enquire what answer or resolution was offered for Hamlet's predicament, or, in our own century, by *Waiting for Godot* or the plays of Pinter, and whether that 'failure' invalidates those works aesthetically. One perfectly valid task for a writer is to identify and articulate the contemporary crisis, to represent in aesthetic terms the central quandary of the time, often as yet unperceived by the general public, just as the Cubists were presenting it in the visual arts. In the technique adopted by the painters to express that message they were remarkably close to Huxley. The main distinction in its application lay, as suggested earlier, in an intrinsic difference between the media, whereby the painter, restricted to a single canvas fixed in time, expresses the current concern with the mutual exclusivity of viewpoints through the superimposition of contrary angles of vision, while the novel, unrestricted in that way, could explore that discordant multiplicity in more expanded form, projecting the inner conflict into a series of fictional characters, each symbolising the destructive predominance of one such aspect in a situation that offers no possibility of compromise.

Within that broader aesthetic context, the theme of multiplicity of viewpoint in this novel emerges, therefore, not as an irrelevant structural prank, a series of amusing plot repetitions with minor variations, but as a remarkably effective tool for exploring, through the medium of the novel, the disparate, irreconcilable truths of the new era. To regard *Point Counter Point* as an aesthetic failure on the ground that 'the pattern promised by the title is never achieved'[43] is, I think, to miss the extraordinarily subtle relationship between the characters, who counterpoint each other to provide that 'simultaneous' diversity and contradiction of viewpoint that Cubist art had recognised as the central predicament of its time. In the same way, to regard the musical theme as an extraneous or casual contrivance is to ignore its profoundly symbolic function here, so germane to the central theme of the novel. Like the proliferation of fragmented musical instruments in Cubist painting and the innovation of dual-faceted portraits in their art, Huxley's multiplicity of viewpoints within this novel expresses a new conception of the universe and of mankind's place within it, a tragic sense of cosmic disharmony permeating at that time the consciousness of both artist and writer.

4

Minimalism and
the Hemingway Hero

Modernism, it has been remarked, was essentially reactionary in impulse, its innovations being expressed for the most part as rejections of established modes. Where Victorian literature had been organically connected to its precursors – the emotional subjectivity of Tennyson's poetry forming a natural outgrowth of Romanticism, and the novels of Dickens being consciously modelled on Smollett's fiction – Modernism, in attempting to construct its philosophical and aesthetic creed, tended, in T. S. Eliot's phrase, to murder before it created, to resist overtly the traditional principles or moral assumptions as a prelude to its own fashioning of artistic and ethical precepts believed to be more suited to the twentieth-century scene. That resistance is evidenced not only in the shock tactics adopted by the Vorticists and Dadaists in the 1920s – such as the publication of *Blast*, stridently repudiating traditional typography, or Marcel Duchamp's irreverent addition of a moustache to the *Mona Lisa* – but is also visible in the nomenclature adopted by that generation, the emergence of such terms as *anti-matter, atheistic, a-tonal, a-moral, a-political* to highlight the negation of previous criteria.

The emergence in literature of a further instance of such repudiation, the *anti-hero*, resulted in a fictional figure seeming to contradict the qualities traditionally associated with heroism. Where the protagonists of the novel in the eighteenth and nineteenth centuries had embodied – or, at the very least, achieved by the close of the narrative – the ideals of moral steadfastness, honesty and courage subscribed to by contemporary society, that figure was now being replaced by one conspicuously remiss in those characteristics, a diffident, self-sceptical and disenchanted being. There emerge at this time the seedy central characters of Graham Greene's early fiction, haunted by despair and disillusionment in a dreary world of unrelieved boredom, Faulkner's male Quentin, plagued by incestuous broodings, Scott Fitzgerald's dubious Gatsby, functioning illicitly in a society symbolised by a valley of ash beneath the empty gaze of an

118

optometrist's billboard. That emergent change was to lead to such characteristically twentieth-century antiheroes as Salinger's Holden Caulfield and Bellow's Herzog, both fleeing from a society in which they can no longer function, and both succumbing to a nervous breakdown symptomatic of their inability to cope with the prevailing modes of their time.

The pendular movement of history outlined by Spengler may account to some extent for the reactionary impulse of the period and its rejection of the customary hero of fiction;[1] but the specific form acquired by that figure in the novel was dictated in large part by the contemporary undermining – often invalidation – of the specific virtues and moral principles with which previous heroes had been endowed and by which they had to a large extent been defined. In the light of Freudian analysis, courage in battle had come to be seen less commendably as a suppressed suicidal tendency; chastity, both male and female, was now reinterpreted as impotence, sexual perversion or a residual allegiance to primitive taboos; and even so self-evident a virtue as respect for one's parents, long established in nineteenth-century fiction as a distinguishing trait of hero and heroine, had fallen into disrepute, being now identified in terms of an Oedipal syndrome – witness the contemporary response to D. H. Lawrence's *Sons and Lovers*.

For the literary historian, Hemingway's novels provide, in this connection, a striking exception, his fictional protagonists, to whom the term 'the Hemingway hero' was soon affixed by the public, seeming to emerge in direct contradiction to the antiheroic proclivities of the time. As Sean O'Faolain, in his classic study of the 1920s and 1930s, *The Vanishing Hero*, noted with puzzlement, even with some degree of irritation, Hemingway was alone among novelists of distinction at that time in his preservation and reaffirmation of the mystique of the hero.[2] For in contrast to the intellectually paralysed inhabitants of Huxley's novels or the emotionally warped Pinkie of *Brighton Rock*, Hemingway's central figures remain characterised by positive qualities – by unquestionable courage, by a staunch masculinity, by enviable professional expertise and by unswerving dedication to the ideals that they have espoused; and all this in a period when those former virtues had been challenged not through some passing fashion but in response to the seemingly incontrovertible revelations of scientific and psychological research. It was a mystique soon to be extrapolated – by Hemingway's own desire and often to the detriment of his literary reputation – into the author's public figure, as he sought to embody in his own life as war reporter, wild-life hunter and womaniser the macho quality of his fictional heroes. It is true that the symptoms of androgyny revealed in the posthumous publication of *The Garden of Eden* in 1986 began later to be read back into his life, and thence into his earlier novels, by both biographer and critic, encouraging conjecture about the incidents in his own experience that had prompted the fictional scenes of transvestite behaviour appearing there.[3] Yet whatever psychoanalytical speculations biographical investigation may suggest, each novel must, in the final analysis, be judged as an independent literary artifact, meriting evaluation upon its own terms; and in this regard the way in which the traditional ideal of the hero was, in his widely read fiction, either perpetuated or recreated in defiance of the new debilitating modes deserves special attention.

The rise of semiotics as a major critical tool in our generation has directed attention away from the search for unified meaning within a text to the systems of communication discourse that literary works both employ and generate. As a result it has tended to focus upon the dynamics of exchange within each document, what Bakhtin has termed the 'dialogic imagination'. That exchange or tension may take the form of the author's resistance to preexisting works, as in Harold Bloom's intertextual exploration of the anxiety of influence, or of an inner conflict between text and subtext producing an *aporia*, or unresolved conflict, as pursued in the writings of Derrida and Hillis Miller.[4] One approach that may prove particularly valuable here is that of Hans Robert Jauss, who has discerned a tension within the literary text arising from a conflict between the author's purpose and the reader's 'horizons of expectation', which the author must resist and overcome. In contrast to such reader-reception critics as Wolfgang Iser and Stanley Fish, who, underplaying the authority of the text, have placed major emphasis upon the personal interpretations that each individual brings to the work, Jauss has perceived a two-sided discourse. He begins from an aspect of Karl Popper's theory that is somewhat different in emphasis from the one we recently examined – that while every scholarly or scientific hypothesis develops out of certain presuppositions, it is the disappointment of such anticipations that constitutes the revelation or discovery, a revelation Popper describes as resembling 'the experience of a blind man running into an obstacle and thereby learning of its existence. We gain contact with "reality" by disproving our assumptions.'[5] That same effect, Jauss argues, occurs within literature. The reader in each generation brings to the work a referential framework derived from the established codes or values embedded within contemporary culture. Drawing for his examples on Flaubert and others, he suggests that each author, aware of the body of contemporary assumptions that would predispose the reader to interpret signals received from the text in accordance with the semiotic matrix of the time, is obligated to wean the reader away from such expectations, whether moral, philosophical, social or aesthetic, and to construct a new or modified set of values to replace them. The result is a process of seduction, in which the reader, by subtle manipulation from within the text, is lured from such preconditioning, from the 'horizons of expectation' brought to the work, and encouraged to adopt a new set of standards by which the actions of the fictional protagonists are to be judged.[6]

That strategy for dealing with the dynamics of exchange within the text would seem especially appropriate to the problem occupying us here, once one perceives that Hemingway has not simply ignored the antiheroic tendency of his day – in which case his novels would have been hopelessly outmoded – but has adopted with remarkable shrewdness the kind of procedure identified by Jauss.[7] Hemingway, it is true, did grant a major concession to the negation of traditional ideas of heroism in that the victory of his protagonists is a victory in defeat, the stoic survival of a physically maimed Jake, the rearguard action of a dying Jordan, the patient resignation of an aged fisherman as he loses to predatory sharks the prize he had so laboriously won. But theirs is nonetheless a triumph of the spirit, a display of fortitude against overwhelming odds in a manner that perpetuates, in the climactic scenes of his novels, precisely those moral virtues that had seemed to be invalidated:

> The gun was firing now with the rocket whish and the cracking, dirt-spouting boom.... Then he was out in the open, over the road that was so hard under the hooves he felt the pound of it come up all the way to his shoulders, his neck and his teeth, on to the smooth of the slope, the hooves finding it, cutting it, pounding it, reaching, throwing, going, and he looked down across the slope to where the bridge showed now at a new angle he had never seen...[8]

In turning to the visual arts in search of contemporary changes that may cast light on the methods he employed, there is an initial barrier to be overcome. Emily Watts' study *Hemingway and the Visual Arts*, tracing the numerous references to painting in his published works, has noted that, while he collected canvases by Juan Gris, Miró and Paul Klee, and from other respected painters comparatively recent in time, ranging from the Impressionist period to Picasso, and while he was indeed a friend and admirer of Brancusi, the main references in his writings are to artists of much earlier generations, to El Greco, Velázquez and Goya, to Hieronymus Bosch, Brueghel the Elder and Rubens.[9] That concentration upon the past suggests there may exist little relationship between his own innovations in the genre of the novel and those being introduced in the visual arts of his time. Moreover, when Hemingway does acknowledge a relatively contemporary source of inspiration, it is a painter whom it is difficult, if not impossible, to identify closely with his own work, either in artistic purpose or in technique. As critics have frequently noted, he claimed on a number of occasions that his primary indebtedness as a writer was to Cézanne: 'I'm trying to do the country like Cézanne', he wrote in 1924, 'and having a hell of a time sometimes getting it a little bit'.[10] That same year, in 'Big Two-Hearted River' he depicted Nick Adams as striving to describe landscapes in the way Cézanne had painted them, attempting to reproduce in verbal form the artistic techniques of the painter:

> Cézanne started with all the tricks. Then he broke the whole thing down and built the real thing. It was hell to do. He was the greatest. The greatest for always. It wasn't a cult. He, Nick, wanted to write about the country so it would be there like Cézanne had done it in painting. You had to do it from inside yourself. There wasn't any trick. Nobody had ever written about country like that. He felt almost holy about it. It was deadly serious...

One should note that this passage was in fact excised by Hemingway before publication.[11] In *A Moveable Feast*, published in later years, he recalled how, in the early days of experimentation, he went almost every day to the Musée de Luxembourg (where the Impressionist collection was housed before its removal to the Jeu de Paume) to view the work of Manet, Monet and other artists whom he had first come to know at the Art Institute of Chicago, adding:

> I was learning something from the painting of Cézanne that made writing simple true sentences far from enough to make the stories have the dimensions that I was trying to put in them. I was learn-

ing very much from him but I was not articulate enough to explain it to anyone. Besides it was a secret.

That last phrase itself raises a doubt, a suspicion that Hemingway is teasing the reader. And his admission that he himself could not explain the nature of the indebtedness – an inability that, it would seem, persisted to the time he penned this retrospective account – detracts further from its cogency. Moreover his inclination to joke about his indebtedness reinforces this suspicion, as in his remark that, in the Luxembourg museum, Cézanne's paintings were clearer and more beautiful if you were 'belly-empty, hollow-hungry':

> I used to wonder if he were hungry too when he painted; but I thought possibly it was only that he had forgotten to eat. It was one of those unsound but illuminating thoughts you have when you have been sleepless or hungry. Later I thought Cézanne was probably hungry in a different way.[12]

But the main objection to this theory of indebtedness arises from a close comparison of his writings with the work of the painter and with the principles adopted in the latter's canvases. Alfred Kazin, for example, has in recent years devoted a lengthy essay to the comparison; but all that emerges from the supposed parallel between Hemingway's prose style and Cézanne's artistry is vague in the extreme, the suggestion that the opening of *A Farewell to Arms* reveals a similar 'removal of his subjects from the contingent world'.[13] In fact the salient element in Hemingway's individualistic style, in contrast to the tradition of the nineteenth-century novel, was the very reverse – its accurate, objective depiction of reality in a spare, unsentimental prose, the precise conjuring up of a scene through an unemotional focusing upon detail:

> The taxi went up the hill, passed the lighted square, then on into the dark, still climbing, then levelled out onto a dark street behind St. Etienne du Mont, went smoothly down the asphalt, passed the trees and the standing bus at the Place de la Contrescarpe, then turned onto the cobbles of the Rue Mouffetard. There were lighted bars and late open shops on each side of the street. We were sitting apart and we jolted close together going down the old street. Brett's hat was off. Her head was back. I saw her face in the lights from the open shops, then it was dark, then I saw her face clearly

as we came out on the Avenue des Gobelins. The street was torn
up and men were working on the car-tracks by the light of acetyl-
ene flares.[14]

Can this, in any significant way, be regarded as evocative of a
Cézanne canvas, especially when one recalls that such canvases
were distinguished by their rejection of optical verisimilitude and
depth-perspective, and by the painter's search for structural pattern-
ings based upon juxtaposition of colour patches and shapes, as in his
views of *Mont Sainte-Victoire* or, in closer focus, in *Still Life with Pep-
permint Bottle*? There, as Richard Shiff and others have shown, optical
distortions are deliberately exaggerated, the artist's purpose being not
photographic precision but an essentially new composition or visual
rearrangement of the scene.[15] Moreover Hemingway's comments on
the painter, one should note, are always related to landscape, Nick
Adams adding in the passage quoted earlier that although Cézanne
could do people too, Nick was capable of handling that aspect himself. Hemingway's restriction to landscape of the supposed modelling of his prose upon Cézanne's art suggests, therefore, that there
existed little relationship between the painter's innovations and the
creation of Hemingway's fictional heroes, or indeed the style of his
writing at large.

Hemingway's claim that he had in some sense modelled himself
upon the painter cannot, of course, be ignored; but since there is so
little substantive connection between Cézanne's unique mode and
Hemingway's own stylistic innovations, it seems likely that the
author's comments arose from a desire to follow Gertrude Stein's
advice at a time when he still respected her judgement, coupled
with a youthful ambition to conform in some way to the fashionable
interests of the *avant garde*, of which he was part during the Paris
period. Stein herself did believe that she was following Cézanne's
lead. She had been so impressed in 1905 by the latter's portrait of his
wife, which she and her brother had just purchased, that she laid
aside the novel on which she had been working and attempted to
develop a new style that would mark a 'first definite step away from
the nineteenth century and into the twentieth century in literature'.
She did learn from that painting the principle of disfiguration, of non-
mimetic representation.[16] But her own prose description of Cézanne's
work reveals how remote she was from him, that description characterising not the painter's style, but the convoluted form of writing
she herself developed – the principle of incremental repetition

whereby each restatement reflected the flux of change in the narrator. Like her other writings, not only does it bear little if any resemblance to the Cézanne she ostensibly admired, but it has no resemblance whatever to the highly disciplined verbal economy developed in Hemingway's prose:

> The landscape looked like a landscape that is to say what is yellow in the landscape looked yellow in the oil painting, and what was blue in the landscape looked blue in the oil painting and if it did not there still was the oil painting, the oil painting by Cézanne. The same thing was true of the people there was no reason why it should be but it was, the same thing was true of the chairs, the same thing was true of the apples. The apples looked like apples the chairs looked like chairs and it all had nothing to do with anything because if they did not look like apples or chairs or landscape or people they were apples and chairs and landscape and people.[17]

The theory that Hemingway gained from her any deep understanding of Cézanne is further undermined by the fact that astute visitors, such as the American painter Maurice Sterne, felt that she was signally lacking in appreciation of the visual arts, and attributed to her brother Leo the artistic discrimination that led them to assemble the distinguished collection of canvases by Impressionists and others displayed on the walls of their apartment in Paris. It would be far-fetched, therefore, to assume that she understood Cézanne sufficiently to deduce from his work any valuable pointers that she could pass on to the young writer.[18]

There is, moreover, a chronological element involved. If Hemingway's finely honed prose, the removal of excessive adjectives producing 'simple true sentences', was, as he suggests, derived from Cézanne during the period of his sojourn in Paris, how are we to reconcile this supposed source with the well-known fact that such pruning of vocabulary had, much earlier, formed part of the editorial style-sheet issued to all journalists while he was working at the Kansas City Star in 1917–18: 'Use short sentences. Use short first paragraphs. Use vigorous English. Be positive, not negative. Avoid the use of adjectives, especially such extravagant ones as *splendid, gorgeous, grand, magnificent*'? Concluding with the directive, 'Be brief, be simple, be clear', it was acknowledged later by Hemingway as having offered him 'the best rules I ever learned for the business of writing'. In contrast to the vagueness of his supposed debt to Cézanne, the

patent relevance of these editorial instructions to his own prose style
renders the author's acknowledgment superfluous.[19]

The advice on that style-sheet should, however, be seen as reflecting a much broader change in aesthetic sensibility, which manifested
itself at the turn of the century and reached its apogee during the
years of Hemingway's first public success as a novelist. The advice
emanated from the assistant city editor, Pete Wellington, whom Hemingway greatly respected as 'a stern disciplinarian, very just and
very harsh, and I can never say properly how grateful I am to have
worked under him'; but it was neither an isolated phenomenon nor
merely the personal preference of a journalist with whom Hemingway came into chance contact. The similarity between such stylistic
innovation and the principles being promulgated and applied by
contemporary architects and designers within the movement that
has come to be known as Functionalism suggests that Hemingway's
contribution to the American novel was, as may be expected from
distinguished writers in all eras, an expression within the literary
medium of the altered cultural climate of his time, of new aesthetic
criteria emerging concurrently in the plastic arts.[20]

It has been rightly remarked that Functionalism, the concept that
the design of an object should be dictated strictly by the purpose for
which it is intended and the materials from which it is constructed,
was not a sudden eruption on the architectural scene but the outgrowth of tendencies developing during the latter decades of the
nineteenth century. Even within the Arts and Crafts movement of
William Morris, with its indulgence in elaborate ornamentation and
the whirls and curlicues of its vegetative forms, may be perceived, as
Stella K. Tillyard has pointed out, the first stirrings of such proclivities, especially during the later years of the association's existence. A
call was heard for 'Truth to Materials', and for a recognition, however
embryonic at that stage, that a china vase made to resemble wicker-
work was a hybrid and hence an aesthetically invalid construct. As
L. F. Day claimed in 1886, 'form is best appreciated in its naked purity'.
But as one can see from the elaborately decorative designs by Morris,
and the ornamental items offered for sale at stores such as Liberty's
and Tiffany's, which provided an outlet for Arts and Crafts prod-
ucts, it was a principle that remained largely theoretical within that
movement.

The main incentive came from the urgent need to redesign tools,
machines and vehicles to ensure that tasks could be performed
more swiftly and more efficiently. Henry Ford's introduction of the

assembly line into the process of automobile manufacture between 1903 and 1913 transformed industry at large by demonstrating how the elimination of superfluous actions on the part of the worker, the standardising of machine-made parts and the resulting speed in construction could reduce costs by almost two thirds, the price of the touring car dropping as a result of Ford's changes from $850 in 1913 to only $300 by 1925. For his famed Model-T, which was to dominate the market, inessential embellishments were eliminated, machine parts were designed to be interchangeable, and even choice of colour was sacrificed (Ford declaring that his customers could choose freely, on condition that they chose black), and all to create practical, affordable transportation with low price and guaranteed durability. The resulting transformation in design affected even such mundane objects as the cash register, remodelled at this time for the American Sales Book Company by Walter Dorwin Teague (Figure 17). The improvements Teague introduced served in this instance, as so often in industrial design, to fulfil an aesthetic purpose in addition to the functional. By relocating within the case the sharp external cog on which a lady's sleeve might catch, Teague not only achieved an improvement in safety and greater practicality but also smoothed out the lines, removing the protruding screw heads from the original version to produce a more sleek, as well as a more efficient item.

A parallel change occurred in furniture. In 1924 Marcel Breuer, inspired by the handlebars of contemporary bicycles, had begun at the Bauhaus to design furniture made of steel tubing, producing seats or stools shaped like an inverted U. On a visit to the Bauhaus, the Dutch architect Mart Stam, turning one of Breuer's chairs on its side, perceived how effective that shape could be, and on his return to Holland he designed the first, rather ungainly 'cantilever' chair, composed of straight pieces of tubular steel connected by elbow corners. Mies van der Rohe then moved the process a stage further, devising in 1926 his own much superior version, for which he obtained the sole patent, smoothing out the lines and simplifying the design in a manner that was to help revolutionise furniture design. In place of the ornate traditional chair assembled from separately fashioned wooden components, it consisted with utter simplicity of a single piece of chrome tubing bent into a graceful double-S shape, the seat and backrest provided by plain pieces of stretched canvas. That design became enormously popular in subsequent years, not least for the simplicity and seamlessness of its construction.[21]

These various changes received an official stamp of approval at L'Exposition International des Arts Decoratifs et Industriels, held in Paris in 1925, which formally advocated geometrical forms in place of the fussiness of previous designs. Such principles were to be applied (as the title of the exhibition specified) not only to industrial items, but to decorative arts too. At this time a discovery concerning the forms in nature intensified the growing interest in functionalist lines, the new concept introduced by Sir D'Arcy Wentworth in a seminal treatise published in 1917, entitled *On Growth and Form*. Wentworth had noted there the smooth, eddying trails left by the movement of air and water over soft, malleable objects: 'The contours of a snowdrift, of a windswept sand-dune, even of the flame of a lamp, show endless illustrations of stream-lines or eddy curves which the stream itself imposes, and which are oftentimes of great elegance.' From that fact he deduced that Nature had, with functional grace, contoured the bodies of birds and fish to ensure minimal resistance as they moved through air or water, those elements being made to flow or stream by, unimpeded by projections. It was a principle, he perceived, that could 'lay the very foundations of the modern science of aeronautics' – as indeed it did.[22] The concept was adopted for modelling the profiles of the new steam-driven ocean liners, which, now relieved of masts and sails, were henceforth provided with funnels and upper decks sloped back to reduce the force of air and wind. Their counterparts on land and in the air, the automobiles, airplanes and dirigibles of the 1920s and 1930s, shared that new profile, bestowing on that generation the nickname 'the streamlined era'. And once the process had been adopted for functional purpose, streamlining soon became the fashion for items where the need to overcome the resistance of the elements was no longer relevant. Such smooth contours now served to symbolise the speed and efficiency of a new age, in which the more leisurely tenor of nineteenth-century society was being replaced by an accelerated tempo, an exploitation of the swiftness of movement and of communication that the inventiveness of engineers and designers was making possible.

The emergence of a more taut and bare prose style in the newspapers of the day as well as in Hemingway's writings was thus not a matter of mere eccentricity or of innovation for the sake of innovation but had wider implications. It reflected the sense of increased velocity in daily life – an aspect of the flapper era captured so effectively in the fiction of Hemingway's friend Scott Fitzgerald, such as Tom and Daisy's swift, restless movements from place to place – and, as part of that impulse, the discarding of non-functional embellishments as impediments to its speed.

In tracing the filaments connecting this demand for purity of line in art design with Hemingway's writings, it should be noted that the true origins of the movement are to be found not on the European scene, as so often occurred in other branches of art at this time, but in his native America, which had retained many of the rudimentary, utilitarian elements introduced by the early settlers. At an 1878 exhibition in Paris, Julius Lessing, the director of the Museum of Industrial Arts in Berlin, had been enchanted by some of the American tools displayed there, tools whose beauty of line was, he enthusiastically remarked, achieved without recourse to decoration, 'simply by moulding the axe to the human hand and to the movement of the body'. In 1913 Walter Gropius, soon to design the influential Bauhaus, was similarly impressed by the clean lines of American grain elevators and coal conveyers, lines dictated by their function in ways that, as he put it, 'present an architectural composition of such exactness that to the observer their meaning is forcefully and unequivocally clear'.[23] The long European tradition reaching back to the medieval trade guilds, whereby artisans were trained in successive generations by qualified mastercraftsmen, had encouraged conservativism there; but America lacked that legacy. Moreover the absence of that tradition, resulting in a shortage of craftsmen, had encouraged a swifter development of mechanisation and of various processes of prefabrication to substitute for the shortage. The so-called 'balloon frame' houses, for example, which enabled Chicago to grow with such incredible rapidity from a village to a city in the 1880s, had demanded minimal expertise as they were constructed of easily assembled wooden-strut frames using standard two-inch cross-sections. As part of that prefabricating process aimed at inexpensive construction, decorative elements had been reduced to a minimum, speed of manufacture and assembly being a prime criterion. Moreover the tradition of austerely plain churches introduced by the early Puritans as part of their protest at the construction of the palatial St Peter's in Rome had encouraged, in secular structures too, the principle of plain walls with simple openings for doors and windows, as in the stone Community House of 1832 in Concord, Vermont. For those various reasons, all contributing to simplicity of design and lack of ornamentation, the Carson Pirie Scott department store, constructed by Louis Sullivan in 1904, was less revolutionary than has often been thought, its austerity of line, if not the innovative structural process it employed, conforming to an established American tradition. As John Root admiringly remarked of such contemporary buildings, 'to lavish upon them profusion of delicate ornament is worse than useless'.[24]

If, in identifying the context of Hemingway's stylistic innovations, our primary comparison will be with the manifestations of Functionalism in architectural and technological design, it should be noted that the desire to prune away superfluous ornamentation was beginning simultaneously to manifest itself elsewhere within literature itself, not least within the contemporary Imagist movement. Although the verse that movement produced was far from simplistic, the latter often verging on obscurity and, at the very least, demanding a conscious intellectual effort on the part of the reader, the principles agreed upon in 1912 by Ezra Pound, Richard Aldington and Hilda Doolittle did contain a demand for a rejection of all words not absolutely essential. As Pound defined their aim in *The Poetry Review*, they sought for verse that was 'austere, direct, free from emotional slither'; and the rules formulated for the movement by F. S. Flint and published in the same journal contained a stern call for poetry to 'use absolutely no word that did not contribute to the presentation'.[25] But such stripping away of inessentials, although reflecting the broader tendencies of the time, tended in Imagism to be submerged beneath the demand for a new type of metaphor, and the movement towards sparseness in literature was to find its major exponent in Hemingway.

I should like to suggest, in line with the semiotic readings of Hans Robert Jauss, that Hemingway did not simply adopt the emergent style of Functionalism in keeping with contemporary taste, but did far more with it. He employed it as a tool to construct for the novel a new aesthetic with moral undertones, using it as a means of countering the negative 'horizons of expectation' brought to the work by the contemporary reader. But before pursuing that approach, we need to examine the nature of that functionalist style in architecture and its relationship to Hemingway.

The fact that he grew up in Oak Park, Chicago, the small suburb in which Frank Lloyd Wright's first studio was located and where the famed 'Prairie' style of architecture, with its smooth lines and utilitarian design, first manifested itself, has been dismissed by his recent biographer, Kenneth Lynn, as irrelevant, on the ground that Hemingway seems never to have referred to the architect directly – although Lynn does admit that the author's silence may have arisen from his well-known antipathy to his home town and his reluctance to say anything complimentary about it.[26] We are, however, considering the author here not as an imitator of plastic forms, but as a creative artist independently expressing the new tendencies within his own medium. And in that context, evidence of direct connection or indebtedness, though helpful, is by no means mandatory. From the geographical proximity one may, at the very least, assume that Hemingway would not have been unaware of these architectural trends, as his uncle, George Hemingway, built a home in Oak Park that was designed by John Bergen in the new Prairie style. But his activity as a journalist would in any case have brought him into contact with the new movement, if one recalls that by 1925, the time of the disastrous fire at Taliesin, Wright had become a personality of major media interest for reasons not only architectural, the scandals of his private life having attracted wide publicity. There is, in addition, the fact that Hemingway, in summarising in *A Moveable Feast* the principle of stylistic economy that he himself developed at this time, resorts to an architectural analogy clearly drawn from the International or Functionalist school as Le Corbusier and others had developed it. Echoing the principle enunciated by the latter's mentor, Perret, who maintained that decoration such as scrollwork always hides an error in construction and must be ruthlessly excised, Hemingway noted of his new system of writing:

> 'All you have to do is write one true sentence. Write the truest sentence that you know.' So finally I would write one true sentence, and then go on from there.... If I started to write elaborately, or like someone introducing or presenting something, I found that I could cut that scrollwork or ornament out and throw it away and start with the first true simple declarative sentence I had written.[27]

By 1909 Wright had completed perhaps the finest of his Prairie-style buildings, the Robie residence in Chicago (Figure 18), rejecting the Victorian-type home so widely adopted in America, with its numerous projecting gables and 'fussy' forms, in favour of a design offering a sleek, uninterrupted horizontal profile. The projecting cantilevered roof, sheltering the glass-walled salon from the midsummer sun, employed an economy of line that was to introduce a new form of artistic integrity to buildings. It deeply influenced Mies Van der Rohe, who met Wright in Germany, prompting him to coin as the principle for his own structures the well-known axiom 'Less is more' – an architectural equivalent of the Kansas Star's directive 'Be brief, be simple, be clear'.[28] Within Oak Park itself, by 1913 (when Hemingway was in his teens) Wright had completed the Harry S. Adams residence, in which a longitudinal plan was again employed, with immaculate straight lines shunning ornamentation.[29] This minimalist process, permitting the viewer to deduce structural form without visual assistance, without, that is, such traditional features as imposing porticoes to mark out the front entrance or gables to identify attics, is of patent relevance to Hemingway's concept of stylistic 'omission', as outlined in his *Death in the Afternoon:*

> If a writer of prose knows what he is writing about he may omit things that he knows, and the reader, if the writer is writing truly enough, will have a feeling of those things as strongly as though the writer had stated them.

And as if to confirm the connection, Hemingway defends there his stylistic paring away of the superfluous with the significant statement: 'Prose is architecture, not interior decoration, and the Baroque is over.'[30]

If Hemingway's style was, from the first, recognised as striving for purity of language uncluttered by superfluity of adjectives, it should be recalled that in 1918 Le Corbusier (at that time primarily a painter, working under his original name Charles-Edouard Jeanneret) published, in cooperation with his fellow artist Amédée Ozenfant, a manifesto advocating in art a style for which they employed the term *Purism*. Under that name they launched a movement whose precepts Le Corbusier soon crystallised in his widely admired treatise *Vers une architecture*, published in 1923, shortly before Hemingway composed *The Sun Also Rises*. Cubism, they argued, had become too playful and art must return to rational forms, free of embellishment. In the same way as every organ in the human body has undergone through the centuries a process of continual adaptation in order to suit its exclusively operational needs, with the relationship between form and function reducing to the minimum the effort required by that organ to fulfil its purpose, so the architectural style they aimed at must reflect such precision in its dedication to its own proposed function. At a time when industrial mechanisation was introducing time-and-motion studies within the factories in order to reduce all wasted effort, Corbusier argued for a similar austerity and economy of form in buildings. As they claimed in the journal they founded in

1920, *L'Esprit nouveau*, art and architecture were to aim at clarity and objectivity.[31] In Holland, isolated from other countries by the First World War, the De Stijl group, with Mondrian as one of its founders, announced in 1918 its intention of cultivating a similar simplicity of design. Initially they considered as the name for their journal, *The Straight Line*, the implications of that ideal for Mondrian's own canvases being self-evident.

Hemingway's narrative style, the words pared down to the minimum, the descriptions brief and factual, free from emotional embellishment, clearly belongs within this emergent mode. It reflected the new ideal of total dedication to proficient performance, to execution of the immediate task in hand, an ideal characterised both by Hemingway as a writer and, by extension, his protagonists as heroes, whose lines of thought must be direct and clearly focused, uncluttered by distractions:

> his mind was thinking of the problem of the bridge now and it was all clear and hard and sharp as when a camera lens is brought into focus. He saw the two posts and Anselmo and the gypsy watching. He saw the road empty and he saw movement on it. He saw where he would place the two automatic rifles to get the most level field of fire ...

Like the new machinery of the industrial age, divested of all superfluity and dedicated to the execution of a crisply defined assignment, his leading characters discard all maudlin, self-indulgent or otherwise extraneous musings in order to concentrate with total clarity upon the facts with which they are required to deal. Thus Jordan, striving to retain consciousness in the last few moments before his death, refuses to allow himself any drift into illusion, falsity or sentimentalism, sternly stripping away such inclinations as he pulls himself back to the simple truth that he is not yet dead and has a final task to perform:

> He looked down the hill slope again and he thought. I hate to leave it, that is all. I hate to leave it very much and I hope I have done some good in it. I have tried to with what talent I had. *Have, you mean. All right, have.*[32]

To the end of his career as a writer, that concept of dedicated expertise, of excluding everything but the bare essentials, motivated

Hemingway's narrative technique, as it did the activities of his protagonists, concentrating, to the exclusion of self-pity or self-indulgence,
upon the efficient performance of their objective, so that the assignment itself emerges as beautiful in the simplicity and directness with
which it can be accomplished. The old fisherman in his final novel
may be entirely alone, far from land, exhausted, battling not only for
his livelihood but for life itself; yet of that nothing need be said:

> ... he loosened his sheath knife and taking all the strain of the fish
> on his left shoulder he leaned back and cut the line against the
> wood of the gunwale. Then he cut the other line closest to him
> and in the dark made the loose ends of the reserve coils fast. He
> worked skillfully with the one hand and put his foot on the coils
> to hold them as he drew his knots tight.[33]

And as he faces the last test, fighting the sharks who are consuming
the marlin, his austere self-discipline remains dominant:

> I am sorry that I killed the fish though, he thought. Now the bad
> time is coming and I do not even have the harpoon. The *dentuso* is
> cruel and able and strong and intelligent. But I was more intelli-
> gent than he was. Perhaps not, he thought. Perhaps I was only
> better armed.
>   'Don't think, old man,' he said aloud. 'Sail on this course and
> take it when it comes.'

Until this point we have merely noted the relationship of Hemingway's style to the new artistic modes of his generation. But as usual
our main interest should be focused on the insights such knowledge
can offer into the nature of the literary works themselves. It is time,
therefore, to examine more closely the method by which Hemingway weaned the reader away from the contemporary antiheroic
prejudice, from the current conception of man as a Prufrockian figure characterised by timidity, moral confusion and spiritual para-
lysis, and succeeded in revalidating the traditional values of courage
and dedication to ideals, employing the new functionalist mode as
a means of achieving that aim.

Within each of his fictional works, Hemingway, one should note,
created an enclave, isolated from everyday existence – the marlin
waters far from the mainland, a battlefield remote from the everyday world. There, sequestered from the encroachments of science

and the chilling scrutiny of the psychoanalyst for ever fixing and formulating human behaviour in a reductive phrase, he was free to
erect a new set of standards, a new series of semiotic significations
based upon functionalist principles, and then, with sleight of hand,
to transfer or extend them to the 'real' world outside the enclave.
The subtlety of that process of exchange is fascinating to watch.

It would, of course, be absurd to suggest the following proposition: that, in an age when established moral standards and traditional
modes of behaviour have been disqualified, when rules no longer
seem to operate with any validity, the game of chess or basketball
can no longer be played. Such games are segregated from contemporary cultural norms, their rules dependent not on social, moral or
logical justification but on arbitrary regulations agreed upon by both
sets of players and confirmed by generations of predecessors. There
is no *reason* why a bishop on the chess board may only move diag-
onally, other than the accepted conditions of the game. With any
change in those conditions, the game simply ceases to be chess. In
the same way, there is no logical reason why a bullfighter should
not, at the climactic moment, draw out a revolver and shoot the bull;
but were he to do so it would cease to be a Spanish bullfight. It is the
ritualised code, the ceremonial procession of matadors, toreadors
and picadors in elaborate costumes, and the formalities instituted
before, after and during the fight that define the occasion. In that
respect, therefore, whatever is within the bullring is immune to the
kind of behavioural analysis that had paralysed the intellectual outside the ring. Hemingway, brilliantly perceiving this distinction,
accordingly established within the bullring itself, or within the parallel enclaves within his other novels, a newly devised moral code
whereby his heroes are to be judged, a code based, initially at least,
on the principle of functional efficiency. Those standards, as we
shall see, are then made to eddy out from within that protected area
into his larger fictional world, where they regulate the actions and
define the moral principles of his leading characters, having drawn
their authority, in a manner unnoticed by the reader, from that
inner enclave.

If in this novel the immunity of the enclave consists of the ceremonial of the bullring, its equivalent in the other novels is invariably
an area of activity whose rules are dictated not by moral criteria but
by their effectiveness in achieving the purpose undertaken (the
functionalist principle). There is in *For Whom the Bell Tolls* a central
concern with the craft of guerilla warfare, the blowing up of enemy

bridges being treated there in terms of the precision and coolness of temperament requisite for the task, irrespective of the nature of the enemy or the morality of the cause for which the act is performed. As has often been noted, if Hemingway's sympathies are primarily with the communists, they shift back and forth in the course of the novel, the communists, as in the chilling account of the village massacre, being represented as no less guilty of ruthlessness and inhumanity. In *The Old Man and the Sea* such professionalism is located in the art of marlin fishing, where knowledge of tides, the technicalities of rod and line, and the exercise of patience and self-restraint employed for maximum effectiveness in catching the prey determine the degree of success. But for the moment let us concentrate on the first of these novels, *The Sun Also Rises*, where the principle was so fully and effectively developed.

A central passage for defining such skill occurs at the moment when Jake introduces Brett to the subtleties of the bullring and the superiority of Romero's artistry. It deserves to be quoted in full:

> Romero never made any contortions, always it was straight and pure and natural in line. The others twisted themselves like corkscrews, their elbows raised, and leaned against the flanks of the bull after his horns had passed, to give a faked look of danger. Afterward, all that was faked turned bad and gave an unpleasant feeling. Romero's bullfighting gave real emotion, because he kept the absolute purity of line in his movements and always quietly and calmly let the horns pass him close each time. He did not have to emphasize their closeness. Brett saw how something that was beautiful done close to the bull was ridiculous if it were done a little way off. I told her how since the death of Joselito all the bull-fighters had been developing a technic that simulated this appearance of danger in order to give a fake emotional feeling while the bull-fighter was really safe. Romero had the old thing, the holding of his purity of line through the maximum of exposure, while he dominated the bull by making him realize he was unattainable, while he prepared him for the killing. (pp. 165–6)

Obvious enough is the connection of this passage with the purity of line in contemporary art, as in the graceful sculpture by Hemingway's friend Brancusi, *Bird in Space* (cf. Figure 7), first exhibited in 1919, or the principle regulating the De Stijl movement of Purism. In contrast to the 'corkscrew' twistings of the lesser bullfighters,

Romero's movements are 'straight' and 'pure' in his pursuit of 'absolute purity of line' – a term occurring twice in this passage – and in each case devoted to the functional purpose of killing the bull with masterly skill. All simulation of danger aimed at impressing the crowd, all mere embellishment of his actions is rigorously avoided.

In the course of this passage, however, there is a subtle transference, which was to prove of major importance for the novel at large. It is the use of elision, a sliding across from the patent meaning of a term to its connotation or association, in a manner that obliquely sets up within the bullring a set of moral standards, no longer based upon religious or social imperatives, but on the prescriptive rules of the ring. Technically the word *straight*, as employed here, is anatomical in denotation, defining Romero's arm as unbent at the elbow during the moment of final thrust. But the word carries with it the moral association of 'honest', straight as opposed to devious or corrupt. In the same way, the word *pure*, while ostensibly diagrammatic here, denoting a movement free from deviations, again cannot be divorced from its ethical connotations. And as the passage continues, the contrast between the straight, pure lines of Romero's skills and the corkscrew efforts of his colleagues takes on a more conspicuous moral force, as we learn that the poorer fighters 'fake' their effects and 'simulate' the appearance of bodily risk in order to deceive the uninitiated. Hemingway has thus tangentially authenticated within the ring, upon exclusively ceremonial grounds related to the ritualistic regulations of the game, the qualities of ethical integrity, of total dedication to art, and of the courage associated with maximum exposure to danger.

From this fictional centre, those standards of behaviour, as we shall see, radiate outwards, to be absorbed by the society beyond the stockade of the bullring, and through them into the world at large. Hence Hemingway's careful manipulation of the reader into identifying him- or herself as an aficionado of the game. In real life the reader may (like myself) find the sport of bullfighting obnoxious. But under the spell of the work we are made to dissociate ourselves from the vulgar Biarritz crowd, ignorant of the subtleties of the bullring, misconstruing the skill and danger of Romero's sidesteps and hence ignorantly preferring 'Belmonte's imitation of himself or Marcial's imitation of Belmonte.' We are thereby made to feel privileged in aligning ourselves with the élitist sect consisting of the discriminating Montoya, Jake and Romero. Montoya himself smiled again. He always smiled as though bull-fighting were a very special secret between the two of us; a rather shocking but really very deep secret that we knew about. He always smiled as though there were something lewd about the secret to outsiders, but that it was something that we understood. It would not do to expose it to people who would not understand. (p. 131)

The fact that each of the 'enclosed' areas in Hemingway's novels involves the pitting of man against the primitive forces of nature, facing alone the challenge of death and compelled to rely on his personal resources and expertise, forms part of this functionalist approach. Where the linking of civilised man to his ancient origins had, in contemporary anthropological and evolutionist theory, been essentially pejorative in its implications, assuming for that earlier period a subjection to irrational taboos and barbaric impulses in a manner robbing him of the dignity of choice, Hemingway sees in such confrontation an opportunity for twentieth-century man to return to his roots, to fulfil, for however brief a period, the original *function* of man, the struggle for survival against the forces of nature in the hunt or in warfare, either as the fighter himself or, vicariously, as the aficionado experiencing the challenge through him. And in that process Hemingway, again in accordance with the new artistic mode, accords aesthetic as well as moral preeminence to the kind of protagonist who, with the strictest economy and dedication, applies to the performance of his task the skills, the valour and the powers of endurance with which nature had equipped him.

The aesthetic implications of the conflict produce a circular effect within the novel. For if the principles Hemingway adopted as a stylist helped to create verbally the economy and beauty of Romero's movements within the ring, Romero himself functions as a paradigm for the innovative style Hemingway was striving to create within the novel, his adoption of exact, unsentimental, unimbellished depictions in line with Romero's economy of movement. On the struggles Hemingway experienced as an author during this period he wrote: 'I found the greatest difficulty, aside from knowing what you really felt, and not what you were supposed to feel, and had been taught to feel, was to put down what really happened in action. . . . I was trying to learn to write, commencing with the simplest things . . .'[34] As the narrator remarks in *A Farewell to Arms*, abstract words 'such as glory, honour, courage, or hallow were obscene beside the concrete names of villages, the numbers of roads, the names of rivers, the numbers of regiments and the dates'. But he applied this principle of economy not only to the nouns he used but also to the structure of his writing, avoiding complex sentences and subordinate clauses in favour of simple, direct juxtaposition. He produced as a result those unornamented vignettes, terse statements linked only by the word 'and' that became recognised as the distinctive Hemingway style:

> It was a warm spring night *and* I sat at a table on the terrace of the Napolitain after Robert had gone, watching it get dark *and* the electric signs come on, *and* the red and green stop-and-go traffic-signal, *and* the crowd going by, *and* the horse-cabs clippety-clopping along at the edge of the solid taxi traffic, *and* the poules going by, singly and in pairs, looking for the evening meal. I watched a good-looking girl walk past the table *and* watched her go up the street *and* lost sight of her, *and* watched another, *and* then saw the first one coming back again. She went by once more *and* I caught her eye, *and* she came over *and* sat down at the table. (p. 14) [my italics]

Hemingway once remarked, 'that's how I learned to write – by reading the Bible', adding that he was referring to the Old Testament.[35] And one may suspect that it was this specifically Hebrew sentence structure that he learned from it, an element preserved in the translation of the authorised version with which he was so familiar:

> *And* the earth was without form, and void; *and* darkness was upon the face of the deep. *And* the Spirit of the Lord moved upon the face of the waters. *And* God said, Let there be light: *and* there was light.

That propensity of both Jake and Romero for simplicity, directness and fidelity to truth in their contrasting vocations creates the natural bond existing between them, Jake seeing within the young bull-fighter's professional dedication the embodiment of his own ideals as a writer.[36]

The way that the principles established in the ring eddy out into society can best be seen at the moment of their transition beyond the stockade into the 'real' world. Montoya, the ideal aficionado, is totally committed to the finest that the bullring represents. He himself is no matador, only an innkeeper; but in managing his inn he follows a series of moral principles derived directly from the code of the ring.

With the same purity of purpose we have learnt to associate with Romero, he waives all considerations of financial profit in favour of dedication to art, selecting only those clients whom he can respect and discouraging the others from returning, however eager they may be to pay for the privilege.

> All the good bull-fighters stayed at Montoya's hotel, that is, those with aficion stayed there. The commercial bull-fighters stayed once, perhaps, and then did not come back. The good ones came each year. In Montoya's room were their photographs. The photographs were dedicated to Juanito Montoya or to his sister. The photographs of bull-fighters Montoya had really believed in were framed. Photographs of bull-fighters who had been without aficion Montoya kept in a drawer of his desk. They often had the most flattering inscriptions. But they did not mean anything. One day Montoya took them all out and dropped them in the waste-basket. He did not want them around. (pp. 131–2)

Especially notable in this passage is the subtle elision from surface meaning to connotation in the term the 'good' bullfighters, a usage that offers in miniature form – compressed, indeed, into a single word – a paradigm of the larger principle suggested here. At the surface level a 'good' bullfighter is one professionally competent within the ring, just as one speaks of a 'good' workman or a 'good' teacher, irrespective of their ethical standards outside the performance of their vocation. But a moment later the word is endowed with moral associations as their austere commitment to their art is contrasted with the acquisitive motivation of the 'commercial' bullfighters, eager for material gain. Hence Montoya's contemptuous discarding of photographs bearing flattering dedications, whose display might have provided valuable publicity for his hotel. And implicit in that weaning out of the photographs is the implication, so relevant to the principles of functionalism we have been examining, that the lesser matadors compose false and flowery dedications, egregious embellishments, while the 'good' are minimalists, restricting their comments to the barest truths.

Whatever personal envy may, in real life, have prompted Hemingway to portray Harold Loeb in so unsavoury a light in this novel, in the process of fictionalising him as Robert Cohn he made the new character serve the structural requirements of the novel. In effect he recreated him to function as a contrast or foil to the true aficionado, and by association to the true functionalist.[37] Hence the lengthy section devoted to him in the opening chapter, even though he is not scheduled to emerge as a central character in the story; for he provides there a negative background against which the positive traits of the new dispensation can be constructed. A romantic by nature, Cohn finds his supposed truths not in the factual world, in the frank, unflinching confrontation of reality characteristic of Romero and Jake (or the pared-down practicality of Le Corbusier and Mies van der Rohe), but in the lush, idealised world of W. H. Hudson's *The Purple Land*, sarcastically described by Jake as recounting the 'splendid imaginary amorous adventures of a perfect English gentleman in an intensely romantic land', with the added comment that as a guide book to what life holds it was about as safe as it would be to enter Wall Street direct from a French convent. A novelist himself, Cohn judges his own book not by the rigorous standards of his art but, like the inferior bullfighter playing to the applause of the Biarritz crowd, by the flattery of his associates. The praise of his publishers, we are told, 'rather went to his head'. In himself, he is an incorrigible sentimentalist, imagining that one night spent with Brett means the eternal possession of her love. He is melodramatic, tearful in his apologies, and constantly informing others of his own emotions. Indeed throughout the novel he is the epitome of fuzzy non-discernment, of a failure to face truths, of continued attempts to embellish or disguise reality. Even his Jewishness serves that purpose in the novel, an aspect introduced, I suspect, less for anti-Semitic reasons (in real life, Loeb, like Cohn in this novel, had been welcomed by the group until personal frictions over Brett disrupted relations) than from Cohn's attempt to be something he is not, to conceal or minimise his alien background. Defensive and oversensitive when apprised of that difference at Princeton, he studied boxing there not through enthusiasm or aficion for that art but, like the 'commercial' bullfighters, for the use he could make of it, as a means of bolstering his social standing.

> He cared nothing for boxing, in fact he disliked it, but he learned it painfully and thoroughly to counteract the feeling of inferiority and shyness he had felt on being treated as a Jew at Princeton.

The only time Cohn employs functionalist terminology he is absurdly in error, that is, in his romantic misreading of the dissolute Brett as 'absolutely fine and straight'.

In the midst of the lost generation, the real world existing outside the ring, Jake alone remains true to his art. While retaining the appearance of professional negligence necessary for acceptance into this group, he is, like Romero, scrupulous in fulfilling his obligations, slipping away from the others on some mild excuse in order to ensure that his journalistic despatches will leave on time. The dreadful wound he has suffered is not easy to accept, and there are moments in the beginning of the novel when at night he weakens temporarily; but it is a wound he confronts at all times with honesty and directness, refusing to conceal it from others or to minimise it to himself, as well as refraining at all times from sentimentalising his predicament. Such directness forms a central part of the code he has developed as an aficionado of the bullring, reflecting the qualities represented there by Romero.

That new code, constructed upon functionalist principles, is reflected even in minor scenes of the novel. When Jake and Bill are at last free from Cohn, vacationing away from the sick world typified by the rest of the group – with their addiction to drunkenness, their financial sponging on others and their casual sex – and are escaping instead into the beauty of unspoilt nature, their meeting with the humorous, generous Basques provides a second game enclave, reinforcing the standards of the bullring, a game element both ritualistic and artistic, again carrying moral implications. The newcomers offer the peasants their bottles of wine but the Basques, politely accepting a sip in order not to offend their guests, prefer their rustic leather wineskins, whose use requires a degree of expertise:

> 'No! No!' several Basques said. 'Not like that.' One snatched the bottle away from the owner, who was himself about to give a demonstration. He was a young fellow and he held the wine-bottle at full arms' length and raised it high up, squeezing the leather bag with his hand so the stream of wine hissed into his mouth. He held the bag out there, the wine making a flat, hard trajectory into his mouth, and he kept on swallowing smoothly and regularly.
>   'Hey!' the owner of the bottle shouted. 'Whose wine is that?'
>   The drinker waggled his little finger at him and smiled at us with his eyes. Then he bit the stream off sharp, made a quick lift with the wine-bag and lowered it down to the owner. He winked at us. The owner shook the wine-skin sadly. (p. 103)

Even within this minor art form, the art of drinking from a wineskin, one perceives the functionalist pattern, the need to achieve a *flat, hard trajectory*, the stream of wine hissing directly into the mouth smoothly and regularly, to be bitten off with a sharp, quick movement. And again that skill is associated with moral traits, with the honesty, generosity and good humour of the Basques in contrast to the quarrelsome self-indulgence of the group Bill and Jake have just left behind.

These moral criteria, established obliquely through the 'game' scenes, are of central importance for the climactic scenes of the novel, as well as the critical interpretation of those scenes, in comprehending what will emerge as the ultimate test of Jake's integrity. Viewed without the contextual reading offered here, the ending of the novel has been widely understood as indicating Jake's failure, his 'emotional adolescence' in succumbing to Brett's entreaties and weakly handing over to her corrupting Circe-like power (thereby acting as a mere pander) the young Romero who represents the ideals to which he supposedly subscribes.[38] Carole Vopat, in summarising that approach, argues that in those final scenes Jake has discovered that he is little different from Cohn after all, that he is, like him, merely a romantic dreamer. By surrendering to Brett's pleas, we are told, he proves 'his inability to take charge, to control and master, to live with that courage, dominance, independence, and stamina which for Hemingway is the essence of masculinity'.[39] If that reading were correct, Jake would indeed be a failure.

That misunderstanding of his actions – both on Cohn's part (in accusing Jake of being a pimp) and on that of the critics who have accepted Cohn's comment as justified – arises, I would suggest, from their inability to perceive one of the central aspects of the aficionado's and the functionalist's code as it is developed within the novel. The decision by Mies van der Rohe and the proponents of De Stijl to reject all embellishments to their art, and the refusal by the 'good' bullfighters in this novel to spoil their purity of movement by the fake corkscrew twists demanded by the uninitiated Biarritz crowd, is essentially the same principle as directs Jake's response in this instance. He allows his actions to stand bare of any alleviating comment, any sentimentalising, any extenuations, even though he knows beyond doubt that those actions will be misinterpreted to his detriment by the non-aficionado Cohn, as they will by any reader who has failed to absorb the new principles.[40] Above all, he knows that even his fellow aficionado Montoya, deprived of the inside knowledge available to us, will condemn him as a traitor to the cause:

> Just then Montoya came into the room. He started to smile at me, then he saw Pedro Romero with a big glass of cognac in his hand, sitting laughing between me and a woman with bare shoulders, at a table full of drunks. He did not even nod.

Jake's persistent silence, his unwillingness to explain or justify, even to himself, the reasons motivating his actions, to leave them unexcused and unsentimentalised, create the impression that he has betrayed his trust. But as Hemingway himself claimed, stylistically he was, as author, determined to reveal only one eighth of the iceberg, leaving the remainder to be deduced by the reader. Jake, I would argue, is in fact confronted here with a tragic dilemma, a choice between two incompatible moral absolutes, such as Hegel had perceived to be intrinsic to the genre of tragedy.[41]

Those who have acknowledged the tragic aspect of this novel, including the most recent exponent of that view, Wirt Williams, have focused exclusively upon Jake's eventual acceptance of his wound, his ability to come to terms with his fate.[42] But that, as Williams and others have admitted, is an essentially passive response, and in that regard differs basically from the situation of central figures within the tragic genre, such as Sophocles' Antigone, faced with an impossible choice, who must either commit the sin, so dreadful in the Greek tradition, of leaving her brother's body unburied or transgress the law of her country, which carries the penalty of death. Whether such tragic figures die in consequence of their choice or, like Oedipus, live on as maimed beings, they bear full responsibility for the decisions they have made.

So here Jake is faced with a harrowing choice. On the one hand there is his code as an aficionado, a code that, as we have learnt, functions not as a form of sport or recreation but as the set of ethical and aesthetic precepts that validate both his profession as writer and the concept of honour governing his daily life – the framework that has lent meaning and dignity to an otherwise pointless existence. That is a commitment to which he offers his fullest allegiance. Yet he recognises that the code, however cardinal to his existence, is ultimately a personal, even a selfish concern, the desire for *his own* purity of purpose, against which is now pitted the altruistic principle of compassion for one who has suffered and continues to suffer

so deeply from the destructive forces of the contemporary waste-
land. Brett, as the scene of her instruction in the art of the bullring
has indicated, is in many ways a potential aficionado, responsive to
the subtleties and finesse of Romero's art; but she has been ravaged
by the inexplicable cruelties of life, the sordid death of her fiancé, the
incapacity of Jake to perform as her lover, and her consequent
descent into nymphomania. Initially Jake rejects her request that he
introduce her to Romero, urging her to exercise self-control. 'Don't
do it' he warns her tersely; but to no avail. When finally convinced of
her plight as he sees her hand shaking uncontrollably in desperation,
his duty becomes unavoidable. He sacrifices himself, his individual
credo and his personal reputation to the higher ideal of selfless
compassion:

> 'You ought to stop it.'
> 'How can I stop it? I can't stop things. Feel that?'
> Her hand was trembling.
> 'I'm like that all through.'
> 'You oughtn't to do it.'
> 'I can't help it. I'm a goner. . . . Please stay by me and see me
>   through this.'
> 'Sure.' (p. 183)

Not a word of self-vindication, no 'ornamental' excuses. Instead the
scene continues with a deflection of focus from the emotions (which
a nineteenth-century novel would have described so fully) to the
bare, unadorned facts: 'Together we walked down the gravel path.'
Some, because of that suppression of emotion, have missed the
pathos here, the unspoken agony of his decision; but it is there
for any reader sensitive to the code. As Hemingway remarked after
the reviews began to appear: 'It's funny to write a book that
seems as tragic as that and have them take it for a jazz superficial
story.'

    To highlight, by telling contrast, Jake's self-disciplined silence,
we are offered soon after this scene Cohn's whimpering, self-
pitying outburst, his tearful apology to Jake, not in regret for having called him a pimp but in hope of recovering his supposed
friendship. Apart from the melodramatic tone, the series of
explanations and justifications so different from Jake's silence,
Cohn's utter self-centredness throws into high relief the quiet altruism of Jake's actions. Especially notable is Cohn's total insensitivity,

in bewailing his own troubles with Brett, to Jake's physical disability, which permanently prevents the latter from ever consummating his love. Cohn

> was crying without making any noise.
>   'I just couldn't stand it about Brett. I've been through hell, Jake. It's been simply hell. When I met her down here Brett treated me as though I were a perfect stranger. I just couldn't stand it. We lived together at San Sebastian. I suppose you know it. I can't stand it any more.'
>   He lay there on the bed.
>   'Well,' I said, 'I'm going to take a bath.'
>   ... I could not find the bathroom. After a while I found it. There was a deep stone tub. I turned on the taps and the water would not run.... I found my room and went inside and undressed and got into bed. (pp. 194–5)

Not only style, including the bare presentation of Brett's plea to Jake, but actions and thoughts too are stripped down to their barest minimum as, on sending the reply to Brett's telegram, Jake recognises with grim irony the interpretation that would be placed by others upon his behaviour:

> That seemed to handle it. That was it. Send a girl off with one man. Introduce her to another to go off with him. Now go and bring her back. And sign the wire with love. That was it all right. I went in to lunch.

This is, in the finest sense, the principle of 'omission' that Hemingway recognised as characterising his writing, whereby the author 'may omit things that he knows, and the reader, if the writer is writing truly enough, will have a feeling of those things as strongly as though the writer had stated them'. To ignore what is unstated here, what is deliberately excluded from the narrative – Jake's anguish both in making his choice and in executing it – is to fail to respond to the principle of minimalism motivating the novel both stylistically and thematically.

   Once Jake's decision is made, he attains calm, in the symbolic scene of his bathing at San Sebastian: 'After a while I stood up, gripped with my toes on the edge of the raft as it tipped with my weight, and dove cleanly and deeply, to come up through the lightening water, blew the salt water out of my head, and swam slowly and steadily in to the shore'. (p. 238) The clean, deep dive, with its simplicity of line, the slow, steady swim form an act of self-purification, a rebaptism settling and steadying the nerves.

The adoption of the 'functionalist' mode achieves its fulfilment in the closing lines of the novel, not only in the famed final line itself but, even more so, in the way Hemingway prepares for it. Alone with Brett in the taxi, now that she is no longer involved with another man, he could, theoretically, be tempted to dream, to interpret the pressing of Brett's body against him as a spontaneous expression of her love, a gesture making everything worthwhile. But by forcing himself to focus his attention upon the bare facts, upon the whiteness of the houses and the movement of the policeman's baton with the same uncompromising directness as was motivating the architects and designers of his era, he invokes in that process the self-discipline demanded by the new mode. With all romantic emotionalism stripped away, he recognises that her movement towards him has resulted only from the movement of the vehicle. He is empowered thereby to accept the full implications of his own physical condition and firmly to dismiss any sentimental imaginings of what might have been:

> We sat close against each other. I put my arm around her and she rested against me comfortably. It was very hot and bright, and the houses looked sharply white. We turned out onto the Gran Via.
>
> 'Oh, Jake,' Brett said, 'we could have had such a damned good time together.'
>
> Ahead was a mounted policeman in khaki directing traffic. He raised his baton. The car slowed suddenly pressing Brett against me.
>
> 'Yes.' I said. 'Isn't it pretty to think so?'

By anchoring the new code within the ritual of the bullring, immune to the debilitating effects of psychological analysis, and by extrapolating from within it a set of moral imperatives, Hemingway was able to counter the 'horizons of expectation' brought to the novel by readers steeped in the antiheroic tendencies of contemporary thought. Paralleling within the medium of literature the functionalist mode then prevailing in art and architecture – austerity of line, the discarding of ornamentation and commitment to a defined purpose – Hemingway succeeded in creating, both thematically and stylistically, an essentially new type of hero. It was a hero divorced from the nineteenth-century tradition, yet revalidating the ideals of courage, integrity and professional dedication in a manner both aesthetically and intellectually more appropriate to the needs of his time.

5

Woolf, Joyce, and Artistic Neurosis

Although the principle of *ut pictura poesis* had long lost its authority, in the early decades of the twentieth century the principle itself, no longer reliant on the classical axiom, seems to have regained its strength; for writers repeatedly projected themselves fictionally into their works in the guise of painters, on the assumption that the two media were essentially kindred. D. H. Lawrence, in his semi-autobiographical *Sons and Lovers*, depicted his younger self as Paul Morel embarking on a career as a painter, long before he himself took up painting as an avocation;[1] James Joyce entitled the fictional-ised account of his own decision to become a writer *A Portrait of the Artist* ..., naming his central character after the 'cunning artificer' Daedalus, whose artistic creations, according to legend, were so real-istic that they appeared to come alive; and Virginia Woolf's own attempt to reconstitute the English novel was projected into the figure of the painter Lily Briscoe, agonising over the structural com-position of a canvas.

The writer's identification of the novel with the visual arts at this time was particularly remarkable as it was a period when painting was moving towards the abstract and non-figural – techniques inim-ical to the creation of credible human characters, which had always been of central importance to the genre of the novel and was due to remain so in most of its subsequent development. It is true that the visual arts at this time were not entirely non-representational, the tradition of mimetic accuracy being preserved by some of the more radical and innovative of the Modernists. There were the lifelike portrait-busts by Jacob Epstein, contrasting with his more revolu-tionary works, the painstakingly accurate vignettes by Magritte, and the canvases of Paul Delvaux, scrupulously realistic in their repres-entation of detail. Yet even those instances reveal the artist's deter-mination to dissociate himself from the kind of verisimilitude that had distinguished painters of previous eras, such as De Hooch's depictions of middle-class home interiors or the scenes of everyday

life by Courbet. Delvaux's nude females, for all their appealing realism, wander unselfconsciously through incongruously inappropriate settings, among formally dressed males in ballrooms or parks, as
if existing in some remote dreamworld;[2] Epstein characteristically
left rough chisel marks on his portrait-busts, as though to remind us
that they are artifacts; and Magritte, while meticulously reproducing
a commonplace pair of boots, ironically subverted the familiar by
endowing the boots with human toes.

   To attribute this dissociation from reality to the advent of photography, to the assumption that the artist, now that visual accuracy
could be achieved more effectively by mechanical means, needed to
redefine the purpose of art, is a theory not supported historically.[3]
The appearance of the Daguerrotype in the 1850s had, as Aaron
Scharf has shown, been regarded by artists not as rivalling their art
but as a valuable aid to its execution. Delacroix, Corot, Manet, Dégas
and their contemporaries learned much from the insights the new
process offered, such as the blurring of figures caught in movement,
adopted by the Impressionists as the principle of optical 'halation'.[4]
From the series of sequential photographs provided by Eadweard
Muybridge, artists discovered how incorrectly they had previously
depicted the positioning of horses' legs in full gallop; while Dégas,
who frequently employed photographs in designing his own paintings, inaugurated from his study of such camerawork an essentially
new subgenre. Stimulated by such photographic series as Muybridge's *Girl Picking up a Towel*, which recorded the movements of
the human body in their natural sequence, he developed his own
artistic interest in portraying similar moments of unaffected spontan-
eity – a ballet dancer tying a shoe off-stage, a young woman, her
clothes untidily scattered about her, bathing in the privacy of her
room – in a manner free from the academic tradition of carefully
posed figures.[5] And it was, we should recall, the photographer
Alfred Stieglitz who served as a primary patron and advocate of
Modernist painting in America, his gallery at 291 Fifth Avenue serving from 1905 as the focal point for such artists as Picabia, Duchamp
and Georgia O'Keefe, whose work he promoted in his magazine
Camera Work, and in its successor, named after the street number of
his own gallery, *291*.[6]

   One reason why the potential rivalry with photography failed to
materialise, even during the next generation, was that the accurate
reproduction of reality the Daguerreotype and camera provided
coincided with a shift of interest among painters. The Impression-

ists' fascination with changing light was intimately related to colour and the interplay of adjacent hues, in line with the discoveries of Eugène Chevreul and others. For that interest, photography, restricted as yet to monochrome, could be only tangentially relevant, offering no serious competition and helpful primarily in the insights it could offer into bodily movement. As Svetlana Alpers has suggested, the advent of photography during the 1850s should be seen as paralleling not the work of the Impressionists but the contemporary resurgence of interest in seventeenth-century Dutch painting, to which it more closely approximated. She argues that

> many characteristics of photographs – those very characteristics that make them so real – are common also to the northern descriptive mode: fragmentariness; arbitrary frames; the immediacy that the first practitioners expressed by claiming that the photograph gave Nature the power to reproduce herself directly unaided by man. If we want historical precedence for the photographic image it is in the rich mixture of seeing, knowing, and picturing that manifested itself in seventeenth-century images.[7]

In those instances where photography did, during its subsequent development, desert mere mechanical reproduction to experiment with montage, with illusionist double exposure and with other creative manipulations of camera images, both in stills and in the early cinema, its innovations were welcomed enthusiastically by the painter as creative art forms to be incorporated as far as possible within their own medium. Max Ernst produced in *The Sunday Spectre Makes Shrill Sounds* of 1929 an ironically incongruous photo-montage in which he inserted the figure of a naked woman in front of a group of spectators idly watching a road repair; and Man Ray constructed a drawing-plus-photocollage in 1933 to illustrate Count Lautréamont's famous remark on 'the chance meeting upon a dissecting table of a sewing-machine and an umbrella'.[8] The recognition in the recent work of Umberto Eco and other postmodern critics that even strictly mimetic camera productions are not objective but reveal the prejudices of the photographer in the framing and angle of viewpoint, seems in fact to have been acknowledged much earlier, not least by painters reacting to the new process at the time of its first appearance. Dégas, once again, proved immediately responsive in the absorption into his own work of the photographic technique of 'cut-off', whereby, in his depiction of unposed figures, he used the framing to slice off part of the scene in order to increase the effect of realistic immediacy. The new medium was thus regarded not as a mechanical substitute threatening to replace painters, but as a creative art form paralleling their own.[9]

If figural painting continued, as we have noted, in the works of Delvaux, Magritte and others, it now did so with transposed mimetic fidelity, a fidelity not to the visible and tactile but to the processes of human thought, to the creations of free association uncensored by reason. Chagall's *I and the Village* of 1911 evoked his home town of Vitebsk in images defying logic, related only by mental association. A cow's head encloses within it a scene of milking, as though the sight of the animal has triggered off recall of a related scene; objects reverse themselves in the mind; and colours, like the green face of the peasant, depict emotional identification in place of actuality, the real world being recreated as if screened through the memory. Chagall would, on principle, never explain his paintings, maintaining that they were simply 'a pictorial arrangement of images that obsess me'. That same process of representing in art not the factual but the cerebral found its most obvious parallel in Joyce's account of a day in the life of two Dubliners, recorded with similar vividness but with the events filtered and distorted through the restlessly active minds of the participants, in the manner that psychological research had begun to reveal.

There is, however, an anomaly here that may serve as a starting point for this present chapter – that while the so-called 'stream of consciousness' novel, with its focus upon the flow of uninhibited inner thought, demonstrated so powerful an indebtedness to the new principles of psychoanalysis, both Joyce and Woolf consistently expressed a marked antipathy to that discipline. Joyce, it has been discovered, owned, as early as 1915, two books by Freud, one by Jung and one by Ernest Jones, all of which have been registered as being in his personal library before he left Trieste.[10] Yet his interest in such theories was singularly limited. Although he was himself fascinated by dreams and carefully recorded the details of those that he and others experienced, he recurrently dismissed psychoanalysis itself as being absurd, declaring that its symbolism was merely mechanical, a rigid system. To the psychoanalyst, he maintained, a house invariably symbolises a womb, a fire inevitably represents a phallus. And while he admitted that in *Ulysses* he had 'recorded simultaneously what a man thinks, and what such seeing, thinking, saying does to what you Freudians call the subconscious' (the 'you

Freudians' evidencing his conscious dissociation from them), he had added mordantly, 'but as for psychoanalysis, it's neither more nor less than blackmail'.[11] More relevantly to his own work, he remarked on one occasion, 'Why all this fuss and bother about the mystery of the unconscious? What about the mystery of the conscious?' In 1919 he rejected vehemently the suggestion that he be psychoanalysed by Jung, remarking to a friend that 'It was unthinkable', and later fictionalising the incident in *Finnegans Wake* in a form of scornful parody:

> You have homosexual catheis of empathy between narcissism of the expert and steatopygic invertedness. Get yourself psychoanolised!

He was clearly sensitive concerning his antagonism to the new science, and when Mary Colum asked him forthrightly why he consistently denied his indebtedness to Freud and Jung, he tightened his lips, we are told, became obviously annoyed and refused to answer her question.[12]

Virginia Woolf revealed a similar hostility, even though she was surrounded by people who viewed the new theories with favour. Her father, Leslie Stephen, had been closely associated with psychological research even before the advent of Freud through his acquaintance with James Sully, whom Virginia knew well. Sully, of whom Freud was later to write with admiration, had fascinated Stephen by his early interest in the subconscious, as in his 1884 comment:

> At any time there is a whole aggregate or complex of mental phenomena, sensations, impressions, thoughts, etc., most of which are obscure, transitory, and not distinguished. With this wide obscure region of the subconscious, there stands contrasted the narrow luminous region of the clearly conscious. An impression or thought must be presumed to be already present in the first or subconscious region before the mind by an effort of attention can draw it into the second region.[13]

Although we have no firm evidence, it seems likely that such ideas may have laid the groundwork for Virginia's own narrative technique. Her husband, Leonard Woolf, reviewed Freud's *The Interpretation of Dreams* for *The New Weekly* as early as 1914 when that treatise was scarcely known in England, and studied other works by Freud in order to broaden his knowledge in preparation for writing the review.

Strachey, another close friend from within the Bloomsbury group, was among the first to apply Freud's ideas to history in composing his *Eminent Victorians* of 1918, winning high praise from Freud himself for providing in his *Elizabeth and Essex* a model of 'psycho-history'. And others of her circle were drawn into the new studies. Her younger brother, Adrian, became a professional psychiatrist, while Lytton's brother, James, again closely involved with the group, after travelling to Vienna to study psychoanalysis under Freud, became the official translator of his collected works, eventually to be published by the Hogarth Press, which Virginia Woolf had cofounded and continued to direct.[14]

Yet despite this intimate contact with critics and scholars laudatory of Freud, colleagues whose opinions she generally admired, she spoke of psychoanalysis with an icy coolness, even with contempt. In a letter dated 1921 she remarked: 'The last people I saw were James and Alix [Strachey], fresh from Freud – Alix grown gaunt and vigorous – James puny and languid – such is the effect of 10 months psychoanalysis.' On another occasion she stated categorically that 'Fantasticality does a good deal better than sham psychology'; and she was at times considerably more vigorous in expressing her antipathy, James Strachey remarking in 1924, after dining with the Woolfs, that Virginia had made 'a more than usually ferocious onslaught upon psychoanalysis and psychoanalysts, more particularly the latter'. In a letter she wrote that same year she records how, at the Hogarth Press, where Freud's works were being prepared for publication, her eye was caught by a passage analysing an incident concerning one of his female patients, where Freud attributed the patient's habit of repeatedly spilling red claret on the tablecloth to certain previous sexual experiences. Woolf's response was acidic: 'We could all go on like that for hours; and yet these Germans think it proves something – besides their own gull-like imbecility.' One notes, moreover, that although she herself experienced a number of nervous breakdowns and mental disturbances indicating her urgent need of care, she firmly rejected all suggestions that she consult a psychiatrist.[15] Only in the late 1930s, after Freud's death, did her resentment abate.

Nor were she and Joyce alone in their antipathy. Although D. H. Lawrence, as one might have expected, approved of Freud's theories about the sexual source of most human activity, he displayed a similar antagonism to psychoanalysis itself. He rejected its concern with the hidden or repressed elements of the human mind, claiming that 'it *was* fair to jeer at the psychoanalytic unconscious, which is truly a negative quantity and an unpleasant menagerie'.[16] If writers, who owed so much to the new theories and were so conscious of that indebtedness, proved so hostile to Freud, one may suspect there was some serious reason prompting them to denigrate his contribution to twentieth-century thought.

The problems posed by Freudian theory – the fragmentation of the human personality into the component parts of ego, id, libido and super-ego, the debilitating sense of being controlled by unknown forces, whether hereditary or resulting from childhood traumas – weighed even more heavily upon the creative artist than upon other intellectuals,[17] especially as those theories emanated from a researcher who was himself remarkably well-versed in both literature and painting. Freud frequently quoted in his writings passages from Shakespeare and other major authors in support of the ideas he was presenting, as though such literary citations lent his theories added validity; and he devoted one complete work to the study of a Renaissance painter. But like Plato, whose philosophical principles had compelled him reluctantly to exclude from the ideal Republic the poetry he loved, so, it would seem, the psychoanalytic process inevitably led Freud, despite his instinctive admiration of literature and painting, to see all art in terms of neurosis, as a form of substitute gratification for the artist's inability to achieve success in the real world. In marked contrast to the deep reverence for the writer that had permeated the Victorian era, often to an exaggerated degree, with its Browning societies solemnly discussing the Master's every word or the legendary hush in Tennyson's house when he was engaged in composing poetry in his study, the psychoanalyst's picture of the writer and artist, at least in the earlier part of the century, proved considerably less flattering. No longer was he regarded as a visionary discerning, through the superficialities of daily life, profound truths obscured from the ordinary run of men. Instead he was, it now transpired, the heir to a tradition traceable back to primitive tribes, where it was always the weakest, the most incompetent member, the man unable to participate effectively in the hunt, who remained behind to sublimate his impotence and frustration by drawing the chase on the wall of the cave, attempting to 'capture' through representation the animals he was so inept at capturing in real life. In subsequent developments of the theory, it is true, sublimation began to be seen as an essentially healthy activity, whereby instinctual drives deprecated by society or by the cultural environment could be deflected to the pursuit of achievements socially more acceptable, such as artistic or scientific endeavour. But as Freud defined it during the earlier decades of the century, the terms were distinctly pejorative.

In his *Three Contributions to the Theory of Sex* (1905) he had already attributed the main source of artistic activity to excessive sexual excitation, adding that, 'whether such sublimation is complete or incomplete, a characterological analysis of a highly gifted individual, in particular one of an artistic disposition, may reveal a mixture, in every proportion, of efficiency, perversion, and neurosis'.[18] That in itself was sufficiently disparaging. But the passage most damning to the artist's image was to appear in his *Introductory Lectures on Psychoanalysis* (1917). There he suggested that the artist possesses

> an introverted disposition and has not far to go to become neurotic. He is one who is urged on by instinctive needs which are too clamorous; he longs to attain to honour, power, riches, fame, and the love of women; but he lacks the means of achieving these gratifications. So, like any other with an unsatisfied longing, he turns away from reality and transfers all his interest, and all his Libido too, on to the creation of his wishes in the life of phantasy, from which the way might readily lead to neurosis...

The true artist, he explains, eventually learns to elaborate his day-dreams so that they become enjoyable to others. And having thereby obtained the public's gratitude and admiration, he has succeeded in winning 'through his phantasy – what before he could only win in phantasy: honour, power, and the love of women'.[19]

There is, indeed, a degree of respect here for the *method* whereby the creative artist, both writer and painter, translates his frustrations into imaginative form and thereby learns to cope with his disability; but it is, according to Freudian theory, from a nervous disability that the primary motivation for the artistic process arises, from mental disturbance due to the 'inexorable repressions' of his inner being. The purpose of such literary or pictorial creativity is thus not the noble pursuit of truth and beauty, but the need to compensate for a personal psychic deficiency. In that context the 'divine' Michelangelo, as he was called by his contemporaries, together with his fellow artists and poets throughout the generations, emerged as introverts bordering upon insanity, coping, it is true, a little more successfully than the demented by eventually managing to work out their psychoses through play or illusion, but mentally disturbed nonetheless.

Freud in fact provided a prototype for such analysis in his monograph on Leonardo da Vinci, published in 1910, in which he argued that the essentially new depiction of the Madonna and Child in Leonardo's paintings, so influential for subsequent High Renaissance art, was not, as had been believed, an expression of the changing concepts of that era. It arose instead, he suggested, from a personal handicap, Leonardo's repressed longing for his natural mother, a peasant from whom, as an illegitimate child, he had been separated at an early age, to be raised in his father's house by a stepmother. Subconsciously needing to compensate for the traumatic inadequacies of his childhood experience, Leonardo imaginatively merged the two female figures, the true and the substitute mother, introducing into his Madonna paintings a second representative of maternity, the Madonna's mother St Anne. And to that childhood crisis Freud also attributed the origins of what he claimed were homosexual leanings on the part of the artist. It should be noted, incidentally, that subsequent analysts have reversed the process by suggesting that Freud's theory on Leonardo, as well as his further paper on Michelangelo's *Moses*, were actually projections of Freud's own father–son neuroses.[20] But that idea had not of course been mooted during these earlier years, when Freud's theories were being first promulgated.

Freud's psychoanalytical readings of art and literature constituted, to quote Paul Ricoeur's terminology, a striking example of the 'hermeneutics of suspicion' since they discarded traditional notions of high culture as being idealistic or transcendental, alleging instead that they were merely the outcome of baser impulses. His studies of Leonardo and Michelangelo opened the way for others to develop the process much further, not always with the sensitivity Freud himself had employed. Thus Albert Modell declared categorically in 1919, in *The Erotic Motive in Literature*, that the source of creative genius is generally to be traced to 'the infantile love life' of authors. He classified Byron as 'a good example of hysteria in literature', and identified the genre of satire at large as traceable to sadistic instincts suppressed during childhood.[21] Yet even in Freud's own theory, however sensitively presented, the implication was clear, as in his statement that children experience incestuous or narcissistic impulses that, if not directed into suitable channels during puberty, are liable to transform them in adulthood 'into neurotics, perverts, artists, or madmen' – a grouping in which, to say the least, it was somewhat uncongenial for the artist to find himself placed.

In our own day the application of such psychoanalytical principles to authorship has resulted in critical observations reflecting
more favourably upon the writer. Harold Bloom's conception of the
author as oedipally struggling to overcome the powerful influence
of literary predecessors has drawn attention to the subtlety whereby
those previous literary works become rewritten or, to employ his
terminology, are consciously 'misread' in order to create essentially
new works of art. In that Oedipal struggle the splendour and power
of the earlier work is fully acknowledged, as well as the victory of its
successor in surmounting the challenge. Moreover, even within that
distinctly favourable view of artistic creativity, Bloom has acknowledged certain major exceptions, recognising that such 'strong'
writers as Shakespeare, Milton and Goethe seem to have suffered
from no such anxiety. In France, Jacques Lacan, basing himself upon
Freud's theory of narcissism, has extrapolated the concept to argue
that a child's first recognition of its image in a mirror produces a recognition of the duality of self. The creative author, dissatisfied with
that duality, achieves self-unity by structuring a 'mythical self' in
language, by mastering reality through the act of writing.[22] But such
interpretations, infinitely more soothing to the artist's *amour propre*,
were to be developed only in the latter part of the century, while in
the period we are examining the implications of Freudian theory,
not least in the terms in which it was first presented, proved gravely
disparaging to the social and intellectual standing of both writer and
artist.

Freud was well aware of the negative impact of his theories,
responding to the charge of critics by insisting, 'one can only char-
acterize as simple-minded the fear that all the highest goods of
humanity, as they are called – research, art, love, ethical and social
sense – will lose their value or their dignity because psychoanalysis
is in a position to demonstrate their origin in elementary and
instinctual impulses'.[23] But in this response he made, significantly,
no attempt to substantiate the denial, to explain why the description
of the artist as neurotic should not be seen as damaging to his or her
dignity, relying instead on a dogmatic rebuttal, probably because he
felt the difficulty of disproving the allegation. Even more important
was the reaction of the artists, art historians and writers themselves.
In 1910 Karl Kraus, a leading Viennese *litterateur* initially sympathetic towards psychoanalytical theory, became an implacable enemy
when one of Freud's colleagues described the respected periodical
he edited, *Die Fackel*, as a mere symptom of the latter's neurosis.[24] In

1924 the impact upon the public of this diminished respect for the creative writer and painter prompted Roger Fry to produce a rejoinder, in a lecture delivered to the British Psychological Society and subsequently published under the title *The Artist and Psycho-Analysis*. Quoting in full the passage from Freud cited above, which described the artist as being an introvert verging upon neurosis, Fry argued that, interesting as that theory may be, it has no bearing on the value of the creative act itself. Even if it were possible to prove that art originates from sexual repression, identification of origins does

> not necessarily explain functions. The alimentary canal and the brain both have their origin in the epithelial tissue, but one would give an enquirer a strange idea of the importance of the brain in the economy of the body if one stated that it was originally part of the skin.
>
> So if you were to prove that art originated in the sexual feelings of man . . . it would be no explanation of the significance of art for human life.

Definitions of art as being based on wish fulfilment and sexual repression were, he continued, only relevant to paintings of inferior quality, to the medium of the cinema (which Fry deprecated) and to third-rate novels, since true art, he claimed, is always elevated above dreams, reaching regions where only the pure may follow. And he neatly reversed the implications of Freud by remarking that, if he felt offended by the new definitions, they held no threat for him:

> To be called introverted and on the brink of being neurotic does not seriously affect me. Indeed, ever since I observed that the only people worth talking to, the only agreeable companions, belonged to the class that morbidly healthy, censurious people classed as neurotic and degenerate, these words have lost all terror for me.

That, however, was only the beginning of the battle. A few weeks later Clive Bell brought the dispute into the public domain, following up Fry's lecture with a blistering attack on Freud in the columns of *The Nation and the Athenaeum*, an attack that revealed how affronted the artistic world was by the new theory as Freud had presented it. Quoting the same passage that had offended Fry and dismissing it as a total misconception of the function of the artist, Bell wrote with withering sarcasm:

Art is, to stick to the Freudian jargon,'wish fulfilment'; the artist 'realizes' his own dream of being a great man and having a good time, and in so doing gratifies a public which vaguely and feebly dreams the same dreams, but cannot dream them efficiently.

   Now this, I dare say, is a pretty good account of what housemaids, and Dr. Freud presumably, take for art. Indeed, the novelette is the perfect example of 'wish fulfilment in the world of phantasy.' The housemaid dreams of becoming a great actress and being loved by a handsome earl; Dr. Freud dreams of having been born a handsome earl and loving a great actress. And for fifteen delirious minutes, while the story lasts, the dream comes true. But this has nothing to do with art.... The artist is not one who dreams more vividly, but who is a good deal wider awake than most people. His grand and absorbing problem is to create a form that shall match a conception, whatever that conception may be. He is a creator, not a dreamer...

Dr Freud, he claimed, had made himself ridiculous by talking about things of which he knew nothing, and being ignorant, Bell concluded caustically, he ought to have held his tongue.[25]

   While there is no record of Virginia Woolf's reaction to this article, penned as it was by a prominent member of her circle, we do know that her response to Fry's essay was one of delight, revealing that she had been equally disturbed by the new theory of artistic motivation and had been gratified by its rebuttal. The article, she wrote at once to Fry, 'fills me with admiration.... I am alive with pleasure'.[26] Within her own writings, moreover, she offered, if more obliquely, a similar defence of aesthetic creativity, repeatedly depicting the intensity of the artist's struggle as an attempt to reach beyond the 'cotton wool' of the factual to the pattern that lies beyond. It is, she insisted, 'a constant idea of mine; that behind the cotton wool is hidden a pattern; that we – I mean all human beings – are connected with this; that the whole world is a work of art; that we are parts of the work of art'. And Lily Briscoe's often despairing attempts to redesign her canvas are depicted in her novel as emanating from an ardent endeavour not to sublimate suppressed frustrations, but to actualise through her imaginative powers an elusive verity beyond the everyday, to capture through art 'the truth of things':

   Her mood was coming back to her. One must keep on looking without for a second relaxing the intensity of emotion, the determination not to be put off, not to be bamboozled. One must hold the scene – so – in a vice and let nothing come in and spoil it. One wanted, she thought, dipping her brush deliberately, to be on a level with ordinary experience, to feel simply that's a chair, that's a table, and yet at the same time, It's a miracle, it's an ecstasy.[27]

How far that represented Woolf's own endeavour to apprehend the ultimate truths of human experience through the medium of the novel is indicated by her comment in an essay published only a year before she wrote *To the Lighthouse*, her rejection of mere surface verisimilitude, as she sought to penetrate to the authenticity behind the façade of life:

> Stridently, clamorously, life is forever pleading that she is the proper end of fiction and that the more [the novelist] sees of her and catches of her the better his book will be. She does not add, however, that she is grossly impure; and that the side she flaunts uppermost is often, for the novelist, of no value whatever. Appearance and movement are the lures she trails to entice him after her, as if these were her essence, and by catching them he gained his goal.[28]

There is, one notes, no hint here of the contemporary view that art arises from unconscious sexual repressions. Yet her attempt to counter the effects of Freudian theory, like the more direct rebuttals by Fry and Bell, were to produce little result, as the principles of psychoanalysis had by then become firmly embedded in the public consciousness. As Lionel Trilling summarised the impact of the new concept on his time, wrily employing the jargon of that science, the twentieth-century writer had come to be seen by his generation as merely sublimating 'childhood frustrations by means of escapist fantasy coupled with exhibitionist craving for social approval'.

*   *   *

I should like to suggest, however, that the reductive conception of art that emanated from psychoanalytic theory needs to be seen not merely as a source of irritation or dismay to the artist. It deserves to be recognised as a major factor in motivating many of the far-reaching changes affecting both literature and painting in the early decades of the century, in certain ways moulding the specific art forms that

those changes produced. It is, for example, in the light of the challenge posed to the function of the artist that one should view the
emergence of two of the most influential manifestations in Modernist
art and literature – Dadaism and Surrealism. André Breton, sequentially a founding member of both schools had, before turning to the
arts, been employed as a medical assistant in a clinic for neurotic
patients, and had himself planned at one stage to become a psychoanalyst. When he decided that his future lay in the arts, he not only
brought to that pursuit an intimate knowledge of the new theories
but served as a conduit for them to his circle of friends within the
avant garde, at a time when those theories were still little known to
the wider public.[29] Dadaism, in its strident iconoclasm, may be perceived in that setting as the initial response of artists to the damaging implications of Freudian theory. Founded in Zurich in 1914 and
spreading swiftly to Paris, Berlin, New York and Barcelona, the
movement represented a protest against bourgeois values and the
senseless destructiveness of war; but one of the primary thrusts of
the movement in all those cultural centres was its derisive denial of
all art forms as they had been previously conceived, a nihilistic
debunking of everything hitherto considered aesthetically valid, as
though there no longer existed any logical justification for artistic
creativity. Duchamp's urinal, provocatively entitled *Fountain* and
mockingly signed 'R. Mutt' (the name of a firm of sanitary engineers), which he submitted for display in 1917 knowing that it would
be rejected by the committee, challenged the basic principle of art
exhibitions as such. It was intended to repudiate the assumption
that any cogent criteria existed for establishing aesthetic value.

Yet it is significant that the Dadaists, in the midst of the ridicule
they poured upon art, continued, if with heavy sarcasm and self-irony,
to function as artists. Such continued aesthetic activity suggests that
Dadaism was in effect the desperate cry of frustrated writers and
painters who had with dismay seen the basis of their art collapse
beneath them and the authorisation of their vocation nullified. As
artists they experienced the urge to create, but were intellectually
hampered by a baffling sense of the pointlessness of their supposed
profession, as posited in the new disparaging view of the artist's
place in society. Like the disturbed patients Breton had witnessed in
the clinics, they proceeded to smash out wildly at whatever was left,
offering such lunatic performances as the one held in the *Cabaret
Voltaire* in 1916, when Richard Huelsenbeck and Tristan Tzara simultaneously recited a poem in different languages, while Marcel Janco

crooned a popular American song alongside, to ensure the performance's total intelligibility for the audience:

> ...the big drum is brought in... the people protest shout smash
> windowpanes kill each other demolish fight here come the police
> interruption. Boxing resumed: Cubist dance, costumes by Janco,
> each man his own big drum on his head, noise, Negro music/
> trabatgea bonoooooo oo ooooo/5 literary experiments: Tzara in
> tails stands before the curtain, stone sober for the animals, and
> explains the new aesthetic: gymnastic poem, concert of vowels,
> bruitist poem, static poem chemical arrangement of ideas...[30]

The direction that their creativity took after this phase indicates how
sensitive they were to the Freudian classification of the artist. Jean
Arp, dissatisfied with a drawing he had made, tore it to pieces, and
then noticed with interest the pattern that the pieces formed on fall-
ing to the floor. From that moment, chance became a major factor in
their art, largely because it seemed to *exclude* the artist from the act of
creativity and hence safeguarded him from exposing the hidden
impulses that Freud claimed to be the motivating force for such
work. As Hans Richter, a leading member of the group, remarked,
'Chance appeared to us a magical procedure by which one could
transcend the barriers of causality and of conscious volition.'[31] The
artist as artist in that context ceased to exist, the fortuitous alone
determining the nature of the art. As with the concept of *objets trouvés*
or 'readymades' now characterising the movement – such as the
snow shovel that Duchamp purchased from a hardware store and
provocatively placed on display as a work of art – the constructive
contribution of the artist was reduced to the minimum, thereby providing him with protection against any tracing of the work to the
effects of his childhood repressions. And together with the readymades, they began experimenting with poetry consisting of words
uttered in random sequence, allowing such chance juxtaposition to
spark off new meanings, with no intentional meaning being
imposed on them by the poet. It was that same reluctance of artist or
poet to be involved in the creative process that lay behind Count
Lautréamont's famous categorisation of beauty as the accidental
meeting of a sewing machine with an umbrella on an operating
table, the causal in art now being replaced by the casual.

   On the other hand, the fact that these artists continued to perform
and to produce – however cynical and self-derisive their methods of

presenting such art may have been – suggests a covert hope that out of the ruins produced by their iconoclastic ridicule might emerge some more valid art form, in some way exempt from the charges Freud and others had levelled. And such was in fact the result, the next stage in their development proving fascinating against this background of their response to Freud. It was Breton himself who, having helped inaugurate Dadaism and having participated actively in its nihilistic protests, gradually led it towards Surrealism, wresting his justification of the new art form out of those very theories that had disqualified the old. The psychoanalytical denigrating of the arts had been based on the supposition that writers and artists were essentially victims, *unknowingly* sublimating their neuroses at the very time when they imagined they were in creative control. The new art form that Breton introduced, by encouraging artists to exploit, with full awareness, the dream experiences and free associations of their subconscious, was calculated to restore the creative artist to a position of superiority. It located him no longer as the neurotic patient impelled by recondite repressions of which he had no knowledge and over which he could exert no control, but as a responsible explorer, mapping and scouting out mental territories as yet uncharted.

The first 'automatic' text produced jointly in 1919 by André Breton and Philippe Soupault, *Les Champs magnétiques*, in fact adopted the method that had been introduced by Pierre Janet – the professor of psychology and the most famous of Charcot's pupils, with whom Breton had come into contact during his medical days. Janet had, in advance of Freud, advocated for the neurotically disturbed patient a total relaxation of the mind, which would allow submerged thoughts to surface and express themselves in a manner free from inhibitions, and he had encouraged the patient to record those thoughts in writing: 'Let the pen wander automatically on the page even as the medium interrogates the mind.'[32] The adoption of that technique, one should note, still categorised the writer as a mental patient, or at least as a person subject to neurotic disturbance; but it did offer the possibility of a more consciously active role, marking a first stage in the movement's regaining of artistic self-respect. This first attempt by Breton and his colleague was embryonic, a work of little literary or artistic value, and the reason lay in his insistence during that initial phase that the writer remain entirely passive, free from 'any control exercised by reason, exempt from any aesthetic or moral concern', merely transcribing the ideas that surfaced under those conditions.

We become in our work, he declared, 'the dumb receptacles of so many echoes, modest *recording devices*'.[33] He and his colleagues experimented with drugs and other techniques intended to relieve inhibitions and to allow suppressed thoughts to rise freely into the mind without any interference from the conscious self. The *Surrealist Manifesto* of 1924 defined their aim as 'Pure psychic automatism through which it is intended to express, either verbally or in writing, the true functioning of thought. Thought dictated in the absence of all control exerted by reason, and outside any aesthetic or moral pre-occupation.' Typical of this first phase were the paintings of Yves Tanguy – haunting, ambiguous landscapes dotted with blob-like fetal forms, their significance mysterious and left unexplained, re-corded unaltered as they have emerged directly from the recesses of dream-experience. There was nonetheless a sense that the artist, even through this process of recording, was making a contribution to knowledge, and hence justifying art, since such paintings, as Breton remarked, 'yield us images of the unknown as concrete as those which we pass around of the known ... the first non-legend-ary glimpse of the considerable area of the mental world ...'

The more substantial justification of Surrealism, however, may be seen to have emerged during the second stage of its aesthetic devel-opment, as writer and painter transformed this passive recording of mental experience, still connected with a form of therapeutic treat-ment intended for the mentally disturbed, into an independent art form, which placed the artist not in the role of patient but of analyst, perceptively investigating his own thoughts and dreams, or those of others, and suggesting – either directly or by implication – the psy-chological significance of the scene depicted and the impulses con-cealed within it. By that altered and more positive function, the second-stage Surrealist acquired what the Dadaist and early Surreal-ist had lacked, a means of rising above the disparaging Freudian role assigned to the painter and of adopting instead the more dignified function of analyst.

Salvador Dali, as we know from a drawing that surfaced only in 1980 at an exhibition of his works at the Pompidou Centre, did at first experiment with passive automatism, but he found it unsatis-factory. His subsequent work, however, represented a major change of direction, a conscious exploitation of psychoanalysis in his work, marking the next phase in the development of the movement. In the film he produced in collaboration with Luis Buñuel in 1929, *Un Chien andalou*, his purpose was, he declared, to produce a work that 'would carry each member of the audience back to the secret depths of adolescence, to the sources of dreams, destiny, and the secret of life and death'.[34] But even more important was the form of art he introduced in his own paintings, immediately recognised by Breton as an innovation, a departure from their established programme and hence arousing the latter's strong disapproval. In a telling phrase Breton condemned Dali for establishing himself 'as both judge and party' to the actions produced by psychological impulse, that is, for moving beyond a mere recording of psychic phenomena into the analysis and interpretation of their significance.[35] Dali, fully aware of the nature of his innovation, defined his method in his *Conquest of the Irrational* (1935) as 'paranoiac-critical' activity, the term 'critical' in that definition indicating his intention that the artist should consciously interfere in the automatic process, displaying his paranoias while at the same time rising above them by functioning as their decoder.

His *Metamorphosis of Narcissus* of 1937 (Figure 19) is, one may perceive, no mere transcribing of a dream vision but an exercise in psychological self-analysis, with the hints of his interpretive conclusions embedded in the painting for the perceptive viewer to discern. Freud's *The Ego and the Id* of 1923 had proposed that we begin life as narcissists, gradually transforming the early erotic interest in the mother figure into ego-identities without which relations with others could not be effected. And such is the theme of this painting. Narcissus's dejected pose here, as he gazes into the pool, is echoed in the outline of the ghostly hand to the right, a hand swarming with ants (a recurrent image of putrefaction and death in Dali's work) and is attended by an emaciated dog chewing on a skeletal ribcage. The hand, however, holds an egg, the symbol of life, from which emerges the flower that will bear Narcissus's name. In the background stands (as was described in Dali's poem of the same name) a 'heterosexual group' in attitudes of 'preliminary expectation' representing the act of love into which the narcissist hopes to mature. The entire painting thus reveals Dali's conscious application to himself of the Freudian and Surrealist *Eros/thanatos* concept, echoed in so many of his works at this time – his belief that his love for his mistress, Gala, would succeed in countering his own despair, his narcissistic self-absorption and suicidal tendencies, eventually metamorphosing him, like Narcissus, from death to life. Similarly paintings such as his *William Tell* of 1930 had multiple mythic allusions, as he himself explained: 'What we have here is "Saturn devouring his own children; God the Father sacrificing Jesus Christ; Abraham sacrificing Isaac; Guzmán the Good with a dagger in his hand ready to kill his son; and William Tell pointing his arrow at the apple on the head of his own son."'[36] But, as he confirmed elsewhere, the painting also symbolised, his own Oedipal relationship with his father and his consequent castration complex. Hence the depiction of himself turning away, protected only by a fig leaf, from the virile figure of his father, who threateningly wields a pair of scissors. Freud, incidentally, was not Dali's only source, his reading of Krafft-Ebbing's *Psychopathia sexualis* of 1899 offering him insights into various forms of sexual aberration and sexual fetishism that he began to incorporate into his art, with an understanding of the way they functioned within his own troubled psyche.

To accuse Dali in such works of 'unknowingly' sublimating his repressions (in line with Freud's concept of the artist) becomes absurd, not because he is failing to respond to recondite impulses but because they are no longer recondite to him. He has taken control, adopting the commanding position of the self-analyst. Indeed Freud himself immediately recognised the altered artistic role in Dali's works, remarking astutely, when introduced to Dali in London by Stefan Zweig in 1938, that 'It is not the unconscious I see in your pictures, but the conscious. While in the pictures of the masters – Leonardo or Ingres – that which interests me, that which seems mysterious and troubling to me, is precisely the search for unconscious ideas, of an enigmatic order, hidden in the picture, your mystery is manifested outright. The picture is but a mechanism to reveal it.'[37] That *but* is significant, suggesting that Freud was a trifle disappointed by the artist's new role, being robbed thereby of his usual mission, to reveal the hidden motives of the artist, his function having now been expropriated by the artist himself.

In turning to literature, one may discern within the novels produced at that time a similar annexation of that role, as authors, too, began to commandeer the function of the analyst. As usual there is no intention on my part of suggesting any direct influence of art upon literature, but rather a concomitant response in the two media. It is true that Joyce may in fact have had some acquaintance with the new art movements during the time he was resident on the continent, while living in Trieste, Paris and Zurich; but there is no definite evidence to support the supposition.[38] There was in Britain some limited contact with the literature of the Dadaists, partly through the adoption of their more truculent tactics by Wyndham Lewis and the Vorticists; Edith Sitwell, to her annoyance, often being associated with Dadaist writers by her decriers because of her similarly provocative acts. But as regards painting, Britain's first real contact with Dada and Surrealism took place as late as 1936, after the major works of Joyce and Woolf had already been published. The art exhibition held in the New Burlington Galleries in that year, at whose opening ceremony Breton appeared dressed in green, Dali wearing a diving-suit (in which he almost suffocated) and Dylan Thomas offering to guests boiled string in teacups, produced a near-hysterical reaction from the public – some twenty thousand visitors flocked to see it, mainly in order to scoff. But if there was little direct contact until then, writers in Britain were independently developing their own responses to the changing intellectual milieu, responses closely paralleling the work of those continental painters in their resistance to the Freudian derogation of the creative artist.

The characters in Virginia Woolf's *The Waves* (1931), although slightly individualised and diverse in personality, are, as critics have long recognised and as she herself indicates in the text, patently projections of herself. In his concluding monologue, Bernard remarks: 'I have been talking of Bernard, Neville, Jinny, Susan, Rhoda and Louis. Am I all of them? Am I one and distinct? I do not know.... There is no division between me and them.' But if the novel is so clearly an expression of her own inner being, she functions there, like Dali, not as the unwitting sublimator of her hidden repressions but as their conscious decipherer, acting as a discriminating guide to the uncharted areas of human personality as she exposes the complex impulses within herself and traces them to their causes. The temperament of each of the fictional characters in adulthood is integrally related to their childhood experiences in accordance with the new doctrines. Thus Louis's oppressive sense of social vulnerability is linked to the traumatic moment in his childhood when Jinny, discovering him hiding behind a bush, invades his privacy and, to his horror, forces a kiss upon him: 'She has kissed me. All is shattered.'

For a male to be 'raped' or psychologically damaged by an undesired kiss from a girl may seem farfetched; but with allowance for gender transference – part of the process of fantasy substitution revealed by psychological theory, and central to her *Orlando* – that scene deserves to be seen as a reflection of the sexual abuse Woolf herself experienced in childhood, when, to her great disgust, she was erotically embraced and fondled in bed on a number of occasions by her older stepbrother, George Duckworth, experiences so traumatic as to leave her sexually frigid throughout her life.[39] Her recognition of the parallel impact upon Louis marks her acknowledgment of the psychological patterns governing her own life. And the double gender transference later in the novel, as Louis, when recollecting that incident from his childhood, mentally substitutes a male for the supposed female attacker, leaves no doubt that the author was fully aware of the relevance of that scene to her own experience. In recalling the event in adulthood, Louis employs an image whose phallic connotations can scarcely be missed, the image patently identifying the scene with the cause of Woolf's own psychological distress:

> I woke in a garden, with a blow on the nape of my neck, a hot kiss, Jinny's; remembering all this as one remembers confused cries and toppling pillars and shafts of red and black in some nocturnal conflagration. . . . It is a stigma burnt on my quivering flesh by a cowled man with a red-hot iron.[40]

If, fictionally, that image is 'unconscious' on Louis's part, on Woolf's part it constitutes a fully conscious attribution of her own neuroses to their source, a process of psychoanalytical self-exposure in literature paralleling the paranoiac-critical art form developed by Dali. The effect of her own childhood traumas upon her mental development into adulthood she presents by means of Louis's sense of terror, of a social vulnerability so closely resembling the problem from which she herself suffered. Attempting to mislead his interlocutor by an assumed confidence, he acknowledges to himself the trembling inner being concealed behind his protective exterior, the quivering self within the outwardly sanguine façade:

> But I beg you also to notice my cane and my waistcoat. I have inherited a desk of solid mahogany in a room hung with maps. Our steamers have won an enviable reputation for their cabins replete with luxury. We supply swimming-baths and gymnasiums. I wear a white waistcoat now and consult a little book before I make an engagement.
>   This is the arch and ironical manner in which I hope to distract you from my shivering, my tender, and infinitely young and unprotected soul. For I am always the youngest; the most naïvely surprised; the one who runs in advance in apprehension and sympathy with discomfort or ridicule – should there be a smut on a nose or a button undone. I suffer for all humiliations.[41]

That same tendency within herself to withdraw from reality into a protective cocoon, to hide behind walls through which there filtered only muffled echoes of the actual world, she depicts frequently in her writings – a metaphor echoing the environment Marcel Proust had created in reality, constructing for himself a sequestered room, insulated from all outside sounds and activities. The contrast she employs in *To the Lighthouse* is with Ramsay who, in the opening chapter entitled 'The Window', gazes through it to establish the facts about the weather. He sees reality without illusion: 'What he said was true. It was always true. He was incapable of untruth; never tampered with a fact; never altered a disagreeable word to suit the pleasure or convenience of any mortal being . . . ' Her world, on the other hand, is represented by a window through which no facts beyond it can be discerned, a window darkened by night, reflecting the room in which she finds herself. It constitutes an alternative existence into which she mentally recedes, retreating there into her interior self, absolved from the burden of social participation and the unwelcome intrusion of others. The spoken words that reach her ears disintegrate into an almost meaningless babel as they pass through the mental barrier separating her from that world:

> She looked at the window in which the candle flames burnt brighter now that the panes were black, and looking at that out-side the voices came to her very strangely, as if they were voices at a service in a cathedral, for she did not listen to the words. The sudden bursts of laughter and then one voice (Minta's) speaking alone, reminded her of men and boys crying out the Latin words of a service in some Roman Catholic cathedral. She waited. Her husband spoke. He was repeating something, and she knew it was poetry from the rhythm and the ring of exaltation and melancholy in his voice . . . [42]

Her sense of their speech as mere noise conforms closely to the theory of Jacques Lacan mentioned earlier, his perception of the period of maturation occurring after one recognises the 'otherness' of persons separate from oneself, a process in which language too is eventually perceived as essentially 'other.' Words become acknowledged as mere signifiers whose meaning depends on further signifiers, and which are therefore never available to be possessed in their fullness. In Lacan's reading, that process is linked to the feeling of loneliness when a child first discovers that it is an entity separate from its mother and longs to be reunited with her – a process of especial relevance for a reading of this novel, permeated as it is by the narrator's yearning to recapture the lost presence of her mother. And in this passage the 'otherness' of language is caught remarkably accurately as the words reaching her seem to disintegrate, failing to register any meaning.[43]

Many attempts have been made to connect Virginia Woolf's innovative style to the growing admiration for Post-Impressionist painting, which, although dating back to the 1870s, did not become known in Britain until her time. Cézanne's landscapes, Bettina L. Knapp maintains, encouraged her 'to connect the disparate, give shape to the chaotic, and depict past, present and future in unwinding patterns'; but such terms are, one should note, too vague to be meaningful.[44] Attempts to establish such affinity have drawn most of their authority from Woolf's cryptic comment about the new forms of fiction, that 'in or about December 1910, human character changed . . .' – a date coinciding with the Post-Impressionist exhibition at the Grafton Gallery. Her close friendship with Roger Fry, the organiser of the exhibition and the man most responsible for introducing those French artists to England, seems to invite inquiry into her own stylistic indebtedness. But an examination of her writings and diaries reveals in contrast how markedly unresponsive she was to painting and the visual arts. Time after time she records the gulf separating her sensibility from that of the discriminating art lovers surrounding her – art lovers that included such practising painters as her sister Vanessa and their friend Duncan Grant, as well as two of the leading art critics of the day, Clive Bell and Roger Fry. She admitted early in her life to an innate distaste for painting, and her subsequent attempts to benefit from the guidance of her friends only left her with a conviction of her own inadequacy. In 1904 she travelled to Italy for the first time, visiting with her sister the art galleries in Florence and Venice; but while Vanessa was thrilled by what she saw, being especially excited by the Tintorettos, there was very little that pleased Virginia. During a second visit to Italy in 1909, she included in her diary almost no reference to the art of that country, preferring to record impressions of the people she met there; and after a series of quarrelsome moods culminating in what Vanessa described as a 'tiresome' scene in the Bargello, she cut short her Italian trip and returned to England. Painters themselves, she declared in exasperation, 'are an abominable race. The furious excitement of these people all the winter over their piece of canvas,

coloured green and blue, is odious.' In 1918, after a visit to the
National Gallery under Fry's guidance, she bemoaned her lack of
sophistication in responding to the paintings: 'I thought a Rembrandt "very fine" which to him was mere melodrama ... the Ingres
was repulsive to me; & to him one of the most marvellous of
designs.' And with an amusing mordancy, no doubt reflecting her
own feelings, she spoke on another occasion of that 'most extreme
of penalties, the most exquisite of tortures – to be made to look at
pictures with a painter'.[45]

To return, then, to that seminal essay in which she located the
major transformation in fictional characterisation as having occurred
around December 1910, since when, she argued, 'all human relations have shifted – those between masters and servants, husbands
and wives, parents and children', one should note that it was not to
the Impressionists or Post-Impressionists that she originally attributed that far-reaching change, but to Freud. She commented in the
course of that essay that the modern novelist has a distinct advant-
age in searching for the hidden ambitions and motives of human
beings: 'If you read Freud you know in ten minutes some facts ... or
at least some possibilities ... which our parents could not possibly
have guessed for themselves.' The fact that she suppressed that
remark, omitting it from the final draft, leads one to suspect once
again that it was an attribution she was reluctant to acknowledge.
The date she offered as the turning point in human characterisation
would thus, if one bears her original comment in mind, have
referred to the arrival of Freudian theory on the English scene,
rather than to an exhibition of Post-Impressionist painters that
influenced her so little.[46] Even in the use of the amateur painter,
Lily Briscoe, to represent her own attempts at restructuring the
novel, the solutions at which Lily arrives have no connection with
Impressionism, consisting merely of the use of the lighthouse as a
divider, a solution that scarcely required a profound understanding
of painting, nor was in any way indebted to the new modes in art:

> With a sudden intensity, as if she saw it clear for a second, she
> drew a line there, in the centre. It was done; it was finished. Yes,
> she thought, laying down her brush in extreme fatigue, I have had
> my vision.

Another of Woolf's comments on the change occurring in the modern novel has also been seen in terms of an indebtedness, if not to

the Post-Impressionists, then at least to such predecessors as Monet: 'Life is not a series of gig-lamps symmetrically arranged; life is a luminous halo, a semi-transparent envelope surrounding us from the beginning of consciousness to the end. Is it not the task of the novelist to convey this varying, this unknown and uncircumscribed spirit, whatever aberration or complexity it may display, with as little mixture of the alien and external as possible?'[47] But Monet would have strongly rejected that attribution. The Impressionists had insisted that their purpose was optical accuracy, an attempt to capture the way light altered objects or affected the human retina. It was in no sense to present the inner world of the individual, cut off by a semitransparent envelope from reality, an image that suggested the modern writer's need to present not actions nor details of the social scene – which are merely 'alien and external' – but the hidden impulses producing action.

The adoption of the innovative role of probing analyst among writers, whether in the fictional characters they created or (by process of conscious self-examination) through projection of the author's own personality, holds eminently true for Joyce. A number of psychoanalytical studies of his work have appeared in recent years, notably those by Mark Shechner and Shelton Brivic; but their focus has been upon the *subliminal* elements in his personality, those latent associations and psychic patterns, unacknowledged by him, that may be revealed through a study of his writings. They do not examine his conscious application, both to his characters and to himself, of the Freudian and Jungian principles he had absorbed.[48] Here too, however indebted he may have been to Freudian theory, Joyce himself staunchly repudiated and indeed ridiculed Freud's interpretation of recondite sexual excitation as the motive force of art. What, one may ask, is Stephen Dedalus' lengthy lecture on Shakespeare in *Ulysses* if not a delightful parody of Freud's conception of the creative artist, an amusing debunking of the idea that the writer is merely sublimating his repressions through fantasy? In a protracted scene set in Dublin's National Library, Stephen facetiously proposes the theory that the bard had been traumatised in his youth on being raped by a lusty and older Ann Hathaway:

> He was overborne in a cornfield first (a ryefield, I should say), and he will never be a victor in his own eyes after nor play victoriously the game of laugh and lie down.

The rest of Shakespeare's career was, we are gravely informed, simply a vicarious working out of this early trauma of the 'beast with two backs', expressed through the substitute personalities of Adonis, of Lucrece and of Imogen, as well as of a Hamlet whom woman delights not. And extrapolating the thesis, Stephen, with tongue in cheek, proceeds to argue that Shakespeare was, like Hamlet's father, cuckolded in real life by his own brother, his repressions, created by these fraternal rivalries within the family, being worked out obsessively within the plays:

> The note of banishment, banishment from the heart, banishment from home, sounds uninterruptedly from *The Two Gentlemen of Verona* onward till Prospero breaks his staff, buries it certain fathoms in the earth and drowns his book.... It is between the lines of his last written words, it is petrified on his tombstone ... in *Hamlet*, in *Measure for Measure* – and in all the other plays which I have not read.
> He laughed to free his mind from his mind's bondage.[49]

The absurd argument at the conclusion, that the theory holds true for 'all the other plays which I have not read', should provide sufficient indication of the flippant intent of this passage; but to confirm this reading, when Stephen is asked by a somewhat gullible listener if he believes the implausible theory he has elaborated, his answer is unequivocal: 'No, Stephen said promptly.'

Like Dali and Woolf, Joyce too responded to Freud's disparaging view of the artist as a neurotic casualty by usurping the role of the psychoanalyst. For in addition to creating the illusion that we are listening to the untrammelled flow of thoughts within a human mind, he embeds within the supposed recording of those thoughts insights into the motivation of his characters, motivations essentially different in quality from those previously provided in fiction. Such motivation is seen now as deriving from subconscious stimuli of which the character is incognizant, but which are made available within the text for the alert reader to discern – a process that leaves no doubt of the author's awareness of those hidden impulses, and of Joyce's conscious direction of the reader's attention to them. The refreshing realism in the account of Leopold Bloom's attendance at Paddy Dignam's funeral, for example, owes its effectiveness, I would suggest, in large part to our growing recognition of the hidden psychological impulse directing Bloom's responses to the scene, an impulse of which those thoughts function, with remarkable effect, as fantasy substitutes:

> Mr. Bloom moved behind the portly kindly caretaker. Well-cut frockcoat. Weighing them up perhaps to see which will go next. Well, it is a long rest. Feel no more. It's the moment you feel. Must be damned unpleasant. Can't believe it at first. Mistake must be: someone else. Try the house opposite. Wait, I wanted to I haven't yet. Then darkened deathchamber. Light they want. Whispering around you. Would you like to see a priest? Then rambling and wandering. Delirium all you hid all your life. The death struggle. His sleep is not natural. Press his lower eyelid. Watching is his nose pointed is his jaw sinking are the soles of his feet yellow. Pull the pillow away and finish it off on the floor since he's doomed. Devil in that picture of sinner's death showing him a woman. Dying to embrace her in his shirt. Last act of *Lucia. Shall I nevermore behold thee?* Bam! He expires. Gone at last. People talk about you a bit: forget you. Don't forget to pray for him. Remember him in your prayers. Even Parnell. Ivy day dying out. Then they follow: dropping into a hole one after the other.
>
> We are praying now for the repose of his soul. Hoping you're well and not in hell. Nice change of air. Out of the frying pan of life into the fire of purgatory.
>
> Does he ever think of the hole waiting for himself? They say you do when you shiver in the sun. Someone walking over it. Callboy's warning. Near you. Mine over there towards Finglas, the plot I bought. Mamma poor mamma, and little Rudy.
>
> The gravediggers took up their spades and flung heavy clods of clay in on the coffin. Mr. Bloom turned his face. And if he was alive all the time? Whew! By Jingo, that would be awful! No, no: he is dead, of course. Of course he is dead. Monday he died. They ought to have some law to pierce the heart and make sure or an electric clock or a telephone in the coffin and some kind of canvas airhole. Flag of distress. Three days. Rather long to keep them in summer. Just as well to get shut of them as soon as you are sure there's no. The clay fell softer. Begin to be forgotten. Out of sight, out of mind. (p. 91)

The inappropriateness of Bloom's thoughts to the occasion, his irrepressible sense of the comic while in the presence of a solemn interment, accurately capture the mind's unruly tendency to resist the pressures of social conformity, as well as its proclivity for wandering away from the subject in hand into peripheral fields. In that, Joyce discards the sentimental tradition of the nineteenth-century novel – such as the burial of Little Nell in *The Old Curiosity Shop*, which conforms so closely to the behaviour expected at such scenes by Victorian society, where not an eye is dry, many a stifled sob is heard and all present recall her angel-like qualities. Instead we are offered here not only the seemingly random, unsubduable flow of thought behind the mourner's solemn exterior but, even more effective in attaining that credibility, a sequence of associations revelatory of a hidden trepidation that never achieves overt expression – Bloom's inability to confront the suppressed fear of his own death, a fear awakened by the solemn occasion. In a manner closely matching Freud's transference theory, whereby the mind, recoiling from unpleasant memories, temporarily projects them into fantasy or wit until capable of coping with them, so Bloom's thoughts clothe his fear in comedy, thrusting it away from direct encounter, while his mind nonetheless unconsciously circles ever closer to the central dread itself. Earlier in the novel Joyce had prepared the reader by indicating Bloom's innate terror of dying. The sight of an old woman, a 'bent hag' arousing thoughts of age and death, produces in him a powerful reaction:

> Grey horror seared his flesh.... Cold oils slid along his veins, chilling his blood: age crusting him with a salt cloak.

In the funeral passage, the first hint of that subdued theme occurs at the very opening, as Bloom idly imagines the undertaker assessing, for professional reasons, which of the present mourners will next need his services; but before Bloom can actually visualise himself as the next candidate, his mind, by a process of substitution, sidetracks itself away from that danger into an ironic picturing of the deathbed scene of some other person, a scene in which Bloom has the more secure role of detached, amused observer, gazing at, but not identified with, the moribund patient. But instantaneously there arises the thought, defensively couched in the third person: 'Does he ever think of the hole waiting for himself?' A momentary consideration of his own grave awaiting him in the plot towards Finglas, together with the flinging of clods of earth on to the coffin – a sight from which Bloom, flinching, instinctively 'turned away his face' – again induces him to resort to drollery, as he ponders various ludicrous means of avoiding underground suffocation, the nearest his mind dares approach a confrontation with the ultimate terror of his own burial.

Again, therefore, there is a reversal of roles, in which the tensions created by unacknowledged neuroses and repressed fears have been transferred from the author, where Freud had firmly placed them, to his fictional characters, the author now functioning creatively as diagnostic investigator or perceptive recorder. As Dorrit Cohen has pointed out, the stream-of-consciousness novel does not reproduce, as has so often been imagined, a preverbal flow of thought. It presents instead the flow of thought at a stage just beyond the border line with the subconscious, at the phase when the thinker verbalises his or her musings.[50] But to redefine the situation even more precisely than she does, it constitutes rather the *author's* verbalisation of the character's flow of thought in a manner calculated to reveal the psychological motivations of which the character itself may be totally unaware. The unawareness is thus transferred from the writer, where Freud had placed it, to the fictional character.

In Joyce's writing, the same process holds true for his self-portraiture, echoing in that respect the strategy revealed in Dali's canvases and in Woolf's fictionalised projections of self. A primary attraction of Joyce's two early novels derived not just from the process of mental thought, revealed in a manner free from adjustment to social formalisation. It lay rather in the *quality* of Stephen's mind, in the privilege it offered the reader of witnessing the thoughts of a highly intelligent and artistically sensitive being exploring ideas fascinating in their perceptiveness and range. But together with that newer form of realism was its revelation, however painful to the author, of the psychological motivation of his inner self, a motivation bordering on neurosis, as in the obsessive guilt complex concerning Stephen's and, by extension, Joyce's own mother:

Ghoul! Chewer of corpses!
No, mother. Let me be and let me live.[51] (p. 9)

This was fundamentally different from the rebellion against parents in such nineteenth-century works as Butler's *The Way of All Flesh* and Edmund Gosse's *Father and Son*, which had marked the standard ideological conflict between generations, the rebellion against parental authority, usually involving a rejection of oppressive standards or beliefs felt to be no longer applicable to the new age. Here the conflict takes on psychological proportions close to Dali's syndrome – the castration syndrome in relation to his father and the love–hate relationship with his mother. As regards the latter, Dali frequently affirmed his passionate devotion to her, but coupled that sentiment with a vicious antipathy, admitting that he often spat upon her portrait, his hostility resulting in the representations of her in his paintings as a praying mantis emasculating or consuming her sons.[52] So here Joyce's conflict takes on neurotic proportions, patently reflecting Freud's new theory about the growing child's complex relationship with its parents, including the identification in the male child of a tendency to transform the loved mother into an object of sexual desire, a bond from which the child needed to break away into maturity, that desire for release frequently expressing itself in violent animosity.[53]

Therein lay the new justification for the creative artist, his function as analyst instead of unknowing victim revealing in monologic form psychic depths never previously articulated; or, in painting, portraying through dream visions the transference of those psychic elements by means of fantasy substitution. As Proust had declared of the contemporary novel, it was no longer sufficient for a writer to present human behaviour and emotions vividly and persuasively. The modern author now needed to interpret and decipher such experiences, whether his own or those of his fictional characters, in order to reveal their hidden meaning:

> One experiences, but what one has experienced is like these negatives which show nothing but black until they have been held up before a lamp, and they, too, must be looked at from the reverse side; one does not know what it is until it has been held up before the intelligence. Only then, when one has thrown light upon it and intellectualized it can one distinguish – and with what effort – the shape of what one has felt.[54]

If Ortega y Gasset once defined Modernist painting, literature and music as constituting the 'dehumanization of art', remarking that, if many young men have fallen in love with La Gioconda, none has done so with a Cubist painting,[55] that axiom does not function effectively for literature, where Stephen Daedalus, Quentin Compson and Louis are anything but dehumanised forms, coming wonderfully alive, even though entirely Modernist in their stylistic presentation. They are so precisely because of this penetration into the inner world of their being and the psychological perception with which they are characterised, often in terms of projected authorial self-portraiture, including a new emphasis on the traumas of childhood experience:

'Now Miss Hudson,' said Rhoda, 'has shut the book. Now the terror is beginning. Now taking her lump of chalk she draws figures, six, seven, eight, and then a cross and then a line on the blackboard. What is the answer? The others look; they look with understanding.... But I cannot write. I see only figures.... The world is entire, and I am outside of it, crying, "Oh, save me from being blown for ever outside the loop of time!"'[56]

If such conscious and responsible application of psychological principles formed one response of the discomfited writer to the Freudian definition, a further phenomenon in both art and literature, tending in exactly the opposite direction, was no less indebted to Freud. Paul Klee has rightly been recognised as among the most intellectually sophisticated of artists working in this period. Selected by Walter Gropius to join the prestigious teaching staff at the Bauhaus, he produced astute pioneering essays on aesthetics and the new principles to be adopted by Modernism. In one such essay he urged the artist, when studying objects, 'by optico-physical means to deduce, from the exterior, conclusions of an affective nature which can intensify the impression of the phenomenon to the point of functional interiorization'.[57] If we today have become immune to the shock effects of Modernist art, it was no doubt difficult for his contemporaries to associate that intellectually ratiocinative passage with the producer of such 'infantile' paintings as his *Idol for House Cats*, or *Dance, You Monster, to my Soft Song* of 1922 (Figure 20). The subject matter seemed unbecoming for a sober artist, the drawing 'crude' by traditional standards, and the proportions of the figure absurd – a huge purple-nosed head resting on a tiny body. And such was, indeed, the general reaction. When the senior students of the Stuttgart Art Academy urged its governing body to appoint Klee to a teaching position, the governors rejected the proposal on the ground that the work he produced was 'frivolous'. But for those more perceptive students, responsive to the new theories, his attempt in such paintings and drawings to recall the imaginative world of the child and to employ it as a new model for art was welcomed as a serious project, paralleling the exploration of the subconscious in the work of Dali and Joyce. It echoed the remark by the Dadaist, Hugo Ball, that art should depict 'everything childlike and phantastic, everything childlike and direct, everything childlike and symbolical in opposition to the senilities of the world of grown-ups'.[58]

In an important study, some years ago, Robert Goldwater identified Klee's childlike drawings as attributable to the influence of
Primitivism in twentieth-century art, a continuation of the movement examined in an earlier chapter in connection with Gauguin
and Conrad.[59] But it is significant that, although he had been active
in the *Blaue Reiter* group since 1912, it was only in the 1920s that his
interest in such drawings became dominant. It was in the new
Freudian dispensation, whereby childhood traumas were seen to pre-
determine the configuration of the adult psyche, that Klee began to
resort to the child's vision of the world, a vision that might, he
believed, offer a more valid picture of human experience than that of
the adult inhibited by social pressures and the demands of rationality.
As Klee remarked to his colleague, Lothar Scheyer, rejecting the current censure of his work by the establishment:

> Child's play! Those gentlemen, the critics, often say that my
> pictures resemble the scribbles and messes of children. I hope they
> do! The pictures that my little boy Felix paints are often better than
> mine, because mine have often been filtered through the brain,
> which regrettably I cannot always avoid, as sometimes I work too
> much. We must serve honestly and loyally the shift of conscious-
> ness that our generation has experienced and experiences...[60]

As that closing comment suggests, he acknowledged the shift of
consciousness that psychology had introduced to his generation. It
is in that sense that the principle behind Klee's technique differed
fundamentally from the Wordsworthian concept of the child as
father to the man. That earlier idea, relying upon the Platonic theory
of *anamnesis*, had assumed that the child enters the mortal world
'trailing clouds of glory', still partly conscious of the truths of eternity
with which it had been in contact before birth, its sense of that lost
world becoming dulled as it matures. For Freud, in contrast, there
was no such enriching myth, no ideal truths in an eternity existing
outside the mortal; only a pathetically vulnerable child, susceptible
to fears and traumas that impressed themselves deeply upon the
mind and created the complexes and repressions liable to emerge as
neuroses in later life. Klee's painting attempts to capture that shift of
consciousness, the renewed respect for the simplicity of childhood
before those traumas have been experienced. In this painting,
a child seated at a piano is playing to an imagined monster – a monster lacking any terrifying or even threatening aspects, its clownish

quality implying the artist's desire to explore the emotions of childhood before fears and terrors, precursors of adulthood, have left
their mark. And the paintings of Klee's admirer Joan Miró, especially
his *Nursery Decorations* of 1938 and his play with biomorphic forms,
similarly aimed at capturing the fantasy world of childhood, the
naive and unschooled art of the very young. And clearly, both
instances represented not involuntary revelations of hidden repressions but conscious attempts on the part of mature adults to recreate
childhood experiences.

In literature the same phenomenon emerged. It was in the 1920s
that e. e. cummings, himself a practising painter closely following
contemporary movements in art, began publishing poems of which
some, like *Chanson Innocente*, sought to blend kindergarten thoughts
with the sophistication of experimental Modernist typography in
order to break through linguistic and metrical protocol and offer
a refreshingly new perception of the world. It captured the thought
processes of a child not yet trammelled by convention and, he
implies, not yet corrupted by society:

> in Just–
> spring when the world is mud–
> luscious the little
> lame balloonman
> whistles far and wee
>
> and eddieandbill come
> running from marbles and
> piracies and it's
> spring
>
> when the world is puddle-wonderful...[61]

In one of his best-known poems he employs the sing-song rhythms
of the nursery rhyme and the simplistic language of the kindergarten to create a caustic satire on a society that he, as a staunch indi-
vidualist, saw as crushing the natural love and altruism of mankind:

> anyone lived in a pretty how-town
> (with up so floating many bells down)
> spring summer autumn winter
> he sang his didn't he danced his did.

Women and men (both little and small)
cared for anyone not at all
they sowed their isn't they reaped their same
sun moon stars rain

children guessed (but only a few
and down they forgot as up they grew
autumn winter spring summer)
that noone loved him more by more...[62]

Just as the paintings of Klee and Miró questioned by implication the intellectual sophistications of Cubism, Expressionism and Surrealism, so Cummings, while preserving the standpoint of the adult, temporarily adopted the perspective of the child as a means of reassessing the mores of his generation. The self-centred hypocrisies of adulthood include, he suggests, an egocentricity that neglects the needs of the young; and, he wrily adds, even the child's perception 'that noone loved him' will itself be forgotten or repressed as it matures into the mendacious world of adulthood.

Here too, then, one may perceive the strategy whereby the withering implications of Freud's definition of the creative artist came to be countered by the painters and writers of the time, as they began to appropriate the function of the psychoanalyst in their work and thereby reestablish their self-respect as authentic creators, in place of being typecast as passive sublimators of hidden neuroses. The Dadaists in painting and poetry, and Joyce, Woolf and others in literature, reacted with dismay and even anger to the derogatory implications for art in Freud's identification of its neurotic source – hence the contemptuous comments or outright condemnation of psychology on the part of the artists themselves. Yet, paradoxically, they succeeded in denying those damaging implications by importing its principles into their own work, introducing thereby a new depth of characterisation to their creations and, not least, to their semi-autobiographical analyses of self. For in so doing they in effect reversed the Freudian definition, proving themselves to be not unconscious victims of hidden repressions but creative and discriminating observers and recorders of the complex inner motivations of human behaviour, both within their own personalities and within those of their fictitious figures.

Recognition of that process, moreover, reveals how far the dismaying challenge provided by Freud's definition determined the

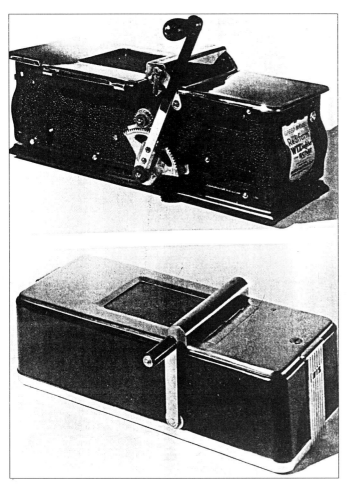

17. The 'Wiz' cash-register, before and after its remodelling by Walter Dorwin Teague.

18. Wright, Robie House, Chicago.

19. Dali, *Metamorphosis of Narcissus*.

20. Klee, *Dance, You Monster, to My Soft Song*.

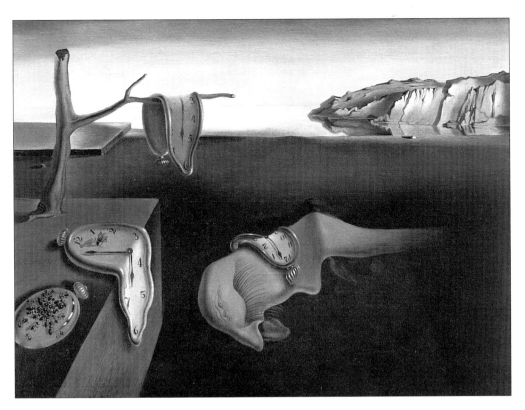

21. Dali, *The Persistence of Memory*.

22. Dali, *Apparition of Face and Fruit Dish on a Beach*.

23. Dali, *Slave Market with the Disappearing Bust of Voltaire.*

24. Escher, *Day and Night.*

25. Magritte, *Reproduction Prohibited*.

26. Dali, *Christ of St John of the Cross*.

27. Calder, Mobile.

28. Lewis, *The Crowd*.

29. Epstein, *Torso in metal from 'The Rock Drill'.*

30. Epstein, *The Risen Christ.*

31. Moore, *Mother and Child*.

32. Moore, *Two Forms*.

direction that painting and literature were to take at that time. If it initially produced a frustration with the revealed purposelessness of art, expressed within Dadaism as the artist's nihilistic rebellion against the basic principles and values of the profession, it led eventually, in Surrealism, to the remarkable paranoiac-critical paintings of Salvador Dali and, in literature, to the innovative stream-of-consciousness novels of Joyce and Woolf, offering thereby an essentially new view of the function of the artist.

6

The Twentieth-Century Dyad

With the Modernist focus upon inner experience, where incidents from the past involuntarily surge into the mind triggered either by mental association or by the promptings of some suppressed anxiety, time in terms of a fixed calendar or of a regularly advancing chronometer disintegrates. Even before Freud, Bergson had prepared the way by his identification of subjective chronology – *durée réelle*, he termed it – as being ultimately more valid than the measured variety. He had even, with remarkable foresight, suggested in his *Time and Free Will* (1889) that such a conception of inner time might form the basis for a new type of fiction, more true to human experience than traditional modes:

> Now, if some bold novelist, tearing aside the cleverly woven curtain of our conventional ego, shows us under this appearance of logic a fundamental absurdity, under this juxtaposition of simple states an infinite permeation of a thousand different impressions which have already ceased to exist the instant they are named, we commend him for having known us better than we knew ourselves.[1]

Bergson's growing influence during the early part of the century had merged into the Freudian, since both acknowledged the non-temporality of inner human experience and its ignoring of ordered sequence, as past arbitrarily impinges upon present within the uninterrupted flow of human thought. This questioning of logicality as the directing factor of the mind was reflected in science itself, which, as we have seen, had begun at this time to desert its basic precept of defining elements in fixed and measurable terms. Bohr's Principle of Complementarity now argued with a new sense of equivocality that the electron must be regarded both as a wave and as a particle, its nature fluctuating in accordance with its context; and quantum theory acknowledged the random unpredictability of the electrons as they leap, seemingly haphazardly, from orbit to orbit. It was in that setting that the sequence of human thought began to be seen as based not upon rational progression but upon a more arbitrary process of associative memory and experiential linkage. Wyndham Lewis cited an interesting parallel in the human response to music, which he contrasted with the examination of a statue. Although one may move around a work of sculpture and regard it from different view-points, the statue itself remains present in its entirety throughout the process; whereas music, at each individual moment, exists only as a single note or chord. 'When you are half-way through the piece of music, or it is halfway through you, if you did not *remember* what you had just heard you would be in the position of a clock ticking its minutes, all the other ticks except the present one no longer exist-ing.' It is thus only through our holding the previous notes in the mind and creating a context for the isolated note or chord that the music can be apprehended.[2] Analogously, human thought should be perceived as functioning not in terms of a logical advance from point to point, but by a process resisting sequential time, continually calling up the past in order to apprehend the present.

It was this altered perspective, it would seem, that Dali aimed to capture in his remarkable canvas *The Persistence of Memory* of 1931 (Figure 21). The scene he depicts there is the landscape of the psy-che, where clocks and watches, intended to record fixed time, 'melt' and droop, unable to function within this mental terrain. One time-piece drapes uselessly over a fetus-like figure, the latter representing the human mind linked irrevocably to the primal period of its shel-tered existence within the womb. As Virginia Woolf remarked of time in *Orlando* (1928):

> though it makes animals and vegetables bloom and fade with amazing punctuality, it has no such simple effect upon the mind of man.... An hour, once it lodges in the queer element of the human spirit, may be stretched to fifty or a hundred times its clock length; on the other hand, an hour may be accurately represented on the timepiece of the mind by one second.

That she saw this change as forming part of the new science is revealed by the image she employed in advocating the principle that should underlie modern fiction: 'Let us record the atoms as they fall, let us trace the pattern, however disconnected and incoherent in appear-ance, which each sight or incident scores upon the consciousness.'[3]

Jean Piaget, the cognitive psychologist, has shown that as a child
matures it learns to correct optical impressions by logical inference,
perceiving, for example, that when water is poured from a short
wide container into a tall thin one, the higher water level does not
indicate a larger quantity. In the mature adult, as part of this developing process, visual perception never functions alone but is always
structured by an operating mechanism that corrects and refines it so
that, for example, scenes recalled from the past and events perceived in the present are often cerebrally arranged into temporal
sequence. But it should be added to Piaget's theory that such controlling mechanism can itself undergo change in accordance with
the altered concepts of the period. Where Cubism and Surrealism
had created a new spatial perspective by according equal validity to
foreground, middle distance and background, allowing them to be
seen simultaneously as though through transparent planes of reality,
so the stream-of-consciousness novel began to replace the traditional
mechanism for separating past from present and for selectively clas-
sifying events into chronological order, and instead bestowed equal
and concurrent authenticity upon memory, upon present cognition
and upon mental association in a manner truer to the actual experience of the individual than was the order imposed by the mechanism of selectivity.[4]

In 1929, Faulkner's novel *The Sound and the Fury* gave fictional
expression to this rejection of rigid temporal progression. Quentin,
obsessed by incestuous thoughts linked to his childhood, sadly
reflects that clocks slay real – that is, subjective – time; that 'time is
dead as long as it is being clicked off by little wheels; only when the
clock stops does time come to life'. Symbolically, he tears off the
hands of the watch he has inherited from his grandfather:

> I went to the dresser and took up the watch, with the face still
> down. I tapped the crystal on the corner of the dresser and caught
> the fragments of glass in my hand and put them into the ashtray
> and twisted the hands off and put them in the tray. The watch
> ticked on. I turned the face up, the blank dial with little wheels
> clicking and clicking behind it, not knowing any better.

In that damaged form he carries it with him until the moment of his
suicide, a timepiece continuing its mechanical ticking but unable to
disturb by its strict chronometricality the feverish ranging of his
mind through past and present:

Thinking it would be nice for them down at New London if the weather held up like this. Why shouldn't it? The month of brides, the voice that breathed *She ran right out of the mirror, out of the banked scent. Roses. Roses. Mr and Mrs Jason Richmond Compson announce the marriage of. Roses.* Not virgins like dogwood, milkweed. I said I have committed incest, Father I said. Roses. Cunning and serene. If you attend Harvard one year, but don't see the boat-race there should be a refund ...[5]

Within the same novel Faulkner introduced, as an imaginative device representing this conflict, the 'idiot' boy Benjy, his impaired intelligence functioning by a process of association untrammelled by the regularity of clock or calendar, whose movements he cannot follow. As he and his attendant wander near a golf course, the word 'caddy' called out by a player conjures up for him from the distant past a desolating image of his sister Candace, known to him affectionately as Caddy, a sister comforting to him in his childhood but no longer with him. His inarticulate moaning is prompted by a mental connection incomprehensible to those around him, and by that incomprehensibility emphasising even further the isolation of the individual's inner experience from the prosaically fixed temporality of the outside world.

Bergson recognised that fluid inner time was an entity needing in some way to be related to the external world, expressed in language that does not formulate it as a rational process; and that perception had led him to remark that 'the writer's art consists above all in making us forget that he uses words. The harmony he sees is a certain correspondence between the movements of his mind and the phrasing of his speech, a correspondence so perfect that the undulations of his thought, borne by the sentence, stir us sympathetically; consequently, the words, taken individually, no longer count.'[6] It was a statement that may have held true for Virginia Woolf's mode of writing, where, as in a passage examined earlier, words seem to disintegrate as they enter the consciousness of the listener. But it was inapplicable to a further aspect of the new mode, of which Joyce's writing formed a main exemplar, where words, far from being forgotten as such, attained central significance in the form of verbal play based on assonance, connotation or mental correlation.

The emergence of such a mental correlation of words that, like memory, is seen to transcend the limits of time and place, was more closely related to Freudian theory than has been recognised. In that respect, this present chapter may be seen as an extension of the last, exploring a further aspect of the impact of psychology on literature and the arts. In this instance the effect upon them involved the convergence of two seemingly unconnected principles. The first, propounded in *The Psychopathology of Everyday Life* and arousing wide interest as it gradually percolated into the public consciousness, was Freud's revelation that both the forgetting of names and unintentional slips of the tongue should be seen not as fortuitous failures of memory nor the result of awkward articulation but as at all times dictated by subconscious stimuli, in certain cases indicative of grave psychic disturbance. The mind, in such instances, either suppresses an undesired recollection by temporary oblivion or diverts attention from it by substituting an alternative word, a word similar to it either in sound or association.

There are, he maintained, three main stages of development in this process. At the earliest stage, children tend to play with nonsense sounds that resemble in rhyme or rhythm words they have just learned; and they do so as a form of temporary rebellion, a resistance to the pressures of discipline and of rational thought. In subsequent years, that same process expresses itself in a more sophisticated form, in the indulgence in punning so characteristic of adolescents, such word substitution marking a reluctance to move from childish pleasures into adult responsibility. It constitutes an attempt to 'appease the protesting reason, which strives to suppress the pleasant feeling of play'. In the final or adult stage, wordplay marks a more mature desire for compromise, for a more fundamental reconciliation of these two antithetical impulses of reason and recreation by making possible that which reason forbids, that is, by allowing two different meanings or associations to exist concurrently.[7]

The second theory, published by Freud at almost the same time and producing no less an impact upon the broader public as its implications began to be absorbed, was his demonstration in *The Interpretation of Dreams* that essentially the same principle functions in sleep – the process of displacement or fantasy transference, whereby the memory, suppressing repugnant or perturbing incidents, again replaces them by surrogates, the ego acting as a censor and directing this strategy of substitution in a manner beyond the control of the dreamer.

The filaments connecting these two separate theories, filaments of especial relevance here, derive from the fact that the process of dream transference, like that of speech error, is frequently based on verbal resemblance – on assonance, alliteration or rhythmic similarities subliminally connecting the name or designation of the repressed object with its replacement. Both processes are thus dictated to a large extent by the merging of lexical substitutes.

In the German originals of his essays, Freud offered numerous examples of such subconscious wordplay; but those instances were either untranslatable or, at the very least, cumbersome in English. For that reason his translators, including James Strachey who edited the Collected Works, generally omitted them. But the leading translator of Freud's works into English prior to Strachey, the American Dr A. A. Brill, who was himself an experienced psychoanalyst, chose a different method, providing examples taken from his own English-speaking patients. In his 1913 translation of *The Interpretation of Dreams*, readers would have come across instances such as the following. A female patient recalled a particularly bizarre scene from a dream, her vision of a signboard bearing the seemingly incomprehensible message *'uclamparia – wet'*. The analyst explains that the message constituted a subconscious merging of lexical substitutes for the words, ideas and names that her conscious mind was afraid to confront:

> The word *'uclamparia'* then resolves itself into *eucalyptus* and *malaria*, and the word *wet* refers to the former swampy nature of the locality. Wet also suggests dry. *Dry* is actually the name of the man whom she would have married but for his over-indulgence in alcohol. The peculiar name of *Dry* is of Germanic origin (*drei* = three) and hence, alludes to the monastery of the Three (*drei*) Fountains.[8]

The science of linguistics has, in recent years, taken Freud's thesis as a starting point for numerous studies of polysemes, homophones and portmanteau words, instances in which one signifier has two or more possible signifieds; and a major conference on the semantic function of puns was organised in 1985 by Jonathan Culler.[9] But our interest here is less in the nature of puns themselves than in the aesthetic implications of Freud's insights, the influence they exerted upon literature and painting during the 1920s and 1930s as his theories began to be assimilated into the public consciousness.

The most striking effect of this process of transference, both verbal and non-verbal, was the sense of equivocality it introduced, the disturbing and yet stimulating recognition that words and objects

might, while retaining their own identity, be functioning simultaneously as metamorphosed substitutes for other words or objects.
Here too there was a parallel with the natural sciences as the latter
began to desert their trust in the reliability of empirical verification,
recognising that the apparently solid may be illusory. In such a
period there was an especial attraction in the realisation that language
and thought, too, might contain more than appears on the surface,
that however lucid and rational they might seem, they could often
comprise twofold or even multiple meanings concealed within the
text, meanings often mutually exclusive. Such verbal interchange,
Freud had demonstrated, possessed a very positive function, not
only in providing, by the process of substitution, a temporary deflection from the unpleasant but in offering thereby a valuable pointer
for the analyst in attempting to trace the cause of the hidden trauma:

> in a line of associations ambiguous words (or, as we may call
> them, 'switch-words') act like points at a junction. If the points are
> switched across from the position in which they appear to lie in
> the dream, then we find ourselves upon another set of rails; and
> along this second track run the thoughts which we are in search of
> and which still lie concealed behind the dream.[10]

It is surely within that contemporary context that Salvador Dali's
Apparition of Face and Fruit Dish on a Beach of 1938 (Figure 22) should
be seen, translating into art this new conception of the multiple signification of words and objects, whereby one reading or denotation
displaces the other while yet remaining present in the mind. Dali
had been impressed by Jean Arp's experiments in the 1920s, in
which he had attempted to create shapes concurrently suggestive of
more than one object, and Dali began to take the experiment further
in his own work. In this painting Dali provides a complex dream
vision in which each element seems to disappear and merge into
alternatives. The dog's head at the top right of the canvas becomes
transformed, as one gazes at it, into a river flowing past a rocky spur,
its collar, in that context, changing into an aqueduct; and as the eye
moves to the centre of the canvas the dog's body becomes metamorphosed into a fruit dish, which in its turn is optically displaced
by the emergence of a female face. In paranoiac phenomena, Dali
declared soon after discovering psychoanalytical theory, 'common
images have a double figuration – the figuration can be theoretically
and practically multiplied'. He envisaged at that time producing

a canvas (apparently never executed) in which 'six simultaneous images would be represented without any of them undergoing the least figurative deformation', the images blending into each other, just as fantasy transference in dreams provided substitutions of the originals even though the original painful object remained covertly present as the motive force of the scene.[11] A similar experiment was provided in his *Slave Market with the Disappearing Bust of Voltaire*, produced two years later (Figure 23), the group of figures in the centre, by visual sleight, interchangeably becoming a bust of Voltaire. With Voltaire as the classic representative of the Age of Reason, Dali here offers a subtle suggestion that the rational may be seen to disintegrate and dissolve in the thoughts of the figure meditating at the side of the scene.

Optical illusionism, or *trompe l'oeil*, had been employed often in previous eras, but its purpose there had been fundamentally different. In 1513 Baldassare Peruzzi, in the loggia of the Villa Farnesina, had painted on one wall a handsome verandah opening on to a broad vista of Rome. Carlo Carloni had, with similar realism, portrayed on a wall in the Villa Lechi near Brescia a majestic stairway with figures descending. But those depictions had a practical aim; they were intended to add a sense of grandeur, the optical illusion designed to enlarge visually the dimensions of the room, in the same way as Fra Pozzo's impressive ceiling fresco *The Glorification of St. Ignatius* of 1690 was designed to create the impression that the ceiling had opened up to provide a view of the vast heavens at that apocalyptic moment. Here, in contrast, the *trompe l'oeil* is intended not to persuade the viewer of its actuality, but to cast doubt. The viewer is invited to shift from one reading to another in order to be taken beyond the tactile world, where objects remain solid and static, into the world of psychological displacement, where items have dual or multiple signification as they merge into associate forms. There had indeed been certain instances in the past when *trompe l'oeil* had been intended to encourage a dual reading, but there too the purpose had been different. Hans Holbein's *The Ambassadors*, with its weird anamorphic image in the foreground, offers, as I have suggested elsewhere, a remarkable representation of contemporary concepts. In a frontal viewing it provides a picture of Renaissance achievement and splendour, the ermine robes and scientific instruments symbolising the power, wealth and learning to be attained in this world; but the viewer is invited also to gaze at the painting from the side, at an angle almost level with the surface of the canvas, when the anamorphic blur resolves itself into a skull, a reminder of the alternate view of this world in terms of *media vita in morte sumus*, as a mere corridor leading to the Day of Judgment.[12] The new usage introduced by Dali, however, has no connection with such Renaissance concerns. It is a response to an essentially new conception, arising from the fantasy substitutes disclosed as motivating mental processes.

The idea of multiplicity of meaning in Freudian psychology in fact goes beyond fantasy substitution. A turning point in the development of his theories was the moment, recorded in his *Interpretation of Dreams*, when Freud realised with astonishment that the central figure in his own 'Irma' dream was in fact a mental amalgam of *two* of his patients, Anna Lichtheim and Emma Eckstein.[13] To this discovery was added a further component, his discovery that while children recall their dreams with exactitude on awakening, the adult mind, at the moment of transition into the real world, imposes a censorship that suppresses or transforms aspects of the dream itself. The result is that the analyst must regard each element not merely as an act of substitution but as an element of multiple or layered significance. It is scarcely surprising that, as these concepts filtered through to the public, there arose a fundamentally new sense of the uncertainty of objects, which blend or dissolve their import as one gazes upon them.

It was during this same period of the 1930s, one may note, that M. C. Escher, whose works have become so popular in our own day, began experimenting with a type of graphic work that cast doubt on the reliability of human optics and demonstrated the uncertainty of visual verification.[14] A woodcut such as Figure 24, one of the first of those experiments, dating from 1937, is essentially an exercise in equivocation, the drawing susceptible to two mutually exclusive interpretations. It depicts with equal validity a flight of white birds moving to the right against a dark background and, alternatively, of dark birds moving to the left against a light background, the merger occurring in the centre where each individual bird can be 'read' either as background or foreground. The eye, unable to grasp both interpretations simultaneously, shifts uncomfortably from one impression to the other, sensing that each reading, while temporarily excluding its alternative, nonetheless acknowledges the other's authenticity. It was a technique that was to reach its culmination in his famed representation of two life-like hands, each holding a pencil and drawing the other, so that each is seen both as the creative hand of the artist and as the artifact produced by it.

Nor were Escher and Dali alone in responding to this cultural shift. The paintings of the latter's colleague, René Magritte, often regarded by the public as mere entertaining oddities, have in recent years come to be recognised by historians as of far deeper significance, especially as he was highly cognisant of contemporary art movements, having himself experimented with Cubism, Futurism and Art Deco, and having become part of the Dada group before developing his own interests. His graphic depiction in 1926, for example, of a smoker's pipe above the seemingly absurd statement 'This is not a pipe', was, Foucault has pointed out, an extraordinary adumbration of postmodernist theory, paralleling the contemporary work of Wittgenstein (with whom Magritte had not then come into contact). As the provocative rubric of the painting declares and as we come to recognise after a moment's thought, what we see is indeed not a pipe; it is only the *depiction* of a pipe. In that, he anticipated the theory of representationalism, the concept, advocated by Gombrich in the 1960s and by the semioticists at approximately the same time, that words and pictures are not equivalents or fixed substitutes for objects or ideas but merely signs suggestive of them, loosely connected and needing to be interpreted by the receptor.[15] The title Magritte assigned to the painting, *The Treachery of Images*, leaves no doubt that those implications were intentional.

On the other hand, what has not been sufficiently acknowledged is the connection between the teasing equivocality of his canvases and the new Freudian theories. His paintings and their titles frequently employ the kind of wordplay Freud was then focusing upon, constituting visual puns connected with the subject matter of the paintings – as in *Le Soir qui tombe* of 1934, with its droll suggestion that the 'fall' of evening has shattered the glass window. The marks of the landscape still attached to the broken glass again undermine here the mimetic tradition of the picture as a window on reality.

Even more interestingly, he toys in his canvases with the principle of fantasy substitution. A favourite theme in his work is the dislodgement of the familiar and its replacement by those mental associations the object evokes – such as his depiction of a rifle incongruously dripping with blood; and such associations at times create new entities. One of his most effective treatments of that theme was *The Rape* of 1934. It depicts a woman's face in which the normal features have been replaced by erogenic portions of her body – her eyes consisting of twin breasts, her nose replaced by a navel, her mouth by a mound of pubic hair. The painting both portrays and at the same time parodies the male's vision of the female as sex-object. It represents a mental superimposition of covert desire upon actuality, a supplanting of the real by the meta-real, the two views of the female existing, as in Dali's work, concurrently and yet independently; for although only the erotic dream vision is displayed on the canvas, its dislodgement of the norm inevitably induces recollection of the standard female visage, allowing the two to coexist in the mind of the viewer.[16]

That duality or dyad, the impinging of the psychological upon the actual, is hinted at in another of his paintings from this period, his *Reproduction Prohibited* of 1937 (Figure 25), where a figure gazing into a mirror confronts not the reflection of his face but a vision of the back of his own head, even though the book on the shelf is reflected mimetically. Here too the artist is not being facetious, but would seem to be expressing a changed concept. In contrast to such traditional self-portraits as those by Da Vinci, Dürer and Rembrandt, the assumption that a person's facial features provide a key to personality has here been discarded. Like the characters in Virginia Woolf's novels, Magritte's figure contemplates what has now become a more important indication of individuality, the thoughts passing through his own mind, gazing, as it were, at the back of his own head. Where the nineteenth-century novel customarily introduced its characters by a detailed description of their physical appearance, the human countenance being seen as offering clues to personal traits:

> her brow was broad and fine, her grey eyes were bright and full of intelligence, her nose and mouth were well formed, and there was not a mean feature in her face. But there was withal a certain roughness about her...[17]

for the new generation of writers, focusing upon the flow of unarticulated thought, external appearance had come to be regarded as a mere façade. As T. S. Eliot had noted in a phrase fundamental for an understanding of the Modernist era, individuals no longer establish rapport on meeting but remain isolated within themselves, able only to 'prepare a face to meet the faces that you meet'. Only the masks of personality make visual contact while the complex inner beings, the psyches remain insulated from view, locked up, as it were, behind a protective externality. Accordingly the authorial voice of the earlier novel is replaced by an internalised, subjective rendition of self, as in *The Waves*, a rendition of the stream of ideas and sensations passing through the mind and unperceived by the other characters in the novel. In Magritte's painting the displacement of the facial reflection by a view of the back of his head once again allows both images to remain simultaneously in the spectator's mind, creating a suggestive interplay between the conventional facial self-portrait and the new concern with interior monologue.

To return to the more specifically Freudian concept of shifting ambivalence (as reflected in Dali's *Apparition of a Face* and *Voltaire*) and its concomitant, verbal substitution, one may perceive counterparts in literature even before the exuberant wordplay of *Finnegans Wake*. Stephen in the *Portrait*, representing the author during his early years, plays with words in the manner Freud had attributed to that stage of adolescence, their sounds blending and separating in his mind with little relation to their meaning. But now that Stephen is beginning to mature, to emerge from that pre-adult stage, such wordplay reliant upon assonance or alliteration tends to exasperate him by the mere nonsense it creates:

> His own consciousness of language was ebbing from his brain and trickling into the very words themselves which set to band and disband themselves in wayward rhythms:
>
> > *The ivy whines upon the wall*
> > *And whines and twines upon the wall . . .*
>
> Did any one ever hear such drivel? Lord Almighty! Who ever heard of ivy whining on a wall?[18]

Hugh Kenner's influential study, *The Pound Era*, attributed Joyce's growing interest in wordplay to contemporary developments within philology, noting that while Samuel Johnson had regarded words as fixed entities, more recent lexicographers such as Skeat had come to see them as more malleable, evolving from generation to generation.[19] But that philological change does not account for Joyce's delight in deliberately fusing words together, in creating new verbal entities pregnant with manifold allusions. The source for that tendency lay, it would seem, in the psychological principle of verbal substitution. Indeed Joyce made that debt explicit in a statement to his friend Edmond Jaloux, stating that in his prospective novel,

Ulysses, he intended to employ the dream process of verbal transference as the basis for his narrative experiment. The new novel, he claimed would be designed to suit the esthetic of the dream, where the forms prolong and multiply themselves, where the visions pass from the trivial to the apocalyptic, 'where the brain uses the roots of vocables to make others from them which will be capable of naming its phantasms, its allegories, its allusions'.[20] The unfettered sequence of ideas within the new novel would thus rely, in part at least, upon mental associations triggered by verbal correspondence. But as the above comment indicates, such associations would be dependent not on chance but on the hidden 'phantasms' for which they were to serve as surrogates. Accordingly, lexical transmutation appears frequently in *Ulysses*, correlations of similar-sounding words, seemingly fortuitous, producing combinations resonant with meaning, matching associations of deep import: 'His lips lipped and mouthed fleshless lips of air: mouth to her womb, Oomb, all wombing tomb' – the final assonance echoing the birth/death theme central to the novel at large.

Such verbal mergers in Joyce's work, as well as his irrepressible indulgence in puns, have often been attributed by critics to his admiration of a similar practice in the writings of Lewis Carroll. But there is, one should note, a fundamental difference in the function of such wordplay. Carroll's writings, the avocation of a professional mathematician, are essentially a play with logic, such as his droll assumption that 'mock turtle soup' entails the existence of a Mock Turtle, or the Mad Hatter's objection to Alice's cruelty in 'beating Time' in music. It is a surface play, a transference of verbal meanings free from serious undercurrents. As Humpty Dumpty remarked in a comment beloved of modern linguists, he used words to mean anything he chose them to mean, and always paid them extra for carrying especially heavy loads. His wordplay, he implies, is thus entirely arbitrary. In contrast, the emergence of such verbal elisions in Joyce's work, concurrent with the illusionist experiments of Arp and Dali and the visual punning of Magritte, have a more contemporary motivation, importing the mechanism of subconscious displacement, which Freud had revealed as functioning, often with profound significance, within the human psyche.

That concept of transference in the thought processes of his characters emerges in Joyce's writings not only in the form of wordplay but also as visual substitution, as when Bloom, gazing at a dog, finds his subconscious transforming it into the figure of his late father, its shaggy canine coat being metamorphosed into beard and caftan:

> The retriever approaches sniffing, nose to the ground. A sprawled form sneezes. A stooped bearded figure appears garbed in the long caftan of an elder in Zion and a smokingcap with magenta tassels. Horned spectacles hang down at the wings of the nose. Yellow poison streaks are on the drawn face. (p. 357)

To connect such images with Joyce's poor eyesight, as John Gordon does,[21] or even with the influence of film montage, is to miss their deeper significance. The father image, with which Bloom is obsessed throughout the work, here forces its way uninvited into his consciousness, imposing itself upon the actual object perceived.

There was, however, another area in which Freud's concept of verbal relationships and name substitution was to have a major impact, namely the sphere of literary analysis and criticism. In Freud's *Wit and its Relation to the Unconscious*, published in 1905 and translated into English in 1922, wordplay continued to occupy a central position. But in that work he introduced an additional aspect of considerable significance – the doctrine that such verbal displacement often involves a process of condensation, for which Freud cited Shakespeare as his authority, the axiom that 'brevity is the soul of wit'. Such wit, Freud suggested, involves not the substitution of a disturbing idea, its removal from the person's memory as in the case of *'uclamparia'*, but its temporary displacement into a subordinate position, with both the substitute and the original being simultaneously acknowledged:

> If we delve more deeply into the variety of 'manifold application' of the same word, we suddenly notice that we are confronted with forms of 'double meaning' or 'plays on words' which are universally acknowledged as belonging to the technique of wit.

Irony, defined by him as a subspecies of the comic, exploits this duality more patently, as the speaker or writer expresses the opposite of what he intends while negating the impression by an inflection of voice, by a concomitant gesture or, in literary versions, by stylistic hints that countermand the more explicit text, both elements being present concurrently. But his main concern in this work is with

condensation of double meanings into a single word, which function, as does irony, by a process of dyad, by the compression of
divergent or opposite ideas. As a very simple illustration of the latter
type, he quotes the story of Louis XV, who asked a courtier known
for his wit to concoct a joke, this time about the monarch himself.
Realising the danger involved, the courtier neatly sidestepped the
request with a pun, remarking that 'A King is not a *subject*'.

Although the connection has never been noted by historians, it
was surely not fortuitous that William Empson's seminal study,
Seven Types of Ambiguity, appeared at this time – in 1930, shortly after
the English publication of Freud's study – ushering in a fundamentally new approach to literature, and creating in effect a revolution
in critical theory that was to lead to the emergence of New Criticism.[22] The reputation of that critical school has been somewhat
eclipsed in recent years by the advent of postmodernism, with structuralism, semiotics and deconstruction often questioning its basic
tenets; but as Frank Lentricchia acknowledged in his *After the New
Criticism*, that earlier approach has been neither disqualified nor
rejected, remaining like a powerful father figure looming over the
present scene.[23]

Our interest here, however, lies less in the intrinsic merits of New
Criticism than in its place in history, the situation at the time of its
appearance and the relationship of its new practices to the themes we
have been examining. In that regard, even the most committed oppon-
ents of New Criticism would acknowledge the enormous advance
it represented over the attitudes prevailing before its advent. The
function of the literary critic, as represented by such eminent scholars as George Saintsbury and Sir Arthur Quiller-Couch, had not
been to provide close analyses of specific works, nor to develop critical principles for distinguishing good literature from bad, but rather
to pronounce authoritatively, to guide opinion on the basis of their
own enlightened and discriminating judgment. They tended, in the
tradition of Samuel Johnson, to dogmatise, employing a commanding rhetoric to convince the reader of the efficacy of their judgment,
Saintsbury offering, for example, the categorical and unsupported
statement:

> Pope is much more superficial than Young; yet some of those who
> hold Pope's poetry cheapest as poetry, would confess that they
> never tire of the special pleasure which, as literature, it is fitted to
> give and does give to them.[24]

The lack of any clear guidelines for determining how literature functions produced lamentable results. I. A. Richards, astonished to discover the inability of intelligent university students to agree even on the simplest level of meaning in a poem, began in the 1920s to search for more firmly based criteria, his *Practical Criticism* recommending closer attention to prosody and to a questioning of stock responses. But it was only with the appearance of Empson's book that a new basis for literary analysis could be seriously developed. In fact the innovative approach of his book can be traced directly to the impact of the new psychoanalytical principles, coinciding with the emergence of the parallel phenomenon in the arts, the visual ambiguities in the works of Dali and Magritte that we have been examining. Empson himself mentioned explicitly that he was exploring in that book 'an association of opposites such as would interest the psycho-analyst'.[25]

The keyword in Empson's title, *Ambiguity*, challenged the previously pejorative associations of that term, the assumption hitherto that any double meaning within a literary work was either an unconscious error on the part of the writer or mere adolescent humour. The classic instance in that regard was Johnson's castigation of Shakespeare, over whose mind, he argued, a 'quibble' (as the doctor disdainfully termed such wordplay) held a malignant power. 'A quibble poor and barren as it is, gave him such delight, that he was content to purchase it by the sacrifice of reason, propriety, and truth. A quibble was to him the fatal Cleopatra for which he lost the world and was content to lose it.'[26] Empson now argued, in direct contrast, that such ambiguity functioned as one of the most basic ingredients of literature at its best and, no less important, that an appreciation of that ingredient could provide an extraordinarily valuable tool for analysis. As Lacan has developed that theory for us in post-structuralist terms, relying heavily upon the Freudian distinction between the ego and the unconscious, language is to be seen as consisting not of firmly defined signs but as a collection of sliding, multiply relevant signifiers. Our desire in reading a text for some ultimately gratifying reality provided by the author is constantly frustrated, to be replaced by a sense of paradox.[27] And it was that paradox in literature, the richness of a more complex view of the world, that Empson first revealed.

The filaments connecting his literary interest with contemporary psychoanalytic theory can in fact be clearly traced. Robert Graves, who had suffered from shell shock during the war, became, in the course of his medical treatment, familiar with the new theories through his analyst W. H. Rivers, a disciple of Freud; and Graves soon began applying those principles to literary criticism. It was his revelation, in a study published in collaboration with Laura Riding in 1929, of the multiple meanings in Shakespeare's sonnet 'The expense of spirit...' that inspired Empson to embark on his own challenging venture, extending that approach to an examination of the equivocal elements in poetry at large and the frequent condensation of disparate concepts even within a single word.[28]

He revealed, as a result, a previously unobserved verbal intricacy in literature and, just as importantly, offered thereby a more object-ive and hence more scientific method of analysis. In *Measure for Measure*, for example, he perceived, compressed into a single word, not only a hint of the subsequent development of plot (that is, the dramatist's subtle preparation of his audience for what is to follow) but also, as part of Shakespeare's insight into character, Claudio's unconscious revelation of his submerged motive in sending his sister to plead with Angelo for his life. Claudio urges Lucio to

> Acquaint her with the danger of my state;
> Implore her in my voice, that she make friends
> To the strict deputy; bid herself assay him.
> I have great hope in that; for in her youth
> There is a prone and speechless dialect
> Such as move men.

The word *prone* here, Empson noted, means not only 'tending to' or 'prone to' but also lying on one's back as with a lover, a foreshadow-ing of the sexual attraction she will exert over Angelo. Similarly, in the opening line of a Holy Sonnet by Donne, *What if this present were the world's last night?* he discerned the conflation of two separate and quite contradictory meanings, both of them integral to the poem. *What if...*, he pointed out, can be read as an exclamation of alarm, expressing the speaker's dread at the prospect of an immediate con-frontation with the Day of Judgment; yet it can also, he added, be read in a manner adumbrating the poem's concluding trust in divine mercy, a shrugging off of such concern, in the sense of *So what if...?* with the latter reading expressing confidence that all will be well. In poems of wit, Empson remarked, such duality functions with especial force, providing twofold readings which add to the effectiveness of the lines, as when Belinda wins at cards in Pope's *Rape of the Lock*:

> The Nymph exulting fills with Shouts the Sky,
> The Walls, the Woods, and long Canals reply.
> Oh thoughtless Mortals! ever blind to Fate,
> Too soon dejected, and too soon elate!
> Sudden, these honours shall be snatch'd away,
> And curs'd for ever this Victorious Day.

The word *reply*, he noted, can be read transitively or intransitively, the subsequent lines to be regarded either as an interpolated authorial comment proclaiming the moral message, or as the delayed object of the word *reply*, as a choric response by the environs of Hampton Court, accustomed as they are to witnessing the fall of favourites and the brevity of human glory – both readings functioning simultaneously to reinforce the mock-epic message.

   This concern with 'wit' was to become central in the criticism and poetry of Empson's time, not least in his own poems, such as the play with 'symbol' and 'retort' (the glass tube in the laboratory) and the double meaning of 'force' within this stanza from his 'Bacchus':

> The laughing god born of a startling answer
> (Cymbal of clash in the divided glancer
> Forcing from heaven's the force of earth's desire)
> Capped a retort to sublime earth by fire . . .

What emerges from these and similar instances of wordplay is that, to the alert reader, both readings are concurrently present, functioning with the same alternating, mutual exclusivity as the contrary views elicited by the Dali paintings. The effect of Empson's book was so widespread that, by 1936, I. A. Richards could declare categorically:

> the old Rhetoric treated ambiguity as a fault in language, and hoped to confine or eliminate it; the new Rhetoric sees it as an inevitable consequence of the power of language and as an indispensable means of most of our important utterances.[29]

In Cleanth Brooks' *The Well-Wrought Urn*, that critical process reached its culmination with his contention that poetry at its best employs the 'language of paradox', exploiting the connotations and associations of words to merge and eventually harmonise essentially antithetical concepts. By noting, for example, that in the sixteenth and seventeenth centuries the word *die* carried the connotative meaning of sexual intercourse (in a belief that each sexual act shortened one's life), he revealed a subtlety and resonance in the lines from Donne's 'Canonization' that had previously been missed, a daring blending of the sexual act with the Resurrection, both sharing in a sense of ecstasy, of rising above the physical into the spiritual :

> Wee dye and rise the same, and prove
> Mysterious by this love.

> Wee can dye by it, if not live by love.
> And if unfit for tombes or hearse
> Our legend bee, it will be fit for verse;[30]

That perception of enriched double-meaning, the merger within the word *die* of the seemingly inconsistent ideas of procreation and decease, took on a deeper force for Brooks' generation in the light of Freud's revelation of the perpetual conflict between the life instinct and the death wish within the human personality. It was this proclivity of the Metaphysical poets to express the paradoxes of the human situation through such dualities that accounted to no small extent for the spectacular rise in their popularity during the 1930s and 1940s – those same poets who had in the past been condemned for this very failing, for producing verse in which, as Johnson had remarked disapprovingly, 'the most heterogeneous ideas are yoked by violence together'. The new interest in verbal paradox, in the fruitful ambiguity of contrasting meanings and connotations, endeared these poets to a generation made newly aware of the discordant elements constantly warring within the human psyche, and the role played, in the mechanism of fantasy transference, by verbal condensation, syllabic inversion and wordplay. Puns were no longer aberrations or childish 'quibbles', but seen as deeply serious attempts to explore the contradictory yet intertwined worlds of the corporeal and the etherial, as in the lines:

> Dull sublunary lovers love
> (Whose soul is *sense* cannot admit
> *Absence*, because it doth remove
> Those things which elemented it.[31]

or the ironic contrast in the double meaning of 'vain' ('self-pride' and 'in vain') in the opening line of Marvell's *Garden*, a duality reinforced by the use of 'upbraid'('to rebuke' as well as 'to bind') in relation to the athletes' 'Toyles' ('toiling' and 'toiletry') towards the close of the stanza:

> How vainly men themselves amaze
> To win the Palm, the Oke or Bayes;
> And their incessant Labours see
> Crown'd from some single Herb or Tree.
> Whose short and narrow verged Shade
> Does prudently their Toyles upbraid;

Nor was the principle seen as restricted to the seventeenth century but valid for all eras, as in Blake's lines:

> How the chimney-sweeper's cry
> Every blackening church appalls...

where Brooks perceived that the chimney sweeper's cry not only shocks the church but at the same time throws a *pall* over it, denoting it as dead.[32]

T. S. Eliot's advocacy of the Metaphysical poets, as recorded in an earlier chapter, relied in part upon his perception that they acknowledged a reality beyond the tactile, and were able effectively to integrate that supernatural world with the physicalities of everyday human experience, to hold the two entities in a mutually enhancing relationship. But his perception of the method whereby they conveyed the duality of existence was perhaps even more influential for the future development of twentieth-century poetry, when he identified as one of their main and most admirable characteristics their 'telescoping of... multiplied associations'. Such compression of images, often their condensation within one word, demanded a form of mental and verbal dexterity that Eliot saw as essentially different from that of other writers, a distinct kind of 'wit' exemplified by the Puritan, Andrew Marvell, a wit that needed in the twentieth century to be revalidated for his own generation:

> Wit is not a quality that we are accustomed to associate with 'Puritan' literature, with Milton or with Marvell. But if so, we are at

fault partly in our conception of wit and partly in our generaliza-
tions about the Puritans. And if the wit of Dryden or of Pope is not
the only kind of wit in the language, the rest is not merely a little
merriment or a little levity ...

He defined that earlier version as a special 'agility' of mind, a rapid
association of thought establishing connections not normally implicit in the words or images used.[33]

Such seventeenth-century wit might at times be humorous in
intent, but more often expressed a profound sense of the paradoxicality of the universe, a religious faith in spiritual ambiguities
that transcend the limitations of physical reality and outreach the
bounds of time and space. In Donne's verse, such twofold images –
evoking the Christian God both in corporeal form at Calvary and as
deity controlling the vast universe – are merged by means of
intensely serious wordplay, the 'poles' signifying at one level the
spars of the wooden cross and at the same time the poles of the universe, the nadir and zenith of the vast cosmos:

> Could I behold those hands which span the poles,
> And tune all spheres at once, pierced with those holes?[34]

How far such double vision, this sense of a twofold authenticity of
viewpoint, affected the twentieth century may be seen in the painting produced by Dali during his religious phase, his impressive
Christ of St John of the Cross (Figure 26), which, based on a tradition
close to that of Donne's time, as the title suggests, captures that same
sense of lambent duality, of a Crucifixion that, at one and the same
time depicts Christ in the flesh nailed to the cross and as a divine
entity reigning over the universe.

While this new concept of ambiguity was being absorbed into the
analytical apparatus of the critic, it was beginning to emerge concurrently in the literary works appearing during the early decades
of the century, as this validation of the dyad began to permeate
the consciousness of creative writers. Ford Madox Ford had been
amongst the earliest authors to employ such new theories in his
writings, perhaps because his strong German connections allowed
him to come into contact with Freudian theories even before their
appearance in English translation. His fictional trilogy on the love of
Katherine Howard and Henry VIII in fact forestalled Lytton Strachey in its application of psychological insights to historical figures.

But in his finest novel, *The Good Soldier: a tale of passion*, published in 1917, this sense of ambiguity functions as its most distinguishing quality. The novel is animated by the author's ironic use of an obtuse narrator, a narrator sexually dispassionate yet recounting a tale of unbridled sexual lust, perplexed by the contradictions and incongruities in his tale, and thereby conveying a sense not only of the irresolvable enigma of human affairs but also of the possibility of viewing the same events from quite contrary, yet perhaps equally valid viewpoints:

> Upon my word, yes, our intimacy was like a minuet, simply because on every possible occasion and in every possible circumstance we knew where to go, where to sit . . .
>
> No, by God it is false! It wasn't a minuet that we stepped – it was a prison – a prison full of screaming hysterics, tied down so that they might not outsound the rolling of our carriage wheels as we went along the shaded avenues of the Taunus Wald.
>
> And yet I swear by the sacred name of my creator that it was true. It was true sunshine; the true music; the true plash of the fountains . . . [35]

If here the equivocality lies in the process of narration, that process reflected a change in the contemporary attitude to love itself. In his discussion of infantile sexuality, Freud had noted the polarity that develops during a child's early years, a polarity adumbrating the mingling of sadism and affection that would, he argued, manifest itself in the adult experience. It is of some significance that the term *ambivalence*, soon adopted by literary critics in place of Empson's use of the still-pejorative *ambiguity*, was borrowed directly from the world of psychology. On first discussing this phenomenon of mingled sadism and affection, Freud had explained that the symptom had been 'happily designated by Bleuler by the term *ambivalence*', and the word now entered the vocabulary of the critic. Virginia Woolf remarked in 1939:

> It was only the other day when I read Freud for the first time that I discovered that this violently disturbing conflict of love and hate is a common feeling and is called ambivalence. [36]

And she noted how relevant the term was to her own condition, remarking in a letter written that same year, 'I dislike this excitement, yet enjoy it. Ambivalence as Freud calls it . . .' [37]

There had been precedents in earlier eras – as there were, of course, for all the patterns of behaviour that psychoanalysis had begun to classify and label – but the simultaneous experiencing of contradictory emotions had in previous generations been regarded as an aberration, in no sense a behavioural norm. Catullus, lamenting the incongruity of his passion for Lesbia, acknowledged in touching terms the sense of wonder it would arouse in the reader of his poem:

Odi et amo, quare id faciam	I love and I hate. Perhaps you will ask
fortasse requiris. nescio	Why this is so. I do not know;
sed fieri sentio et excrucior.	But that it is so, I feel and am tormented.

And in Trollope's 1865 novel of a young lady drawn towards a cousin whom she both idolises and abhors, whom she dislikes intellectually yet finds in some strange way attractive, her predicament is presented throughout as an unfortunate abnormality for which it may be difficult for the reader to experience any sympathy, as the title, *Can You Forgive Her?* indicates. But the concept of the paradoxicality of the love experience, the essential equivocality of human passion, was in fact to emerge during the Modernist period as a primary constituent. We have already mentioned Dali's repeated affirmation of his passionate affection for his mother coupled with his vicious antipathy towards her, a complex relationship vividly expressed in his paintings. And within literature, such love–hate relationships began to be accepted as a norm, functioning in fact as a primary theme in D. H. Lawrence's novels. In *The Rainbow*, the conflicting and often simultaneous sensations of attraction and repulsion, of tenderness and cruelty, swiftly alternating or emanating concurrently in a manner unprecedented in the nineteenth-century novel, denote the dyadic quality of human experience that Freud had revealed to his age:

> She lifted her shoulders and turned aside her face in a motion of cold, indifferent worthlessness. He felt he would kill her.
> When she had roused him to a pitch of sadness, when she saw his eyes all dark and sad with suffering, then a great suffering overcame her soul, a great, inconquerable suffering. And she loved him. For oh, she wanted to love him. Stronger than life or death was her craving to be able to love him; and at such moments, when he was mad with her destroying him, when all his

complacency was destroyed, all his everyday self was broken, and only the stripped, rudimentary, primal man remained, demented with torture, her passion to love him became love, she took him again, they came together in an overwhelming passion.... But it all contained a developing germ of death.[38]

Such ambivalence came to be acknowledged, therefore, in the realm of emotional relationships. Within the specific area of verbal dualisms, Joyce's *Finnegans Wake* was, in due course, to consummate this interest, proving that the exploitation of lexical association and connotation could function effectively not only in the realm of poetry, as closely explored by Empson and Brooks, but in prose too, a genre that until then had not been especially associated with semantic subtleties. In his earlier work, Joyce had occasionally revealed his penchant for the enriching effects of wordplay. In the funeral scene from *Ulysses* quoted earlier, Bloom, visualising a death-bed scene, is reminded of the cautionary picture familiar to the Catholics amongst whom he lived, a picture in which the Devil, attempting to trap the moribund patient into devoting his final moments to lust instead of repentance, taunts him with the vision of a voluptuously naked woman. Bloom comments drolly that the unfortunate victim was '*Dying* to embrace her in his shirt', the pun once again playing on the merger of the procreative life instinct with the death wish, the poignancy here reinforced by Bloom's suppressed fear of his own death, which motivates the passage at large.

That dualism within the human psyche, with its frequent expression through wordplay in terms of a subconscious fantasy transference seeking for associative, similar-sounding substitutes, found its fullest literary acknowledgment in *Finnegans Wake*. The work is presented as a dream sequence, in which the half-dozing mind, only partially grasping the names, ideas, and allusions flowing through it, uninhibitedly splices them into multilingual puns and hybrid hapaxlegomena, such as references to 'abcdminded' readers or 'the Great Shapesphere'. Those syntheses, sanctioned by psychoanalysis, are no longer to be regarded as inconsequential slips but as valid, if often amusing insights into the subconscious personality of the thinker. The dreamer here, tired of his wife, has hopes of a last fling with some younger woman, his thoughts turning incestuously to his own daughter. But the closest his mind can approach the intimidating word *incest* is, by consonantal transposition, through the word *insect*, suggesting his own suppressed disgust at the despicable direction his thoughts have taken. Accordingly, and arising in part from that word substitution, the name he sleepily adopts for himself – Humphrey Chimpden Earwicker – indicates the hidden promptings of his conscience, the hump of guilt that he acknowledges, and the reduction of his human dignity to the level of ape or insect. And from his subconscious arise also the irreverent recastings of society's clichés in such phrases as 'The flushpots of Euston and the hanging garments of Marylebone.' The presence of an author sensed by the reader as existing behind that dream account, consciously controlling and manipulating it, in no way detracts from the authenticity accorded to the new principles of psychology, since the fecund verbal capering throughout the dream account offers a glimpse of the correlation of ideas existent in Joyce's own mind. If Joyce is ultimately to be credited for the ingenious substitutions attributed to his dreamer, the results are no less fascinating to read than if they had belonged to his fictional character.

Often within the work, such verbal transference results in sly humour, as in the sleepy inversion, 'Where the bus stops there shop I', which belongs within that new concept of wit as condensation that had manifested itself in the criticism and poetry of the time – in this instance amusingly contrasting Ariel's celebration of the freedom and joys of nature with the commercial activities of a later, urban generation. Such wit involves a new respect for mental ingenuity, often as two or more verbal meanings appear to contradict each other but are enrichingly reconciled. In the work of Joyce's colleague, Samuel Beckett, that sense of equivocation was to reach its consummation as, in his prose trilogy and in the plays, his speakers repeatedly negate in the second half of their statements what had been asserted in the first, in a manner suggesting the ultimate paradoxality of all experience:

Winnie: Oh this is a happy day! This will have been another happy day! [pause] After all. [pause] So far.[39]

In the plastic arts, that sense of ambiguity was to find parallel expression not only in the paintings cited above but also in a medium that might seem singularly uncongenial to such experimentation – the medium of sculpture. Wit, especially when reliant upon paradox, functions on the principle of ideas that appear to clash, yet surprisingly resolve their conflict at the last moment, reconciling the contradictions once the element of compatibility is discerned. Describing Belinda's toilet in the *Rape of the Lock*, Pope comments, 'The Tortoise here and Elephant unite' – creating a monstrous image of incongruous copulation. But the incongruity is happily resolved by the explanation in the following line: 'Transformed to *Combs*, the speckled and the white' (2: 135–6). It was in the early 1930s that Alexander Calder began to introduce his innovative 'mobiles' (as Duchamp was to name them). Closely associated with Arp and Picasso during his lengthy stays in Paris, as well as with the Constructivist Naum Gabo, Calder developed his sculpture into one of the earliest forms of kinetic art, producing figures or flanges moved by mechanical propulsion or, in a second stage of his constructions, by the wind. In such mobiles as the one produced in 1936 (Figure 27), varied shapes move in subtle relationship to each other as they turn in the breeze, repeatedly threatening – like the disparate meanings of ambivalent words – to be about to collide, yet gracefully avoiding conflict as their carefully balanced movement ensures an ultimately integrated and harmoniously devised art-work. They were in a very real sense not only manifestations of wit, constructs demonstrative of mental agility and ingenious design, but expressions within the plastic arts of the same qualities as were now being demanded from poetry.

By interweaving such assumptions into the fabric of the artifact, the two media once again succeeded in producing modes responsive to the changing concepts of the time. The incorporation of the theory of fantasy substitution into the paintings of Dali and Magritte, with the consequent ambiguity of viewer response resulting from the mutual exclusivity of the alternating readings, expressed their awareness of a profound duality now revealed within the human imagination and within the human subconscious. And in the same way, the discovery that verbal transference fulfilled a central function in that process of mental substitution opened the way for an essentially new form of literary analysis and, by extension, of literature itself, a focus in New Criticism upon the hitherto unrecognised exploitation by poets of the submerged connotations and associations of words. Just as the psychoanalyst searched for the recondite idea or object suppressed by the fantasy substitute, so the critic now scrutinised the poem for the hidden connotations that could reveal the writer's perception of the paradoxality of the human condition. It is that essentially new sense of ambivalence and duality – in critical theory, in the twentieth-century versions of *trompe-l'oeil* painting, and in the complex love–hate relationship depicted in the novel – that forms a major unifying factor in the art and literature of the Modernist period. Freud himself acknowledged that the denominator common to all his theories was his sense of the binary nature of human experience, the clash between opposite forces within humankind, such as 'the familiar ambivalence of love and hate in erotic life'. 'Our views', he added in an essay published in 1920, 'have from the very first been *dualistic*, and today they are even more definitely dualistic than before.'[40]

7

Palpable and Mute

I should like, for a moment, to return to the origins of Modernism, to an overview of its development, in order to focus upon a curious inconsistency.

At the beginning of the century, painting in Britain and the United States had, as is well known, lagged seriously behind France in breaking away from established traditions. Whistler, who had studied in Paris in his youth and had associated there with Fantin-Latour and Dégas, had brought to London some hint of Impressionism; but the night-time setting of his *Nocturnes* revealed how little he shared that movement's central concern with the changing effects of sunlight. And John Singer Sargent, although he had been a friend of Monet during his Paris days and had sanctioned the latter's artistic experiments intellectually, did not himself adhere to the same tenets. He helped found the New English Art Club in 1886, its members 'in utter revolt against the prettiness and anecdotal nature' of works exhibited at the Royal Academy; but, as Barbara Novak has rightly noted, while his rougher brushwork has often been classed as Impressionistic, the brilliant portraits he produced remained markedly traditional both in the placing and the treatment of his subjects.[1]

The impact and reverberations produced by the 1910 Grafton Galleries exhibition in Britain and by the 1913 Armory Show in the United States demonstrated how isolated the two countries had been from the aesthetic innovations being introduced on the continent. For the overwhelming majority of the public in both countries, those exhibitions constituted a first exposure not only to the contemporary changes being introduced by Cubism but even to the work of the Post-Impressionists who, by then, had been active for over thirty years. The initial hostility the exhibitions aroused was soon followed by a growing, if hesitant recognition that a new era had dawned.[2] But if the new modes were a revelation to the public, both artists and art historians were shown to have been equally out of touch. The very few who had indeed been responsive, such as the small group stimulated by Alfred Stieglitz in New York, had anticipated the exhibition by only a small margin of time, as he began introducing the works of contemporary French artists in his magazine *Camera Work* only from around 1908. In England, even Roger Fry, the initiator and organiser of the London exhibition, had, as late as 1906, still written of Cézanne's work with confident disapproval as touching 'none of the finer issues of the imaginative life'.[3]

The creative response, when it did materialise, manifested itself simultaneously on two fronts, as an avowedly interdisciplinary venture involving both literature and the visual arts. Among writers, there had emerged just around that time an uncomfortable sense that some fundamental change was required, a break from nineteenth-century traditions; but the direction of that change had been difficult to specify. The simultaneous advent of the telegraph, radio, cinema and gramophone had created an uneasy sense that traditional literary forms, predominantly linear and sequential in design, were no longer adequate. 'Nineteen-twelve was a bad year', Ezra Pound remarked of that period, 'we all ran about like puppies with ten tin cans tied to our tails. The tin cans of Swinburnean rhyming, of Browningisms, even in Mr. Ford's case, of Kiplingisms...'[4] Moreover the older forms seemed no longer productive of any satisfying results. Frank Lentricchia has recently reminded us how bare the poetic scene was in America during the opening decade of the century, as the vacuous 'Fireside' poets – who from the 1880s had controlled the publication of poetic collections, occupied university chairs and to a large extent dictated the tastes of the public – continued to exert their lamentable influence. As T. S. Eliot was to recollect of his early years as a writer, during the first decade of the century there was not 'a single living poet, either in England or America, then at the height of his powers, whose work was capable of pointing the way to a young poet conscious of the desire for a new idiom'. With the hindsight of history and our knowledge of the revolution taking place in painting at that time and about to take place in poetry, it is ironic to recall Wallace Stevens' comment on the remarkable insularity of America, that when he was a student at Harvard 'it was a commonplace to say that all the poetry had been written and all the paintings painted'.[5] On the other hand, when the new ideas being generated in painting and sculpture on the European continent did finally find expression on the British and American scene, the main artistic stimulus came, somewhat surprisingly, not from the shock of exposure to the French Post-Impressionists or Cubists, but from the Futurist movement in Italy.

In Britain, it was the visit of Marinetti in 1912 that was to provide the turning point for Ezra Pound and others, not merely exciting interest among the British and American avant garde (some leading American figures being then resident in Britain), but prompting them to respond almost immediately with a programme of their own. Marinetti, in his manifesto of 1909 (not widely known in Britain until his visit there) had called for a totally new approach in the visual arts, contending even then that the innovations he was advocating should be extended to writing too. He demanded, in place of the traditional search for lyric beauty, a strident dynamism, reflecting the exciting technological innovations of the time:

> Up to now, literature has exalted a pensive immobility, ecstasy, and sleep. We intend to exalt aggressive action, a feverish insomnia, the racer's stride, the mortal leap, the punch and the slap. We say that the world's magnificence has been enriched by a new beauty: the beauty of speed. A racing car whose hood is adorned with great pipes, like serpents of explosive breath – a roaring car that seems to ride on grapeshot – is more beautiful than the Victory of Samothrace.

The Futurist exhibition that his visit was intended to publicise, an exhibition transferred in 1912 from the Bernheim-Jeune Gallery in Paris to the Sackville Gallery in London, contained tantalisingly unconventional works by Boccioni, Balla, Carrà, Russolo and Severini, which, instead of ignoring the advent of the machine age as irrelevant to the sequestered world of aesthetics – the 'genteel' world fostered by nineteenth-century European poets – embraced it enthusiastically as the authentic symbol of Modernism. Russolo's canvas *Revolution*, although somewhat Cubist in form, went beyond the static still-lifes produced by Picasso and Braque to capture a new sense of vigour and conflict, depicting a wedge-like mass of human figures in collision with a powerful contrary force, as if within some massive, steam-driven forge. Such works accorded with Marinetti's call for vivid imagery expressing the power and energy of industrialism:

> the nightly fervour of arsenals and shipyards blazing with violent electric moons; greedy railway stations that devour smoke-plumed serpents; factories hung on clouds by the crooked lines of their smoke; bridges that stride the rivers like giant gymnasts, flashing in the sun with a glitter of knives; adventurous steamers

that sniff the horizon; deep-chested locomotives whose wheels paw the tracks like the hooves of enormous steel horses bridled by tubing; and the sleek flight of planes whose propellers chatter in the wind like banners...[6]

How foreign such ideas were to Britain at that time is perhaps evidenced by E. M. Forster's *Howards End*, published only a year before the London exhibition. In that novel the motor car functions throughout as a repugnant symbol of mechanisation – a smelly, noisy contraption destroying the countryside, terrifying children, dogs and chickens as it raises choking clouds of dust along the previously picturesque country lanes, and transforming charming horse paddocks into unhygienic, oil-stained garages. A journey through the country within that swift-moving vehicle Forster's heroine regarded as a form of torture: 'She looked at the scenery. It heaved and merged like porridge. Presently it congealed. They had arrived.'[7] But that distaste for the world of machines was swept aside by the invasion of Futurism. For Percy Wyndham Lewis and, by extension, his friend and colleague Ezra Pound, the arrival of Italian Futurism provided the incentive for which they had been waiting.

Marinetti's support for Mussolini in later years and Pound's parallel drift towards fascism have cast a retrospective shadow over their work, encouraging a tendency among historians to play down their contribution, especially as their deplorable political sympathies were to some extent intrinsic to their aesthetic espousal of mass technology and power.[8] But the extent of their impact upon leading writers and artists in their own day cannot be retrospectively expunged. The explosive vigour of the Futurists, functioning simultaneously at all levels – provocative public lectures, startling exhibitions, blaring posters, innovative typography and derisive calls for the destruction of conventional art museums – appealed to Wyndham Lewis's pugnacious spirit, as well as to his own multifaceted abilities. With his reputation already established as one of the most original painters of his time and involved as he was in numerous and variegated activities, he was able to describe himself with considerable justice as an all-round creative artist: 'I am a novelist, painter, sculptor, philosopher, draughtsman, critic, politician, journalist, essayist, pamphleteer, all rolled into one, like one of those portmanteau-men of the Italian Renaissance.' He has been acknowledged by historians as having been the first painter in England to respond positively to Cubism within his work, his *Smiling Woman Ascending*

a Stair of 1911–12 representing a startling break with previous traditions, the sitter's face and figure broken down into geometric forms
free from the subtle shadowing required for illusionist perspective,
and suggesting a hardness of outline indicative of the direction his
work was to take. But his impact was to leave its mark on literature
no less than painting and sculpture. After a brief and rhapsodic
involvement in Futurism, his independent spirit led him to repudiate certain elements in Marinetti's platform, the Vorticist movement
that he founded concentrating less on the speed and violence of
modern life and more specifically on the hard, polished surfaces, the
sharp edges and the bare, precise shapes associated with the
machine age, although he did preserve in his own programme the
Futurists' abrasiveness, their iconoclastic vitality and their voci-
ferous demand for a totally new philosophy of art.

For many years, quite apart from the distaste for the movement's
political associations, British Vorticism had been dismissed by historians as a minor incident because of its brief duration. The group
made a great deal of noise, primarily through its short-lived journal
Blast, but disintegrated within two years of its foundation when its
leading members, in contrast to the pacifist Bloomsbury Group,
were absorbed into the army at the outbreak of the First World War.
Some, like the philosopher–critic T. E. Hulme and the promising
sculptor Henri Gaudier-Brzeska, were destined to die in the trenches,
while others, such as Richard Nevinson, having been conscripted as
war artists, drifted away from their original aesthetic affiliations,
especially as the War Office, which had hired them, was interested
in their providing a documentary record of the war and had hence
encouraged a return to some degree of realism in their work.

Recent years, however, have seen the appearance of a number of
studies revealing how profound was the impact of Lewis on the
leading writers and artists of his day, despite the brevity of the
movement's cohesive operation, and indicating that the repercussions of *Blast* and the principles it had advocated in fact continued
long after the journal, and indeed Vorticism itself, had ceased to
exist.[9] In his own day Ezra Pound, so central to the literary revival in
the early decades of the century, lauded Lewis as the 'most articulate voice' of that period, adding that his friend and collaborator
had 'invented more in Modern art than any living man save possibly Picasso'.[10] More recently, in a retrospective exhibition held in
1980, John Rothenstein described Wyndham Lewis unreservedly as
'the most fascinating personality of our time'. It has been rightly

noted that *Blast*, with its innovative typography, helped to inaugurate the Modernist poetic practice of employing radical juxtaposition of words and ideas in place of the logical or rhetorical
transitions of the past.[11] By means of that seemingly random typography, employing words in screamingly flamboyant fonts set at
startling angles to each other, Lewis introduced into England
a foretaste of the techniques to be adopted for commercial advertising and, not least, an adumbration of our present-day computer-
created art, no longer limited to the sober Gutenberg tradition, but
offering instead an unlimited range of typefaces, diversified ori-
entations, text boxes and colour as means of personal expression. And
he would no doubt have added sound-blaster accompaniment had
that utility then been available.[12]

Lewis himself had offended many by his aggressive and disputa-
tious nature but, perhaps because of his rebellious streak, he succeeded in stimulating, even in revolutionising the media of his day.
Long before Joyce and Woolf had appeared on the scene, he had, for
example, foreseen that some radical change was due to take place in
the form of the novel, declaring on his first meeting with Ford
Madox Ford in 1912, 'You and Mr. Conrad, and Mr. James and all
those old fellows are done.... Exploded!... *Fichus!*.... *Vieux jeux!*...
No good!... Finished!' His own novel, *Tarr*, published in 1918 and
praised by T. S. Eliot in *The Egoist*, set new standards, not least in its
uncompromising masculine aggressiveness, reflected in both content and style. The male truculence of Kreisler in that novel, forming
part of the Vorticist fascination with physical power, was, for
example, to inspire the passage in D. H. Lawrence's *Women in Love*
(1921) in which Gerald Crich sadistically tyrannises a terrified mare,
forcing it at a railway crossing to confront the screaming hubbub
of a passing locomotive and relentlessy digging his spurs into its
bleeding sides – a scene symbolising his attitude towards women.
With mingled horror and fascination, Ursula and Gudrun watch the
'strong, indomitable thighs of the blond man clenching the palpitat-
ing body of the mare into pure control; a sort of soft white magnetic
domination from the loins and thighs and calves, enclosing and
encompassing the mare heavily into unutterable subordination ...'
And later in the novel, Loerke, the artist–sculptor through whom
Lawrence expressed the views he himself held at that time, echoes
the new aesthetic of Lewis's Vorticism in his disgust at the ugliness
of English factory buildings, so unsuited to the machinery within,
which he admired as 'maddeningly beautiful'.[13]

Lewis's own contribution to *Blast I*, his surrealist play *Enemy of the Stars*, was acknowledged by contemporaries as the most original contribution in the journal, confirming that the new movement aimed at revitalising literature no less than the visual arts. Moreover his literary impact was integral to his work as a painter. His 1914 canvas *The Crowd* (Figure 28), with its view of the common people as a teeming, uniform mass in a depersonalised cityscape, was an early adumbration of T. S. Eliot's élitist disdain for the populus; and it was in the second issue of *Blast* that Eliot's early poems in fact achieved their first British publication, a reflection of Pound's and Lewis's perceptiveness rather than, as mentioned earlier, any sense of artistic identity on Eliot's part. T. E. Hulme was an enthusiastic supporter of Vorticism, as well as one of its main propagandists; and his insistence upon 'hardness' of imagery in poetry, which was to serve as a major plank in the doctrine of Imagism, would seem to have derived in large part from that association.

The close intertwining of art and literature in this movement is perhaps best evidenced by Pound's remark, patently relevant to his own poetic experimentation in the *Cantos*:

> Vorticism, especially that part of Vorticism to do with form – to wit, Vorticist painting and sculpture – has brought me a new series of apperceptions.... What was a dull row of houses is become a magazine of forms. There are new ways of seeing them. There are ways of seeing the shape of the sky as it juts down between the houses. The tangle of telegraph wires is conceivable not merely as a repetition of lines; one sees the shapes defined by the different branches of wire. The lumber yards, the sidings of railways, cease to be dreary ... [14]

In a letter to Lewis in 1916, Pound, normally considered an exclusively literary figure, mentioned that he was planning a book on four modern artists – Brancusi, Picabia, Picasso and Wyndham Lewis himself. In that same year he did in fact publish an important monograph on the sculptor Gaudier-Brzeska, and he also served, under the pseudonym 'B. H. Dias', as the art critic of *The New Age*.[15]

Whether these changes occurring in England are to be attributed directly to Wyndham Lewis or should be viewed as articulating the general cultural shifts of his day, there can be no doubt that the period immediately prior to the First World War marked a turning point in the development of British and American art and literature, a decisive break with the traditions of the past, the presence of a number of expatriate Americans such as Eliot, Pound and Epstein ensuring the connection between activities in the two countries. *Prufrock*, composed before Eliot's meeting with Pound, had in fact derived its main inspiration from the French poets, especially Laforgue; but it was, of course, *The Waste Land*, published soon after the war under the rigorous editorship of Ezra Pound, that was to proclaim the advent of a new era for poetry, not only in the discon- certingly fragmented juxtapositions of the verse and the disturbingly Protean shifts between the speakers, but also in such unconventional imagery as the 'sound of horns and motors', drawn, in accordance with Vorticist principles, from the hitherto unpoetic world of science and technology. The literary revolution initiated in England at that time was to eddy outwards, leading in the 1920s and 1930s not only to the advent of Imagism and the emergence of an essentially new type of poetry but also to fundamental changes in the form and con- tent of the novel.

*   *   *

The anomaly to which little attention has been paid, and which will form the subject of this present chapter, is the remarkable brevity of the literary revolution that came into being at this time, the brevity not of Vorticism itself (the movement's swift disintegration has long been recognised) but of the major upheaval in poetry and fiction and the conscious break with the past that Vorticism helped to inaug- urate. The debt of Imagism to that movement has already been noted, with Pound acting as a primary intermediary. John Dos Passos's tri- logy *U.S.A.*, which appeared in the 1930s, was clearly evocative of the typography of *Blast* in its employment of newspaper headlines and telegraphic flashes to convey the energy inherent in the swift- moving communication scene emerging across the seas. And as part of the larger reaction of past modes there were the experimental novels of Joyce, Woolf and Faulkner in the 1920s and 1930s; Ivy Compton-Burnet's fiction, strictly élitist in its appeal, exploring the silent inner world in a manner indebted to, but not quite the same as the stream of consciousness, with the unstated thoughts of her char- acters recorded in place of the actual words they must have uttered; and Nathanel West's experiments with the surrealist novel.

But the mainstream novel in both countries, however startling in changed moral perspective – especially in its less-inhibited treatment of sex, a change frequently arousing the ire of the censors – remained remarkably conservative in stylistic form during the Modernist period. The fiction of Ford Madox Ford, D. H. Lawrence, Aldous Huxley, Evelyn Waugh, Scott Fitzgerald, Ernest Hemingway, Sinclair Lewis, John Steinbeck and numerous others continued imperturbably to preserve the basic narrative techniques of the nineteenth century, ignoring such startling innovations as interior monologue and disjointed progression by means of mental association. Those writers continued, despite the startling innovations of Joyce and Woolf, to employ logically developed plots, rounded characters, realistic settings and authorial narrators. If, as was discussed in an earlier chapter, Aldous Huxley provided a fascinating experiment in multiplicity of viewpoint, introducing a structural interplay of mirror characters, the anecdotal form of presentation itself remained fully traditional in that novel, free from the unformulated thought flow, the confusing time changes, the fragmentation and the multiple-page sentences that had characterised the work of Joyce, Woolf and Faulkner. Graham Greene, one of the most rewarding novelists of the Modernist era, fully responsive to the spiritual alienation of his day and to the contemporary collapse of conventional values, had no hesitation in employing in *Brighton Rock* (1938), as he was to employ in his subsequent novels, a narrative technique essentially unchanged from that of the conventional novel. In a typical passage, an anonymous 'authorial' voice summarises Rosa's thoughts and fears not at the moment when they surge up uncontrolledly and haphazardly from the subconscious but, as in the earlier tradition, after they have been verbally articulated in the mind and translated into formal terms as she considers her difficult moral choice:

> If it was a guardian angel speaking to her now, he spoke like a devil – he tempted her to virtue like a sin. To throw away the gun was a betrayal; it would be an act of cowardice; it would mean that she chose never to see him again for ever. Moral maxims dressed in pedantic priestly tones remembered from old sermons, instructions, confessions – 'you can plead for him at the throne of Grace' – came to her like unconvincing insinuations. The evil act was the honest act, the bold and the faithful – it was only lack of courage, it seemed to her, that spoke so virtuously.[16]

Evelyn Waugh's *Brideshead Revisited* of 1944 returned so completely to the narrative patterns of the nineteenth century that it even preserved the nostalgic reminiscing and evocations of nature so often permeating earlier fiction:

> 'I have been here before,' I said; I had been there before; first with Sebastian more than twenty years ago on a cloudless day in June, when the ditches were white with fool's-parsley and meadow-sweet and the air heavy with all the scents of summer; it was a day of peculiar splendour, such as our climate affords once or twice a year, when leaf and flower and bird and sun-lit stone and shadow seem all to proclaim the glory of God; and though I had been there so often, in so many moods, it was to that first visit that my heart returned on this, my latest.[17]

For some critics, that repudiation of the experimental novel of the 1920s marked a failing on the part of those novelists, Bernard Bergonzi accusing them of having 'sold out. Though they subscribe in principle to the notion of originality at all costs, and avoid overt plagiarism, they are still broadly content to write much the same kind of novel . . .'[18] But it is surely significant that the same conservatism may be perceived in the poetry of that time, suggesting that it was a broader cultural phenomenon, not to be so easily dismissed as a personal aberration. If critics of the modern novel have (as Malcolm Bradbury and David Palmer have noted) customarily concentrated on the period of Joyce and Woolf, after which they acknowledge that 'the remaking of the novel into an instrument of modern expression seemed to come to an end',[19] that trait holds no less true for critics of Modernist poetry, who have generally focused almost exclusively upon the experimental verse writing of T. S. Eliot, the *Cantos* of Ezra Pound, the innovative techniques of William Carlos Williams, and Wallace Stevens' 'Peter Quince at the Clavier' as characterising the poetic style of the twentieth century. Those poets were indeed acutely aware of contemporary change in the arts, Williams himself having being closely allied with Stieglitz and the experimental painters resident in the New York area; we shall return to them later. But one should bear in mind how selective such an approach may be, excluding the main body of poetry published both in Britain and America during the first half of the century, in which, after a brief period of innovation, a similar conservatism asserted itself as had occurred in the novel.[20] T. S. Eliot, although less influential during his acknowledgedly religious phase, did, it is true, continue to occupy a major position in Anglo-American writing,

and as late as 1941 was still dominating the scene with such chal-
lengingly elliptical and intellectually allusive poetry as his *Burnt
Norton*:

> Garlic and sapphires in the mud
> Clot the bedded axle-tree.
> The trilling wire in the blood
> Sings below inveterate scars
> And reconciles forgotten wars . . .

But other leading poets, while admiring his achievement, were consciously resisting his influence. In 1939 Stephen Spender remarked
that writers were tending 'today to turn outwards to reality, because
the phase of experimenting in form has proved sterile . . .'[21] The
most prominently acclaimed and most widely anthologised verse of
that period, including his own poem, *The Express*, while turning to
more modern themes, deliberately reverted to older poetic forms, to
verse free from the startling juxtapositions, recondite imagery and
abrupt transitions of the new mode:

> After the first powerful plain manifesto
> The black statement of pistons, without more fuss
> But gliding like a queen, she leaves the station.
> Without bowing, and with restrained unconcern
> She passes the houses which humbly crowd outside,
> The gasworks and at last the heavy page
> Of death, printed by gravestones in the cemetery . . .

The poem's conclusion, while extolling the dignity of the modern
locomotive continues, like so many other poems of this period, to
employ as the criterion for assessing true beauty an old-fashioned,
Wordsworthian admiration of the loveliness of nature:

> Ah, like a comet through flames she moves entranced
> Wrapt in her music no bird song, no, nor bough
> Breaking with honey buds, shall ever equal.

As a poet, D. H. Lawrence had broken with tradition by dispensing
with fixed metre in favour of free verse; but the resulting artifacts,
rich in emotional timbre, subjective in experience and vividly

representational, were by no means revolutionary in their poetic mode:

> A snake came to my water-trough
> On a hot, hot day, and I in pyjamas for the heat,
> To drink there.
>
> In the deep, strange-scented shade of the great dark
>   carob-tree
> I came down the steps with my pitcher
> And must wait, must stand and wait, for there he was
>   at the trough before me ... [22]

A major proportion of the verse produced at that time moved in the same direction, including such widely anthologised poems as Allen Tate's 'Ode to the Confederate Dead', John Crowe Ransom's 'Bells for John Whiteside's Daughter', Richard Eberhart's 'The Ground-hog' and W. H. Auden's 'Musée des Beaux Arts', with its meditation on Brueghel's painting, *The Fall of Icarus*:

> About suffering they were never wrong,
> The Old Masters: how well they understood
> Its human position; how it takes place
> While someone else is eating or opening a window or just
>   walking dully along;
> How, when the aged are reverently, passionately waiting
> For the miraculous birth, there always must be
> Children who did not specially want it to happen, skating
> On a pond at the edge of the wood ...

As Geoffrey Hartman and others have argued, Modernist poetry contained a surprisingly large residue of Romantic sensibility, an enduring concern with subjective consciousness and the intensity of personal experience. [23]

In marked contrast to this stubborn conservatism both in Modernist poetry and in the Modernist novel, the genre of painting moved un-hesitatingly into the starkly revolutionary modes of Cubism, Abstract art, Expressionism and Orphism, the less-daring painters of the time being simply dropped by the wayside as incompatible with the new aesthetic dispensation. Painters wholeheartedly rejected the past, banishing the anecdotal, the subjective, the historical and the mimetic as irrevocably outmoded.

That disparity between the media would seem, at first sight, to suggest a startling failure on literature's part, an inability to respond effectively to the contemporary pressures for cultural change. It would appear to cast doubt on the basic assumption motivating synchronic enquiry, that creative artists in all media, while they may react a little differently to shared, contemporary pressures because of the specific demands of their own art form, reveal nonetheless a considerable degree of unity in the ways they express their response aesthetically.

The stylistic conservatism of literature in this era poses a further problem, its contradiction of the view – first presented by Worringer, as discussed in an earlier chapter – that periods of equilibrium tend to produce naturalistic art, while in times of disequilibrium, art moves in the direction of the linear and geometric. He argued that in such periods as the Renaissance, when civilisation was essentially at peace with the cosmos and mankind was able to control or at least to be reconciled to organic nature, painters had striven for illusionist representation and mimetic accuracy of perspective; while in periods such as the medieval, when the external world was seen as a nugatory prelude to eternity or, in ancient Egypt, as a threatening chaos, art adopted stylised and non-mimetic forms. The patent applicability of that theory to twentieth-century painting had accorded it an especial attractiveness in the 1940s, and Joseph Frank's widely admired essay on 'Spatial Form in Modern Literature' redefined Worringer's argument in terms of the contemporary situation, lending added force to it.[24] The generally harsh, geometric abstractions of Cubist and Expressionist art seemed to confirm the distinction, so that the findings of Darwin, Freud and the physicists, having seemingly demolished all sense of mankind's harmony with nature, could now be seen as stimulating the painting of the time to move towards the non-figural. The effectiveness of that theory, however, would be significantly lessened if its definition of such overall cultural change were to prove relevant only to the visual arts of the time, and not to its literature, especially as the declared purpose of Frank's essay had been to justify, by comparison with the history of painting, the radically new forms being adopted by contemporary poets and novelists such as T. S. Eliot and Virginia Woolf. The theory would thus function only for the more obviously experimental writings of the twentieth century, leaving

outside its parameters those poets and authors alluded to above
who declined to conform to that pattern and yet have attained recognition as major literary figures of their time.

Stephen Spender, aware of the discrepancy between the media,
offered the following explanation in his study of Modernism:

> The Imagists tried to turn poetry into word-painting or sculpture.
> They wanted to release poetry from the burden of past conven-
> tions and traditional ways of thinking by concentrating upon
> reproducing the image which springs naked into the mind from
> the impact of modern life. Yet the most intelligent of them soon
> realized that poetry could not be completely modern and new in
> the way that the other arts could be, because it uses as its material
> words which are old and social, and which only to a limited extent
> can be used in new ways.[25]

But one would have thought that Hopkins and Eliot had provided
ample proof that words could indeed be used in startlingly new
ways if the poet so wished, as in Hopkins' lines:

> Cloud-puffball, torn tufts, tossed pillows | flaunt forth, then
>   chevy on an air –
> Built thoroughfare: heaven-roysterers, in gay-gangs | they
>   throng; they glitter in marches.
> Down roughcast, down dazzling whitewash, | wherever an
>   elm arches,
> Shivelights and shadowtackle in long | lashes lace,
>   lance, and pair.[26]

An explanation of the anomaly may, perhaps, be found by exploring a well-known theory of art – by adopting, however, the negative
implications of that theory rather than the principle it aimed to pro-
pound. In a seminal essay published in 1965, Clement Greenberg
suggested that the distinguishing factor of Modernist painting lay in
its rigorous attempt to limit itself to components unique to each specific genre, a self-imposed discipline that insisted upon emphasising
those elements exclusively and unequivocally appropriate to its own
medium. At a time when the arts had, like religion, come under
attack as being extraneous to the prevailing scientism of the day, as
being dependent merely upon personal, emotional response, there
arose a conviction among painters, Greenberg argued, that the arts

could be rescued only if they demonstrated the singularity of the experience they provided. They needed to prove that each medium and each genre could supply an aesthetic encounter valuable in its own right, an experience not to be obtained from any other kind of activity. Accordingly, where the Old Masters had consciously camouflaged the means whereby they achieved their effects (*'ars est celare artem'*) or at the very least attempted to deflect the viewer's attention from the tools of their trade – hoping that the viewer would ignore the surface brushwork and the two-dimensional limitations of the canvas in order to be imaginatively transported to a heroic, mythological scene, or to gaze through the frame of the painting into a world beyond – Modernist painters, from the Post-Impressionists onward, reversed the procedure, deliberately drawing attention to the artifactuality of their work. They abjured underpainting and glazing, in order to leave the eye in no doubt of the technical means employed, highlighting the tactile presence of paint either by wide brushmarks upon the canvas or by squeezing it directly from the tube. Van Gogh, for instance, applied pigment in thick ridges in order to thrust to the fore its material presence, reminding the viewer that he was really gazing at a stretched piece of canvas and recalling the process whereby the work was produced.

By drawing attention to those physical elements, Modernist art aimed above all, Greenberg suggested, at cultivating its exclusivity as a *visual* medium. Cubist painters flattened their images in order to assert the two-dimensional quality of the canvas. They introduced *collage*, attaching pieces of chair-caning or newspaper to the painted surface as a means of jolting the viewer out of any expectation of illusionism. The new purpose, as Picasso defined it, was to demonstrate that 'different textures can enter into a composition to become the reality in the painting that competes with the reality in nature. We tried to get rid of *trompe l'oeil* to find a *trompe l'esprit*.' 'Cubism', he added, 'has kept itself within the limits and limitations of painting never pretending to go beyond it.'[27] Rigorously eschewing anecdotalism, mimesis, mythology and historical scenes as more appropriate to literature, it divested itself of everything that other media and other genres could supply in order to entrench itself within its own area of competence, and to proclaim the validity of the act of painting as an independent craft. Greenberg's theory, in its turn, stimulated the important further work of Michael Fried and Richard Wollheim, both of whom have drawn attention to the emphasis on materiality in Modernist painting, whereby awareness of the canvas surface was no longer minimised nor eclipsed but consciously asserted.[28]

If, however, we focus on the reverse implications of that theory, applying this Modernist desire for the exclusivity of each art form to the verbal in place of the visual arts, literature may be perceived not to have deserted the Modernist aim but to have followed the same principle. It was affirming its own identity and determining the parameters of its own medium by cultivating precisely those elements of which painting wished to divest itself. The reason painters had disdained the anecdotal, the subjective and the fictionally realistic was *because* those elements belonged more naturally to literature, to the verbal genres of epic, lyric, novel and drama. Painting, they argued, should explore geometric relationships, colour juxtapositions and abstract patterning as the domain proper to a visual medium, even when attempting to represent extant forms, such as those believed to exist in hyperspace. If a divergence seemed to have manifested itself in the twentieth century after so long a period of close relationship between these two art forms, that bifurcation could, in this context, be seen to arise not from a disparity in their contemporary purpose but from a shared cultural impulse, a desire in each medium to confirm the individuality of its art form. And in that context the mainstream of Modernist literature was indeed restricting itself to the qualities most naturally belonging to its medium by *not* venturing into the world of Cubist forms and Abstract patterning. It is perhaps significant that the eventual return of the novel to radical experimentation – as in the works of Thomas Pynchon, Alain Robbe-Grillet, Anthony Burgess, Donald Barthelme and Tony Morrison – occurred from the 1960s onwards, when the Modernist desire for the exclusivity of each medium had waned, and when innovation in style and content had become an ideal in itself. But such experimentation had not held true for the novels of the 1930s and 1940s, the period of our present concern.

The initial phase in Modernism had, as we have noted, been manifestly interdisciplinary, an aspect that would seem to account for those experimental forms of poetry to which historians have tended to pay most attention. Vorticism, during that early period, made a calculated attempt to correlate all the arts and to encourage painters, writers and sculptors to apply to their own work the experiments being conducted in the other media. There were in fact no composers within the Vorticist group and, whether that was fortuitous or not, the medium of music tended to be excluded; but synaesthesia, a belief in the intimate association of literature, painting and sculpture, became a central theme of the movement. It was evidenced most clearly in Ezra Pound's monograph on Gaudier-Brzeska, which was not simply a memorial tribute to the sculptor but an exploration of the filaments connecting Vorticist sculpture with poetry, especially in their innovative approach to plane surfaces. T. E. Hulme, too, the main theoretician of Imagism, had planned to write a book-length study entitled *Jacob Epstein and the Aesthetics of Sculpture*, a plan interrupted by his conscription into the army and his early death. And in 1914 Richard Aldington, defining the poetic objectives of the Imagists, turned to sculpture as the most apt illustration. A basic objective of their poetry, he explained, was to achieve a

> hardness, as of cut stone. No slop, no sentimentality. When people say that Imagist poems are 'too hard,' 'like a white marble monument,' we chuckle; we know we have done something good.[29]

As a result of that synaesthetic impulse, Imagist poetry and the stream-of-consciousness novel echoed the dominant proclivities of the plastic arts even more closely than in other eras. The Modernist painter's bold exposure of the physical texture of the paint was paralleled in literature by a deliberate focus upon the technical processes of verbal communication. There arose a provocative play with typography, the dropping of capitals in poetry, the desertion of regular metre in favour of free verse. Within the novel one perceives an ingenious juggling with words. And Dos Passos' trilogy, *U.S.A.*, not only imported headlines borrowed from the newspapers of the day but did so in a manner reminiscent of the Cubist practice of glueing foreign objects on to the canvas. All those elements achieved prominent expression in literature during that initial phase. Hence such instances as the following passage from Joyce's *Ulysses*, which thrusts to the fore the technical processes in the act of writing:

ORTHOGRAPHICAL
Want to be sure of his spelling. Proof fever. Martin Cunningham forgot to give us his spellingbee conundrum this morning. It is amusing to view the unpar one ar alleled embarra two ars is it? double ess ment of a harassed pedlar while gauging au the symmetry with a y of a peeled pear under a cemetery wall.[30]

Once past that initial synaesthetic phase, however – important as it was for twentieth-century writing – both poetry and the novel reverted to the patterns more naturally germane to literature and more integral to its art form. Even Joyce himself, the arch-innovator, could, in his own verse writing, return unembarrassedly to the Romantic sensibilities of the past, as in a poem he produced in 1927, some five years after the publication of *Ulysses*:

> Rain on Rahoon falls softly, softly falling,
> Where my dark lover lies.
> Sad is his voice that calls me, sadly calling,
> At grey moonrise.

If the Modernists were convinced that each art form should be contained within the boundaries of those elements most appropriate to it, one may note the contrast in the reaction by the public at large. On the one hand viewers, after a brief period of hesitation, accepted the startlingly new contents of art galleries with enthusiasm, the public eagerly purchasing reproductions (when they could not afford originals) of Post-Impressionist and Cubist works to display in their own homes, while on the other hand, only a small proportion of the reading public did more than dip into such experimental works as *Ulysses*. Although those new literary works stimulated wide public interest, not least because of the legal battles over their supposed pornographic content, their reception as a new form of art was in no way commensurate with that of Picasso and his fellow painters. As Stuart Gilbert recorded in 1930, the heavy demands that *Ulysses* imposed on the reader's attention, memory and endurance made it a book that was widely discussed and sampled but very rarely read. Apart from the considerable difficulties he mentions, there was the problem of the structural framework. On the seemingly disconnected Dublin experiences of Dedalus and Bloom, Joyce imposed a mythic allusiveness to Homer's epic in order to provide some degree of developmental sequence that the associationist principle of stream-of-consciousness precluded. But that process assumed a detailed knowledge of the Homeric account, which was lacking in the vast majority of potential readers. Only the scholar would identify Bloom's encounter with the xenophobic Citizen in the public house as echoing Ulysses' confrontation with the Cyclops, or would recognise that the following episode, describing the flirtatious Gerty MacDowell responding to Bloom's erotic interest, was intended to echo the meeting, subsequent in the epic, when the princess Nausicaa eyes the hero as a potential amorous conquest.[31] And, one should note, the difficulty in reading such novels was no less than that involved in interpreting a Cubist or Abstract painting.

With her usual perceptiveness, Virginia Woolf realised that the changes both she and Joyce were introducing to the novel would not prevail for long, that they constituted only a passing, experimental phase:

> Ah, but I'm doomed! As a matter of fact, I think that we all are. It is not possible now, and never will be, to say I renounce. Nor would it be a good thing for literature were it possible. This generation must break its neck in order that the next may have smooth going. For I agree with you that nothing is going to be achieved by us. Fragments – paragraphs – a page perhaps: but no more. Joyce to me seems strewn with disaster. I can't even see, as you see, his triumphs. A gallant approach, that is all that is obvious to me; then the usual smash and splinters.[32]

Readers betrayed a similar hesitancy in their response to Faulkner. Malcolm Cowley noted as late as 1945 that the latter's novels, although frequently cited (usually disparagingly at that time), were in fact little read, all seventeen novels being in that year completely out of print. Only when Cowley persuaded the author to write an Appendix summarising the complex histories of his fictional characters, in order to help the reader find a way through the bewildering temporal shifts in that innovative narrative mode, did a revival of interest become possible, the Appendix henceforth appearing as a standard introduction in subsequent reissues of the novels.[33] Where painting, now defined as an exclusively visual experience devoid of message or story, left viewers free to construct their own personal response with no fear of contradiction, the novel, dependent even in its experimental form upon some degree of anecdotal progression and demanding many hours of concentration, left the public disconcerted when that intrinsic element was either missing, disordered or obscured. And poetry, with its long tradition of expressing subjective emotion and providing lyrical appeal, proved no less discomfiting when those aspects were replaced by ambiguously interchangeable speakers, fragmented images and recondite allusions.

In that latter regard, one may note how even so innovative a poet as William Carlos Williams emerges, in hindsight, as far less consistent in his revolutionary Modernism than critical studies have allowed, even than he himself foresaw. In 1920, in the prologue to 'Kora in Hell', he had, in defining his own conception of poetry, scorned the traditional characteristics of the genre, arguing that the 'associational or sentimental value is the false. Its imposition is due to lack of imagination, to an easy lateral sliding...' And he had implemented that ideal in his well-known 'Red Wheelbarrow' of 1923, justly celebrated for its innovative attempt to capture in verse the new artistic principle of *objet trouvé*, of an item seen in isolation, divorced from emotional associations:

> so much depends
> upon
>
> a red wheel
> barrow
>
> glazed with rain
> water
>
> beside the white
> chickens.

He had thereby granted the banal a new meaning, in the manner he had come to admire so much in the work of his artist friends.[34] Williams acknowledged the source of his inspiration.

> In Paris, painters from Cézanne to Pisarro had been painting their revolutionary canvases for fifty or more years but it was not until I clapped my eyes on Marcel Duchamp's *Nude Descending a Staircase* that I burst out laughing from the relief it brought me! I felt as if an enormous weight had been lifted from my spirit for which I was infinitely grateful.[35]

Williams, therefore, consciously sought at that time to remove internal progression from poetry, whether emotional or logical, finding his inspiration in the more challenging aspects of Cubist painting and the cinema. In an unpublished manuscript describing the kind of poetry he was attempting to produce, he wrote that some intimation of the process he aimed at could be demonstrated there – 'the much greater interest felt in the snatches of pictures shown at the movies between the regular films, to advertise pictures coming the following week, than the regular features themselves is because the banality of the sequence has been removed'.[36]

All this is true. Yet within a brief time, it should be noted, he deserted this concern with objectivity and distancing, finding them essentially inimical to the nature of poetry itself, and began to revert to a more conventional and more emotionally involved representationalism, as in his celebrated poem 'The Yachts' of 1935. There he describes how, in the

> brilliance of cloudless days, with broad bellying sails
> they glide to the wind, tossing green water
> from their sharp prows while over them the crew crawls
> ant-like, solicitously grooming them, releasing,
> making fast as they turn, lean far over and having
> caught the wind again, side by side, head for the mark...[37]

To suggest, as I have here, that the discrepancy between literature and art in this period arose ultimately from a shared contemporary impulse, from a common desire for the specificity of each genre, might, without further confirmation, appear no more than an unsubstantiated theory. But for corroboration we may turn to a third medium, that of sculpture, which falls neatly into a category between painting and literature, a category especially relevant to our theme in a period when painting was moving into abstract forms. For, while belonging to the visual arts and therefore possessing obvious affinities to painting, its tactile quality, dependent upon the physical solidity of marble or bronze, connects it firmly with the materiality of nature. Unrestricted to the two-dimensional limitation of a canvas, the limitation that led Modernist painting towards abstraction and colour juxtaposition, sculpture is, in that regard, related at the same time to literature's concern with the three-dimensional actualities of existence in this world.

Within sculpture a progression can be discerned that is very similar to that which occurred in literature. There too, the initial interdisciplinary impact of Vorticism had produced revolutionary changes in both the conception and form of the medium. In both Britain and America, nineteenth-century sculpture had, like painting, been lacking in innovative ideas, the major occupation of sculptors being sepulchral or commemorative statuary, generally of a conservative nature, together with the ever-popular genre of nudes, both male and female, sanctioned by their titles as representations of classical myth. Especially influential in the Victorian period were Sir Frederick Leighton's sculpture of a nude male entitled *Athlete Struggling with a Python* of 1877, and Alfred Gilbert's similar study of *Perseus Arming* of 1882. The main criterion for such art was anatomical realism, applied with equal diligence to the highly popular genre of animal sculpture, of which Sir Edwin Landseer became the foremost exponent. And in America, Augustus Saint-Gaudens' huge statue of a nude *Diana* drawing her bow, originally placed at the top of a tower in Madison Square Garden in 1893 but eventually moved to the Philadelphia Museum, came to be regarded as the outstanding sculptural achievement of its time.

The contrast between such works and Jacob Epstein's dramatic *Rock Drill* of 1913 (Figure 29) speaks for itself. Epstein first became interested in primitive sculpture during his stay in Paris – an interest heightened by his friendship with Modigliani. On his return to England he became closely involved in the work of the Vorticists, producing in 1913 this startling sculptural piece that was to serve, together with the productions of Gaudier-Brzeska, as a paradigm of Vorticist sculpture. Originally affixed above a real rock drill (a reconstruction can be seen in Birmingham Museum), it represented their concern with Machine Expressionism and, to some extent, the ruthless belligerence underscoring Futurist art that had made it attractive to Mussolini, and that tended to be adopted by the Vorticists. T. E. Hulme accorded high praise to Epstein's work in an article in 1913, and at the time of his death he was, it has been discovered, engaged in preparing a fuller study of this piece of sculpture as epitomising the new aesthetic. But Epstein's own comment concerning the origin of *Rock Drill* contains within it significant corroboration of our present theme – how brief that interest was to be, the grotesque and harsh lines of such art being of only temporary relevance to his deeper interests as a sculptor. It marked a passing responsiveness to the interdisciplinary innovations of Vorticism, before he returned to those elements which he felt to be more integral to his medium:

> It was in the experimental pre-war days of 1913 that I was fired to do the rock drill, and my ardour for machinery (short-lived) expended itself upon the purchase of an actual drill, second-hand, and upon this I made and mounted a machine-like robot, visored,

menacing, and carrying within itself its progeny, protectively en-sconced. Here is the armed, sinister figure of to-day and to-morrow. No humanity, only the terrible Frankenstein's monster we have made ourselves into.... Later I lost my interest in machinery and discarded the drill. I cast in metal only the upper part of the figure.[38]

In 1916, therefore, Epstein dismantled the original work, removing the drill entirely and preserving only the figure of the driller himself, with even that section being cast in a modified form, minus most of the right arm. Those alterations robbed it of much of its menace, the work producing in its final form an effect of human vulnerability rather than Vorticist aggression.

Gaudier-Brzeska, too, seems to have been only temporarily attr-acted to the new mode, enthusiastic as he was during the initial stages. To the first issue of *Blast* he contributed a manifesto celebrat-ing the 'sculptural energy' and 'intensity' of Vorticist art; but there are indications, even though his life was cut short before he could develop his ideas further, that his advocacy of Vorticism was to be brief. The direction he would have taken may be conjectured from two striking sculptural works that he did manage to complete, his *Crouching Figure* and *Maternity* from 1914, both of which deserted geometric forms in favour of less rigid, more naturally flowing lines. And there is the further interesting fact, recorded by Pound, that for the second issue of *Blast* Gaudier-Brzeska had been planning an essay entitled 'The Need for Organic Forms in Sculpture', a title that suggests a repudiation of one of the basic Vorticist principles. It defied Wyndham Lewis's contemptuous maxim that nature 'is a blessed retreat in art, for those artists whose imagination is mean and feeble...'[39]

In Epstein, however, we have a sculptor who did survive the war, was able to develop his ideas, and was to become one of the leading practitioners of the Modernist era; and the direction of his work was, as in so much of the poetry of his time, a turning back to conservat-ive principles. His work elicited numerous protests from critics. There was the furore raised by the exposed genitals on his Oscar Wilde memorial (Sir Frederick Leighton had circumspectly arranged for the python's coils to cover those of his nude *Athlete*), and there were repeated attacks upon him throughout his career – for the series of works provided for the building of the British Medical Asso-ciation in the Strand, as well as for the uncomfortable feeling that an

avowedly Jewish sculptor was providing some of the most important contemporary depictions of the central themes of Christianity.
But it was not recourse to Vorticist principles that produced the hostility, for he did not provide in his art any continuation of the
non-human abstractions or jagged patternism associated with the
Rock Drill. As R. H. Wilenski has noted, Epstein, although at first
deeply influenced by T. E. Hulme's theories about geometric forms,
changed direction after the latter's death and 'developed his amazing powers as a Romantic modeller'.[40] The contrast with his Vorticist
phase is strikingly illustrated by *The Risen Christ* (Figure 30) of 1919,
the figure, wrapped in the shrouds of death, pointing to the mark of
the nail as evidence of his suffering. It provoked outraged condemnation from many, Father Bernard Vaughan complaining in mock
terror that if it were to spring to life, he would flee from it 'in dread
and disgust, lest perhaps he might pick my pockets, or worse, do
some deed of violence in keeping with his Bolshevik appearance',[41]
an objection testifying to the disturbing realism of the figure. The
term 'Bolshevik' may appear strange in that context, but during this
period and well into the 1920s, Modernist art was frequently seen as
anarchistic, identified with Marxist attempts to overthrow tradition.
An article in the *New York Times* of 3 April 1921, for example, argued
that Cubists and Futurists 'would subvert or destroy all the recog-
nized standards of art and literature by their Bolshevist methods'.

In fact this statue by Epstein was, as Father Vaughan failed to
recognise, a return to traditional art forms rather than an attempt to
depose them. In many of his works, it is true, he continued to be
inspired by primitive art, and in his brilliant *Genesis* of 1931 there are
clear hints of a conscious indebtedness to tribal fertility totems. Yet
the work is no abstraction. It is recognisably and powerfully human,
the figure placing one arm protectively over the swollen belly, the
breasts enlarged in preparation for providing nutriment, and the
female face brooding over the approaching birth.

The interdisciplinary impact of the Cubist–Vorticist phase in sculpture was, as with the poetry of T. S. Eliot, to continue to flourish,
notably in the work of such continental sculptors as Jaques Lipschitz
and Archipenko, whose non-human, geometric forms employed
the kind of associative compression characterising Imagist verse.
Umberto Boccioni, the Futurist sculptor, in 1913 defined that compression and complexity as the distinguishing factor of the new
mode: 'Our own primitivism should have nothing in common
with that of antiquity. Our primitivism is the extreme climax of

complexity, whereas the primitivism of antiquity is the babbling of *simplicity*.'[42] But in English sculpture a romantic conservatism reasserted itself.

In the discussion of art that forms the culmination of Lawrence's *Women in Love*, that dichotomy in sculpture emerged as a major theme, reflecting a primary concern of that time. His artist protagonist Loerke, although engaged, as a committed Futurist, in carving a huge sculpted frieze for a granite factory and thereby emphasising the beauty of the industrial world, produces for inspection, somewhat incongruously, a photograph of a small bronze statuette he has sculpted, a representation of *Lady Godiva*, which becomes the focus of an argument over aesthetics. As in Epstein's *Genesis*, Loerke has here deserted the principle of geometric abstraction, choosing for the female figure a naturalism that modifies and softens the Vorticist power confined to the stallion upon which she is seated:

> Her limbs were young and tender. Her legs, scarcely formed yet, the legs of a maiden just passing towards cruel womanhood, dangled childishly over the side of the powerful horse, pathetically, the small feet folded one over the other, as if to hide. But there was no hiding. There she was exposed naked on the naked flank of the horse.
>
> The horse stood stock still, stretched in a kind of start. It was a massive, magnificent stallion, rigid with pent-up power. Its neck was arched and terrible like a sickle, its flanks were pressed back, rigid with power.[43]

Ursula, for whom even such softening of Vorticism is insufficient, vehemently castigates Loerke for depicting the horse as a mere 'idea', a falsity of his own invention. And although opposing her and defending the stylisation of the horse, Gudrun, with whom Lawrence clearly identifies here, is nonetheless thrilled by the exquisite tenderness in the modelling of the girl, in the gentle, lifelike quality that it achieves.

It is perhaps significant that, although Lawrence was at this time himself a dedicated painter as well as novelist, he selected sculpture as the model through which to express the aesthetic aims embodied in his novels. For, as has been noted, unlike painting, sculpture was by its nature dependent to a large extent upon the sensory world of physicality, evoking, even when only observed optically, associations of texture and touch, just as the novel, however concerned with the flow of inner thoughts, could not dispense completely with the actuality of human beings located in their human settings.

Jacob Epstein was by no means alone in his desertion of an original Vorticist impulse and his adoption of a moderating naturalism; for a major sculptor of the following generation in Britain, Henry Moore, followed the same path. Profoundly moved in his younger years by Ezra Pound's study of Gaudier-Brzeska, he produced a number of works indebted to Vorticist principles, such as his *Standing Woman* of 1923 and his *Head and Shoulders* of 1927, in which, incidentally, he echoed Picasso's 'dual-facet' experimentation, superimposing the profile upon the frontal view. Exhibited in 1928 and 1931, they provoked the familiar public outcry that they were 'immoral and bolshevistik', together with demands that he be dismissed from his teaching post at the Royal College of Art. Unrepentant, he continued there till the end of his appointment, the College's director, William Rothenstein, who admired his work, resisting public pressures.

Moore, however, records that during that period he began reading with 'excitement' the novels of D. H. Lawrence, and, whether as a result of that reading or by his own inclination, he began at the same time to modify some of his own ideas on art. Lawrence had opposed abstract art for much the same reason as he had opposed Christianity's encouragement of celibacy, seeing in both a rejection of physical actuality, a repudiation of the *élan vital* of the body in favour of a remote, immaterial idea. Moore, too, now moved away from the geometric and the abstract – a tendency that had been fostered by an initial attraction to the stylised forms of Aztec sculpture – and began introducing instead a more naturalistic element into his work, a validation of the organic, henceforth basing his sculpture on the shapes and forms inherent in fauna and flora, which he echoed or incorporated into his own works. The passage in which he discusses this propensity in terms of his desertion of abstract art, whether in the form to be found in painting or that exemplified by modern architecture, deserves to be quoted in full, since he defines there the way in which sculpture is, in contrast to painting and architecture, intrinsically part of the natural world:

> Sculpture, for me, must have life in it, vitality. It must have a feeling for organic form, a certain pathos and warmth. Purely abstract sculpture seems to me to be an activity that would be better fulfilled

in another art, such as architecture. That is why I have never been tempted to remain a purely abstract sculptor. Abstract sculptures are too often but models for monuments that are never carried out, and the works of many abstract or 'constructivist' sculptors suffer from this frustration in that the artist never gets around to finding the real material solution to his problems. But sculpture is different from architecture. It creates organisms that must be complete in themselves. An architect has to deal with practical considerations, such as comfort, costs and so on, which remain alien to an artist, very real problems that are different from those which a sculptor has to face.... A sculpture must have its own life. Rather than give the impression of a smaller object carved out of a bigger block, it should make the observer feel that what he is seeing contains within itself its own organic energy thrusting outwards – if a work of sculpture has its own life and form, it will be alive and expansive, seeming larger than the stone or wood from which it is carved. It should always give the impression, whether carved or modelled, of having grown organically, created by pressure from within.[44]

At a time when Abstract art and Cubism were striving to convey the mathematical essence of objects in a manner detached from external appearance or physical form, Moore sought to capture, as in his *Mother and Child* of 1932 (Figure 31), a sense of the natural curves of the human body. Indeed his choice of two major themes recurrent throughout his career – parent–child relationships and the recumbent human figure – itself suggests the human interest in his sculptural work. As a twentieth-century artist he did adopt certain non-representational tendencies in Modernist art and, partly under the influence of Brancusi and Modigliani, whom he greatly admired, remained indebted to the totemistic styles of earlier eras, his recumbent figures being derived from a statue of the Mayan Rain Spirit, *Chac Mool*, of which he had seen a copy in Paris in 1925. Yet a comparison of his own reclining figures with that prototype reveals the romantic quality that has entered his work, his dilution of the hieratic in favour of softer moulding, rhythmic curves and more sensuous lines. As he remarked in 1937, the forms he incorporated into his work, even when non-mimetic, were intended to recall the cycle of nature's seasons and mankind's place within it:

The meaning and significance of form itself probably depends on the countless associations of man's history. For example, rounded forms convey an idea of fruitfulness, maturity, probably because the earth, women's breasts, and most fruits are rounded, and these shapes are important because they have this background in our habits of perception. I think the humanist organic element will always be for me of fundamental importance in sculpture, giving sculpture its vitality. Each particular carving I make takes on in my mind a human or occasionally animal, character and personality, and this personality controls its design and formal qualities, and makes me satisfied or dissatisfied with the work as it develops.[45]

Even what was to become the hallmark of his recumbent figures – the unrealistic hole or aperture in the body – was not an abandonment of naturalism but an attempt to retrieve a naturalistic quality liable to be lost in the statuary form. It was, as he himself pointed out, designed to counteract the effect of monumental frontality associated with sculpture, the sense of impenetrable solidity conveyed by the marble, bronze or other material of which it was composed. By carrying the eye through the figure towards the plane on the opposite side, he sought to restore a sense of the roundness or integrality belonging to the human body in its natural form. And the shapes and figures that he incorporated into his sculpture were generally derived from the countryside and seashore, from the pebbles, rocks, driftwood and shells that he found on his frequent walks along the beach and which always lined his studio:

Although it is the human figure which interests me most deeply, I have always paid great attention to natural forms, such as bones, shells, and pebbles, etc. Sometimes for several years running I have been to the same part of the sea-shore – but each year a new shape of pebble has caught my eye, which the year before, though it was there in hundreds, I never saw. Out of the millions of pebbles passed in walking along the shore, I choose out to see with excitement only those which fit in with my existing form-interest at the time.

Such responsiveness to the beauty of the natural world is as far removed from the geometric abstractions of Cubist art as Elinor Wylie's poetry is from the compressed, cerebral allusiveness of *The Waste Land*, as, in her 'Wild Peaches' and other poems, she reverts to the subjective lyricism traditionally associated with poetry:

I love the look, austere, immaculate,
Of landscapes drawn in pearly monotones.
There's something in my very blood that owns
Bare hills, cold silver on a sky of slate,
A thread of water, churned to milky spate
Streaming through slanted pastures fenced with stones.
I love those skies, thin blue or snowy gray,
Those fields sparse-planted, rendering meagre sheaves;
That spring, briefer than apple-blossom's breath,
Summer, so much too beautiful to stay . . .

In Britain, too, W. H. Auden, who had begun to replace Eliot as the model for younger poets,[46] consciously resisted the fragmented forms and convoluted patterns of Imagism, with which he was at that time fully familiar. He writes with an emotional directness and unselfconscious subjectivity closer to the nineteenth-century tradition:

Lay your sleeping head, my love,
Human on my faithless arm;
Time and fevers burn away
Individual beauty from
Thoughtful children, and the grave
Proves the child ephemeral:
But in my arms till break of day
Let the living creature lie,
Mortal, guilty, but to me
The entirely beautiful.

And so did Dylan Thomas in such well-known poems as his

Do not go gentle into that good night,
Old age should burn and rive at close of day,
Rage, rage against the dying of the light . . .

During the 1930s, Henry Moore, in collaboration with his friend and colleague Barbara Hepworth, did begin experimenting with a new form of sculpture – mathematically based figures such as para-boloids, with strings or threads gracefully joining the parts. But he soon deserted that mode, maintaining that such forms were too

abstract, leading him in the direction of mere 'ingenuity rather than
a fundamental human experience'. Instead, paralleling his experimentation with reclining figures, he began an essentially new form
of sculpture, of which his *Two Forms* of 1934 (Figure 32) may be taken
as representative. Technically, such sculpture was non-figural, making no pretence at mimetic fidelity and, as its title suggests, seemingly
unrelated to any object in the real world. Yet as Moore himself
acknowledged, they were not abstractions but metaphors, trans-
formative images of human figures, with the larger form curving
protectively over the smaller in a manner evocative of Mother and
Child. Where Picasso in his Cubist phase sought to transfer the
viewer from the real world into a metaphysical reality beyond,
a cacophonous jumble of harsh, jagged edges and conflicting images,
Moore's aim was to reinforce the viewer's sense of the harmony and
beauty of the organic, the curves and shapes to be found in nature
and, above all, the human body.

It is remarkable how close he came in this to a principle then being
enunciated for poetry. Archibald MacLeish's 'Ars Poetica' was
acknowledged in its day as formulating the new characteristics of
Modernist poetry – even though the poem troubled many readers
because it did not seem relevant to the dry, intellectual precision
advocated by the Imagists. The aesthetic criteria MacLeish articulated
for his generation were in fact far closer to the poetry of this later
group, of Elinor Wylie and W. H. Auden, than of Pound and Eliot;
and by extension, far closer to the sculpture of Moore than to the
paintings of the Cubists:

> A poem should be palpable and mute
> As a globed fruit
>
> Dumb
> As old medallions to the thumb
>
> Silent as the sleeve-worn stone
> Of casement ledges where the moss has grown –
>
> A poem should be wordless
> As the flight of birds...

The criterion for poetry here is no longer anecdotal realism, as in
Tennyson's 'Enoch Arden' or Browning's 'Fra Lippo Lippi', nor the

subjective recalling of a moment of profound emotion, as in Words-
worth's 'Solitary Reaper'. As MacLeish claims a few lines later:

> A poem should be equal to:
> Not true.

The principle of mimesis, or figural fidelity, which had, since the
Renaissance, formed so central a part of the arts, was no longer relevant. Instead Modernist poets tended to employ equivalents, symbols
that evoke without imitating. But within his definition one notes
how such poetry is still to be based upon the objects of this world,
especially the texture, shape and appearance of such objects, mutely
conveying their essential, palpable quality. In the same way Henry
Moore's sculpture abandoned the anatomical accuracy of past tradition such as Rodin's *St. John the Baptist Preaching* (a sculpture so lifelike
that Rodin was charged with having produced it from life-casts).[47]
But in deserting the mimetic tradition, Moore did not move towards
abstract art. Instead he conveyed the mute palpability of his reclining figures by evoking the curves, hollows and undulations of the
human body itself.

To conceive of Modernist literature as reflecting the fragmentation of the human personality, the intellectual allusiveness and the
psychological associationism dominating the Cubist, Abstract and
Surrealist painting of the era may be justified in application to certain areas of twentieth-century writing, notably to Imagist poetry
and the stream-of-consciousness novel. But such classification not
only ignores a major portion of English and American literature produced during the first half of this century; it excludes from that category some of the most important novelists and poets of the time. So
serious an omission must cast doubt on the authenticity of the classification itself. On the other hand, by applying Clement Greenberg's
theory in both its negative as well as its positive implications, it
becomes possible to perceive two stages in the literary development
of Modernist literature.

The first stage, consciously interdisciplinary in intent, manifested
itself during the Vorticist period in its attempt to unify art and literature and produce a collective response to the new age, as well as in
the more general need among writers to absorb the impact of their
first stimulating contact with Post-Impressionist and Cubist painting
during the period of the Grafton Gallery exhibition and the Armory
Show. Such was the period of most intense experimentation in the

works of T. S. Eliot, Joyce, Woolf and Faulkner. But, together with
the aesthetic innovations introduced by that interart pursuit and,
with growing force, subsequent to it, literature, it becomes apparent,
began to discard many of those experimental innovations, returning
instead to traditional narrative processes and the lyrical tradition in
poetry. It did so not through the writers' inability to incorporate the
new techniques – as the high quality of the novels by D. H. Lawrence, Hemingway, Fitzgerald and Graham Greene suggest – but
through their sense that those innovations were ultimately inappropriate to the genre of literature. Instead, poets and authors responded
more directly to the contemporary principle that each medium
should emphasise the qualities intrinsic to its own specific art form.
If, for painting, that meant highlighting the two-dimensional aspect
of the medium and rigorously excluding the anecdotal, the figural
and the mythological on the ground that the latter were more suited
to literature, then literature itself was fully justified, on that same
principle, in cultivating those elements recognised as integral to
poetry and the novel. In so doing, writers were not deserting the
tenets of Modernism but were, independently and authentically,
applying its doctrines to their own autonomous medium.

However stylistically dissimilar the works produced in the visual
and verbal media may appear to have been during this second
phase, the desire of their creators to remain within the parameters
specific to their respective art forms reveals an underlying unity of
motivation. In that regard it confirms the principle we have been
investigating throughout this study, that, with all due regard for the
individuality of such writers as Conrad, Eliot, Huxley, Hemingway,
Woolf and others, their responses to the shared challenges of their
day, to the urgent problems posed for their generation by discoveries
in physics, psychology, astronomy and anthropology, produced in
their writings discernible parallels to the stylistic and thematic
innovations of contemporary architects, painters and sculptors, affinities whose identification can prove stimulating for an understanding
of their work.

Notes and References

INTRODUCTION (pp. 1–9)

1. 'A poem is like a picture: one strikes your fancy the nearer you stand; another, when further away. This prefers the shade, while that needs to be viewed in the light, unafraid of critical judgment. This pleases but once; that, although ten times called for, will always please', *Ars Poetica*, 361f. Horace's equation of poetry and painting echoed an aphorism of much earlier origin, probably traceable to Simonides of Ceos.

2. The quotations are from Leonardo Da Vinci's *Notebooks* (London, 1954), 2:211, and Joseph Warton, *An Essay on the Genius and Writings of Pope* (London, 1806), 1:52. The widespread use of the phrase in the Renaissance is discussed in Joel E. Spingarn, *A History of Literary Criticism in the Renaissance* (New York, 1920), p. 42. See also Rensselaer W. Lee, *Ut Pictura Poesis: the humanistic theory of painting* (New York, 1967).

3. 'In reality poetry and rhetoric do not succeed in exact description so well as painting does; their business is, to affect rather by sympathy than imitation; to display rather the effect of things on the mind of the speaker, or of others, than to present a clear idea of the things themselves. This is their most extensive province, and that in which they succeed best.' Edmund Burke, *A Philosophical Enquiry into the Origin of our Ideas of the Sublime and the Beautiful* (London, 1798), p. 3.

4. Exceptions include the attempt by Jacob Burckhardt and Heinrich Wölfflin in the nineteenth century to revive the principle in terms of a *Zeitgeist*, the idea that there exists in each generation a 'Spirit of the Time', a concept briefly revived in the mid twentieth century by such historians as Wylie Sypher and Mario Praz. The effectiveness of that recent revival was severely undercut in 1972 by Alistair Fowler's powerful attack (*New Literary History*, 3:488) in which, with considerable justice, he castigated Sypher and Praz for their failure to substantiate their comparisons, mordantly describing their vague gesturing towards supposed similarities as a 'this-reminds-me-of-that' approach.

5. Stephen Greenblatt, *Shakespearean Negotiations: the circulation of social energy in Renaissance England* (Berkeley, 1988), p. 86, and Michel Foucault, *The Order of Things* (London, 1970), p. xi. Wendy Steiner, *The Colors of Rhetoric: problems in the relation between modern literature and painting* (Chicago, 1982), has seen in semiotic theory renewed justification for comparisons between art and literature in the modern period; but the principle clearly needs to be extended to include past eras too.

6. Michael Baxandall, *Painting and Experience in Fifteenth Century Italy* (Oxford, 1972), p. 40. His approach developed further in his *Patterns of Intention: on the historical explanation of pictures* (New Haven, 1985). See also Norman Bryson, *Vision and Painting: the logic of gaze* (New Haven, 1983), especially pp. xii–xiii, and his introduction to *Calligram: essays in New Art History from France* (Cambridge, 1988), p. xxv, as well as Donald

Preziosi, *Rethinking Art History* (New Haven, 1989), especially pp. 48–50, the useful collections of essays in A. L. Rees and Frances Borzello (eds), *The New Art History* (London, 1986), and Salim Kemal and Ivan Gaskell (eds), *The Language of Art History* (Cambridge, 1993).

7. The jacket quotation is from Alan Brien of the *Sunday Telegraph*. John Galbraith's essay is reprinted in Philip C. Kolin and J. Madison David (eds), *Critical Essays on Edward Albee* (Boston, 1986).

8. Edward Albee, *Who's Afraid of Virginia Woolf?* (Harmondsworth, 1986), p. 113.

9. Ibid., pp. 124–5.

10. Cf. Peter Nicholls, *Modernisms: a literary guide* (Berkeley, 1995) and the valuable collection of essays in Malcolm Bradbury and James McFarlane (eds), *Modernism: a guide to European Literature, 1890–1930* (London, 1991). Raymond Williams, *The Politics of Modernism*, published posthumously (London, 1989), like most Marxist criticism, attributes all developments in the period – literary, artistic and philosophical – to exclusively economic or socioeconomic causes.

1   CONRAD'S STYLISTIC 'MISTINESS' (pp. 10–42)

1. Ford Madox Ford, *Joseph Conrad: a personal remembrance* (London, 1924), p. 6. Ford's 1913 essay 'On Impressionism' was an earlier and briefer application of the term to Conrad's fiction. It is reprinted in Frank MacShane (ed.), *Critical Writings of Ford Madox Ford* (Lincoln, 1964), p. 37. Until 1914 Ford was still writing under his original name, Hueffer, but to avoid confusion I have used throughout the name by which he is best known.

2. Eloise Knapp Hay, 'Impressionism Limited' in Norman Sherry (ed.), *Joseph Conrad: a commemoration* (London, 1979), pp. 54–64. Ford acknowledged his own unreliability as a historian, declaring in the Preface to his *Personal Remembrance* that factual errors discovered after its composition were left uncorrected in the text in order not to spoil its validity as a private impression. He also admitted later in the work (p. 198) that in certain areas 'the writer's memory is not absolutely clear as to the points on which he and Conrad were agreed'.

3. As late as 1923 Ezra Pound still used that older view of Impressionist painting as reproducing external appearances to attack Ford's inappropriate transfer of its principles to the medium of literature: 'Nearly everything he says applies to things *seen*. It is the exact rendering of the visible image, the cabbage field *seen*, France *seen* from the cliffs.' *Criterion* 1 (January, 1923), p. 146. For the suggestion that Ford's own novel *The Good Soldier* derives from the Impressionist painters, see Michael Levenson, *Modernism and the Fate of Individuality: character and novelistic form from Conrad to Woolf* (Cambridge, 1991), p. 102.

4. Brunetière's essay, 'Impressionism dans le roman' appeared in *La revue des deux montes*, 15 November 1879, and was reprinted in his *Le roman Naturaliste* (Paris, 1883).

5. Letter to Edward Gannett, 5 December 1897, in *Collected Letters of Joseph Conrad*, ed. Frederick R. Karl and Laurence Davies (Cambridge, 1983), 1:416. Only much later, when his own novels were all completed, did he praise Crane's impressionism unreservedly, in his *Notes on Life and Letters* of 1919.

6. Letter to Marguerite Poradowska, 2 July 1891, *Collected Letters*, op. cit., 1:84.

7. Ford Madox Ford, *Joseph Conrad: a personal remembrance* (London, 1924), p. 182. The lacunas are in the original. For the development of the allied movement, see Maria E. Kronegger, *Literary Impressionism* (New Haven, 1973).

8. Joseph Warren Beach, *The Twentieth Century Novel: studies in technique* (New York, 1960), pp. 337–65. His reservation about the applicability of the term appears on p. 383.

9. Ramon Fernandez, 'L'Art de Conrad', *Nouvelle Revue française*, 12 (1924), 732. Quotations are from the translation by Charles Owen in Robert W. Stallman (ed.), *The Art of Joseph Conrad: a critical symposium* (East Lansing, 1960), pp. 8–13. Ian Watt examines this aspect in his *Conrad in the Nineteenth Century* (Berkeley, 1981), pp. 179–80. Bruce Johnson,' Conrad's Impressionism and Watt's "Delayed Decoding"', in Ross C. Murfin (ed.), *Conrad Revisited: essays for the eighties* (Alabama, 1984), p. 51, questions Watt's hesitation concerning the indebtedness to Impressionism, claiming that Conrad's descriptions reflect its subjectivism, echoing Laforgue's definition of that art form in 1883 as attempting to capture what the eye sees in its natural or primitive state, before the intervention of intellectual or conventional associations.

10. Hugh Clifford, 'Joseph Conrad: Some Scattered Memories', *The Bookman's Journal*, 11:3.

11. Aaron Scharf, *Art and Photography* (New York, 1983), pp. 165f. He notes (p. 89) that it was Corot who first adopted into painting the blurring 'halation' effect of photography produced both by the movement of objects within the scene and, on the negative, by the encroachment of light areas upon the periphery of adjacent darker sections, the Impressionists taking up the technique from him. The account of the attempt to use magnesium flash is by Adolphe Julien, *Fantin-Latour . . . sa vie et ses amitiés* (Paris, 1909), p. 155, quoted in Scharf, *Art and Photography*, op. cit., p. 62.

12. The interchangeability of the terms 'impressionism' and 'symbolism' in this period is discussed in Richard Shiff, *Cézanne and the End of Impressionism* (Chicago, 1984), p. 40f.

13. John Rewald, *Post-Impressionism: from Van Gogh to Gauguin* (New York, 1956), p. 150.

14. Gustave Kahn, 'Réponse des Symbolistes', *L'Evénement* (Paris), 28 September 1886.

15. The Rimbaud translation appears in Maynard Mack (ed.), *World Masterpieces: continental edition* (New York, 1966), 2:995.

16. Watt, *Conrad*, op. cit., pp. 198–9. Donald C. Yelton, *Mimesis and Metaphor: an inquiry into the genesis and scope of Conrad's symbolic imagery*

(Mouton, 1967), connects Conrad with literary symbolism, of which he regards Flaubert as the main representative.

17.   Michael Fried, 'Almayer's Face: on "Impressionism" in Conrad, Crane, and Norris', *Critical Inquiry* (Autumn, 1990), pp. 193–236. See also Donald R. Benson, 'Impressionist Painting and the Problem of Conrad's Atmosphere', *Mosaic*, 22 (1989), 29, which attributes the fictional mistiness to Impressionism, and the discussion in *Critical Inquiry*, Winter 1992, pp. 387–410.

18.   E. M. Forster, *Abinger Harvest* (London, 1945), pp. 134–5. The review originally appeared in 1921 in *The Nation and the Athenaeum*, and was subsequently reprinted in shortened form in the above collection.

19.   F. R. Leavis, *The Great Tradition: a study of the English Novel* (New York, 1954), pp. 211–20. For the persistence of this view in subsequent criticism, compare, in addition to the critics discussed below, H. M. Daleski, *Joseph Conrad: the way of dispossession* (London, 1977), p. 65. Albert J. Guerard, *Conrad the Novelist* (Cambridge, Mass., 1958) attributed the 'fumbling' adjectives in this story, which he also disliked, to the dream element of Conrad's journey into his inner self.

20.   Edward W. Said, *Joseph Conrad and the Fiction of Autobiography* (Cambridge, Mass., 1968), p. 4. Said argued that the source of Conrad's guilt was a personal history filled with shameful things ranging from his 'desertion of his Polish heritage to the seemingly capricious abandonment of his sea life' (p. 98). But that latter charge ignores the fact that the advent of steamships was making obsolete the sailing vessels for which Conrad had received his master's certificate, and that he had experienced a long period of unemployment and loss of income before reaching his decision to change careers. In fact he continued to seek berths long after he became a published author, as Ian Watt notes (Watt, *Conrad*, op. cit., pp. 16–19). And as regards Said's attribution of Conrad's 'guilt' to his desertion of his homeland, Avrom Fleishman has countered that in his *Conrad's Politics: community and anarchy in the fiction of Joseph Conrad* (Baltimore, 1968), which offers an illuminating analysis of the historical facts, noting that Conrad's family, as land-owning gentry in a section of the Ukraine only temporarily under Polish rule, was entirely alienated from the peasant nationalist movement, and that Conrad himself had been embarrassed at the ineptitude of his father's political activities.

21.   James Guetti, *The Limits of Metaphor: a study of Melville, Conrad, and Faulkner* (Ithaca, 1967), especially pp. 46f. Bruce Johnson, *Conrad's Models of Mind* (Minneapolis, 1971), in an existentialist reading, sees Conrad's inability to articulate (p. 71) as reflecting the white man's distancing from a nature that has become incomprehensible to him, while it remains intelligible to the natives who form an organic part of it. But there is no indication in Conrad's story that the latter, even though they live in the jungle, are in any real sense capable of comprehending its profound mystery. Allon White, *The Uses of Obscurity: the fiction of early modernism* (London, 1981), pp. 108–29, attributes the enigmatic quality of Conrad's writings to the attenuation of form and feature in the descriptions, the effacing of boundary

limits, which produces a haziness of imaginative as well as spatial parameters.

22. J. Hillis Miller 'Heart of Darkness Revisited' in Murfin, *Conrad Revisited*, op. cit., pp. 31f. For a further deconstructionist reading, see Arnold Krupat, 'Antonymy, Language, and Value in Conrad's Heart of Darkness', *Missouri Review*, 3 (1979), 63, who argues that the story conveys the futility of truth-seeking.

23. Daphna Erdinast-Vulcan, *Joseph Conrad and the Modern Temper* (Oxford, 1991), pp. 86f. The Christian allusions in the story are examined in Joan E. Steiner, 'Modern Pharisees and False Apostles: ironic New Testament parallels in Conrad's Heart of Darkness', *Nineteenth Century Fiction*, 37 (1982), 75.

24. Jerry Wasserman, 'Narrative Presence: the illusion of language in *Heart of Darkness*', in Ted Billy (ed.), *Critical Essays on Joseph Conrad* (Boston, 1987), pp. 102f.

25. Wilhelm Worringer, *Abstraction and Empathy: a contribution to the psychology of style* (New York, 1963, orig. 1908). For a discussion of this point, cf. Joseph Frank, *The Widening Gyre: crisis and mastery in modern art* (New Brunswick, 1963), pp. 51f. The Alberti quotation is from his *De aedificatoria* of 1452. Linda Nochlin, *Realism* (New York, 1976), pp. 40f., also examines the relationship between that art form and scientific empiricism. In this instance too, Ford's comment on Conrad's aims is unreliable, when he insists that he and Conrad employed a simple, colloquial style, and that their chief masters were Flaubert and Maupassant (Ford, *Joseph Conrad*, op. cit., pp. 195–6). While that statement may hold true for Ford, it certainly does not apply to Conrad, as Thomas C. Moser pointed out in *The Life in the Fiction of Ford Madox Ford* (Princeton, 1980), pp. 151f.

26. Cf. Cleanth Brooks' seminal essay on 'The Language of Paradox', reprinted in *The Well-Wrought Urn* (New York, 1947).

27. Although Gauguin declined to formulate his aesthetic theory in writing, he dominated the café discussions of the group, which supported him enthusiastically and regarded his 1893 exhibition as a manifesto of its ideas. Albert Aurier's important essay on the movement, in the *Mercure de France* (March 1891), was based largely upon remarks by Gauguin culled from these informal meetings. Cf. Georges Boudaille, *Gauguin* (London, 1964), p. 194.

28. Julia Kristeva, 'Giotto's Joy' in Leon S. Roudicz (ed.), *Desire and Language* (New York, 1980).

29. Norman Bryson (ed.), *Calligram: essays in new art history from France* (Cambridge, 1988), especially pp. xxvi–xxviii.

30. Alfred Haddon, *Evolution in Art* (London, 1895), especially pp. 317–18. The classic study of this aspect, originally published in 1938, is still Robert Goldwater, *Primitivism in Modern Art* (New York, 1967).

31. Owen Jones' *Grammar of Ornament* of 1868 was a rare exception in its praise for what he termed 'the true balance of both form and colour' in primitive decorative art. Criticism of the condescension within the primitivist movement has persisted, as in the controversy surrounding William Rubin's famed exhibition of Modernist Primitivism at the

Museum of Modern Art which, it was charged by many, ignored the political aspects of colonialism and the damaging ways in which tribal cultures had been disrupted in the process of collecting such works.

32. *Lettres de Gauguin à Daniel de Monfreid* (Paris, 1950), p. 113, the letter dated October 1897. Gill Perry, in his essay in C. Harrison, F. Frascina and Gill Perry (eds), *Primitivism, Cubism, Abstraction: the early twentieth century* points to such paintings as Dinet's *Sur les terraces* (1898) to substantiate the view that primitivism was already of interest to Western artists when Gauguin began his work, but the paintings he cites are clear instances of Western condescension in the tradition of the ethnologists.

33. Cf. Jill Lloyd, *German Expressionism: primitivism and modernity* (New Haven, 1991), which examines certain aspects of this validation of primitive art in the West.

34. William Rubin (ed.), *'Primitivism' in Twentieth-century Art: affinity of the tribal and the modern* (Boston, 1984), 1:7. Rubin notes correctly that although the term 'primitivism' was originally pejorative, it has, as Claude Lévy-Strauss has argued in his *Structural Anthropology* (London, 1963), pp. 101–2, by now lost such associations in the general recognition that tribal craftsmen displayed a genius for invention that often outdistanced the achievements of other nations.

35. There are useful collections of reviews and comments representing the English response to the French school in Kate Flint (ed.), *Impressionism in England: the critical reception* (London, 1984) and J. B. Bullen (ed.), *Post-Impressionists in England* (London, 1988). S. K. Tillyard, *The Impact of Modernism 1900–1920* (London, 1988), connects the English response to Post-Impressionism with criteria already established by the Arts and Crafts Movement. There are studies of the British painters who followed the French lead in Simon Watney, *English Post-Impressionism* (London, 1980), and Laura Wortley, *British Impressionism: a garden of bright images* (London, 1988).

36. Chinua Achabe, 'An Image of Africa: racism in Conrad's *Heart of Darkness'*, *The Massachusetts Review*, 18 (1977), 782.

37. Marianna Torgovnick, *Gone Primitive: savage intellects, modern lives* (Chicago, 1990), especially pp. 152f.

38. Joseph Conrad, *Heart of Darkness*, pp. 61–2. All quotations in this chapter are from the Norton text, edited by Robert Kimbrough (New York, 1971).

39. Joseph Conrad, *An Outcast of the Islands* (New York, 1964), p. 155.

40. Paul Gauguin, *The Intimate Journals* (orig. 1903), trans. Van Wyck Brooks (London, 1930), quotations from pp. 128, 125, 143, 175. E. D. Morel, *King Leopold's Rule in Africa* (London, 1904) records, among other instances of ruthless mutilation, the widespread practice of amputating the hands of innocent blacks in order to provide 'evidence' that bullets expended in casual game hunting had been used to suppress 'rebels'. See Andrea White, *Joseph Conrad and the Adventure Tradition: constructing and deconstructing the imperial subject* (Cambridge, 1993).

41. Hoxey N. Fairchild, *The Noble Savage: a study in Romantic naturalism* (New York, 1963).

42.   James Hunt, 'On the Negro's Place in Nature', his presidential address published in the *Memoirs of the Anthropological Society of 1863*, 1:164. The quotations from the Society debate are recorded in George W. Stocking, Jr, *Victorian Anthropology* (New York, 1987), p. 251, which offers a valuable overview of the shift from evolutionism to relativism within nineteenth-century anthropology. The quotation from John Lubbock is from his *Prehistoric Times, as illustrated by Ancient Remains, and the Manners and Customs of Modern Savages* (London, 1865), pp. 410–16, while Edward Burnett Tylor developed his relativist viewpoint in *Primitive Culture: researches in the development of mythology, philosophy, religion, language, art and custom* (London, 1873). On this point, see also John W. Griffith, *Joseph Conrad and the Anthropological Dilemma* (Oxford, 1995), especially pp. 179f.

43.   J. W. Burrow, *Evolution and Society: a study in Victorian social theory* (Cambridge, 1966), especially pp. 245f.

44.   On the relationship between Conrad and Malinowski, see James Clifford, *The Predicament of Culture: twentieth century ethnography, literature, and art* (Cambridge, Mass., 1988), pp. 92–114, and David Richards, *Masks of Difference: cultural representations in literature, anthropology, and art* (Cambridge, 1994), pp. 191f. Frazer's approach and its impact on the twentieth century will be examined in more detail in the following chapter.

45.   Terry Eagleton, *Literary Theory: an introduction* (Minneapolis, 1983), especially pp. 601f.; Richard Rorty, *The Consequences of Pragmatism* (Minneapolis, 1982), p. 92.

46.   Cf. Paul Gauguin, *Noa, Noa*, translated by O. F. Theis (New York, 1920), p. 74 and passim.

47.   J. P. Richter (ed.), *The Literary Works of Leonardo da Vinci* (London, 1939), 1:150.

48.   *Diverses Choses* (1896–97), an unpublished manuscript by Gauguin, quoted in Herschel B. Chipp, *Theories of Modern Art* (Berkeley, 1968), p. 66.

49.   Strindberg's letter to Gauguin, 1 February 1895.

50.   Letter to Fontainas, March 1899, in John Rewald (ed.), *Letters to Ambroise Vollard and André Fontainas* (San Francisco, 1943), p. 22.

51.   Conrad, *Heart of Darkness*, op. cit., p. 62.

52.   Albert J. Guerard, *Conrad the Novelist* (Cambridge, Mass., 1958).

53.   Conrad, *Heart of Darkness*, op. cit.

54.   For the frequency of Christian themes in his work, see Ziva Amishai-Maisels, *Gauguin's Religious Themes* (New York, 1985), pp. 2f.

55.   Cf. Richard Bettell and Peter Zegers, 'The Final Years', in *The Art of Paul Gauguin* (Washington, DC: National Gallery of Art, 1988), pp. 409–10.

56.   In their depiction of *The Meeting of the Magi*, in *Les Très Riches Heures du Duc du Berry*, executed about 1416.

57.   For other instances, cf. his Tahitian Nativity scene in the Hermitage, his *Self-Portrait with the Yellow Christ*, and his *Nave Nave Moe – The Joy of Resting* with its haloed figure.

58.   Michael Levenson, *Modernism and the Fate of Individuality*, especially the opening chapter. See also Karl Miller, *Doubles: studies in literary history* (Oxford, 1985).

59.   Cf. Michel Foucault, *Discipline and Punishment: the birth of the prison*, trans. Alan Sheridan (London, 1977), and Jacques Lacan, *Ecrits: a selection* (London, 1977), as well as his *The Four Fundamental Concepts of Psycho-Analysis* (London, 1977).

60.   Jules Huret, 'Paul Gauguin devant ses tableaux', *Echo de Paris* (23 February 1891), and Gauguin's letter dated 16 November 1889 in Maurice Malingue (ed.), *Lettres de Gauguin à sa Femme et à ses Amis* (Paris, 1946), p. 177.

61.   In a letter dated 8 December 1892, in Malingue, *Lettres de Gauguin à sa Femme*, op. cit., p. 236. The tradition on which the painting relies is discussed in Jehanne Teilhet-Fisk, *Paradise Reviewed: an interpretation of Gauguin's Polynesian symbolism* (Ann Arbor, 1983), pp. 62–72, and Michael Hoog, *Paul Gauguin: life and work* (New York, 1987).

62.   Dorothy Hammond and Alta Jablow, *The Myth of Africa* (New York, 1977), p. 94. Although in a minority among anthropologists, W. Arens, *The Man-Eating Myth* (New York, 1979), suggests that cannibalism never existed at all, while Peggy R. Sanday, *Divine Hunger: cannibalism as a cultural system* (Cambridge, 1986), assumes it to have been a very rare phenomenon. Montaigne made a point similar to Gauguin's in his essay 'Of Cannibals': *Essays of Montaigne*, trans. Charles Cotton (New York, 1947), p. 72. Conrad's reference to eating warriors legitimately slain in warfare, as opposed to innocent victims, occurs on p. 103.

63.   Conrad, *Heart of Darkness*, op. cit.

64.   Ibid., p. 43.

65.   Gauguin, *Noa Noa*, op. cit., p. 93. This work has had doubt cast upon its reliability, as it seems to have been heavily edited by his friend Charles Mortice. But the remark quoted here would seem to have emanated from Gauguin himself. The second quotation is from Gaugin, *Intimate Journals*, op. cit., p. 197.

66.   Conrad, *Heart of Darkness*, op. cit.

67.   Emily Dickinson, *The Complete Poems*, ed. Thomas H. Johnson (Boston, 1960), pp. 506–7.

68.   Conrad, *Heart of Darkness*, op. cit.

69.   Ibid., p. 6.

70.   Rewald, *Post-Impressionism*, op. cit., p. 209.

71.   Letter to Richard Curle dated 24 April 1922, in Richard Curle (ed.), *Conrad to a Friend: 150 selected letters from Joseph Conrad to Richard Curle* (London, 1928), p. 113.

72.   In an unpublished letter from Gauguin to Vincent Van Gogh in 1888, quoted in Rewald, *Post-Impressionism*, op. cit., p. 209. The second quotation is from a letter to Fontainas in March 1899, in Malingue, *Lettres de Gauguin à sa Femme*, op. cit., p. 288.

73.   While my book was already in press, Daniel R. Schwarz's study, *Reconfiguring Modernism* (New York, 1997) appeared, with the interesting suggestion that Conrad may have read Gauguin's *Noa Noa* before writing *The Heart of Darkness* and with an exploration of possible influences upon the novel. I regret that the book reached me too late for the insertion of any fuller acknowledgment.

74.   *Diverse Choses*, in Chipp, *Theories*, op. cit., p. 65.

2 T. S. ELIOT AND THE SECULARISTS (pp. 43–85)

1. Wylie Sypher, *Rococo to Cubism in art and literature* (New York, 1960),
    p. 284; William Skaff, *The Philosophy of T. S. Eliot: from skepticism to sur-
    realist poetic, 1909–1927* (Philadelphia, 1986), pp. 131f. Other early
    explorers of such intermedia connections include Jacob Korg, 'Modern
    Art Techniques in *The Waste Land*', *Journal of Aesthetics and Art Criticism*,
    18 (1960), p. 456, Mario Praz, *Mnemosyne: the parallel between literature
    and the visual arts* (Princeton, 1970), and John Dixon Hunt, 'Broken
    Images: T. S. Eliot and Modern Painting', in A. D. Moody (ed.), *'The
    Waste Land' in Different Voices* (London, 1974), pp. 163–84. Hunt noted
    in that essay how few critics had, until that time, explored or even
    commented on the relationship of Eliot to the visual arts.
2. Werner Haftmann's classic study *Painting in the Twentieth Century: an
    analysis of the artists and their work*, trans. Ralph Manheim (New York,
    1965), 2:8–19, offers a valuable summary of the effects of modern
    physics and psychology upon painting. For certain aspects of science's
    impact on literature in this period, see N. Katherine Hayles, *The Cosmic
    Web: scientific field models and literary strategies in the twentieth century*
    (Ithaca, 1984), and her *Chaos Bound: orderly disorder and contemporary
    literature and science* (Ithaca, 1990).
3. There is an excellent account of the relationship of Eliot's verse to the
    work of Wyndham Lewis, Ezra Pound and James Joyce in Eric Svarny,
    The Men of 1914: T. S. Eliot and early modernism (Milton Keynes, 1988), a
    study which confirms how little Eliot was concerned with the visual
    aspects of Vorticism. The book focuses instead upon the shared intel-
    lectual élitism of this group, and its assimilation of Symbolist poetics.
    On élitism in both art and literature at this time, see Charles Harri-
    son's fine study, *English Art and Modernism, 1900–1939* (New Haven,
    1994), especially pp. 56f.
4. Allen Tate (ed.), *T. S. Eliot: the Man and his Work: a critical evaluation by
    twenty-six distinguished writers* (New York, 1966), pp. 37–8.
5. On his return to America in 1912, Eliot hung a copy of Gauguin's *The
    Yellow Christ* on his wall, but he may have been more interested in the
    religious theme than the artistic representation. Quotations from
    Eliot's poems are from *The Complete Poems and Plays* (London, 1973).
6. Although Eliot was acquainted with Roger Fry and Clive Bell, the
    friendship was never very close, as is recorded in Lyndall Gordon,
    Eliot's Early Years (Oxford, 1977), pp. 77f.
7. T. S. Eliot, *Letters*, ed. Valerie Eliot (London, 1988), 1:363.
8. T. S. Eliot, 'A Note on Poetry and Belief', first published in Wyndham
    Lewis's *Enemy* i (January 1927), pp. 15–17.
9. T. S. Eliot, 'Thoughts After Lambeth', in *Selected Essays* (London, 1949),
    p. 358.
10. George Williamson, *A Reader's Guide to T. S. Eliot* (New York, 1953);
    A. Alvarez, *The Shaping Spirit: studies in modern English and American
    poets* (London, 1967), p. 27; Eloise Knapp Hay, *T. S. Eliot's Negative Way*
    (Cambridge, Mass., 1982), p. 48. Cf. also D. W. Harding, 'What the
    Thunder Said', in A. D. Moody (ed.), *The Waste Land in Different Voices*

(London, 1974), pp. 15f., who sees the poem as essentially secular in orientation, employing the Crucifixion solely in terms of Frazer's fertility cycle.

11. Calvin Bedient, *He Do the Police in Different Voices: 'The Waste Land' and its protagonist* (Chicago, 1986).

12. From the syllabus to Eliot's 1916 Extension Lectures.

13. E. M. Forster, *Abinger Harvest* (London, 1936), pp. 86–96; Malcolm Cowley, *Exile's Return* (New York, 1934), p. 124. For an account of the critical hostility aroused by the poem, see Grover Smith, *The Waste Land* (London, 1983), pp. 133f., which also acknowledges the widespread impact it had upon contemporary readers, stimulated by its vitality and tragic intensity.

14. Cf. his insistence on privacy for the conversion itself: 'He wished for absolute secrecy; he hated, he said, dramatic public conversions. . . . On 23 June 1927 the doors of Finstock Church were firmly locked against idle spectators, and Stead poured the water of regeneration over Eliot's head' (Gordon, *Eliot's Early Years*, op. cit., p. 131).

15. Eliot's widely read review of Grierson's anthology of Metaphysical Poetry was largely responsible for the revival of Donne's reputation. In his Clark lectures, Eliot began to be less positive towards Donne, but not on religious grounds; for he was then developing his theory of impersonality in writing, of objective correlative, in that regard preferring Lancelot Andrewes over Donne. Eliot's essay 'Religion and Literature' (1935), published at a time when Hopkins was only just beginning to be retrospectively recognised, classed the latter as a 'major poet', together with Henry Vaughan, Richard Crashaw and George Herbert, drawn from the group of Metaphysical poets he had recently endorsed.

16. I am of course deeply indebted here to Linda D. Henderson's study *The Fourth Dimension and Non-Euclidian Geometry in Modern Art* (Princeton, 1983), which recounts the emergence of hyperspace theory, together with details concerning the use made of it by painters. Her examination of the theory's effect upon literature (which was never an aim of her book) is restricted, as in most later critical accounts, to the more obvious instances of indebtedness such as the science fiction stories by H. G. Wells and others, or the parody of the theory in Oscar Wilde's 'The Canterville Ghost'. Tom Gibbons, 'Cubism and the Fourth Dimension', *Journal of the Warburg and Courtauld Institutes*, 44 (1981), 130, adds little to her research.

17. Quoted in René Huyghe, *La Naissance du Cubisme* (Paris, 1935), p. 80.

18. Apollinaire's lecture was published the following year as 'Le Peinture Nouvelle' in *Les Soirées de Paris*, April 1912, p. 90. The quotation from Albert Gleizes and Jean Metzinger, *Du Cubisme* (Paris, 1912), p. 17, is from the translation in Robert L. Herbert (ed.), *Modern Artists on Art* (Englewood Cliffs, 1964), p. 8.

19. Quoted in Henderson, *The Fourth Dimension*, op. cit., p. 127. See also the stimulating essays in the catalogue produced for the exhibition entitled 'The Spiritual in Art: abstract painting, 1890–1985', held in the Los Angeles County Museum in 1986.

20. A. S. Eddington, *The Nature of the Physical World* (Cambridge, 1929), pp. xv–xvi, delivered as the Gifford lectures in 1927 (emphasis added).

21. Wyndham Lewis, *Time and Western Man* (Boston, 1957, originally 1927), p. 455.

22. John A. Lester Jr, *Journey Through Despair 1880–1914: transformations in British literary culture* (Princeton, 1968), p. 21.

23. See, for example, Jewel S. Brooker and Joseph Bentley, *Reading 'The Waste Land': modernism and the limits of interpretation* (Amherst, 1990), especially pp. 20–33.

24. L. Revel, '*L'Esprit et l'éspace: La Quatrième Dimension* in *Le Théosophe*, March, 1911. In exploring this connection, we may recall that one of the first published responses to *The Waste Land*, F. L. Lucas's antagonistic review in the *New Statesman*, dismissed it as 'a theosophical tract'.

25. W. F. Tyler, *The Dimensional Idea as an Aid to Religion* (New York, 1910), especially pp. 32, 44.

26. John Dixon Hunt, 'Broken Images', op. cit., p. 169, in an otherwise stimulating article, typifies this approach in the comment that Magritte, together with the Surrealists and Cubists, shared a 'boredom' with illusionist space.

27. Samuel Johnson, *Rasselas* (1759). Joshua Reynolds argued for the same principle in his *Discourses on Art*, 4.

28. Sanford Schwartz, in his excellent study *The Matrix of Modernism: Pound, Eliot, and early twentieth-century thought* (Princeton, 1985), examining the relationship between Modernist literature and such nineteenth-century thinkers as Nietzsche and William James, employs the term 'conceptual abstraction' to describe those mental concepts that censor or filter out sense impressions, and obscure the more valid 'stream of consciousness'. His theme should be distinguished from the more general usage of the term (as employed here), referring to certain 'abstract' truths sensed as existing beyond the tactile world. His book will be discussed more closely in a later chapter.

29. Friedrich Nietzsche, *Philosophy and truth: selections from Nietzsche's notebooks*, ed. and trans. Daniel Breazeale (Atlantic Highlands, NJ, 1979), p. 83.

30. Wilhelm Worringer, *Abstraction and Empathy: a contribution to the psychology of style*, trans. Michael Bullock (New York, 1980), especially pp. 21, 28, 44. Although Eliot was not especially interested in the visual arts, he became aware of Worringer's work through his admiration of Hulme, the latter incorporating Worringer's theories into his own work and thereby encouraging the Imagists' pursuit of the inorganic in verse, a cultivation of 'hardness' or objectivity in imagery. In connection with the religious undercurrent in Modernism, one may note how Hulme, although not a Christian, resuscitated the theme of Original Sin in his philosophy, arguing that the Renaissance humanist concept of man's perfectibility, so influential throughout Western culture, was misleadingly shallow. He urged contemporary art and literature to come to terms with mankind's 'radical imperfections' and to return to the concept behind Original Sin. See his *Speculations: essays*

on humanism and the philosophy of art, ed. Herbert Read (London, 1960, orig. 1924), p. 34.

31. Georges Braque, in an interview reprinted in Edward F. Fry, *Cubism* (London, 1966), p. 53.

32. Olivier-Hourcade, 'La Tendance del peinture contemporaine', *Revue de France et des Pays Français* (February 1912). Joseph Frank's widely admired essay, 'Spatial Form in Modern Literature' (1945), republished in his *The Widening Gyre: crisis and mastery in modern literature* (New Brunswick, 1963), popularised Worringer's view of modern art and literature as based on the concept of fragmentation and discontinuity.

33. Wassily Kandinsky, *Concerning the Spiritual in Art*, trans. Michael Sadleir *et al.* (New York, 1947), p. 29, the earlier quotation from his essay, *'Über die Formfrage'* as translated by Kenneth Lindsay. For a close study of Kandinsky's debt to Theosophy and of the mystical–religious elements in his aesthetic philosophy, see Sixten Ringbom, *The Sounding Cosmos: a study in the spiritualism of Kandinsky and the genesis of abstract painting* (Abo, 1970).

34. Rose-Carol Washton Long, *Kandinsky: the development of an abstract style* (Oxford, 1980), p. 111.

35. Robert Rosenblum, *Modern Painting and the Northern Romantic Tradition: Friedrich to Rothko* (New York, 1975), pp. 173f. The first Mondrian quotation is from Robert P. Welsh and J. M. Joosten, *Two Mondrian Sketchbooks, 1912–14* (Amsterdam, 1969), p. 33, the second from 'No Axiom but the Plastic', *De Stijl*, 6 (1924), 6–7.

36. Cf. Jonathan Rose, *The Edwardian Temperament, 1895–1919* (London, 1986), especially pp. 4–16. Rose correctly notes that, after the war, the Society lost much of its scientific prestige as it pandered to the widespread desire among the bereaved to establish contact with their lost ones. But in the earlier decades of the century it was essentially a movement of intellectuals.

37. The essay was reprinted in Roger Fry's *Vision & Design*, published in 1920.

38. Sheldon Cheney, *Expressionism in Art* (New York, 1934), pp. 313f.

39. Quoted in the catalogue for the exhibition entitled 'Conceptual Art and Conceptual Aspects' at the New York Cultural Center in 1970 (p. 56).

40. The first extract is from Yeats' *Autobiography* (New York, 1958), p. 77, the second from the autobiographical manuscript published in 1972, and the third quotation from his *Memoirs*, ed. Denis Donoghue (London, 1972). Yeats wrote to Ernest Boyd in 1915: 'My interest in mystic symbolism did not come from Arthur Symons or any other contemporary writer. I have been a student of the medieval mystics since 1887.... Of the French symbolists I have never had detailed or accurate knowledge.' Ezra Pound's interest in the occult is discussed in Alan Robinson, *Poetry, Painting, and Ideas, 1885–1914* (London, 1985), especially pp. 150–81.

41. Ezra Pound quoted this remark with approval in 'The New Sculpture', *Egoist*, 16 February 1914, attributing it to an anonymous speaker at a meeting of the Quest Society. For his belief in a 'Theos' and for

a more detailed account of such esoteric interests, see Timothy Materer, *Modernist Alchemy: poetry and the occult* (Ithaca, 1995), pp. 71f.

42. T. S. Eliot, doctoral thesis, (written 1911–14), *Knowledge and Experience in the Philosophy of F. H. Bradley* (London, 1964), pp. 147–8. On his vein of scepticism allowing for such adaptation of viewpoint in his response to other rites and religions, see C. M. Kearns, 'Religion, Literature, and society in the work of T. S. Eliot', in A. David Moody (ed.), *The Cambridge Companion to T. S. Eliot* (Cambridge, 1994).

43. Robert Klein, *Form and Meaning: writings on the Renaissance and modern art* (Princeton, 1981), pp. 184f.; J. Hillis Miller, *Poets of Reality: six twentieth-century writers* (Cambridge, Mass., 1965), p. 9.

44. Meyer Schapiro, 'The Nature of Abstract Art' (1937), reprinted in his *Modern Art, 19th and 20th centuries: selected papers* (New York, 1978), p. 198.

45. The first extract is quoted in Athena T. Spear, *Brancusi's Birds* (New York, 1969), p. 21, and the second in Paul Morand's preface to the catalogue he prepared for the artist's first one-man exhibition at the Brummer Gallery, New York, December, 1926.

46. Yeats, 'Among School Children', (1926). The contemporary account of Loïe Fuller's performance is from Isadora Duncan's autobiography. Numerous artists attempted to capture Loïe Fuller's performances, one of the most successful instances being the Art Nouveau statuette by Raoul-François Larche.

47. Maud Ellmann, *The Poetics of Impersonality* (London, 1987), discusses this aspect of Eliot and Pound, attributing its origin primarily to Bergson's claim for the fugitive quality of the individual self.

48. Cf. James Longenbeach, 'Mature Poets Steal: Eliot's allusive practice' in Moody, *The Cambridge Companion*, op. cit.

49. Eliot, *Knowledge and Experience*, op. cit., p. 30.

50. The principle was explored in Harold Bloom's *The Anxiety of Influence: a theory of poetry* (New York, 1973), his *A Map of Misreading* (New York, 1975) and his *Agon: towards a theory of revisionism* (New York, 1982). In these he counters what he terms the nihilism of deconstructionism by an assertion of the active force of poet or writer, applying in the interpretive reading a conscious 'misprision' of Freud's Oedipal theory, with the powerful author–predecessor viewed as a father figure whom the later author must resist and overpower.

51. Mary Hutchinson's comment, recorded in Anne Olivier Bell (ed.), *The Diaries of Virginia Woolf* (New York, 1978) 2:178.

52. Eugène Jolas, in *Our Exagmination Round his Factification for Incamination of Work in Progress* (1929).

53. T. S. Eliot, '*Ulysses*, Order and Myth', *The Dial*, 75 (1923), 480. See also the discussion of this aspect in David Lodge, *The Modes of Modern Writing: metaphor, metonymy, and the typology of modern literature* (Ithaca, 1977), pp. 138f.

54. See Rodchenko's illustrations to the collection of poems by Mayakovsky, *Pro Eto* (1923). Despite his name, John Heartfield was German, having anglicised it from Helmut Herzfeld in disgust at German militarism.

55. This reading of Botticelli's painting, together with a fuller discussion of the merger of classical and Christian myth, appears in my *Renaissance Perspectives: in literature and the visual arts* (Princeton, 1987), pp. 157–60. The classical elements inimical to Christian tradition that could thereby be imported included a delight in the naked human body, a delight ingeniously justified for both artist and sculptor by the theory that, since the body is conceived as the 'clothing' of the soul, the soul could now be depicted allegorically as a body stripped of its clothing.

56. Franco Moretti, *Signs Taken for Wonders: essays in the sociology of literary forms* (London, 1988), pp. 220f. Moretti's argument leads him to the conclusion that the process fails in this poem, producing myth rather than poetry: '*The Waste Land* is a cultural milestone precisely because it is no longer literature' (p. 236).

57. The passage can be found most conveniently in the abridged one-volume edition of James Gordon Frazer's, *The Golden Bough* (London, 1960), pp. 418–19. The original work appeared in twelve volumes, issued between 1890 and 1915.

58. T. S. Eliot, in *The Dial*, 75 (December 1923), 597.

59. His reservations concerning Frazer's theory appear in *Criterion*, 5 (June, 1927), 283. Maud Bodkin's *Archetypal Patterns in Poetry* (Oxford, 1922) was among the first to recognise the value of using Jung's theory as a critical tool for exegesis, and offered a brief analysis of *The Waste Land* in those terms. But she made no suggestion that in composing the poem Eliot himself had been employing Jung's perceptions.

60. Robert Langbaum, *The Mysteries of Identity: a theme in modern literature* (New York, 1977), p. 98.

61. C. Jung, *Modern Man in Search of a Soul*, trans. W. S. Dell and C. F. Baynes (New York, 1934), p. 215. Although this passage was published in 1933, after the appearance of *The Waste Land*, its principles were of course implicit in Jung's earlier work.

62. D. H. Lawrence, *The Man Who Died* (New York, 1960, orig. 1922), pp. 188, 124. The quoted passages are not contiguous in the story, but their juxtaposition here is in full accord with the story's theme and message.

63. D. H. Lawrence, *Fantasia of the Unconscious* (London, 1933), pp. 9–10.

64. Eliot, *Knowledge and Experience*, op. cit., especially pp. 121f. There is a helpful discussion of this point in William Skaff, *The Philosophy of T. S. Eliot: from skepticism to a surrealist poetic, 1909–1927* (Philadelphia, 1986), pp. 115–16.

65. J. Donne, 'The First Anniversarie', pp. 209f. I have discussed this aspect of Donne's poetry more closely in *The Soul of Wit: a study of John Donne* (Oxford, 1974).

66. Eliot's essay of 1921, 'The Metaphysical Poets', reprinted in his *Selected Essays (1917–1932)* (London, 1934), p. 287.

67. Eliot, *Knowledge and Experience*, op. cit., p. 163.

68. Quoted in Werner Haftmann, *Painting in the Twentieth Century* (New York, 1965) 1:179–80. *The Melancholy and Mystery of a Street* was in fact painted in 1914, before the foundation of the *scuola metafisica*, but the

principles of that school were clearly based on the kind of work De Chirico was producing around that time.

69. Quoted in Hyatt Waggoner, *American Poets* (Boston, 1968), p. 508.
70. Cf. Balachandra Rajan, *The Overwhelming Question: a study of the poetry of T. S. Eliot* (Toronto, 1976), p. 12, which recognises this phrase as a call for commitment.
71. A. Walton Litz (ed.), *Eliot in His Time: essays on the occasion of the fiftieth anniversary of 'The Waste Land'* (Princeton, 1973), p. 7.

3 HUXLEY'S COUNTERPOINT (pp. 86–117)

1. Cf. their tributes in Julian Huxley (ed.), *Aldous Huxley: a memorial volume* (London, 1965), pp. 144–5.
2. David Daiches, *The Novel and the Modern World* (Chicago, 1939), p. 209; Edwin B. Burgum, *The Novel and the World's Dilemma* (New York, 1947), p. 152; Laurence Brander, *Aldous Huxley: a critical study* (Lewisburg, 1969), pp. 370f.
3. The main defenders of Huxley in recent years have been Peter Bowering, *Aldous Huxley: a study of the major novels* (New York, 1969) and Jerome Meckier, *Aldous Huxley: satire and structure* (London, 1969). Both are valuable studies of the author but base their defence of *Point Counter Point* on the play of ideas it contains rather than its achievement as a literary work.
4. Peter Quennell, 'A Critical Symposium on Aldous Huxley', *The London Magazine*, 2 (1955), 51–64.
5. Peter Fichow, *Aldous Huxley: satirist and novelist* (Minneapolis, 1972), p. 95, Others interpreting the counterpoint as mere amusing juxtapositions include Keith M. May, *Aldous Huxley* (London, 1972), pp. 79f., and George Woodcock, *Dawn and the Darkest Hour: a study of Aldous Huxley* (New York, 1972), pp. 150–60. Meckier's more sensitive, although still, I believe, unsatisfactory reading of the musical theme is presented in Meckier, *Aldous Huxley: satire and structure*, op. cit., pp. 43, 132.
6. Sanford Marovitz, 'Huxley and the Visual Arts', *Papers on Language and Literature*, 9 (1973), 172, correctly notes Huxley's acute and perceptive response to painting despite his poor sight.
7. Bertrand Russell, *Our Knowledge of the External World* (Chicago, 1914), p. 89.
8. Olivier-Hourcade argued the case in an article in *La Revue de France et de Pays Français* in February 1912 and another in *Revue Française* in June of the same year. The remark by Braque is recorded in Dora Vallier, 'Braque, la Peinture et Nous', *Cahiers d'Art*, 29:1 (1954). See also John Golding, *Cubism: a history and an analysis* (Cambridge, Mass., 1988), especially pp. 17–18. Although synchronic study is less interested in proving direct influence, it may be noted that Huxley joined the Bloomsbury circle at Garsington in 1914, where Roger Fry and Clive Bell were becoming leading advocates of the contemporary French painters, including the Cubists.

9.   Jacques Rivière, 'Sur les tendances actuelles de la peinture', *Revue d'Europe et d'Amerique*, 1 March 1912, pp. 384f. The idea that the Cubist painters were interpreting each object sequentially, as if they were walking around it, has been disputed, as in Guy Habasque, *Cubism* (New York, 1959), p. 52. It is now generally agreed that it functioned according to the concept of 'simultaneity', the representation of objects concurrently from a number of different angles.

10.   Quoted in Suzi Gablik, *Progress in Art* (London, 1976), p. 81.

11.   Paul M.Laporte, 'Cubism and Science', *Journal of Aesthetics and Art Criticism*, 7 (1949), 243; Laura D. Henderson, *The Fourth Dimension and Non-Euclidean Geometry in Modern Art* (Princeton, 1983), pp. 353f. Cf. also Sigfried Giedion, *Space, Time, and Architecture: the growth of a new tradition* (Cambridge, Mass., 1962), p. 357.

12.   Karl Popper, *The Poverty of Historicism* (London, 1957), and *The Logic of Scientific Discovery* (London, 1959). Darwin, while in the midst of composing his *Origin of Species*, discovered an article by Wallace propounding the identical theory. As perfect gentlemen, they submitted a joint paper to the Linnean Society, after which Wallace generously permitted Darwin to publish the larger treatise and then retired into obscurity. One may note as a similar instance how, at a time when Baroque art and literature were fascinated by dazzling light as an emanance of the divine and interpreting the material massivity of planets and stars as testimony to the Supreme Creator, Newton, instigating an era of rationalist enquiry, devoted his main investigations precisely to those two elements, producing his analytical theories of the spectrum and of gravity.

13.   Albert Gleizes and Jean Metzinger, *Du Cubisme* (Paris, 1912), quoted from the translation in Robert L. Herbert (ed.), *Modern Artists on Art* (Englewood Cliffs, 1964), p. 5.

14.   Cf. Leo Steinberg's valuable discussion in his *Other Criteria: confrontations with twentieth-century art* (Oxford, 1976), pp. 193f. Steinberg traces this element back to earlier forms of recto/verso, such as the representation around 1500 of a skeletal Death behind the carved figures of a couple embracing. But that, I feel, derives from an essentially different impulse, a didactic attempt to nullify or qualify the pleasures of this world in the tradition of *media vita in morte sumus* rather than to experiment with concepts of three-dimensionalism. The non-spatial referentialism of such art and the principle of 'faceting' is discussed in Douglas Cooper, *The Cubist Epoch* (Los Angeles, 1970).

15.   John Atkins, '*Point Counterpoint* and the Uncongenital Novelist', *Studies in the Literary Imagination*, 13 (1980), 69.

16.   Aldous Huxley, *Point Counter Point*, in *Collected Works* (London, 1971), p. 266.

17.   Quoted from the section entitled 'Sexual Selection' in Darwin's *On the Origin of Species*.

18.   C. K. Ogden and I. A. Richards, *The Meaning of Meaning: Study of the influence of language upon thought and of the science of symbolism* (London, 1923) especially Chapter 2.

19.   I. A. Richards, *Science and Poetry* (1926).

20. June Deery, *Aldous Huxley and the Mysticism of Science* (Basingstoke, 1996), makes out a case for Huxley as one of the few Modernists who was able to bridge the cultures, to coordinate literature with science, and to bring them together with the mysticism of religion. But she fails to perceive, as the underlying theme of his work, his conviction of the sheer impossibility of reconciling these diverse cultures.
21. A. Huxley, 'Ninth Philosopher's Song' (1920).
22. Huxley, *Point Counter Point*, op. cit.
23. From the opening page of *Antic Hay* (1923).
24. Cf. Benedick's comment, 'Is it not strange that sheep's guts should hale souls out of men's bodies?' (*Much Ado*, 2:3:611), although in that instance Shakespeare is merely remarking on the queerness of the fact, not struggling with a conflict between empiricism and the intuitive response. On the place of music in fiction during the modern period, see Alex Aronson, *Music in the Novel* (Totowa, 1980), and more specifically, Gerald Cockshott, *Music and Nature: a study of Aldous Huxley* (Salzburg, 1979).
25. Wallace Stevens, 'The Idea of Order at Key West', in *Collected Poems* (New York, 1980), pp. 128–9.
26. See, for example, E. H. Gombrich, *Art and Illusion: a study in the psychology of pictorial representation* (Princeton, 1972), pp. 84f.
27. The close parallel between Huxley's affair with Nancy Cunard and the fictional account of Walter's experience with Lucy Tantamount is noted in Sybille Bedford, *Aldous Huxley: a biography* (New York, 1974), pp. 135–8. Walter Allen, '*Point Counter Point* Revisited', *Studies in the Novel*, 9 (1977), 373, notes that Philip Quarles, Walter Bidlake and Spandrell are all partial projections of Huxley himself, but only to argue that it adds a 'personal' dimension to the novel.
28. Karl Miller, *Doubles: studies in literary history* (Oxford, 1985).
29. Michel Foucault, *Discipline and Punish: the birth of the prison*, trans. Alan Sheridan (New York, 1979), pp. 201–2.
30. Robert Rosenblum, *Cubism and Twentieth-century Art* (New York, 1976), especially p. 90.
31. Aldous Huxley, *Those Barren Leaves* (London, 1950), p. 54.
32. 'D. H. Lawrence' (1932), reprinted in Aldous Huxley, *Stories, Essays, & Poems* (London, 1937), p. 336.
33. Aldous Huxley, 'Water Music', in *The Athenaeum* (1920).
34. Sanford E. Marovitz, 'Aldous Huxley's Intellectual Zoo', *Philological Quarterly*, 48 (1969), 495–507, views the zoological elements in the novel simply as literary devices to display the idiosyncrasies of the characters.
35. From the collection of poems by Delmore Schwartz, *In Dreams Begin Responsibilities*, published by New Directions in 1938.
36. Milton Birnbaum, 'Politics and Character in *Point Counter Point*', *Studies in the Novel*, 9 (1977), 468, for example, follows the usual approach in discussing Spandrell simply as a 'diabolical nihilist', merely noting as an afterthought that there are 'occasional traces of his yearning for some beauty and spiritual ascent'.

37. The comment on Baudelaire appears in his collection of essays *Do What You Will*, published the year after *Point Counter Point*. For an analysis of Spandrell in exclusively Freudian terms, in which the search for God is interpreted as a transposed longing for the mother figure he had idolised in his youth, see Robert S. Baker, *The Dark Historic Page: social satire and historicism in the novels of Aldous Huxley, 1921–39* (Madison, 1982), pp. 112f.

38. T. S. Eliot, 'Baudelaire in Our Time', in *For Lancelot Andrewes* (London, 1928).

39. Aldous Huxley, *Time Must Have a Stop* (London, 1946), p. 289.

40. For a close study of Huxley's view of Lawrence, see Keith May, 'Accepting the Universe: the "Rampion-Hypothesis" in *Point Counter Point* and *Island*', reprinted in Jerome Meckier (ed.), *Critical Essays on Aldous Huxley* (New York, 1996), pp. 229f.

41. In a letter to Jean E. Hare, reprinted in *Letters*, ed. Grover Smith (London, 1969), p. 538.

42. Bowering, *Aldous Huxley*, op. cit., pp. 96–7. Harold H. Watts, *Aldous Huxley* (New York, 1969), p. 64, in an otherwise discriminating and, rarely enough, laudatory reading of the novel, remarks apologetically that, although the contrasts and juxtapositions are presented there with a satiric brilliance, the novel, 'it must be confessed, does not wait for an answer', as if an answer would have improved its effectiveness.

43. Cf. E. K. Brown, *Rhythm in the Novel* (Toronto, 1950), p. 8.

4 MINIMALISM AND THE HEMINGWAY HERO (pp. 118–48)

1. Oswald Spengler, *The Decline of the West*, trans. C. F. Atkinson (London, 1932), which defined cultural movement in terms of oscillatory reactions.

2. Sean O'Faolain, *The Vanishing Hero: studies in novelists of the twenties*, the Christian Gauss lectures delivered at Princeton University in 1953 (London, 1956), p. 154.

3. Cf. Mark Spilka's critical study, *Hemingway's Quarrel with Androgyny* (Lincoln, NA, 1990) and the biography by Kenneth S. Lynn, *Hemingway* (New York, 1987), the latter focusing in large part on the author's presumed sexual inadequacies and childhood fixations, especially those emanating from his relations with his mother.

4. Cf. M. M. Bakhtin, *The Dialogic Imagination*, ed. Michael Holquist (Austin, 1981); Harold Bloom, *The Anxiety of Influence* (New York, 1973) and *A Map of Misreading* (New York, 1975); Jacques Derrida, *Aporias* (Stanford, 1993); J. Hillis Miller, *Fiction and Repetition: seven English novels* (Cambridge, Mass., 1982).

5. Wolfgang Iser, *The Implied Reader* (Baltimore, 1974); Stanley Fish, *Is There a Text in This Class?* (Cambridge Mass., 1980); Karl Popper, *Theorie und Realitat*, ed. H. Albert (Tübingen, 1964), pp. 87–102.

6. Hans Robert Jauss, 'Literary History as a Challenge to Literary Theory', in Ralph Cohen (ed.), *New Directions in Literary History* (Baltimore, 1974), pp. 11–41, developed in such later studies as his comparison of

Racine and Goethe in Rainer Warning (ed.), *Rezeptionsästhetik* (Munich, 1975), pp. 355f., and offered in its fully developed form in his *Toward an Aesthetic of Reception*, trans. Timothy Bahti (Minneapolis, 1982).

7.   For the reception accorded to this aspect of the novels, see Leo Gurko, *Ernest Hemingway: the pursuit of heroism* (New York, 1968) and, more recently, Rena Sanderson's introduction to *Blowing the Bridge: essays on Hemingway* (New York, 1992), especially pp. 6–8.

8.   Ernest Hemingway, *For Whom the Bell Tolls* (Harmondsworth: Penguin, 1955), pp. 421–2.

9.   Emily S. Watts, *Ernest Hemingway and the Arts* (Urbana, 1971).

10.   Ernest Hemingway, *Selected Letters, 1917–1961*, ed. Carlos Baker (New York, 1963), p. 122.

11.   Hemingway wrote to his friend Douglas Ogden Stewart, who had already submitted the manuscript to a publisher, urgently requesting him 'to lop off the last nine pages' of the story. See Carlos Baker, *Ernest Hemingway* (New York, 1969), p. 138. The full text was published by Scribner in 1972. While acknowledging in later years the more general influence upon him of Giotto and Tintoretto, he continued to insist that 'Cézanne is my painter, after the early ones' – his comment recorded in an article by Lilian Ross in *The New Yorker*, 13 May 1950, based upon an interview with him.

12.   Ernest Hemingway, *A Moveable Feast* (New York, 1964), pp. 13, 69. See also Robert L. Lair, 'Hemingway and Cézanne: an indebtedness' *Modern Fiction Studies*, 6 (1960), 165; Charles H. Cagle, '"Cézanne Nearly Did": Stein, Cézanne, and Hemingway', *Midwest Quarterly*, 23 (1982), 268; Eric Nakjavani, 'The Aesthetics of the Visible and the Invisible: Hemingway and Cézanne', *Hemingway Review*, 5 (1986), 1.

13.   Alfred Kazin, 'Hemingway, Painting, and the Search for Serenity', in Donald R. Noble (ed.), *Hemingway: a revaluation* (New York, 1983), p. 61.

14.   Ernest Hemingway, *The Sun Also Rises* (New York: Charles Scribner's Sons, 1986), p. 25.

15.   See Richard Shiff's fine critical study, *Cézanne and the End of Impressionism* (Chicago, 1984), as well as Frank Elgar, *Cézanne* (New York, 1975). My own reading of Cézanne's innovative techniques is presented in more detail than can be offered here within a chapter on Gerard Manley Hopkins in my *Victorian Contexts* (London, 1996).

16.   Malcolm Bradbury discusses this aspect in his interesting essay, 'Putting in the Person: Character and Abstraction in Current Writing and Painting' in Malcolm Bradbury and David Palmer (eds), *The Contemporary English Novel* (New York, 1980), p. 195.

17.   Gertrude Stein, *Lectures in America* (Boston, 1985, orig. 1935), pp. 76–7. It is perhaps significant that in Wendy Steiner's close study of Gertrude Stein's literary innovations and their relationship to Cubist art, *Exact Resemblance to Exact Resemblance: the literary portraiture of Gertrude Stein* (New Haven, 1978), Hemingway is mentioned only peripherally, as a member of Stein's circle but not as a participant in the new styles being created.

18.   Maurice Sterne's comment is quoted in Lynn's *Hemingway*, op. cit., pp. 167–8.

19.   Cf. Glen A. Love, '*The Professor's House*: Cather, Hemingway, and the Chastening of American Prose Style', *Western American Literature* 24 (1990), 295; Charles A. Fenton, *The Apprenticeship of Ernest Hemingway* (New York, 1954), pp. 33–4. For unconvincing attempts to relate Hemingway's style to Impressionism and Expressionism, see Harry Levin, 'Observations on the Style of Ernest Hemingway', *Kenyon Review*, 13 (1951), 63; Raymond S. Nelson, *Hemingway: expressionist artist* (Ames, 1979); Eric Nakjavani, 'The Aesthetics of the Visible and the Invisible: Hemingway and Cézanne', *Hemingway Review*, 5 (1986), 1. For a recent attempt to connect him with the Pre-Raphaelites and other earlier aesthetes, in terms of an art form seen as stretching from Keats to Henry James, see John Gaggin, *Hemingway and Nineteenth-century Aestheticism* (Ann Arbor, 1988).

20.   The connection with functionalism has been briefly but perceptively discussed in Cecilia Tichi, *Shifting Gears: technology, literature, culture in modernist America* (Chapel Hill, 1987), pp. 224–6.

21.   See Peter Blake, *The Master Builders: Le Corbusier, Mies van der Rohe, Frank Lloyd Wright* (New York, 1976), pp. 204f.

22.   Sir D'Arcy Wentworth, *On Growth and Form* (Cambridge, 1963, orig. 1917), 2:961, 966. Details of the impact of this discovery are provided in Douglas J. Bush, *The Streamlined Decade* (New York, 1975), and Arthur J. Pulos, *American Design Ethic: a history of industrial design to 1940* (Cambridge, Mass., 1983).

23.   Quoted in Sigfried Giedion, *Space, Time, and Architecture: the growth of a new tradition* (Cambridge, Mass., 1962), pp. 338f.

24.   John Root, in an article in the *Inland Architect*, June 1890.

25.   Ezra Pound, 'Prolegomena', *The Poetry Review*, February 1912.

26.   'There is no evidence from his boyhood of his having taken an interest in the Prairie School's ideas, and in later years he never once reminisced with an interviewer about the dramatic alterations in Oak Park's appearance which had taken place when he was growing up there.' Lynn, *Hemingway*, op. cit., pp. 17–19. Emily Watts, who also adopts in her *Hemingway and the Arts* a diachronic approach requiring evidence of direct influence, similarly dismisses any connection with architectural functionalism on the ground that Hemingway never refers to the movement (p. 207).

27.   Hemingway, *A Moveable Feast*, op. cit., p. 12. On Perret, see Blake, *The Master Builders*, op. cit., p. 13.

28.   Franz Schulze, *Mies Van Der Rohe: a critical biography* (Chicago, 1985) discusses Wright's visit to Berlin in 1911, and the effect it had upon Mies Van Der Rohe's subsequent work, especially in the 1920s.

29.   Although Wright's work minimised ornamentation at this stage, he did employ it occasionally, as in Hollyhock House in Los Angeles, modelled in 1917 upon the structure of a Mayan temple. But his successors in the movement were rigorous in their eschewing of ornament.

30.   Ernest Hemingway, *Death in the Afternoon* (Harmondsworth, 1966) pp. 181–2. Cf. Susan Beegel, *Hemingway's Craft of Omission* (Ann Arbor, 1988), and Hemingway's further comment in *A Moveable Feast* on his

'new theory that you could omit anything if you knew that you omitted and the omitted part would strengthen the story' (p. 75).

31.   These ideas were originally promulgated in their jointly edited journal *L'Esprit Nouveau*.

32.   Hemingway, *For Whom the Bell Tolls*, op. cit., pp. 161, 428.

33.   Ernest Hemingway, *The Old Man and the Sea*, (London, 1995), pp. 48–9. p. 56.

34.   Hemingway, *Death in the Afternoon*, op. cit., p. 2.

35.   Quoted in Samuel Putman, *Paris Was Our Mistress* (New York, 1947), pp. 128–9. During this period, he and his friend Dos Passos would frequently read aloud to each other passages from the Bible, primarily the Old Testament, enjoying the sounds and rhythms of the text.

36.   Brom Weber, 'Ernest Hemingway's Genteel Bullfight', in Malcolm Bradbury and David Palmer (eds), *The American Novel and the Nineteen-twenties* (London, 1971), p. 151, notes the contrast between the elements of tragi-comedy entering Hemingway's view of bullfighting in *Death in the Afternoon* of 1932 and the solemnity governing his attitude in *The Sun Also Rises*.

37.   Harold Loeb, to Hemingway's chagrin, had outplayed him at both tennis and boxing, had anticipated him in publishing a first novel, and, worst of all, had slipped away for an amorous weekend with the desirable Lady Duff, while Hemingway was held back by the presence of Hadley. Cf., among numerous other accounts, Sheridan Baker, *Ernest Hemingway: an introduction and interpretation* (New York, 1967), pp. 44f.; Bertram D. Sarason, *Hemingway and 'The Sun' Set* (Washington, 1972); and Harold Loeb's own version of the events in *The Way It Was* (New York, 1959). Hemingway, even more than other writers, had a remarkable ability to tailor his experiences to the structural needs of his fiction in a manner that made the original incidents only distantly relevant – witness the fact of his having been jilted by nurse Agnes in Italy in favour of an Italian officer, an incident he metamorphosed into the passionately requited love of the protagonists in *A Farewell to Arms*. It is the work in its final crafted form that interests me here.

38.   Mark Spilka, 'The Death of Love in *The Sun Also Rises*', in Harold Bloom (ed.), *Ernest Hemingway's "The Sun Also Rises": modern critical interpretations* (New York, 1987), p. 25; Arnold E. Davidson and Cathy N. Davidson, 'Decoding the Hemingway Hero in *The Sun Also Rises*', in Linda Wagner-Martin (ed.), *New Essays on 'The Sun Also Rises'* (Cambridge, 1987), p. 83.

39.   Carole G. Vopat, 'The End of *The Sun Also Rises*: a New Beginning', in Harold Bloom (ed.), *Ernest Hemingway's "The Sun Also Rises": modern critical interpretations*, p. 91.

40.   Deconstructionists have predictably identified the contrast between Jake's seeming allegiance to the code and his desertion of it in this 'pimp' episode as demonstrating once again the aporia of literature, the coexistence within one work of opposed and ultimately irreconcilable concepts. See, for example, Davidson and Davidson, 'Decoding the Hemingway Hero' op. cit., pp. 83f.

41. Cf. G. W. F. Hegel, *The Philosophy of Fine Art*, trans. F. P. B. Osmaston, 4 vols (London, 1920).

42. Wirt Williams, *The Tragic Art of Ernest Hemingway* (Baton Rouge, 1981), with earlier, if briefer discussions in Carlos Baker, *Ernest Hemingway: the writer as artist* (Princeton, 1972), and Philip Young, *Ernest Hemingway: a reconsideration* (University Park, PA, 1966).

5   WOOLF, JOYCE, AND ARTISTIC NEUROSIS (pp. 149–83)

1. D. H. Lawrence began painting only in 1926. Marianna Torgovnick, *The Visual Arts, Pictorialism, and the Novel* (Princeton, 1985), although acknowledging the identification of novelist with painter in the work of James, Lawrence and Woolf, dismisses it as a merely 'decorative' element (p. 17). In fact, in Henry James' novels author identification is normally not with the artist but with the connoisseur, watching with interest the painter's or sculptor's progress, as in *Roderick Hudson* or *The Sacred Fount*.

2. There is a very different motivation behind Giorgione's *Pastoral Symphony*, also depicting nude females in the company of fully dressed males, and echoed much later in Manet's *Déjeuner sur l'Herbe*, as discussed in my *Renaissance Perspectives* (Princeton, 1987), pp. 260–2.

3. See, among many such instances, Norman Cantor, *Twentieth-Century Culture: modernism to deconstruction* (New York, 1988), pp. 64f., who supports there the traditional view that the proliferation of photography made it 'necessary for artists to move towards more nonrepresentational portrayals because the camera coopted what had hitherto been the characteristic province of the painter, namely, to depict what the eye saw.'

4. It was later discovered that 'halation' was caused by the slowness of photograph exposures at that time. But the assumption that it was optically valid introduced the blurring effect into their art.

5. Aaron Scharf, *Art and Photography* (New York, 1983), pp. 165f., and on Dégas, pp. 202f. Rodin rejected the lesson offered by Muybridge, endorsing the established method of painting horses' legs as splayed out, since, although inaccurate anatomically, it recreated the optical impression produced on the viewer.

6. Cf. Bram Dijkstra, *Cubism, Steiglitz, and the Early Poetry of William Carlos Williams* (Princeton, 1978), especially pp. 15f.

7. Svetlana Alpers, *The Art of Describing: Dutch art in the seventeenth century* (Chicago, 1983), pp. 43–4.

8. Experiments with composite images began as early as the 1840s and were publicised at the Universal Exposition in Munich in 1855, while in the 1860s W. H. Mumler, an American charlatan, was discovered to have employed double-exposure to produce the illusion of ghostly 'presences'.

9. Umberto Eco, 'Critique of the Image', in Victor Burgin (ed.), *Thinking Photography* (London, 1982); Martin Jay, *The Denigration of Vision in Twentieth-century French Thought* (Berkeley, 1993), especially chapter 3.

10. Richard Ellmann records in his *The Consciousness of Joyce* (Oxford, 1977) that Joyce's library in Trieste contained *The Psychopathology of Everyday Life* and *Leonardo da Vinci: a Memory of his Childhood* by Freud, 'The Significance of the Father in the Destiny of the Individual' by Jung, and *The Problem of Hamlet and the Oedipus Complex* by Ernest Jones.

11. Recorded by Djuna Barnes, a personal friend, in 'James Joyce', *Vanity Fair*, 18 (April 1922), 65.

12. Quotation from James Joyce, *Finnegans Wake* (London, 1939), p. 522 , the Mary Colum reference from Ellmann, *The Consciousness of Joyce*, op. cit., pp. 480, 647.

13. James Sully, *Outlines of Psychology* (London, 1884), p. 74. See also George Johnson, 'Virginia Woolf and Second Wave Psychology', *Twentieth Century Literature*, 40 (1994), 139.

14. Although she wrote in 1939 that she was beginning to read Freud 'for the first time' (see her *Diary*, ed. Anne O. Bell, London, 1948, 5:249), she was clearly referring to a serious reading of his works, as she was fully aware of Freudian theory before then. As early as January 1918, she records with interest that a meeting of the British Sex Society had been openly discussing 'incest between parent and child, derived from Freud' and declared that she was planning to join the group; and in 1920 titled her review of a novel in *TLS*, 'Freudian Fiction'. See her *Moments of Being* (London, 1985), p. 108, and her *Diary*, op. cit., 1:110.

15. Quotations from Richard Ellmann, *James Joyce* (Oxford, 1959), pp. 393, 450, 538; Quentin Bell, *Virginia Woolf: a biography* (New York, 1972) 2:19; Leon Edel, *Bloomsbury: a house of lions* (New York, 1980), p. 255; Nigel Nicolson and Joanne Trautmann (eds), *Letters of Virginia Woolf* (New York, 1978), 2:482, 134–5; Perry Meisel and Walter Kendrick (eds), *Bloomsbury/Freud: the letters of James and Alix Strachey, 1924–25* (New York, 1985), p. 264. James Strachey also mentions her refusal to consult a psychiatrist for her own disorders. There is an interesting discussion of her relationship to psychoanalysis from an exclusively gender viewpoint in Elizabeth Abel, *Virginia Woolf and the Fictions of Psychoanalysis* (Chicago, 1989).

16. D. H. Lawrence, *Fantasia of the Unconscious* (London, 1933, orig. 1921), p. 13.

17. Charles Altieri, *Painterly Abstraction in Modernist American Poetry* (Cambridge, 1989), discusses in general terms the need of the Modernist poet to employ defensive strategies against the sense of dispossession inflicted on the arts.

18. Sigmund Freud, *Collected Psychological Works*, ed. James Strachey (the various volumes appearing in different years), 7:238.

19. Sigmund Freud, *Introductory Lectures on Psychoanalysis* (1917), trans. Joan Riviere (London, 1923), p. 314. As this is a crucial passage, I have used here the translation first published in 1922, which would have been available to writers of that time, rather than that of *The Collected Works*, of which volume 16, containing these lectures, appeared only in 1957. Reviere's was the translation quoted by Roger Fry in his attempt at a rebuttal.

20. Peter Fuller, *Art and Psychoanalysis* (London, 1980).
21. Albert Modell, *The Erotic Motive in Literature* (New York, 1919), pp. 11, 123, 146. For studies of the effect of psychology on art and its theory of the evolution of the artist in society, see Ernst Kris, *Psychoanalytic Explorations in Art* (London, 1953), and Frederick J. Hoffman, *Freudianism and the Literary Mind* (Baton Rouge, 1957).
22. See especially, Harold Bloom, *The Anxiety of Influence* (London, 1975) and *A Map of Misreading* (London, 1975); and Jacques Lacan, *Ecrits: a selection* (London, 1977) and *The Four Fundamental Concepts of Psycho-Analysis* (London, 1977).
23. Freud, *Collected Psychological Works*, op. cit., 18:252.
24. Recorded in Peter Gay, *Freud: a life for our time* (New York, 1988), pp. 214–15.
25. Clive Bell, 'Dr. Freud on Art', *The Nation and the Athenaeum*, 6 September, 1924, an article which gave rise to an exchange of letters in subsequent issues.
26. Nicholson and Trautmann, *Letters*, op. cit., 3:132.
27. Woolf, *Moments of Being*, op. cit., p. 72 and *To the Lighthouse* (London: Hogarth Press, 1977), pp. 228, 309–10.
28. Essay entitled 'Life and the Novelist', published November 1926.
29. Details of Breton's background in psychology are in Anna Balakian, *André Breton: magus of surrealism* (New York, 1971), pp. 29f.
30. Tristan Tzara, *Zurich Chronicle* (1915–19). On Dadaism, see C. W. E. Bigsby, *Dada and Surrealism* (London, 1972); Hans Richter, *Dada: art and anti-art* (Oxford, 1978); Robert Short, *Dada and Surrealism* (London, 1980); Alan Young, *Dada and After: extremist modernism and English literature* (Manchester, 1981).
31. Hans Richter in his recollections of the movement, *Dada, Art and Anti-art* (Oxford, 1978), p. 57.
32. Pierre Janet, *L'Automatisme psychologique* (1889). See also H. N. Finkelstein, *Surrealism and the Crisis of the Object* (Ann Arbor, 1979).
33. A. Breton, *Manifesto of Surrealism* (1924), trans. R. Seaver and H. R. Lane (Ann Arbor, 1981), p. 26 (italics in the original).
34. Quoted in Dawn Ades, *Dau* (London, 1988), p. 50.
35. A. Breton 'The Dali Case' (1936).
36. Salvador Dali, *The Secret Life of Salvador Dali* (New York, 1942). There is an analysis of the function of such legends in Surrealism at large in Whitney Chadwick, *Myth in Surrealist Painting* (Ann Arbor, 1980).
37. Ades, op. cit., pp. 73–4.
38. Archie K. Loss, *Joyce's Visible Art: the work of Joyce and the visual arts, 1904–1922* (Ann Arbor, 1984) attempts, in a brief study, to connect his work with the art of the *fin de siècle*, usually on the basis of rather far-fetched thematic connections. See also Maria E. Kronegger, *James Joyce and Associated Image-makers* (New Haven, 1968).
39. Those incidents, recorded in Bell, *Virginia Woolf*, op. cit., 1:42–4, have long been recognised as related to her subsequent sexual frigidity, although no connection has been made, to the best of my knowledge, with the Louis incident. See Lyndall Gordon, *Virginia Woolf: a writer's life* (New York, 1984), p. 156.

40. Virginia Woolf, *The Waves* (London: Hogarth Press, 1990), pp. 61–2.
41. Ibid., p. 146.
42. Woolf, *To the Lighthouse*, op. cit., pp. 170–1.
43. Jacques Lacan, *The Four Fundamental Concepts of Psycho-analysis* (London, 1977).
44. Bettina L. Knapp, *Word, Image, Psyche* (Alabama, 1985), p. 173.
45. Bell, *Virginia Woolf*, op. cit., 1:89, 143; 2:7; Woolf, *Diary*, op. cit., 1:228, and *The Moment and Other Essays* (New York, 1948, orig. 1925), p. 178. Further discussion of her lack of responsiveness to painting can be found in the essays by various contributors in Diane F. Gillespie (ed.), *The Multiple Muses of Virginia Woolf* (Columbia, 1993), and in Gillespie's own book, *The Sister Arts: the writing and painting of Virginia Woolf and Vanessa Bell* (Syracus, 1988). The more traditional view that Woolf was powerfully affected by the 1910 exhibition whose influence, it is suggested, remained dormant in her consciousness, remains dominant in Marianna Torgovnick, *The Visual Arts, Pictorialism, and the Novel: James, Lawrence, and Woolf* (Princeton, 1985), pp. 62f.
46. Her essay 'Mr. Bennett and Mrs. Brown', first delivered at Cambridge in 1924. This point is also made in Peter Faulkner (ed.), *Modernism* (London, 1977), pp. 34–5.
47. From her essay on 'Modern Fiction' (1925).
48. Mark Shechner, *Joyce in Nighttown: a psychoanalytic inquiry into 'Ulysses'* (Berkeley, 1974); Sheldon R. Brivic, *Joyce Between Freud and Jung* (London, 1980).
49. James Joyce, *Ulysses* (Harmondsworth: Penguin, 1986) pp. 155–75, citations from pp. 174–5. All quotations from *Ulysses* are from the revised Penguin version, the carefully corrected text edited by Hans Walter Gabler.
50. Dorrit Cohen, *Transparent Minds: narrative modes for presenting consciousness in fiction* (Princeton, 1978), especially pp. 86–8.
51. Joyce, *Ulysses*, op. cit., p. 9.
52. Carlos Rojas, *Salvador Dali: or the art of spitting on your mother*, trans. Alma Amell (Pennsylvania, 1993), p. 113. On parent–child relationships in psychoanalytic theory, see especially the chapter on 'The Transformation of Puberty' in Freud's *Three Contributions to the Theory of Sex* (1905).
53. The mother fixation in the works both of D. H. Lawrence and Virginia Woolf are, it may be argued, less indebted to Freud. Apart from the fact that Lawrence seems only to have learnt about Freud at the time of the final revision of *Sons and Lovers* in 1912 – although he could, at the time of writing, have been responding to changes in the intellectual climate created by Freud – in neither instance was the fixation expressed in explicitly sexual or even in neurotic terms, as in the work of Dali and Joyce.
54. Marcel Proust, *Remembrance of Things Past*, trans. C. K. Scott Moncrieff (London, 1949), 3: 896.
55. José Ortega y Gasset, *The Dehumanization of Art*, trans. Helene Weyl (Princeton, 1948), especially p. 21.
56. Woolf, *The Waves*, op. cit., pp. 10–11.

57. Paul Klee, 'Approaches to the Study of Nature', which appeared in a collection of essays published by the Bauhaus in 1923.
58. Hugo Ball, 'Cabaret Voltaire' (1916), in Robert Motherwell (ed.), *The Dada Painters and Poets: an anthology* (Cambridge, Mass., 1989), p. 51.
59. Robert Goldwater, *Primitivism in Modern Art* (New York, 1967), especially pp. 192f.
60. Recalled in Lothar Schreyer, *Erinnerungen an Sturm und Bauhaus* (Munich, 1956), p. 168.

6   THE TWENTIETH-CENTURY DYAD (pp. 184–210)

1. Henri Bergson, *Time and Free Will*, trans. F. L. Pogson (New York, 1970), p. 133. For connections between Modernist poetics and philosophy, see Sanford Schwartz, *The Matrix of Modernism: Pound, Eliot, and early twentieth-century thought* (Princeton, 1985). The centrality of the new time concept in Modernism is discussed in A. A. Mendilow, *Time and the Novel* (London, 1952), Ricardo J. Quinones, *Mapping Literary Modernism: time and development* (Princeton 1985), and Matei Calinescu, *Five Faces of Modernity* (Durham, 1987).
2. P. Wyndham Lewis, *Time & the Western Man* (London, 1927), p. 179.
3. Virginia Woolf, *Orlando* (Harmondsworth: Penguin, 1945), p. 58, and her essay, 'Modern Fiction', reprinted in *The Common Reader* (New York, 1935), p. 155.
4. Jean Piaget, *Genetic Epistemology* (New York, 1970), especially pp. 48f.
5. William Faulkner, *The Sound and the Fury* (New York, 1946), pp. 96, 99.
6. Henri Bergson, *L'Energie spirituelle* (Paris, 1938), p. 49.
7. These concepts are expressed most fully in Freud's essays on 'Childhood and Concealing Memories' and 'Wit and its Relation to the Unconscious'.
8. *The Interpretation of Dreams*, reprinted in *The Basic Writings of Sigmund Freud*, ed. A. A. Brill (New York, 1938), p. 331. In 1904 Carl Jung published the results of a series of experiments conducted under his auspices, the book being translated into English in 1918 under the title *Studies in Word-Association;* but it has little bearing on the theme examined here, concentrating as it does on the word associations of patients suffering from epilepsis, insanity and hysteria.
9. Jonathan Culler (ed.), *On Puns: the foundation of letters* (Oxford, 1988) is a collection of essays based upon the conference. There is also a discussion of wordplay in literature in Derek Attridge, *Peculiar Language: literature as difference* (Ithaca, 1988), especially pp. 188f. Walter Redfern, *Puns* (Oxford: Basil Blackwell, 1984) is a somewhat flippant account of the history of punning.
10. Sigmund Freud, 'Fragment of an Analysis', in *Collected Papers*, ed. Ernest Jones (London, 1943), 3:79n.
11. Quoted in Dawn Ades, *Dali* (London, 1988), p. 126.
12. In *Renaissance Perspectives: in literature and the visual arts* (Princeton, 1987), pp. 254–6, I discuss the relationship of this painting to the shifting viewpoint in Shakespeare's plays.

13. Peter Gay's fine biography, *Freud: a life for our time* (New York, 1988) provides a vivid account of the chronological development of the theories.

14. See, for example, his woodcut entitled *Eight Heads*, dated 1922, which marked an early experiment with this form. It is reproduced in *The Graphic Work of M. C. Escher* (New York, 1967), p. 6.

15. Cf. Michel Foucault's essay, *This is Not a Pipe*, trans. and ed. James Harkness (Berkeley, 1982), the French original published in its earliest form in 1968; and W. J. T. Mitchell, *Picture Theory* (Chicago, 1994), pp. 64f.

16. Magritte made numerous versions of his favourite pictures, continuing the habit well into the 1960s. Here I have used the dates of the first version of each, since it is the period in which the idea originated that interests us here.

17. Trollope's description of Isabel Brodrick in *Cousin Henry* (Oxford, 1929), p. 22.

18. James Joyce, *Portrait of the Artist as a Young Man* (New York, 1956), p. 179.

19. Hugh Kenner, *The Pound Era* (Berkeley, 1971), pp. 96f.

20. Recalled by Edmond Jaloux in the article entitled 'James Joyce' in *Le Temps*, Paris, 30 January 1941 (emphasis added).

21. For further instances, see John Gordon, *James Joyce's Metamorphoses* (Dublin, 1981).

22. Frederick J. Hoffman, *Freudianism and the Literary Mind*, whose main theme is the effect of Freudian theory on literature, dismisses the concern with wordplay in *Wit and its Relation to the Unconscious* as insignificant in its effect on twentieth-century literature (p. 10). Similarly, Stanley Edgar Hyman, *The Armed Vision: a study in the methods of modern literary criticism* (New York, 1955), p. 251, dismisses any relationship of Empson's work to Freud as minor, and William K. Wimsatt, Jr. and Cleanth Brooks, *Literary Criticism: a short history* (New York, 1967), pp. 638f., refers only to his 'psychological' concern with the reader's reaction to ambiguities.

23. Frank Lentricchia, *After the New Criticism* (Chicago, 1980), p. xiii.

24. George Saintsbury, *The Peace of the Augustans* (Oxford, 1946), p. 67, first published in 1916. In the preface to the second edition of Empson's *Seven Types of Ambiguity: a study of its effects in English verse* (New York, 1955), p. xiv, he specified that one of his main aims had been to counter the impression that the first business of a student of literature is the passing of a 'judgement of value', rather than a close analysis of the way words and phrases function within a literary work.

25. Empson, *Seven Types*, op. cit., p. 246. In the Preface to the second edition (p. ix), Empson acknowledged more specifically his indebtedness to Freud, remarking that he may have been too subservient to the latter's views, which underrated the ambiguities arising from more straightforward mental conflicts in favour of those emanating from the subconscious.

26. Samuel Johnson, *Preface to Shakespeare*.

27. Cf. Jacques Lacan, *Ecrits: a selection* (London, 1977), and *The Four Fundamental Concepts of Psycho-Analysis* (London, 1977).

28. The analysis of the sonnet appeared in their joint *Survey of Modernist Poetry*.

29. I. A. Richards, *The Philosophy of Rhetoric* (London, 1936).

30. I. A. Richards, *The Philosophy of Rhetoric* op. cit., p. 40. Cleanth Brooks, *The Well-Wrought Urn: studies in the structure of poetry* (New York, 1947).

31. My italics.

32. In Brooks' *Modern Poetry and the Tradition* (Oxford, 1965, orig. 1939), p. 235.

33. Quotations from T. S. Eliot, *Selected Essays, 1917–32* (London, 1949), pp. 282, 294.

34. 'Goodfriday 1613, Riding Westward', in John Donne, "A Valediction: Forbidding Mourning". (emphasis added)

35. Ford Madox Ford, *The Good Soldier: a tale of passion* (New York, 1955), pp. 6–7. Alan Wilde, *Horizons of Assent: modernism, postmodernism, and the ironic imagination* (Baltimore, 1981), notes Modernism's acknowledgment of the irreconcilable and fundamental diversities in life.

36. Virginia Woolf, *Moments of Being* (London, 1985), p. 108.

37. Virginia Woolf, *Diary*, ed. Anne O. Bell (London, 1948), 5:249.

38. D. H. Lawrence, *The Rainbow* (Harmondsworth, 1958, orig. 1915), pp. 462–3. The Freud quotation is from his essay on 'Infantile Sexuality' in *Three Contributions to the Theory of Sex*.

39. Samuel Beckett, *Happy Days*, Act 1.

40. Sigmund Freud, *Beyond the Pleasure Principle*, in *Collected Psychological Works*, 18:53.

7   PALPABLE AND MUTE (pp. 211–42)

1. Barbara Novak, *American Painting of the Nineteenth Century: realism, idealism, and the American experience* (New York, 1979), p. 243.

2. Picasso's *Mandolin, Wine-glass, and Table*, exhibited in England in 1911, came under especially severe attack, but the animosity gradually tapered off, to be replaced by reluctant admiration. On the British response to the French school, see p. 248 n35 above.

3. Roger Fry's review of the 1906 exhibition, held by the International Society at the New Gallery and containing paintings by Cézanne.

4. Quoted in John Tytell, *Ezra Pound: the solitary volcano* (London, 1987), p. 80.

5. Frank Lentricchia, *Modern Quartet* (Cambridge, 1994). T. S. Eliot and Stevens are quoted in Lentricchia without source.

6. This passage and previous extract reprinted in R. W. Flint and A. A. Coppotelli (eds), *Marinetti: selected writings* (New York, 1972), p. 42.

7. E. M. Forster, *Howards End* (Harmondsworth, 1986), p. 199.

8. Marinetti joined the Italian Fascist party in 1918, became a favourite of Mussolini and was appointed the party's parliamentary candidate. Later, Mussolini, courting the Catholic church for support, disowned Marinetti; but the latter, swallowing his pride, rejoined the party and died defending Bellagio in 1944. For further details see Caroline

Tisdall and Angelo Bozzolla, *Futurism* (London, 1989). Pound's support of fascism requires no documentation.

9. See especially Dennis Brown's stimulating study, *Intertextual Dynamics: within the literary group – Joyce, Lewis, Pound, and Eliot* (London, 1990), to which I am indebted for a number of references; as well as Richard Cork, *Vorticism and Abstract Art in the First Machine Age* (London, 1976); Marjorie Perloff, *The Futurist Movement: avant garde, avant-guerre, and the language of rupture* (Chicago, 1986); R. W. Dasenbrock, *The Literary Vorticism of Ezra Pound and Wyndham Lewis: towards the condition of poetry* (Baltimore, 1985); Eric Svarny, *The Men of 1914: T. S. Eliot and early modernism* (Milton Keynes, 1988). For a study sensitive to the origins of this group's anti-populist and fascist tendencies, see Vincent Sherry, *Ezra Pound, Wyndham Lewis, and Radical Modernism* (Oxford, 1993). Recent book-length studies by Fredric Jameson, Tom Normand, Sue-Ellen Campbell, Daniel Schenker, David Ayers, Toby Foshay and Scott Klein demonstrate a marked revival of interest in Lewis and in the movements he helped foster.

10. Pound's comment in supporting Wyndham Lewis' application for a Guggenheim fellowship; quoted in Noel Stock, *The Life of Wyndham Lewis* (San Francisco, 1982), pp. 326–7.

11. John Rothenstein, in the foreword to Jane Farrington, *Wyndham Lewis: catalogue of the exhibition at the Manchester City Art Galleries* (London, 1980), and Brown, *Intertextual Dynamics*, op. cit., p. 14.

12. This aspect of the computer age is examined in Richard A. Lehan, *The Electronic Word: democracy, technology, and the arts* (Chicago, 1993), especially pp. 31f.

13. D. H. Lawrence, *Women in Love* (Harmondsworth: Penguin, 1961), pp. 126, 477. His response to Futurism is recorded in a letter to Edward Garnett, dated June 1914, in which he approves in principle Marinetti's statement: 'It is the solidity of a blade of steel that is interesting by itself, that is, the uncomprehending and inhuman alliance of its molecules in resistance to, let us say, a bullet. The heat of a piece of wood or iron is in fact more passionate, for us, than the laughter or tears of a woman.'

14. Ezra Pound, in *The New Age*, 14 January 1915.

15. There is a discussion of the relationship between Gaudier-Brzeska's sculpture and Pound's poetry in Marjorie Perloff, *The Dance of the Intellect: studies in the poetry of the Pound tradition* (Cambridge, 1987), pp. 33f.

16. Graham Greene, *Brighton Rock* (Harmondsworth: Penguin, 1956), p. 244.

17. Evelyn Waugh, *Brideshead Revisited* (Boston, 1945), p. 21.

18. Bernard Bergonzi, in *The Listener*, 19 September 1963. Rubin Rabinovitz, *The Reaction Against Experiment in the Novel, 1950–1960* (New York, 1967) takes a similar view, regarding such fictional conservatism as a failing.

19. Preface to Malcolm Bradbury and David Palmer (eds), *The Contemporary English Novel*, Stratford-Upon-Avon Studies 18 (New York, 1980).

20. David Perkins' excellent work, *A History of Modern Poetry*, especially the second volume on 'Modernism and After', does record (pp. 10f.)

the determination among such younger poets as Richard Eberhart, Delmore Schwarz and Karl Shapiro to resist Eliot's inhibiting influence.

21. Stephen Spender, *The New Realism* (London, 1939), p. 8.
22. D. H. Lawrence, 'Snake', from *Collected Poems* (London, 1928).
23. Cf. Geoffrey Hartman, *Beyond Formalism* (New Haven, 1970), Harold Bloom, *Yeats* (New York, 1970) and Robert Langbaum, *The Poetry of Experience* (New York, 1963).
24. Joseph Frank, *The Widening Gyre: crisis and mastery in modern literature* (New Brunswick, 1963), containing his essay 'Spatial Form in Modern Literature', originally published in 1945.
25. Stephen Spender, *The Struggle of the Modern* (Berkeley, 1963), p. 190.
26. Gerard Manley Hopkins, 'That Nature is a Heraclitean Fire'.
27. Françoise Gilot and Carlton Lake, *Life with Picasso* (London, 1965), p. 70. The second remark, made to Marius de Zayas, is quoted in *The Arts*, May 1923.
28. Clement Greenberg, 'Modernist Painting', *Art and Literature*, 4 (1965), 193; Michael Fried, *Three American Painters* (Boston, 1965), especially pp. 19f.; Richard Wollheim, *On Art and the Mind* (Cambridge, Mass., 1973). Modernist artists thereby accentuated a trend already manifesting itself towards the end of the previous century, when Whistler, in *The Gentle Art of Making Enemies* (London, 1890), p. 128, demanded that the arts should appeal to the sense of eye or ear 'without confounding this with emotions entirely foreign to it, as devotion, pity, love, patriotism and the like'.
29. Herbert Read, in his introduction to Hulme's *Speculations*, records his discovery of the book outline amongst the latter's papers. Richard Aldington's comment appears in his article, 'Modern Poetry and the Imagists', *The Egoist*, 1 June 1914, 79.
30. James Joyce, *Ulysses* (Harmondsworth: Penguin, 1986), p. 100.
31. Preface to the 1952 edition of Stuart Gilbert, *James Joyce's 'Ulysses': a study* (New York, 1930), a work providing the reader with a guide to such parallels.
32. To Gerald Brenan, in Virginia Woolf, *Letters*, ed. Nigel Nicholson and Joanne Trautman (New York, 1978) 2:598, dated 25 December 1922.
33. The Appendix, originally written for inclusion in *The Portable Faulkner*, edited by Malcolm Cowley in 1945, was reprinted the following year as the introduction to the Modern Library edition of his two novels, *The Sound and the Fury* and *As I Lay Dying*, contributing significantly to the revival of interest in the author and his eventual incorporation into university curricula.
34. See Terence Diggory, *William Carlos Williams and the Ethics of Painting* (Princeton, 1991), and Peter Halter, *The Revolution in the Visual Arts and the Poetry of William Carlos Williams* (Cambridge, 1994), both of which examine his involvement in the new art movements and his connection with foreign artists who gathered in New York at that time.
35. William Carlos Williams, 'Recollections', *Art in America*, 51 (1963), 52.
36. Quoted in Bram Dijkstra, *Cubism, Stieglitz, and the Early Poetry of William Carlos Williams* (Princeton, 1978), p. 75, from a manuscript at Buffalo.

37. In later years he reverted in his 'Paterson' to a more complex and compressed type of poetry, closer to Pound's *Cantos*; but that was in the late 1940s to the 1960s, when Modernism had already drawn to its close.

38. Jacob Epstein, *Let There Be Sculpture: an autobiography* (London, 1940, revised edition 1955), p. 56.

39. Ezra Pound, *Gaudier Brzeska: a Memoir* (London, 1916).

40. R. H. Wilenski, *The Meaning of Modern Sculpture* (London, 1932).

41. *The Graphic*, January 1920. For a number of references in this section I am indebted to Charles Harrison's fine study of this period, *English Art and Modernism* (New Haven, 1994).

42. Umberto Boccioni, undated letter to Vico Baer, probably written in June 1913.

43. Lawrence, *Women in Love*, op. cit., pp. 482–3.

44. Henry Moore, in an interview recorded by Edouard Roditi in *Dialogues on Art* (London, 1960).

45. Both this passage and the subsequent extract are from his article 'The Sculptor Speaks', *The Listener*, 18 August 1937.

46. The profound influence exerted by Auden on his contemporaries, including C. Day Lewis, Rex Warner, Stephen Spender and Louis MacNeice, is discussed in Valentine Cunningham, *British Writers of the Thirties* (Oxford, 1988), pp. 18–21.

47. The charge was first levelled in connection with Rodin's nude statue entitled *The Age of Bronze*, but the charge was withdrawn after a collective protest by a number of sculptors and painters. The state then made amends by purchasing his *St John the Baptist* and placing it in the Luxembourg museum.

Select Bibliography

Abel, Elizabeth, *Virginia Woolf and the Fictions of Psychoanalysis* (Chicago, 1989).

Achabe, Chinua, 'An Image of Africa: racism in Conrad's *Heart of Darkness*', *The Massachusetts Review* 18 (1977).

Allen, Walter, '*Point Counter Point* Revisited', *Studies in the Novel* 9 (1977), 373.

Altieri, Charles, *Painterly Abstraction in Modernist American Poetry* (Cambridge, 1989).

Alvarez, A., *The Shaping Spirit: studies in modern English and American poets* (London, 1967).

Amishai-Maisels, Ziva, *Gauguin's Religious Themes* (New York, 1985).

Atkins, John, '*Point Counterpoint* and the Uncongenital Novelist', *Studies in the Literary Imagination* 13 (1980), 69.

Baker, Robert S., *The Dark Historic Page: social satire and historicism in the novels of Aldous Huxley, 1921–39* (Madison, 1982).

Baker, Sheridan, *Ernest Hemingway: an introduction and interpretation* (New York, 1967).

Bakhtin, M. M., *The Dialogic Imagination*, ed. Michael Holquist (Austin, 1981).

Baxandall, Michael, *Patterns of Intention: on the historical explanation of pictures* (New Haven, 1985).

Bedford, Sybille, *Aldous Huxley: a biography* (New York, 1974).

Bedient, Calvin, *He Do the Police in Different Voices: 'The Waste Land' and its protagonist* (Chicago, 1986).

Beegel, Susan, *Hemingway's Craft of Omission* (Ann Arbor, 1988).

Bell, Clive, 'Dr. Freud on Art', *The Nation and the Athenaeum*, September 6, 1924.

Bell, Quentin, *Virginia Woolf: a biography* (New York, 1972).

Benson, Donald R., 'Impressionist Painting and the Problem of Conrad's Atmosphere', *Mosaic* 22 (1989), 29.

Bergson, Henri, *Time and Free Will*, trans. F. L. Pogson (New York, 1970).

Bigsby, C. W. E., *Dada and Surrealism* (London, 1972).

Billy, Ted (ed.), *Critical Essays on Joseph Conrad* (Boston, 1987).

Birnbaum, Milton, 'Politics and Character in *Point Counter Point*', *Studies in the Novel* 9 (1977), 468.

Bloom, Harold, *The Anxiety of Influence: a theory of poetry* (New York, 1973).

Bloom, Harold, *A Map of Misreading* (New York, 1975).

Bloom, Harold, *Agon: towards a theory of revisionism* (New York, 1982).

Bloom Harold, (ed.), *Ernest Hemingway's 'The Sun Also Rises': modern critical interpretations* (New York, 1987).

Borzello, Frances and Rees, A. L. (eds), *The New Art History* (London, 1986).

Bowering, Peter, *Aldous Huxley: a study of the major novels* (New York, 1969).

Bradbury, Malcolm, and Palmer, David (eds), *The Contemporary English Novel* (New York, 1980).

Bradbury, Malcolm and McFarlane, James, *Modernism: a guide to European Literature, 1890–1930* (London, 1991).

Brander, Laurence, *Aldous Huxley: a critical study* (Lewisburg, 1969).

Breton, A., *Manifesto of Surrealism*, trans. R. Seaver and H. R. Lane (Ann Arbor, 1981).

Brivic, Sheldon R., *Joyce Between Freud and Jung* (London, 1980).

Brooker Jewel S., and Bentley, Joseph, *Reading 'The Waste Land': modernism and the limits of interpretation* (Amherst, 1990).

Brown, Dennis, *Intertextual Dynamics: within the literary group – Joyce, Lewis, Pound, and Eliot* (London, 1990).

Bryson, Norman, *Vision and Painting: the logic of gaze* (New Haven, 1983).

Bryson, Norman (ed.), *Calligram: essays in New Art History from France* (Cambridge, 1988).

Burgum, Edwin B., *The Novel and the World's Dilemma* (New York, 1947).

Burrow, J. W., *Evolution and Society: a study in Victorian social theory* (Cambridge, 1966).

Bush, Douglas J., *The Streamlined Decade* (New York, 1975).

Butler, Christopher, *Early Modernism: literature, music, and painting in Europe, 1900–1916* (Oxford, 1994).

Cagle, Charles H., '"Cézanne Nearly Did": Stein, Cézanne, and Hemingway', *Midwest Quarterly* 23 (1982), 268.

Cantor, Norman, *Twentieth-Century Culture: modernism to deconstruction* (New York, 1988).

Carlos, Baker, *Ernest Hemingway: the writer as artist* (Princeton, 1972).

Chadwick, Whitney, *Myth in Surrealist Painting* (Ann Arbor, 1980).

Clifford, James, *The Predicament of Culture: twentieth century ethnography, literature, and art* (Cambridge, Ma., 1988).

Cockshott, Gerald, *Music and Nature: a study of Aldous Huxley* (Salzburg, 1979).

Cork, Richard, *Vorticism and Abstract Art in the First Machine Age* (London, 1976).

Curle, Richard (ed.), *Conrad to a Friend: 150 selected letters from Joseph Conrad to Richard Curle* (London, 1928).

Daiches, David, *The Novel and the Modern World* (Chicago, 1939).

Daleski H. M., *Joseph Conrad: the way of dispossession* (London, 1977).

Dali, Salvador, *The Secret Life of Salvador Dali* (New York, 1942).

Dasenbrock, R. W., *The Literary Vorticism of Ezra Pound and Wyndham Lewis: towards the condition of poetry* (Baltimore, 1985).

Deery, June, *Aldous Huxley and the Mysticism of Science* (Basingstoke, 1996).

Diggory, Terence, *William Carlos Williams and the Ethics of Painting* (Princeton, 1991).

Dijkstra, Bram, *Cubism, Stieglitz, and the Early Poetry of William Carlos Williams* (Princeton, 1978).

Edel, Leon, *Bloomsbury: a house of lions* (New York, 1980).

Erdinast-Vulcan, Daphna, *Joseph Conrad and the Modern Temper* (Oxford, 1991).

Fenton, Charles A., *The Apprenticeship of Ernest Hemingway* (New York, 1954).

Fichow, Peter, *Aldous Huxley: satirist and novelist* (Minneapolis, 1972).

Flint, R. W., and Coppotelli, A. A. (eds), *Marinetti: selected writings* (New York, 1972).

Ford, Ford Madox, *Joseph Conrad: a personal remembrance* (London, 1924).

Foucault, Michel, *The Order of Things* (London, 1970).

Foucault, Michel, *Discipline and Punish: the birth of the prison*, trans. Alan Sheridan (New York, 1979).

Foucault, Michel, *This is Not a Pipe*, trans. and ed. James Harkness (Berkeley, 1982).

Frank, Joseph, *The Widening Gyre: crisis and mastery in modern literature* (New Brunswick, 1963).

Fuller, Peter, *Art and Psychoanalysis* (London, 1980).

Gablik, Suzi, *Progress in Art* (London, 1976).

Gauguin, Paul, *The Intimate Journals*, trans. Van Wyck Brooks (London, 1930).

Gay, Peter, *Freud: a life for our time* (New York, 1988).

Giedion, Sigfried, *Space, Time, and Architecture: the growth of a new tradition* (Cambridge, Ma., 1962).

Gillespie Diane F., *The Sister Arts: the writing and painting of Virginia Woolf and Vanessa Bell* (Syracus, 1988).

Gillespie Diane F. (ed.), *The Multiple Muses of Virginia Woolf* (Columbia, 1993).

Gleizes, Albert, and Metzinger, Jean, *Du Cubisme* (Paris, 1912).

Goldwater, Robert, *Primitivism in Modern Art* (New York, 1967).

Gordon, Lyndall, *Eliot's Early Years* (Oxford, 1977).

Gordon, Lyndall, *Virginia Woolf: a writer's life* (New York, 1984).

Greenberg, Clement, 'Modernist Painting', *Art and Literature* 4 (1965), 193.

Griffith, John W., *Joseph Conrad and the Anthropological Dilemma* (Oxford, 1995).

Guerard, Albert J., *Conrad the Novelist* (Cambridge, Ma., 1958).

Guetti, James, *The Limits of Metaphor: a study of Melville, Conrad, and Faulkner* (Ithaca, 1967).

Gurko, Leo, *Ernest Hemingway: the pursuit of heroism* (New York, 1968).

Haftmann, Werner, *Painting in the Twentieth Century*, trans. Ralph Manheim (New York, 1965).

Halter, Peter, *The Revolution in the Visual Arts and the Poetry of William Carlos Williams* (Cambridge, 1994).

Harrison, Charles, *English Art and Modernism, 1900–1939* (New Haven, 1994).

Hartman, Geoffrey, *Beyond Formalism* (New Haven, 1970).

Hayles, Katherine, *The Cosmic Web: scientific field models and literary strategies in the twentieth century* (Ithaca, 1984).

Hayles, Katherine, *Chaos Bound: orderly disorder and contemporary literature and science* (Ithaca, 1990).

Henderson, Linda D., *The Fourth Dimension and Non-Euclidian Geometry in Modern Art* (Princeton, 1983).

Hoffman, Frederick J., *Freudianism and the Literary Mind* (Baton Rouge, 1957).

Hoog, Michael, *Paul Gauguin: life and work* (New York, 1987).

Huxley, Julian (ed.), *Aldous Huxley: a memorial volume* (London, 1965).

Jauss, Hans Robert, *Toward an Aesthetic of Reception*, trans. Timothy Bahti (Minneapolis, 1982).

Johnson, Bruce, *Conrad's Models of Mind* (Minneapolis, 1971).

Kandinsky, Wassily, *Concerning the Spiritual in Art*, trans. Michael Sadleir et al. (New York, 1947).

Kemal, Salim, and Gaskell, Ivan (eds), *The Language of Art History* (Cambridge, 1993).

Klein, Robert, *Form and Meaning: writings on the Renaissance and modern art* (Princeton, 1981).

Knapp, Bettina L., *Word, Image, Psyche* (Alabama, 1985).

Knapp, Eloise Hay, *T. S. Eliot's Negative Way* (Cambridge, Ma., 1982).

Korg, Jacob, 'Modern Art Techniques in *The Waste Land*', *Journal of Aesthetics and Art Criticism*, 18 (1960).

Kris, Ernst, *Psychoanalytic Explorations in Art* (London, 1953).

Kronegger, Maria E., *Literary Impressionism* (New Haven, 1973).

Lacan, Jacques, *Ecrits: a selection* (London, 1977).

Lacan, Jacques, *The Four Fundamental Concepts of Psycho-Analysis* (London, 1977).

Lair, Robert L., 'Hemingway and Cézanne: an indebtedness', *Modern Fiction Studies* 6 (1960), 165.

Langbaum, Robert, *The Mysteries of Identity: a theme in modern literature* (New York, 1977).

Lentricchia, Frank, *After the New Criticism* (Chicago, 1980).

Lentricchia, Frank, *Modern Quartet* (Cambridge, 1994).

Lester, John A. Jr., *Journey Through Despair: transformations in British literary culture 1880–1914* (Princeton, 1968).

Levenson, Michael, *Modernism and the Fate of Individuality* (Cambridge, 1991).

Lewis, Wyndham P., *Time and the Western Man* (London, 1927).

Litz, A. Walton (ed.), *Eliot in His Time* (Princeton, 1973).

Lodge, David, *The Modes of Modern Writing: metaphor, metonymy, and the typology of modern literature* (Ithaca, 1977).

Loeb, Harold, *The Way It Was* (New York, 1959).

Long, Rose-Carol Washton, *Kandinsky: the development of an abstract style* (Oxford, 1980).

Loss, Archie K., *Joyce's Visible Art: the work of Joyce and the visual arts, 1904–1922* (Ann Arbor, 1984).

Lynn, Kenneth S., *Hemingway* (New York, 1987).

Malingue, Maurice (ed.), *Lettres de Gauguin à sa Femme et à ses Amis* (Paris, 1946).

Marovitz, Sanford E., 'Aldous Huxley's Intellectual Zoo', *Philological Quarterly*, 48 (1969), 495.

Marovitz, Sanford, 'Huxley and the Visual Arts', *Papers on Language and Literature*, 9 (1973), 172.

Materer, Timothy, *Modernist Alchemy: poetry and the occult* (Ithaca, 1995).

May, Keith M., *Aldous Huxley* (London, 1972).

Meckier, Jerome, *Aldous Huxley: satire and structure* (London, 1969).

Meckier, Jerome, (ed.), *Critical Essays on Aldous Huxley* (New York, 1996).

Miller, J. Hillis, *Poets of Reality: six twentieth-century writers* (Cambridge Ma., 1965).

Miller, Karl, *Doubles: studies in literary history* (Oxford, 1985).

Mitchell W. J. T., *Picture Theory* (Chicago, 1994).

Moody, A. D. (ed.), *Different Voices* (London,1974).

Nakjavani, Eric, 'The Aesthetics of the Visible and the Invisible: Hemingway and Cézanne', *Hemingway Review*, 5 (1986), 1.

Nelson, Raymond S., *Hemingway: expressionist artist* (Ames, 1979).

Nicholls, Peter, *Modernisms: a literary guide* (Berkeley, 1995).

Noble, Donald R. (ed.), *Hemingway: a revaluation* (New York, 1983).

Novak, Barbara, *American Painting of the Nineteenth Century* (New York, 1979).

O'Faolain, Sean, *The Vanishing Hero: studies in novelists of the twenties* (London, 1956).

Ortega y Gasset, *The Dehumanization of Art*, trans. Helene Weyl (Princeton, 1948).

Perkins, David, *A History of Modern Poetry* (London, 1987).

Perl, Jeffrey M., *Skepticism and Modern Enmity: before and after Eliot* (Baltimore, 1989).

Perloff, Marjorie, *The Futurist Movement: avant garde, avant-guerre, and the language of rupture* (Chicago, 1986).

Perloff, Marjorie, *The Dance of the Intellect: studies in the poetry of the Pound tradition* (Cambridge, 1987).

Philip, Young, *Ernest Hemingway: a reconsideration* (University Park, Pa., 1966).

Popper, Karl, *The Poverty of Historicism* (London, 1957).

Pound, Ezra, *Gaudier Brzeska: a Memoir* (London, 1916).

Praz, Mario, *Mnemosyne: the parallel between literature and the visual arts* (Princeton, 1970).

Preziosi, Donald, *Rethinking Art History* (New Haven, 1989).

Pulos, Arthur J., *American Design Ethic: a history of industrial design to 1940* (Cambridge, Ma., 1983).

Quennell, Peter, 'A Critical Symposium on Aldous Huxley', *The London Magazine*, 2 (1955), 51–64.

Rabinovitz, Rubin, *The Reaction Against Experiment in the Novel, 1950–1960* (New York 1967).

Rajan, Balachandra, *The Overwhelming Question: a study of the poetry of T. S. Eliot* (Toronto, 1976).

Rewald, John, *Post-Impressionism: from Van Gogh to Gauguin* (New York, 1956).

Richards, David, *Masks of Difference: cultural representations in literature, anthropology, and art* (Cambridge, 1994).

Richter, Hans, *Dada: art and anti-art* (Oxford, 1978).

Ringbom, Sixten, *The Sounding Cosmos: a study in the spiritualism of Kandinsky and the genesis of abstract painting* (Abo, 1970).

Robinson, Alan, *Poetry, Painting, and Ideas, 1885–1914* (London, 1985).

Rosenblum, Robert, *Modern Painting and the Northern Romantic Tradition* (New York, 1975).

Rosenblum, Robert, *Cubism and Twentieth-century Art* (New York, 1976).

Ross, Murfin C. (ed.), *Conrad Revisited: essays for the eighties* (Alabama, 1984).

Rubin, William (ed.), *'Primitivism' in Twentieth-century Art: affinity of the tribal and the modern* (Boston, 1984).

Said, Edward, *Joseph Conrad and the Fiction of Autobiography* (Cambridge Ma., 1968).

Sanderson, Rena (ed.), *Blowing the Bridge: essays on Hemingway* (New York, 1992).

Sarason, Bertram D., *Hemingway and 'The Sun' Set* (Washington, 1972).

Schapiro, Meyer, *Modern Art, 19th and 20th centuries: selected papers* (New York, 1978).

Scharf, Aaron, *Art and Photography* (New York, 1983).

Schwartz, Sanford, *The Matrix of Modernism: Pound, Eliot, and early twentieth-century thought* (Princeton, 1985).

Schwarz, Daniel R., *Reconfiguring Modernism: explorations in the relationship between modern art and modern literature* (New York, 1997).

Shechner, Mark, *Joyce in Nighttown: a psychoanalytic inquiry into 'Ulysses'* (Berkeley, 1974).

Sherry, Norman (ed.), *Joseph Conrad: a commemoration* (London, 1979).

Sherry, Vincent, *Ezra Pound, Wyndham Lewis, and Radical Modernism* (Oxford, 1993).

Shiff, Richard, *Cézanne and the End of Impressionism* (Chicago, 1984).

Short, Robert, *Dada and Surrealism* (London, 1980).

Skaff, William, *The Philosophy of T. S. Eliot: from skepticism to surrealist poetic, 1909–1927* (Philadelphia, 1986).

Smith, Grover, *The Waste Land* (London, 1983).

Spender, Stephen, *The Struggle of the Modern* (Berkeley, 1963).

Spilka, Mark, *Hemingway's Quarrel with Androgyny* (Lincoln, Na., 1990).

Steinberg, Leo, *Other Criteria: confrontations with twentieth-century art* (Oxford, 1976).

Steiner, Wendy, *Exact Resemblance to Exact Resemblance: the literary portraiture of Gertrude Stein* (New Haven, 1978).

Steiner, Wendy, *The Colors of Rhetoric: problems in the relation between modern literature and painting* (Chicago, 1982).

Svarny, Eric, *The Men of 1914: T. S. Eliot and early modernism* (Milton Keynes, 1988).

Sypher, Wylie, *Rococo to Cubism in art and literature* (New York, 1960).

Tate, Allen (ed.), *T. S. Eliot: the Man and his Work* (New York, 1966).

Teilhet-Fisk, Jehanne, *Paradise Reviewed: an interpretation of Gauguin's Polynesian symbolism* (Ann Arbor, 1983).

Tichi, Cecilia, *Shifting Gears: technology, literature, culture in modernist America* (Chapel Hill, 1987).

Tillyard, S. K., *The Impact of Modernism 1900–1920* (London, 1988).

Torgovnick, Marianna, *The Visual Arts, Pictorialism, and the Novel* (Princeton, 1985).

Torgovnick, Marianna, *Gone Primitive: savage intellects, modern lives* (Chicago, 1990).

Wagner-Martin, Linda (ed.), *New Essays on 'The Sun Also Rises'* (Cambridge, 1987).

Watney, Simon, *English Post-Impressionism* (London, 1980).

Watt, Ian, *Conrad in the Nineteenth Century* (Berkeley, 1981).

Watts, Emily S., *Ernest Hemingway and the Arts* (Urbana, 1971).

Watts, Harold H., *Aldous Huxley* (New York, 1969).

Weisberger, Edward (ed.), *The Spiritual in Art: abstract painting, 1890–1985* (New York, 1987).

White, Allon, *The Uses of Obscurity: the fiction of early modernism* (London, 1981).

White, Andrea , *Joseph Conrad and the Adventure Tradition* (Cambridge, 1993).

Wilde Alan, *Horizons of Assent: modernism, postmodernism, and the ironic imagination* (Baltimore, 1981).

Williams, Raymond, *The Politics of Modernism* (London, 1989).

Wirt, Williams, *The Tragic Art of Ernest Hemingway* (Baton Rouge, 1981).

Woodcock, George, *Dawn and the Darkest Hour: a study of Aldous Huxley* (New York, 1972).

Worringer, Wilhelm, *Abstraction and Empathy: a contribution to the psychology of style* (New York, 1963).

Wortley, Laura, *British Impressionism: a garden of bright images* (London, 1988).

Yelton, Donald C., *Mimesis and Metaphor: an inquiry into the genesis and scope of Conrad's symbolic imagery* (Mouton, 1967).

Young, Alan, *Dada and After: extremist modernism and English literature* (Manchester, 1981).

Index

Abel, Elizabeth, 265 n15
Achebe, Chinua, 23, 248 n36
Ades, Dawn, 266 n34, n37, 268 n11
Albee, Edward, 5–8
Aldington, Richard, 130, 227
Allen, Walter, 259 n27
Alma-Tadema, 29
Alpers, Svetlana, 151, 264 n7
Altieri, Charles, 265 n17
Alvarez, A. A., 46, 251 n10
Amishai-Maisels, Ziva, 249 n54
Andrewes, Lancelot, 252 n15
anti-hero, 118f.
Apollinaire, Guillaume, 51, 55, 64, 71, 252 n18
Archipenko, 234
Arens, W., 250 n62
Armory Show, 45, 211, 241
Arnold, Matthew, 96–7
Aronson, Alex, 259 n24
Arp, Jean, 163, 190, 196, 209
Atkins, John, 92, 258 n15
Attridge, Derek, 268 n9
Auden, W. H., 49, 222, 239–40, 273 n46
automatic writing, 164
Aztec sculpture, 21, 236

Bacon, Francis, 71, 101
Baker, Carlos, 261 n11, 264 n42
Baker, Robert, S., 260 n37
Baker, Sheridan, 263 n37
Bakhtin, M. M., 120, 260 n4
Balakian, Anna, 266 n29
Ball, Hugo, 179, 268 n58
Barthelme, Donald, 226
Baudelaire, C. P., 14, 15, 45, 112, 260 n37
Bauhaus, 127, 129, 179, 268 n57, n60
Baxandall, Michael, 4, 243 n6
Beach, Joseph W., 12, 245 n8
Bedford, Sybille, 259 n27
Bedient, Calvin, 47, 252 n11
Beegel, Susan, 262 n30

Bell, Clive, 45, 158–61, 171, 251 n6, 257 n8, 266 n25
Bell, Quentin, 265 n15
Bell, Vanessa, 171
Bellow, Saul, 119
Benson, Donald R., 246 n17
Bentley, Joseph, 253 n23
Bergen, John, 131
Bergonzi, Bernard, 220, 271 n18
Bergson, Henri, 184, 187, 255 n47, 268 n1, n6
Berlin, Isaiah, 86
Bernini, Gianbrenzo, 56
Bettell, Richard, 249 n55
Bigsby, C. W. E., 266 n30
Birnbaum, Milton, 259 n36
Blake, William, 203
Blake, Peter, 262 n21, n27
Blaue Reiter, 180
Blavatsky, Helena, 59–60
Bloom, Harold, 69, 120, 158, 255 n50, 260 n4, 266 n22
Boccioni, Umberto, 213, 273 n42
Bodkin, Maud, 256 n59
Bohr, Niels, 43, 184
Borzello, Frances, 244 n6
Bosch, Hieronymus, 122
Botticelli, 73, 256 n55
Boudaille, Georges, 247 n27
Bowering, Peter, 116, 257 n3, 260 n42
Bozzolla, Angelo, 270 n8
Bradbury, Malcolm, 220, 244 n10, 261 n16
Bradley, A. C., 60
Brancusi, Constantin, 65–6, 70, 122, 217, 237, 255 n45
Brander, Lawrence, 86, 257 n2
Braque, Georges, 44, 52, 58, 87–9, 91f., 109, 213, 254 n31, 257 n8
Breton, André, 111, 162f., 266 n29, n35
Breuer, Marcel, 127
Brill, A. A., 189

Drummond, Henry, 27
Duchamp, Marcel, 52, 55, 79, 118,
      150, 162–3, 209, 230
Duncan, Isadora, 66, 255 n46
Dürer, Albert, 194

Eagleton, Terry, 29, 249 n45
Eberhart, Richard, 222
Eco, Umberto, 151, 264 n9
Eddington, A. S., 53, 253 n20
Edel, Leon, 265 n15
Einstein, Albert, 43, 50, 90, 94
El Greco, 113, 118, 122
Elgar, Frank, 262 n15
Eliot, T. S., 43f., 113, 118, 194,
      203–4, 212f.
Ellmann, Maud, 255 n47
Ellmann, Richard, 265 n10, n12, n15
Eluard, Paul, 111
Empson, William, 198f., 269 n24, n25
Epstein, Jacob, 149–50, 227, 232f.,
      273 n38
Erdinast-Vulcan, Daphna, 17,
      247 n23
Ernst, Max, 151
Escher, M. C., 192–3, 269 n14
ethnology, 21
extrasensory perception, 60–1

Fairchild, Hoxey N., 27, 248 n41
fantasy substitution, 188f.
Fantin-Latour, 14, 211
Faulkner, Peter, 267 n46
Faulkner, William, 118, 186–7,
      229, 272 n33
Fauvism, 32
Fenton, Charles A., 262 n19
Fernandez, Ramon, 12–13, 245 n9
Fichow, Peter, 88, 257 n5
Ficino, Marsilio, 72
Finkelstein, H. N., 266 n32
Fireside poets, 212
Fish, Stanley, 120, 260 n5
Fitzgerald, Scott, 118, 128, 219
Flaubert, Gustave, 19, 121, 246 n16,
      247 n25
Fleishman, Avrom, 246 n20
Flint, Kate, 248 n35
Flint, S. F., 130

Ford, Ford Madox, 10, 204–5,
      216, 218, 244 n1, 247 n25
Ford, Henry, 126
Forster, E. M., 16, 49, 214,
      246 n18, 252 n13
Foucault, Michel, 3, 36, 103, 193,
      243 n5, 250 n59, 259 n29,
      269 n15
fourth dimension, 50f.
Fowler, Alistair, 243 n4
Frank, Joseph, 223, 247 n25,
      254 n32, 272 n24
Frascina, F., 248 n32
Frazer, James G., 28, 73f.,
      249 n44, 256 n57, n59
Freud, Sigmund, *passim,*
      especially, 152f., 188f.
Fried, Michael, 15, 225, 246 n17,
      272 n28
Fry, Roger, 23, 45, 61, 159, 161,
      171–2, 212, 251 n6, 257 n8,
      270 n3
Fuller, Loïe, 66, 255 n46
Fuller, Peter, 266 n20
Functionalism, 126f., 272 n28
Futurism, 213f., 271 n13

Gabler, H. W., 267 n49
Gablik, Suzi, 258 n10
Gabo, Naum, 209
Gaggin, John, 262 n19
Galbraith, John, 244 n7
Galileo, 79, 97
Gaskell, Ivan, 244 n6
Gaudier-Brzeska, Henri, 215f.,
      227, 232–3, 236
Gauguin, Paul, 20f., 45, 180, 251 n5
Gay, Peter, 266 n24, 269 n13
Gibbons, Tom, 252 n16
Gidion, Siegfried, 258 n11, 262 n23
Gilbert, Alfred, 232
Gilbert, Stuart, 228, 272 n31
Gillespie, Diane F., 267 n45
Gilot, F., 272 n27
Giotto, 20
Gleizes, Albert, 52, 81, 97,
      252 n18, 258 n13
Goethe, J. W., 158
Golding, John, 257 n8